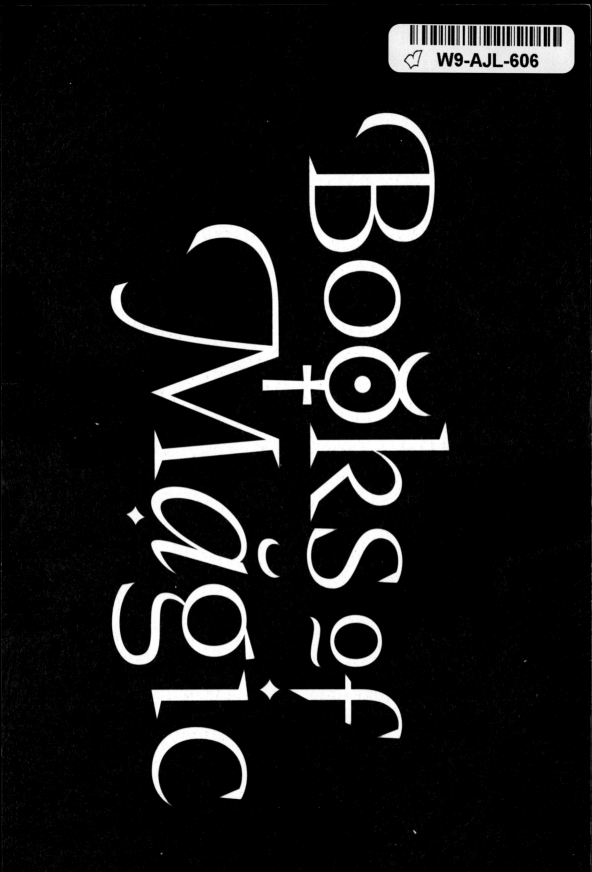

Books of Magic

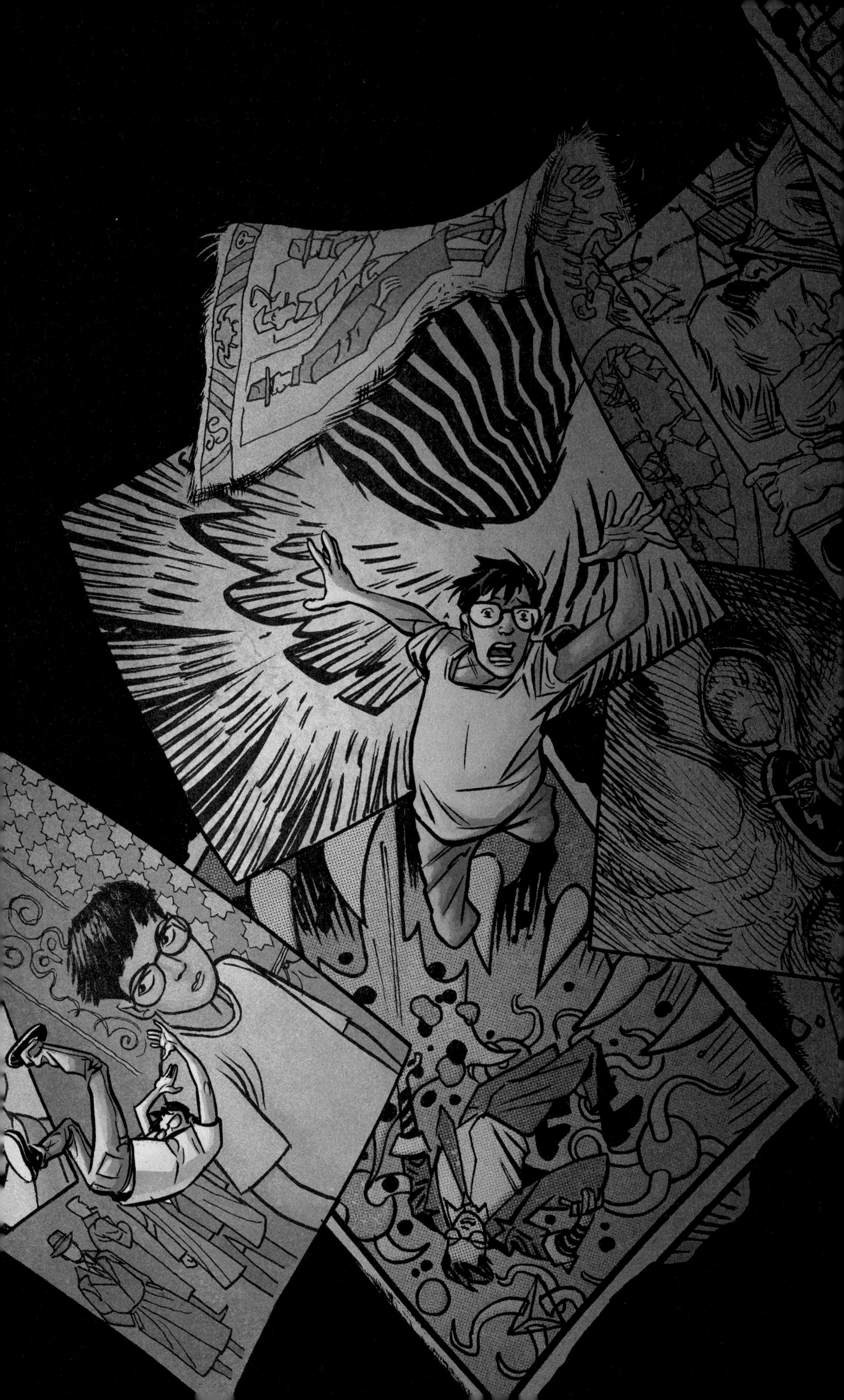

Books of Magic

VOLUME ONE

Moveable Type

WRITTEN BY
Kat Howard
Neil Gaiman
Simon Spurrier
Dan Watters
Nalo Hopkinson

ART BY
Tom Fowler
Bilquis Evely
Max Fiumara
Sebastian Fiumara
Dominike "DOMO" Stanton

COLORS BY
Jordan Boyd
Mat Lopes

LETTERS BY
Todd Klein
Simon Bowland

COLLECTION COVER ART BY
Josh Middleton

ORIGINAL SERIES COVER ART BY
Kai Carpenter
Jill Thompson

Timothy Hunter and the Books of Magic created by Neil Gaiman and John Bolton

The Sandman created by Neil Gaiman, Sam Kieth, and Mike Dringenberg

The Sandman Universe curated by Neil Gaiman

MOLLY MAHAN	*Editor – Original Series*
AMEDEO TURTURRO	*Associate Editor – Original Series*
MAGGIE HOWELL	*Assistant Editor – Original Series*
JEB WOODARD	*Group Editor – Collected Editions*
SCOTT NYBAKKEN	*Editor – Collected Edition*
STEVE COOK	*Design Director – Books and Publication Design*
DANIELLE DIGRADO	*Publication Production*
BOB HARRAS	*Senior VP – Editor-in-Chief, DC Comics*
MARK DOYLE	*Executive Editor, Vertigo & Black Label*
DAN DiDIO	*Publisher*
JIM LEE	*Publisher & Chief Creative Officer*
BOBBIE CHASE	*VP – New Publishing Initiatives & Talent Development*
DON FALLETTI	*VP – Manufacturing Operations & Workflow Management*
LAWRENCE GANEM	*VP – Talent Services*
ALISON GILL	*Senior VP – Manufacturing & Operations*
HANK KANALZ	*Senior VP – Publishing Strategy & Support Services*
DAN MIRON	*VP – Publishing Operations*
NICK J. NAPOLITANO	*VP – Manufacturing Administration & Design*
NANCY SPEARS	*VP – Sales*
MICHELE R. WELLS	*VP & Executive Editor, Young Reader*

BOOKS OF MAGIC VOL. 1: MOVEABLE TYPE

Published by DC Comics. Compilation and all new material Copyright © 2019 DC Comics. All Rights Reserved.

Originally published in single magazine form as THE SANDMAN UNIVERSE 1 and BOOKS OF MAGIC 1-6. Copyright © 2018, 2019 DC Comics. All Rights Reserved. All characters, their distinctive likenesses and related elements featured in this publication are trademarks of DC Comics. The stories, characters and incidents featured in this publication are entirely fictional. DC Comics does not read or accept unsolicited submissions of ideas, stories or artwork. DC – a WarnerMedia Company.

DC Comics, 2900 West Alameda Ave., Burbank, CA 91505
Printed by LSC Communications, Owensville, MO, USA. 6/7/19, First Printing.
ISBN: 978-1-4012-9134-1

Library of Congress Cataloging-in-Publication Data is available.

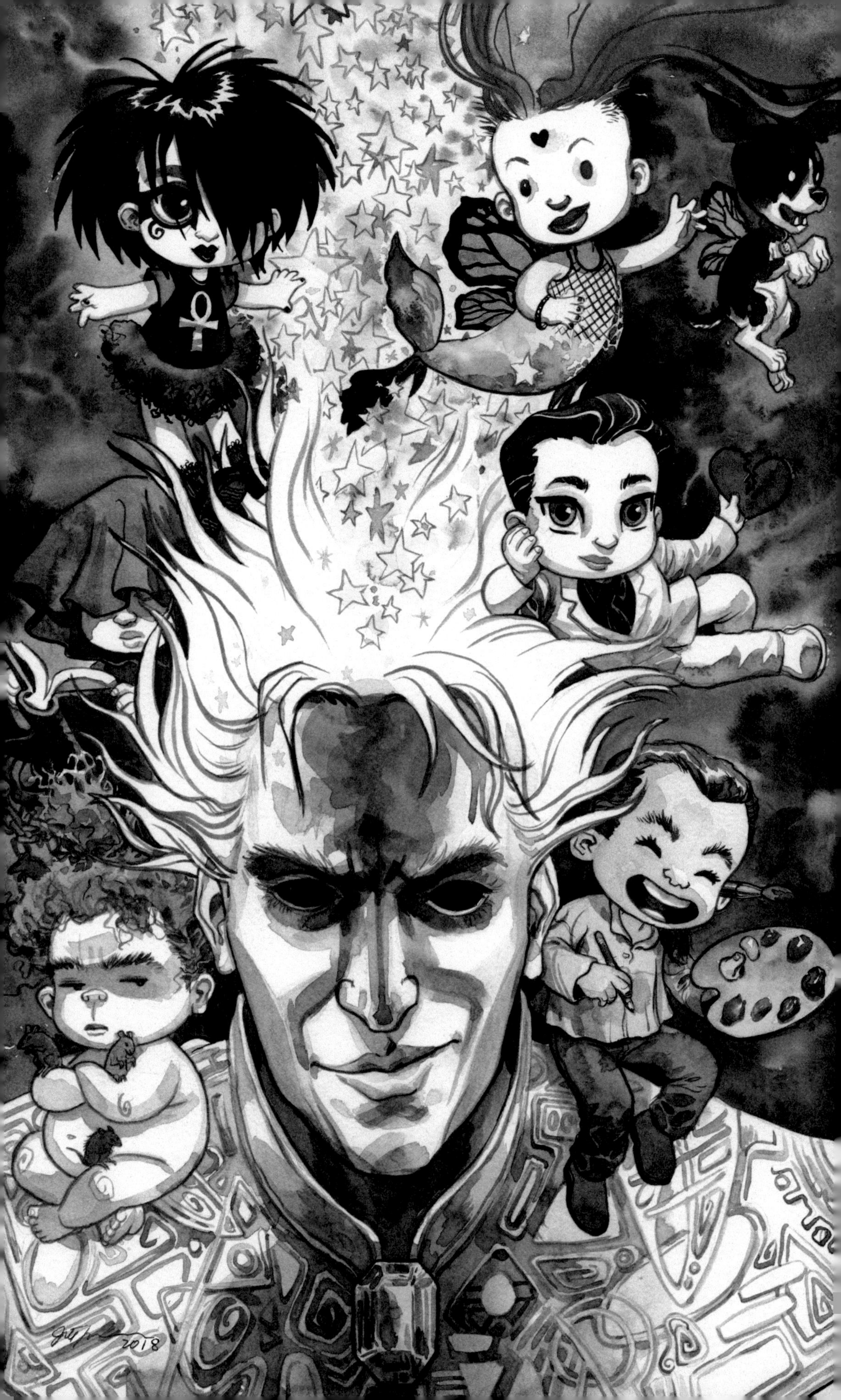

The Sandman Universe

STORY BY
Neil Gaiman

WRITTEN BY
Simon Spurrier
Kat Howard
Nalo Hopkinson
Dan Watters

ILLUSTRATED BY
Bilquis Evely
Tom Fowler
Dominike "DOMO" Stanton
Max Fiumara
Sebastian Fiumara

COLORS BY
Mat Lopes

LETTERS BY
Simon Bowland

COVER ART BY
Jill Thompson

Special thanks to Cat Mihos

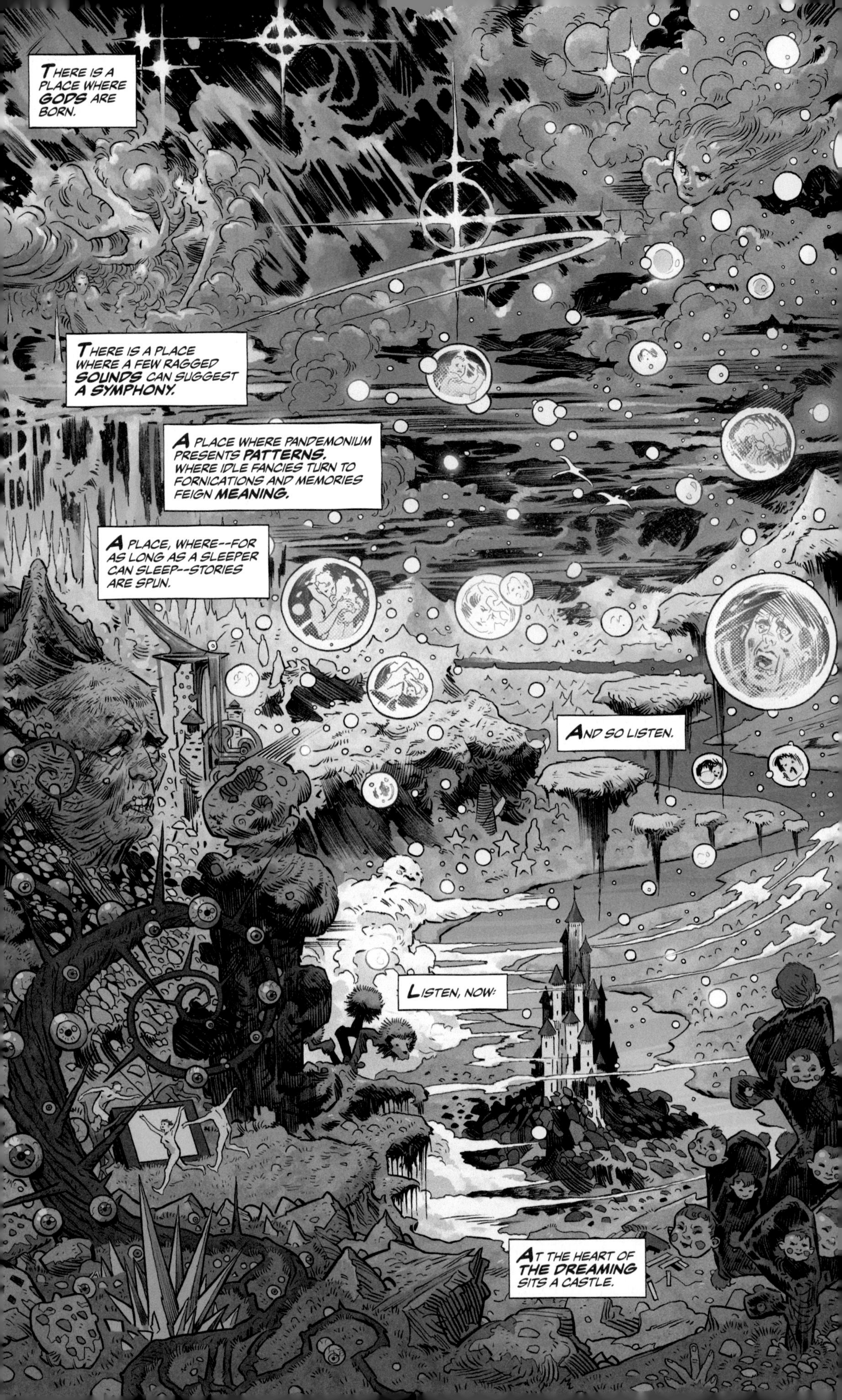

THERE IS A PLACE WHERE GODS ARE BORN.
THERE IS A PLACE WHERE A FEW RAGGED SOUNDS CAN SUGGEST A SYMPHONY.
A PLACE WHERE PANDEMONIUM PRESENTS PATTERNS. WHERE IDLE FANCIES TURN TO FORNICATIONS AND MEMORIES FEIGN MEANING.
A PLACE, WHERE--FOR AS LONG AS A SLEEPER CAN SLEEP--STORIES ARE SPUN.
AND SO LISTEN.
LISTEN, NOW:
AT THE HEART OF THE DREAMING SITS A CASTLE.

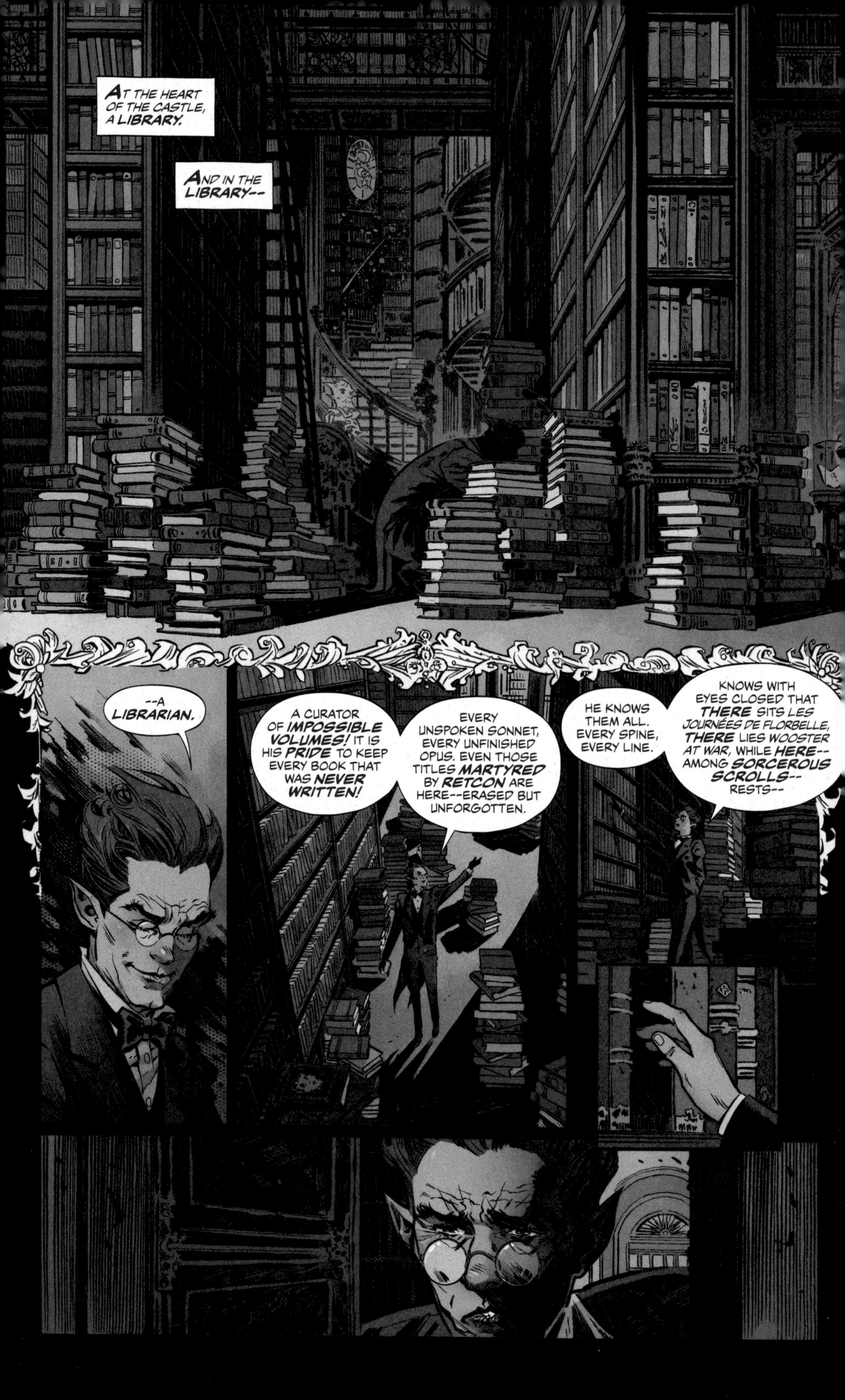
AT THE HEART OF THE CASTLE, A LIBRARY.
AND IN THE LIBRARY--
--A LIBRARIAN.
A CURATOR OF IMPOSSIBLE VOLUMES! IT IS HIS PRIDE TO KEEP EVERY BOOK THAT WAS NEVER WRITTEN!
EVERY UNSPOKEN SONNET, EVERY UNFINISHED OPUS. EVEN THOSE TITLES MARTYRED BY RETCON ARE HERE--ERASED BUT UNFORGOTTEN.
HE KNOWS THEM ALL. EVERY SPINE, EVERY LINE.
KNOWS WITH EYES CLOSED THAT THERE SITS LES JOURNÉES DE FLORBELLE, THERE LIES WOOSTER AT WAR, WHILE HERE--AMONG SORCEROUS SCROLLS--RESTS--

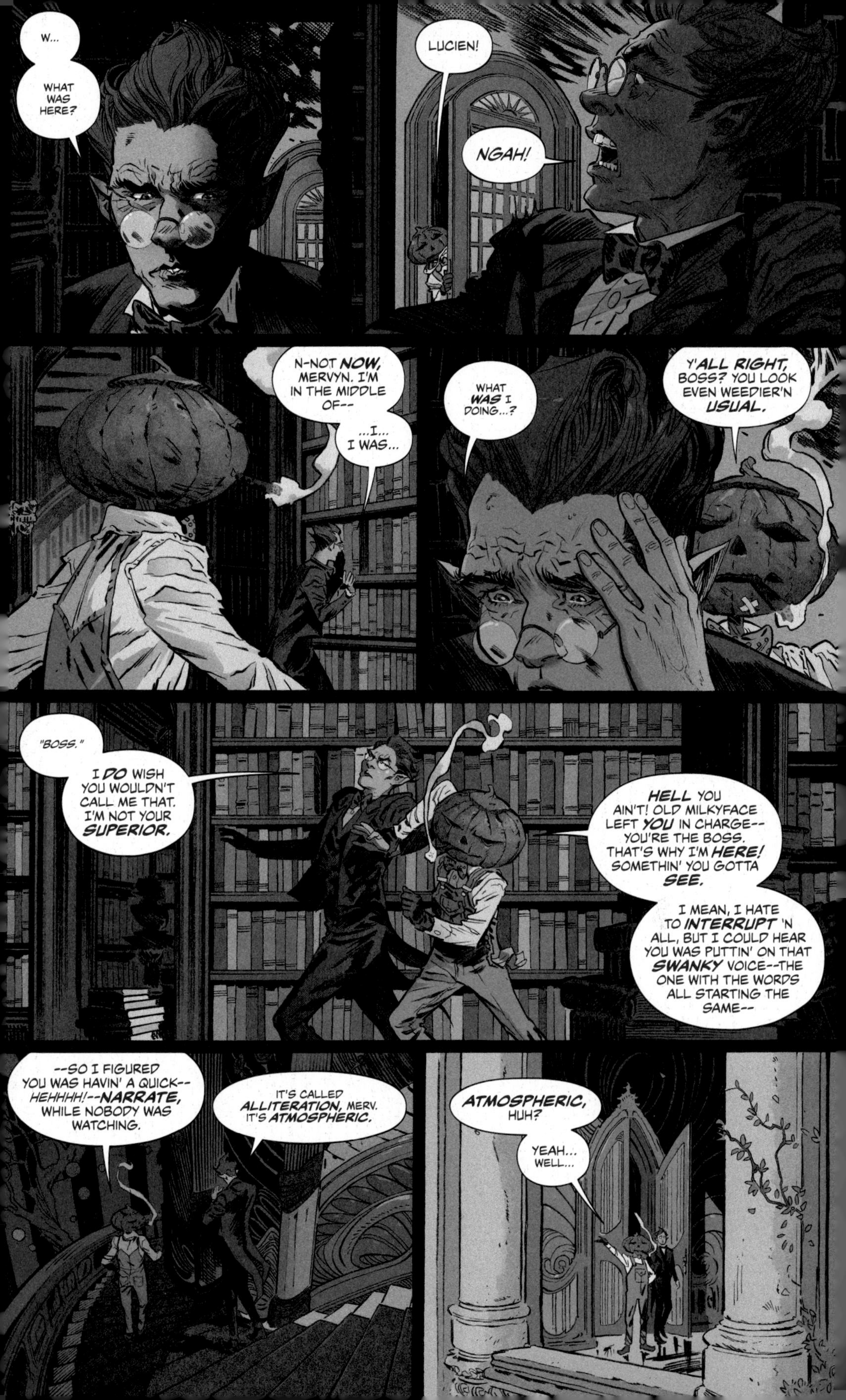
W...
WHAT WAS HERE?
LUCIEN!
NGAH!
N-NOT NOW, MERVYN. I'M IN THE MIDDLE OF--
...I... I WAS...
WHAT WAS I DOING...?
Y'ALL RIGHT, BOSS? YOU LOOK EVEN WEEDIER'N USUAL.
"BOSS."
I DO WISH YOU WOULDN'T CALL ME THAT. I'M NOT YOUR SUPERIOR.
HELL YOU AIN'T! OLD MILKYFACE LEFT YOU IN CHARGE-- YOU'RE THE BOSS. THAT'S WHY I'M HERE! SOMETHIN' YOU GOTTA SEE.
I MEAN, I HATE TO INTERRUPT 'N ALL, BUT I COULD HEAR YOU WAS PUTTIN' ON THAT SWANKY VOICE--THE ONE WITH THE WORDS ALL STARTING THE SAME--
--SO I FIGURED YOU WAS HAVIN' A QUICK--HEHHHH!--NARRATE, WHILE NOBODY WAS WATCHING.
IT'S CALLED ALLITERATION, MERV. IT'S ATMOSPHERIC.
ATMOSPHERIC, HUH?
YEAH... WELL...

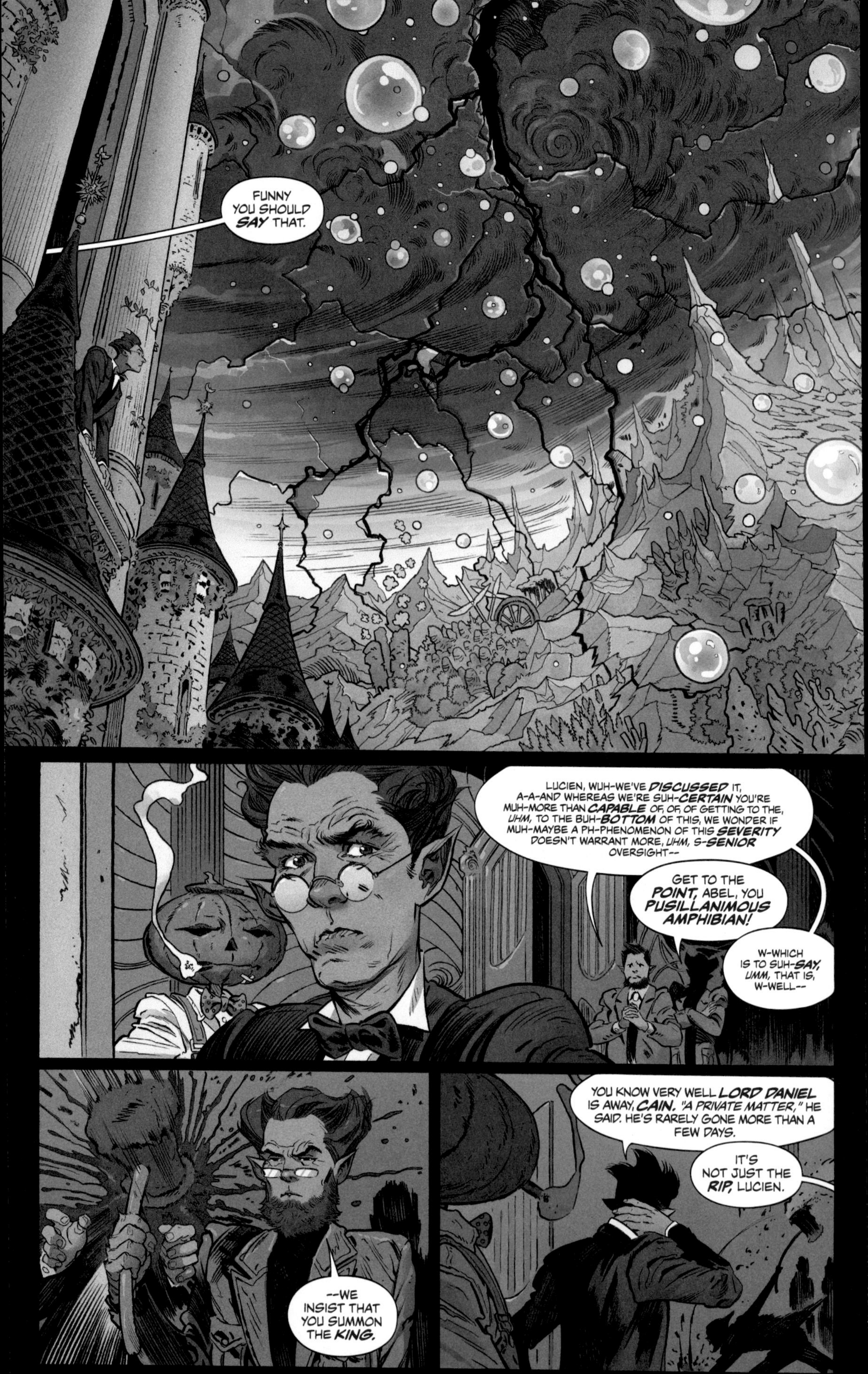
FUNNY YOU SHOULD SAY THAT.
LUCIEN, WUH-WE'VE DISCUSSED IT, A-A-AND WHEREAS WE'RE SUH-CERTAIN YOU'RE MUH-MORE THAN CAPABLE OF, OF, OF GETTING TO THE, UHM, TO THE BUH-BOTTOM OF THIS, WE WONDER IF MUH-MAYBE A PH-PHENOMENON OF THIS SEVERITY DOESN'T WARRANT MORE, UHM, S-SENIOR OVERSIGHT--
GET TO THE POINT, ABEL, YOU PUSILLANIMOUS AMPHIBIAN!
W-WHICH IS TO SUH-SAY, UMM, THAT IS, W-WELL--
--WE INSIST THAT YOU SUMMON THE KING.
YOU KNOW VERY WELL LORD DANIEL IS AWAY, CAIN. "A PRIVATE MATTER," HE SAID. HE'S RARELY GONE MORE THAN A FEW DAYS.
IT'S NOT JUST THE RIP, LUCIEN.

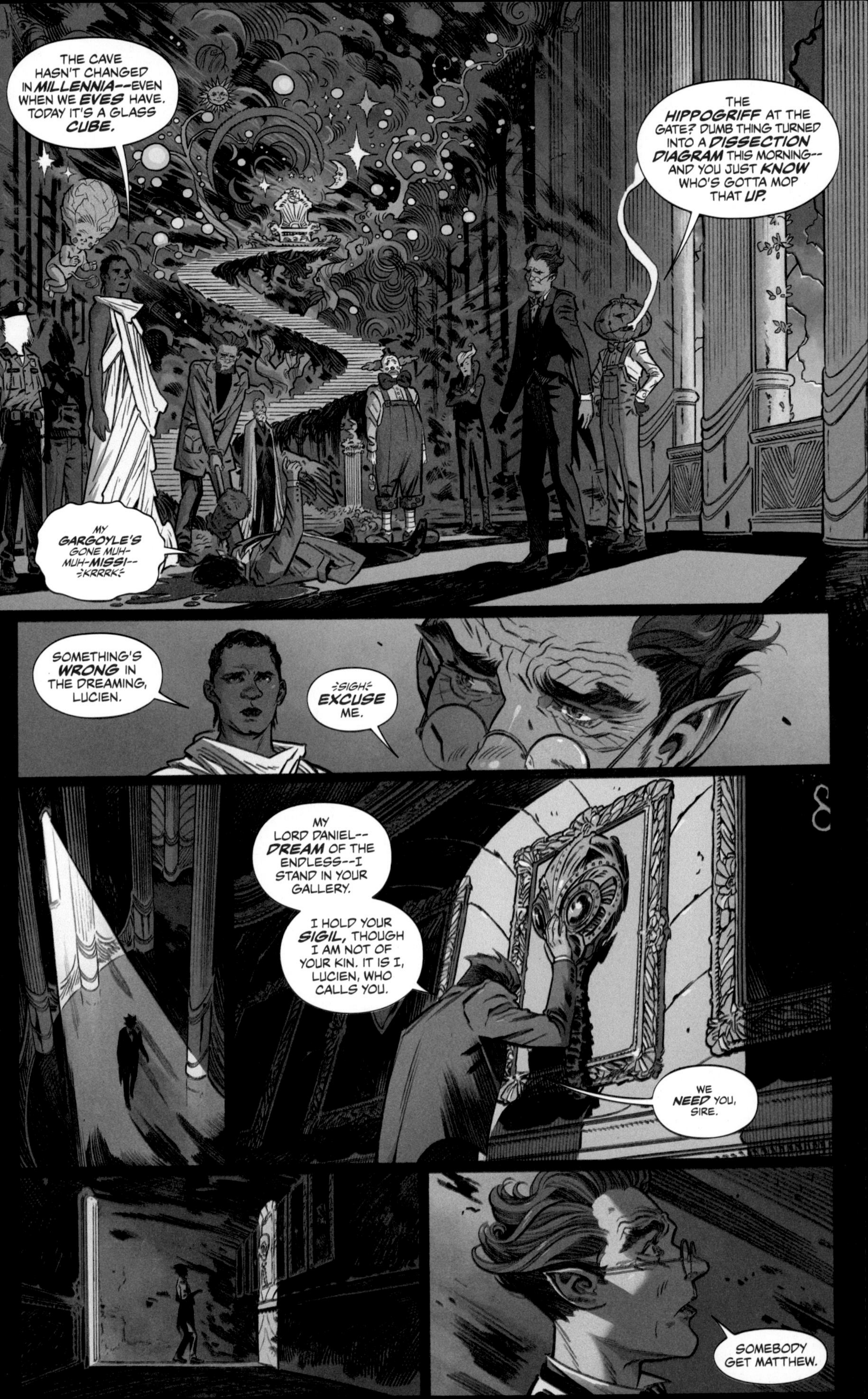
THE CAVE HASN'T CHANGED IN MILLENNIA--EVEN WHEN WE EVES HAVE. TODAY IT'S A GLASS CUBE.
THE HIPPOGRIFF AT THE GATE? DUMB THING TURNED INTO A DISSECTION DIAGRAM THIS MORNING-- AND YOU JUST KNOW WHO'S GOTTA MOP THAT UP.
MY GARGOYLE'S GONE MUH-MUH-MISSI- -KRRRK-
SOMETHING'S WRONG IN THE DREAMING, LUCIEN.
-SIGH- EXCUSE ME.
MY LORD DANIEL-- DREAM OF THE ENDLESS--I STAND IN YOUR GALLERY.
I HOLD YOUR SIGIL, THOUGH I AM NOT OF YOUR KIN. IT IS I, LUCIEN, WHO CALLS YOU.
WE NEED YOU, SIRE.
SOMEBODY GET MATTHEW.

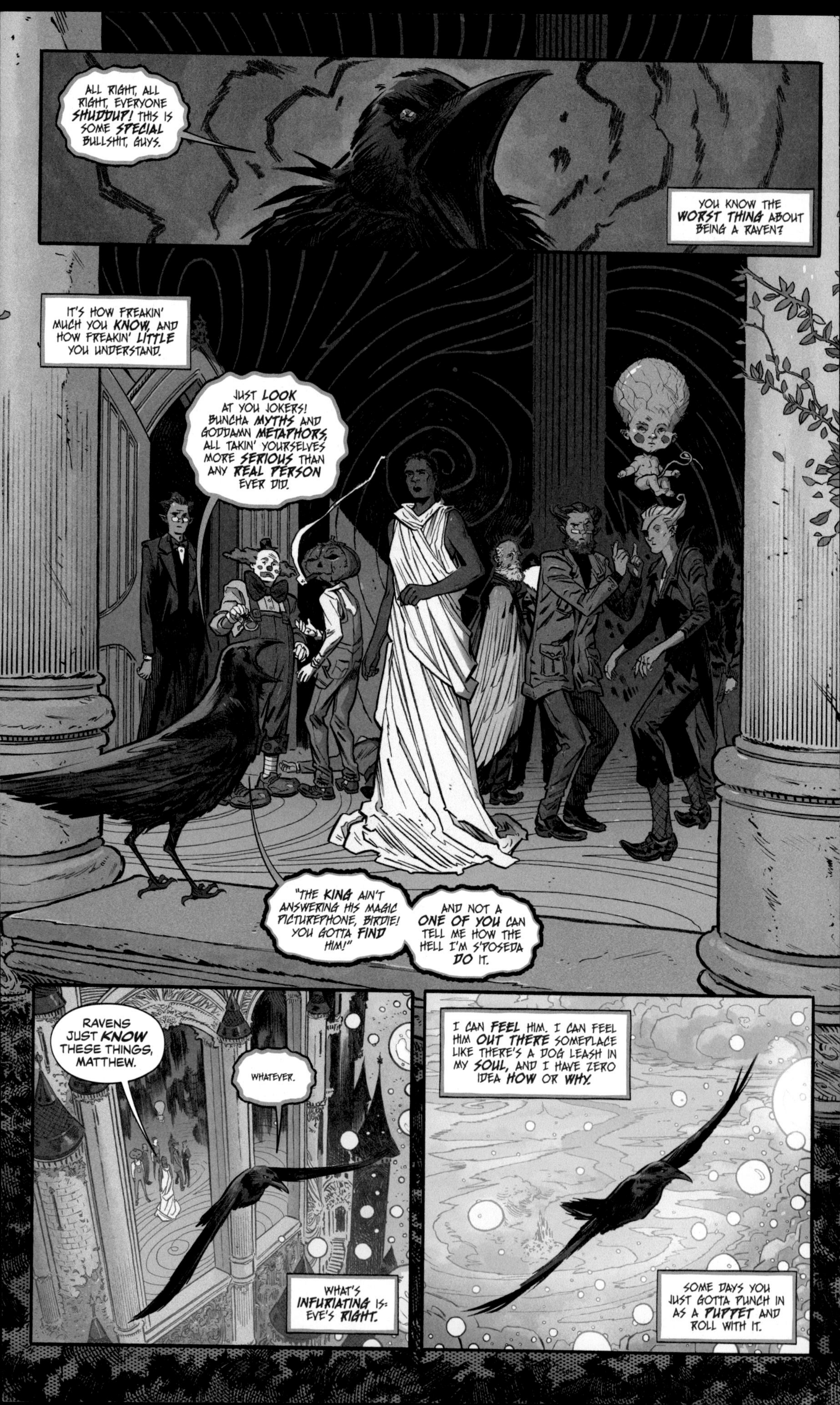
ALL RIGHT, ALL RIGHT, EVERYONE SHUDDUP! THIS IS SOME SPECIAL BULLSHIT, GUYS.
YOU KNOW THE WORST THING ABOUT BEING A RAVEN?
IT'S HOW FREAKIN' MUCH YOU KNOW, AND HOW FREAKIN' LITTLE YOU UNDERSTAND.
JUST LOOK AT YOU JOKERS! BUNCHA MYTHS AND GODDAMN METAPHORS, ALL TAKIN' YOURSELVES MORE SERIOUS THAN ANY REAL PERSON EVER DID.
"THE KING AIN'T ANSWERING HIS MAGIC PICTUREPHONE, BIRDIE! YOU GOTTA FIND HIM!"
AND NOT A ONE OF YOU CAN TELL ME HOW THE HELL I'M S'POSEDA DO IT.
RAVENS JUST KNOW THESE THINGS, MATTHEW.
WHATEVER.
WHAT'S INFURIATING IS: EVE'S RIGHT.
I CAN FEEL HIM. I CAN FEEL HIM OUT THERE SOMEPLACE LIKE THERE'S A DOG LEASH IN MY SOUL, AND I HAVE ZERO IDEA HOW OR WHY.
SOME DAYS YOU JUST GOTTA PUNCH IN AS A PUPPET AND ROLL WITH IT.

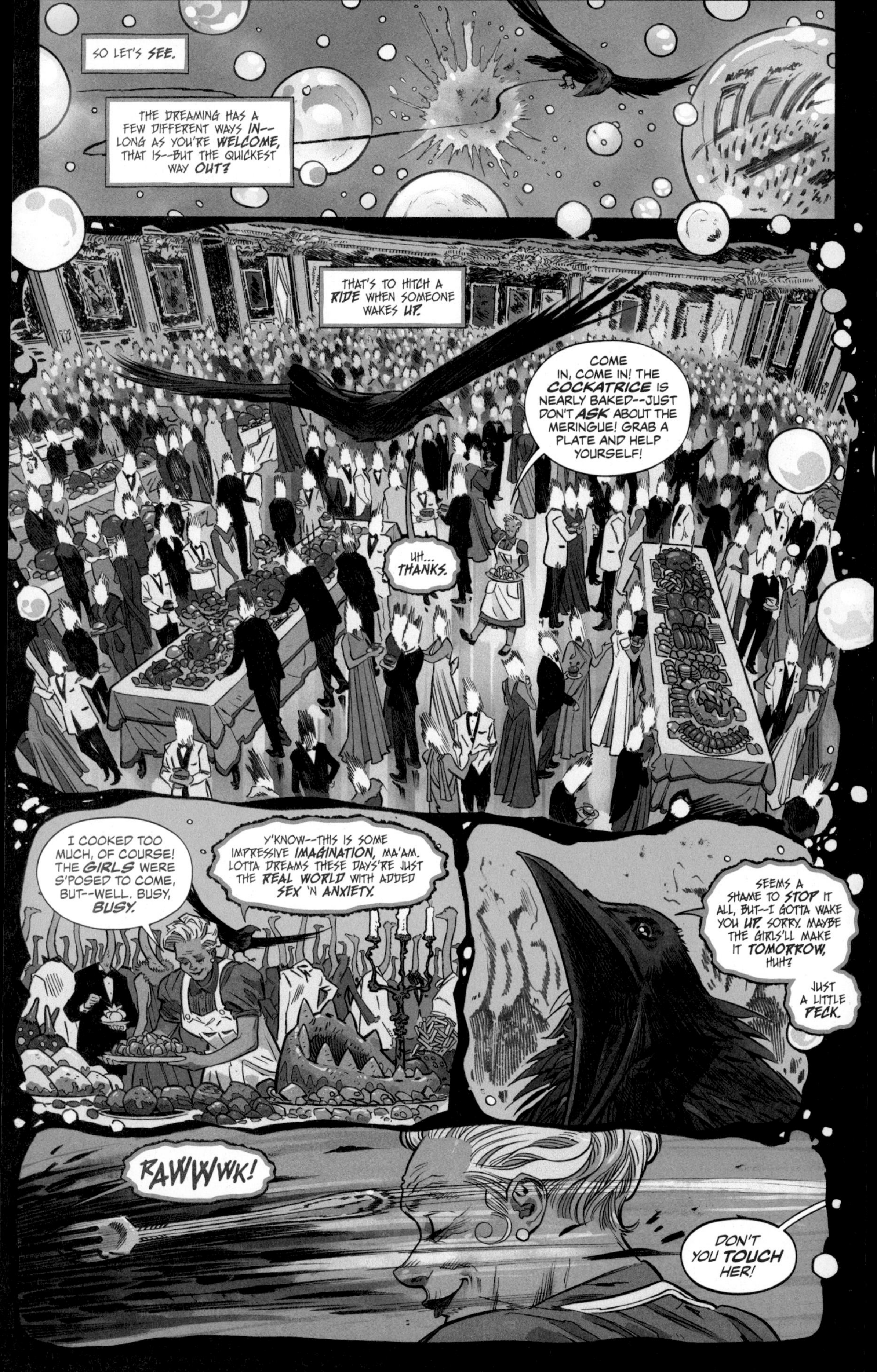
SO LET'S SEE.
THE DREAMING HAS A FEW DIFFERENT WAYS IN--LONG AS YOU'RE WELCOME, THAT IS--BUT THE QUICKEST WAY OUT?
THAT'S TO HITCH A RIDE WHEN SOMEONE WAKES UP.
COME IN, COME IN! THE COCKATRICE IS NEARLY BAKED--JUST DON'T ASK ABOUT THE MERINGUE! GRAB A PLATE AND HELP YOURSELF!
UH... THANKS.
I COOKED TOO MUCH, OF COURSE! THE GIRLS WERE S'POSED TO COME, BUT--WELL. BUSY, BUSY.
Y'KNOW--THIS IS SOME IMPRESSIVE IMAGINATION, MA'AM. LOTTA DREAMS THESE DAYS'RE JUST THE REAL WORLD WITH ADDED SEX 'N ANXIETY.
SEEMS A SHAME TO STOP IT ALL, BUT--I GOTTA WAKE YOU UP. SORRY. MAYBE THE GIRLS'LL MAKE IT TOMORROW, HUH?
JUST A LITTLE PECK.
RAWWWK!
DON'T YOU TOUCH HER!

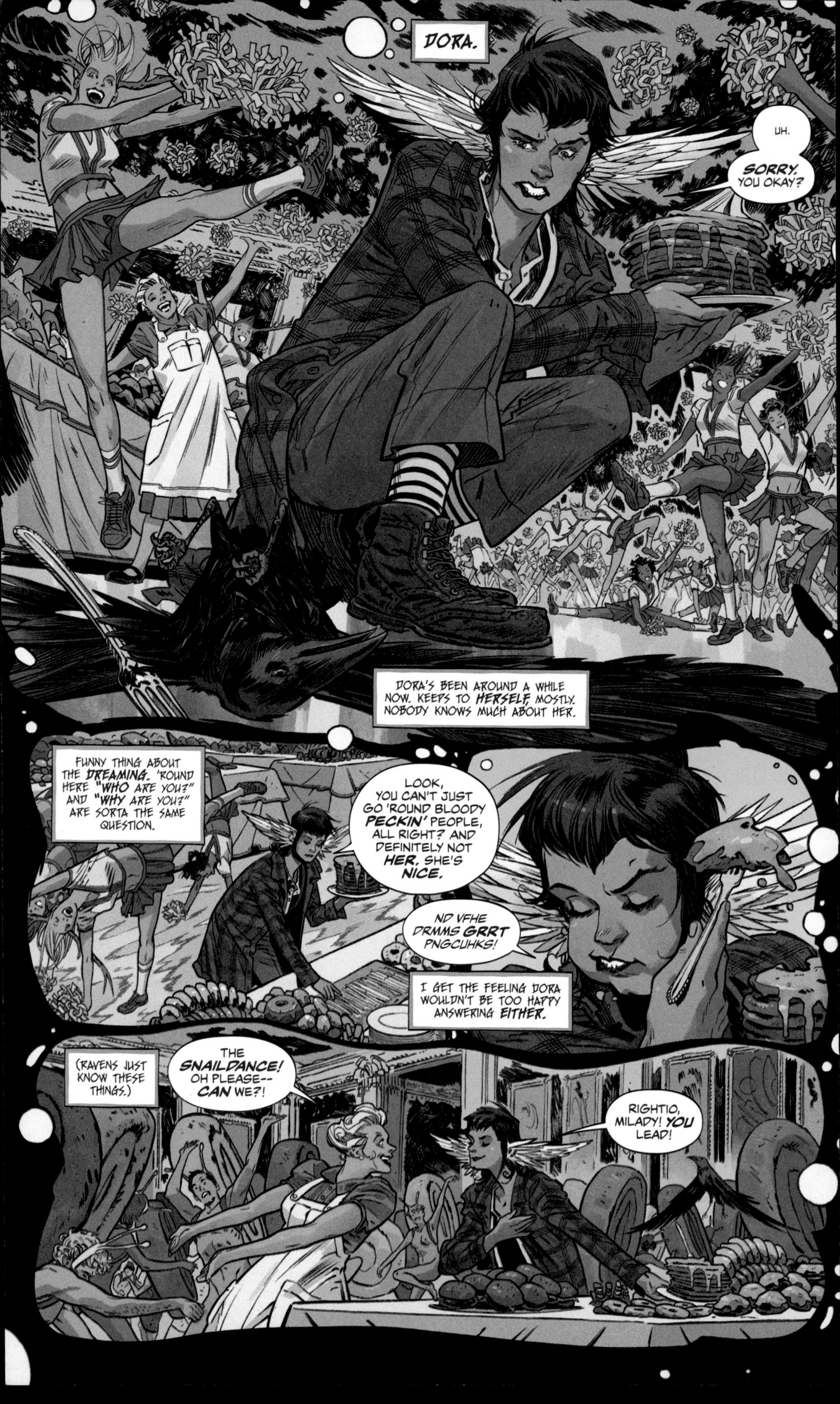
DORA.
UH.
SORRY. YOU OKAY?
DORA'S BEEN AROUND A WHILE NOW. KEEPS TO HERSELF, MOSTLY. NOBODY KNOWS MUCH ABOUT HER.
FUNNY THING ABOUT THE DREAMING. 'ROUND HERE "WHO ARE YOU?" AND "WHY ARE YOU?" ARE SORTA THE SAME QUESTION.
LOOK, YOU CAN'T JUST GO 'ROUND BLOODY PECKIN' PEOPLE, ALL RIGHT? AND DEFINITELY NOT HER. SHE'S NICE.
ND VFHE DRMMS GRRT PNGCUHKS!
I GET THE FEELING DORA WOULDN'T BE TOO HAPPY ANSWERING EITHER.
(RAVENS JUST KNOW THESE THINGS.)
THE SNAILDANCE! OH PLEASE-- CAN WE?!
RIGHTIO, MILADY! YOU LEAD!

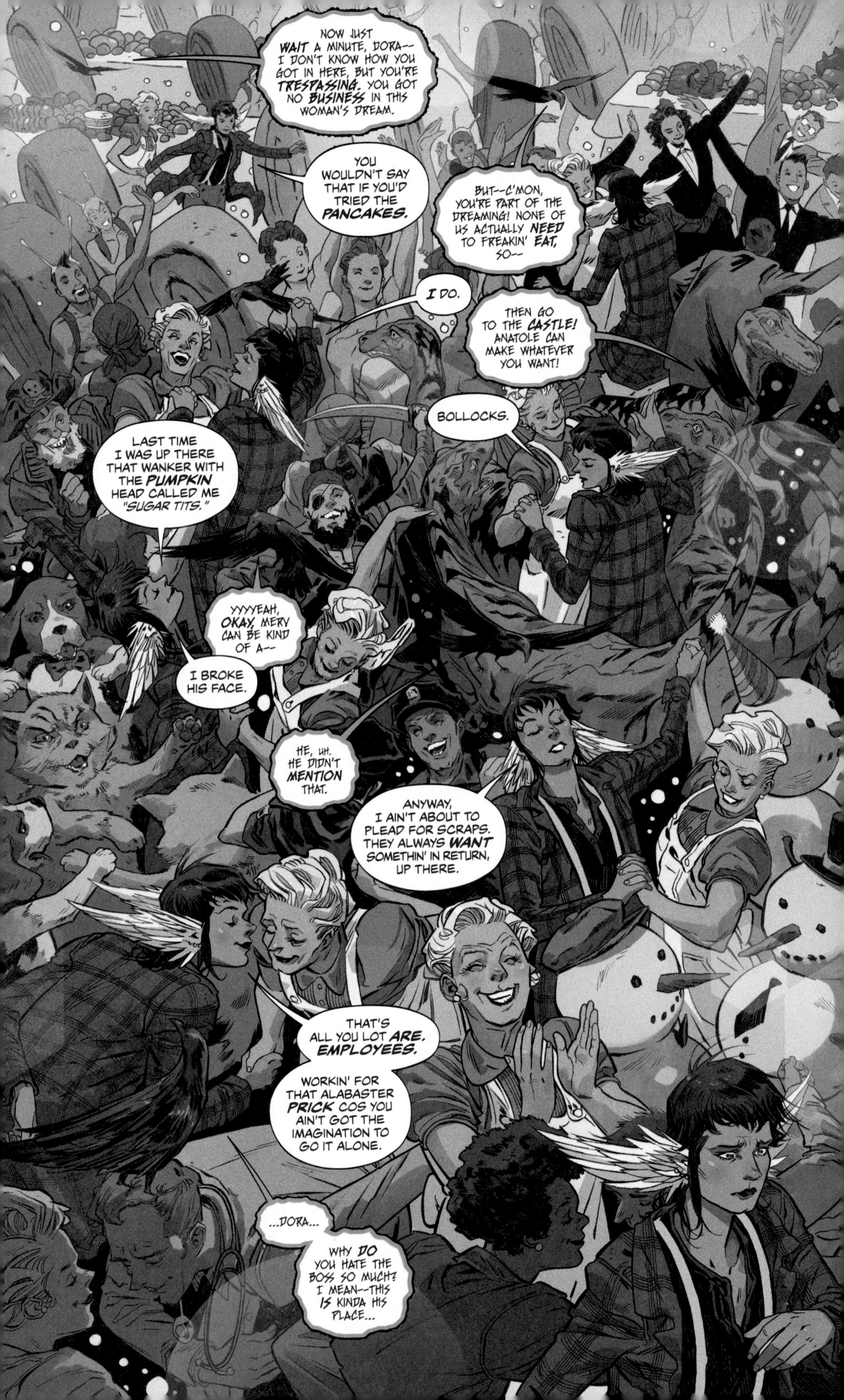
NOW JUST WAIT A MINUTE, DORA-- I DON'T KNOW HOW YOU GOT IN HERE, BUT YOU'RE TRESPASSING. YOU GOT NO BUSINESS IN THIS WOMAN'S DREAM.
YOU WOULDN'T SAY THAT IF YOU'D TRIED THE PANCAKES.
BUT--C'MON, YOU'RE PART OF THE DREAMING! NONE OF US ACTUALLY NEED TO FREAKIN' EAT, SO--
I DO.
THEN GO TO THE CASTLE! ANATOLE CAN MAKE WHATEVER YOU WANT!
BOLLOCKS.
LAST TIME I WAS UP THERE THAT WANKER WITH THE PUMPKIN HEAD CALLED ME "SUGAR TITS."
YYYYEAH, OKAY, MERV CAN BE KIND OF A--
I BROKE HIS FACE.
HE, UH. HE DIDN'T MENTION THAT.
ANYWAY, I AIN'T ABOUT TO PLEAD FOR SCRAPS. THEY ALWAYS WANT SOMETHIN' IN RETURN, UP THERE.
THAT'S ALL YOU LOT ARE. EMPLOYEES.
WORKIN' FOR THAT ALABASTER PRICK COS YOU AIN'T GOT THE IMAGINATION TO GO IT ALONE.
...DORA...
WHY DO YOU HATE THE BOSS SO MUCH? I MEAN--THIS IS KINDA HIS PLACE...

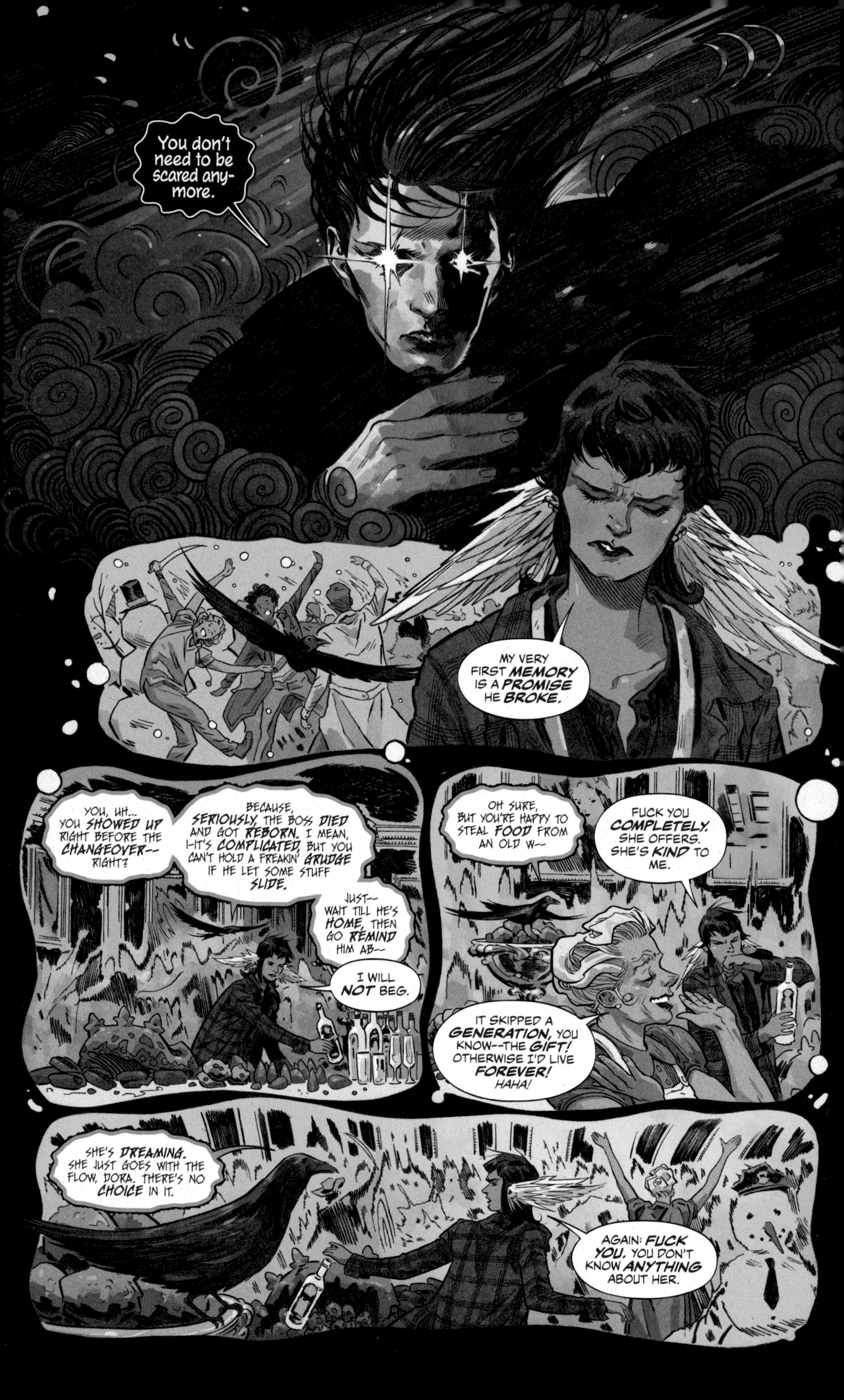

You don't need to be scared any-more.
MY VERY FIRST MEMORY IS A PROMISE HE BROKE.
YOU, UH... YOU SHOWED UP RIGHT BEFORE THE CHANGEOVER-- RIGHT?
BECAUSE, SERIOUSLY, THE BOSS DIED AND GOT REBORN. I MEAN, I-IT'S COMPLICATED, BUT YOU CAN'T HOLD A FREAKIN' GRUDGE IF HE LET SOME STUFF SLIDE.
JUST-- WAIT TILL HE'S HOME, THEN GO REMIND HIM AB--
I WILL NOT BEG.
OH SURE, BUT YOU'RE HAPPY TO STEAL FOOD FROM AN OLD W--
FUCK YOU COMPLETELY. SHE OFFERS. SHE'S KIND TO ME.
IT SKIPPED A GENERATION, YOU KNOW--THE GIFT! OTHERWISE I'D LIVE FOREVER! HAHA!
SHE'S DREAMING. SHE JUST GOES WITH THE FLOW, DORA. THERE'S NO CHOICE IN IT.
AGAIN: FUCK YOU. YOU DON'T KNOW ANYTHING ABOUT HER.

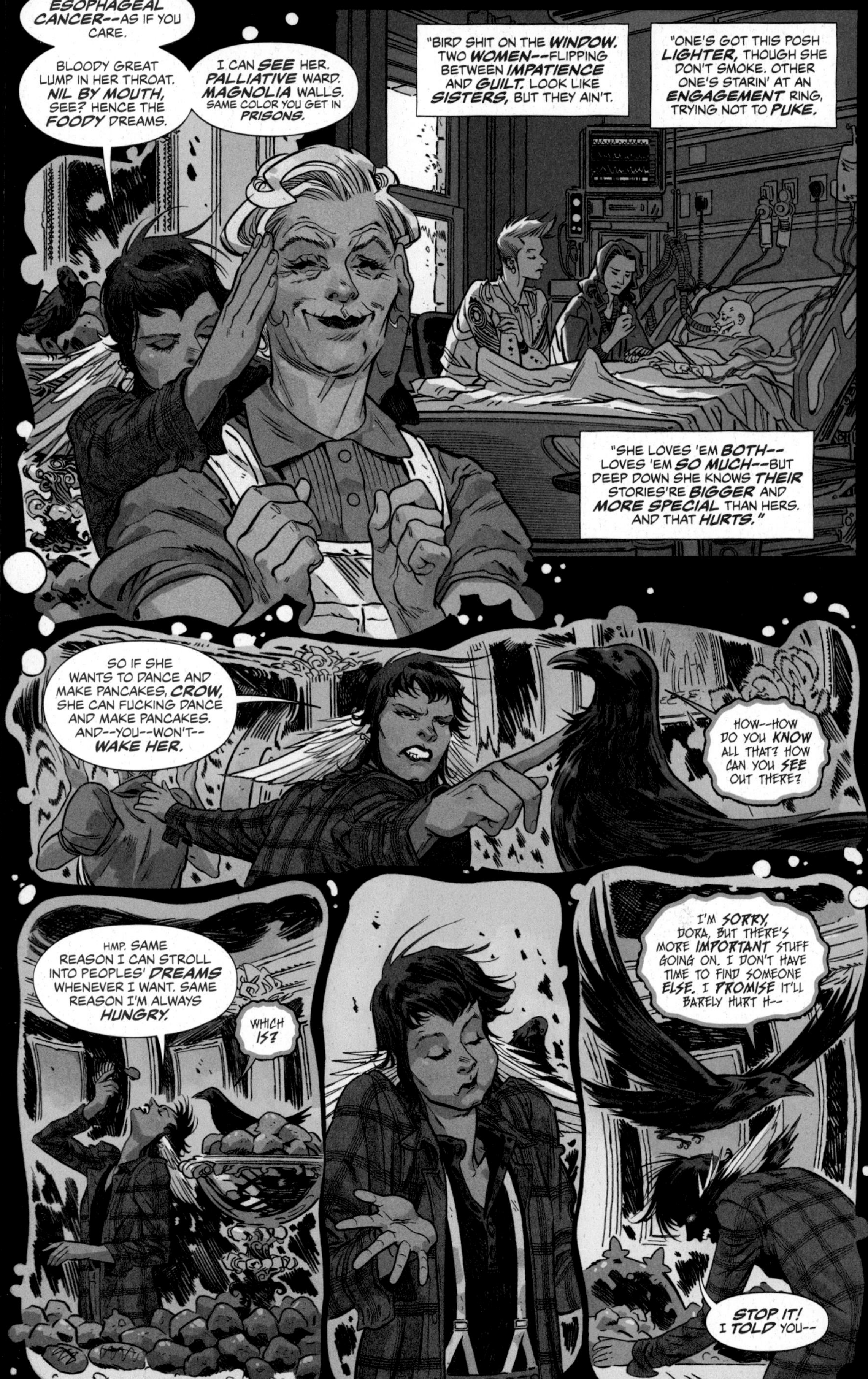

ESOPHAGEAL CANCER--AS IF YOU CARE.
BLOODY GREAT LUMP IN HER THROAT. NIL BY MOUTH, SEE? HENCE THE FOODY DREAMS.
I CAN SEE HER. PALLIATIVE WARD. MAGNOLIA WALLS. SAME COLOR YOU GET IN PRISONS.
"BIRD SHIT ON THE WINDOW. TWO WOMEN--FLIPPING BETWEEN IMPATIENCE AND GUILT. LOOK LIKE SISTERS, BUT THEY AIN'T.
"ONE'S GOT THIS POSH LIGHTER, THOUGH SHE DON'T SMOKE. OTHER ONE'S STARIN' AT AN ENGAGEMENT RING, TRYING NOT TO PUKE.
"SHE LOVES 'EM BOTH--LOVES 'EM SO MUCH--BUT DEEP DOWN SHE KNOWS THEIR STORIES'RE BIGGER AND MORE SPECIAL THAN HERS. AND THAT HURTS."
SO IF SHE WANTS TO DANCE AND MAKE PANCAKES, CROW, SHE CAN FUCKING DANCE AND MAKE PANCAKES. AND--YOU--WON'T--WAKE HER.
HOW--HOW DO YOU KNOW ALL THAT? HOW CAN YOU SEE OUT THERE?
HMP. SAME REASON I CAN STROLL INTO PEOPLES' DREAMS WHENEVER I WANT. SAME REASON I'M ALWAYS HUNGRY.
WHICH IS?
I'M SORRY, DORA, BUT THERE'S MORE IMPORTANT STUFF GOING ON. I DON'T HAVE TIME TO FIND SOMEONE ELSE. I PROMISE IT'LL BARELY HURT H--
STOP IT! I TOLD YOU--

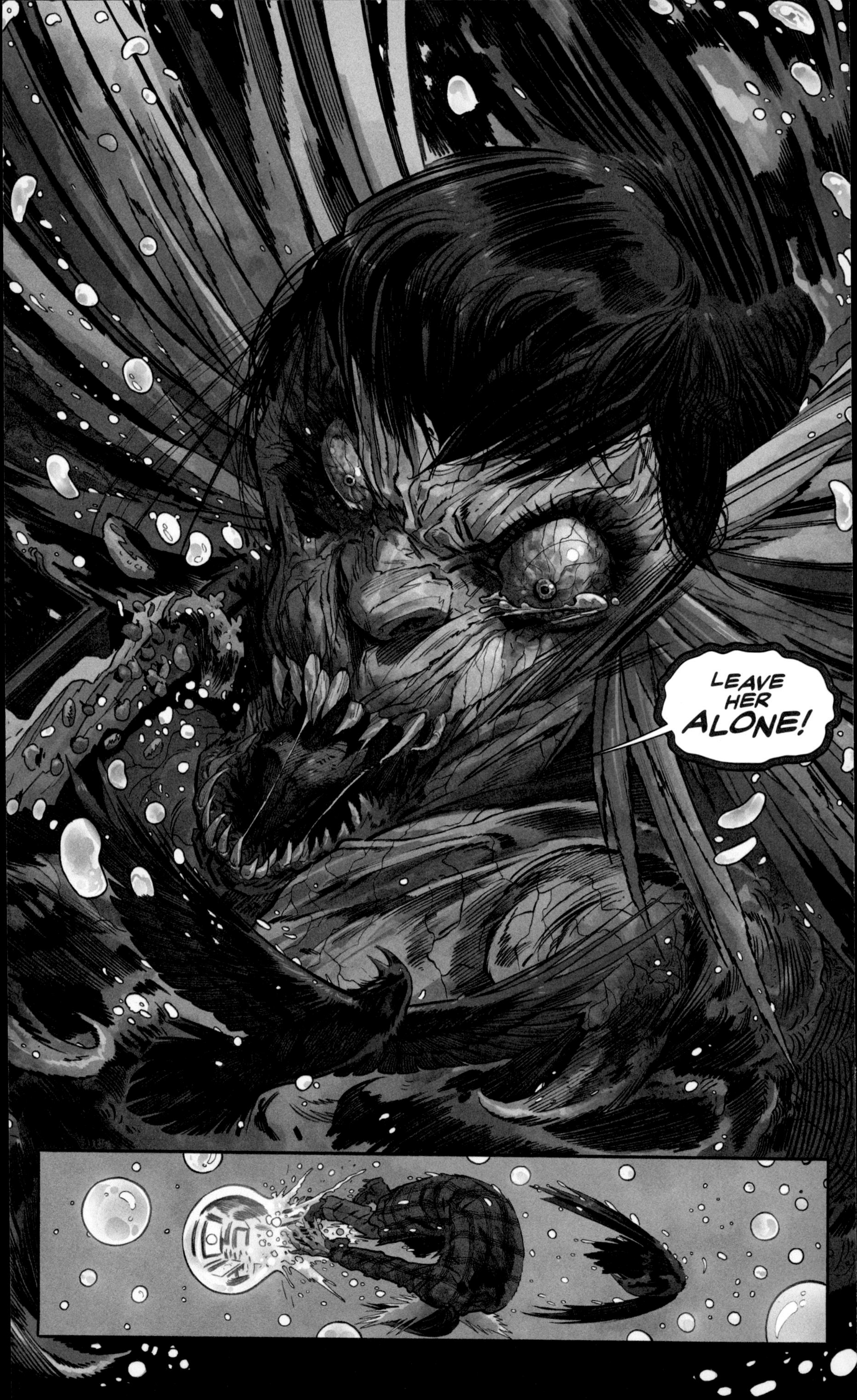
LEAVE HER ALONE!

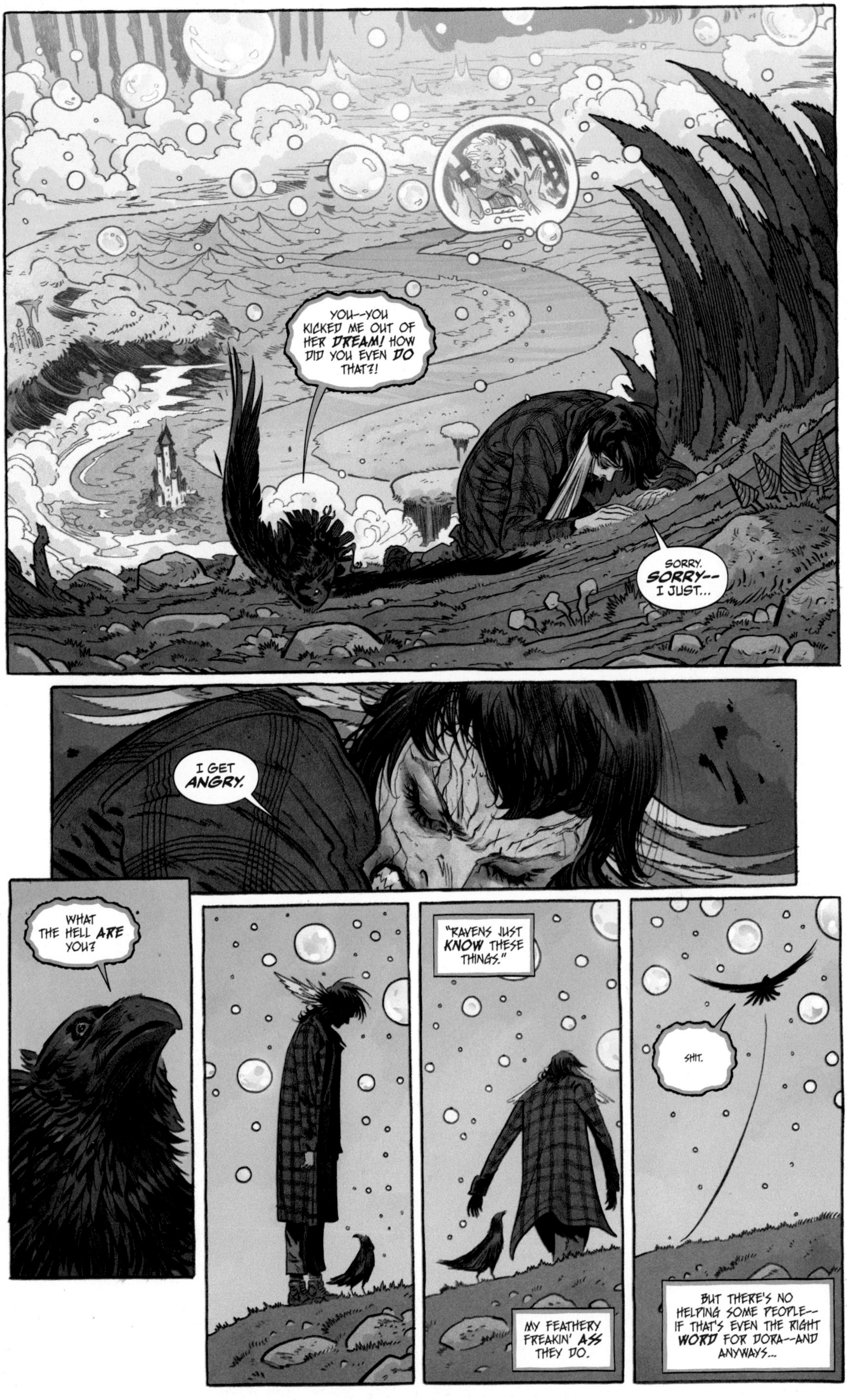

YOU--YOU KICKED ME OUT OF HER DREAM! HOW DID YOU EVEN DO THAT?!
SORRY. SORRY-- I JUST...
I GET ANGRY.
WHAT THE HELL ARE YOU?
"RAVENS JUST KNOW THESE THINGS."
MY FEATHERY FREAKIN' ASS THEY DO.
SHIT.
BUT THERE'S NO HELPING SOME PEOPLE-- IF THAT'S EVEN THE RIGHT WORD FOR DORA--AND ANYWAYS...

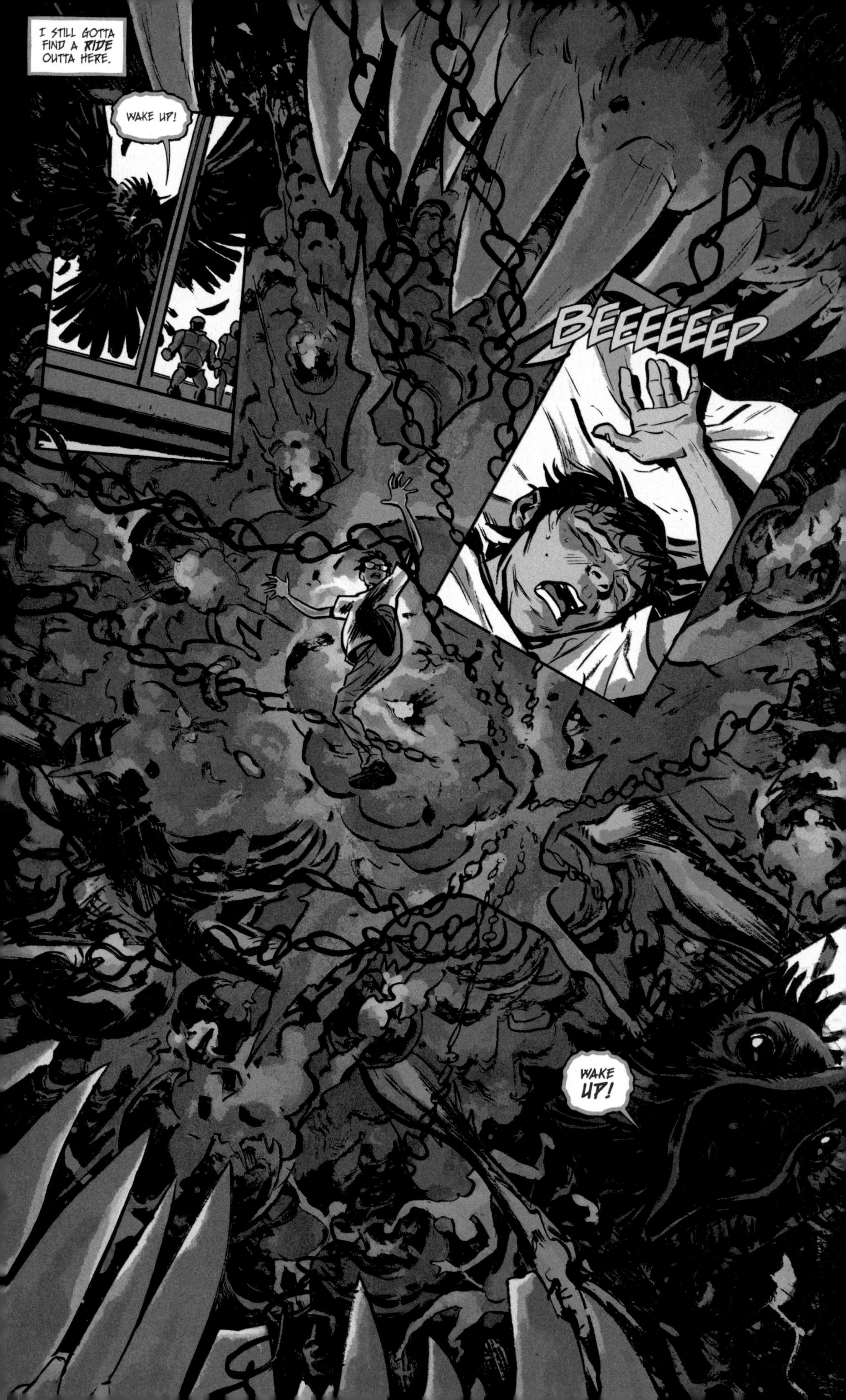
I STILL GOTTA FIND A RIDE OUTTA HERE.
WAKE UP!
BEEEEEEEP
WAKE UP!

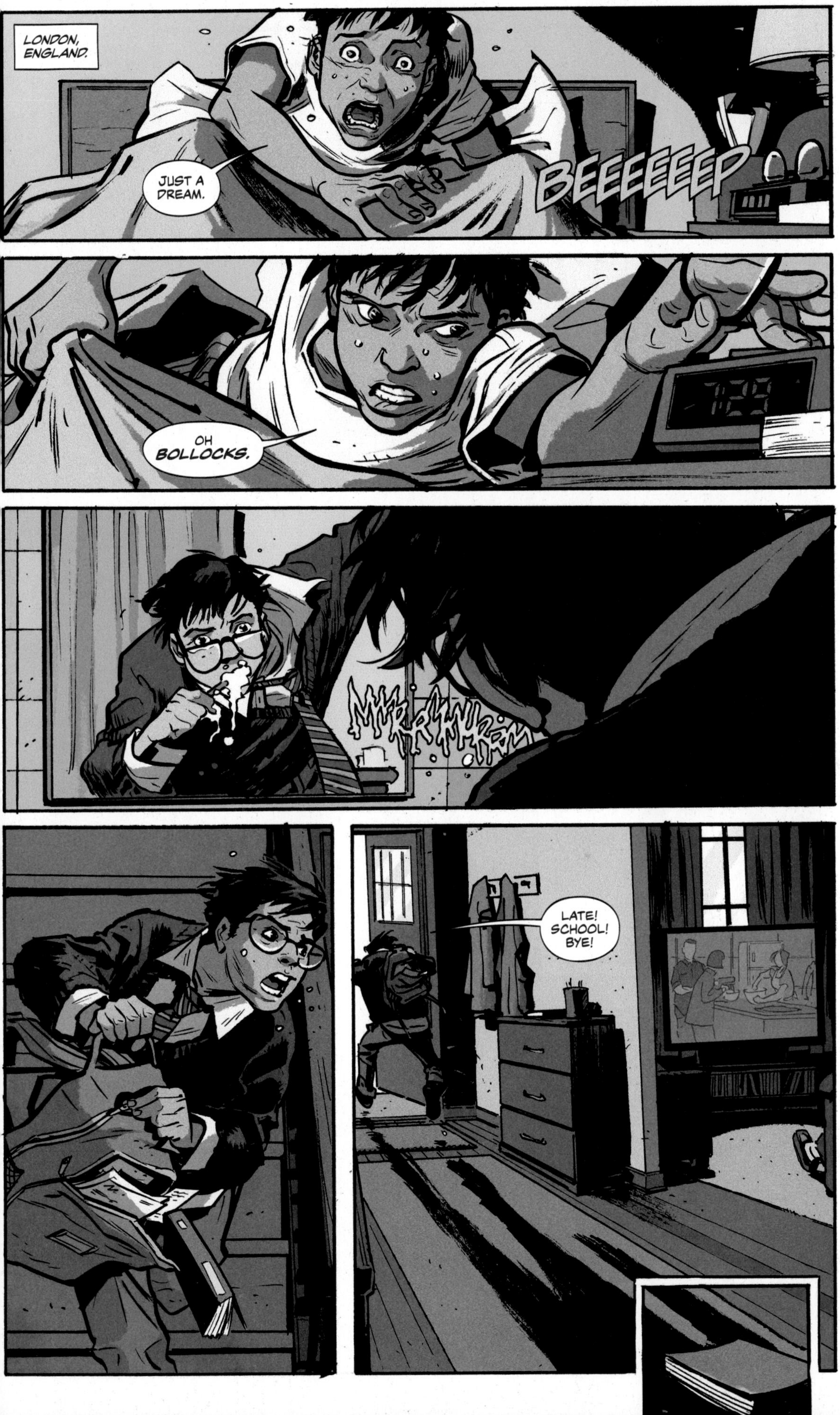
LONDON, ENGLAND.
JUST A DREAM.
BEEEEEEP
OH BOLLOCKS.
LATE! SCHOOL! BYE!

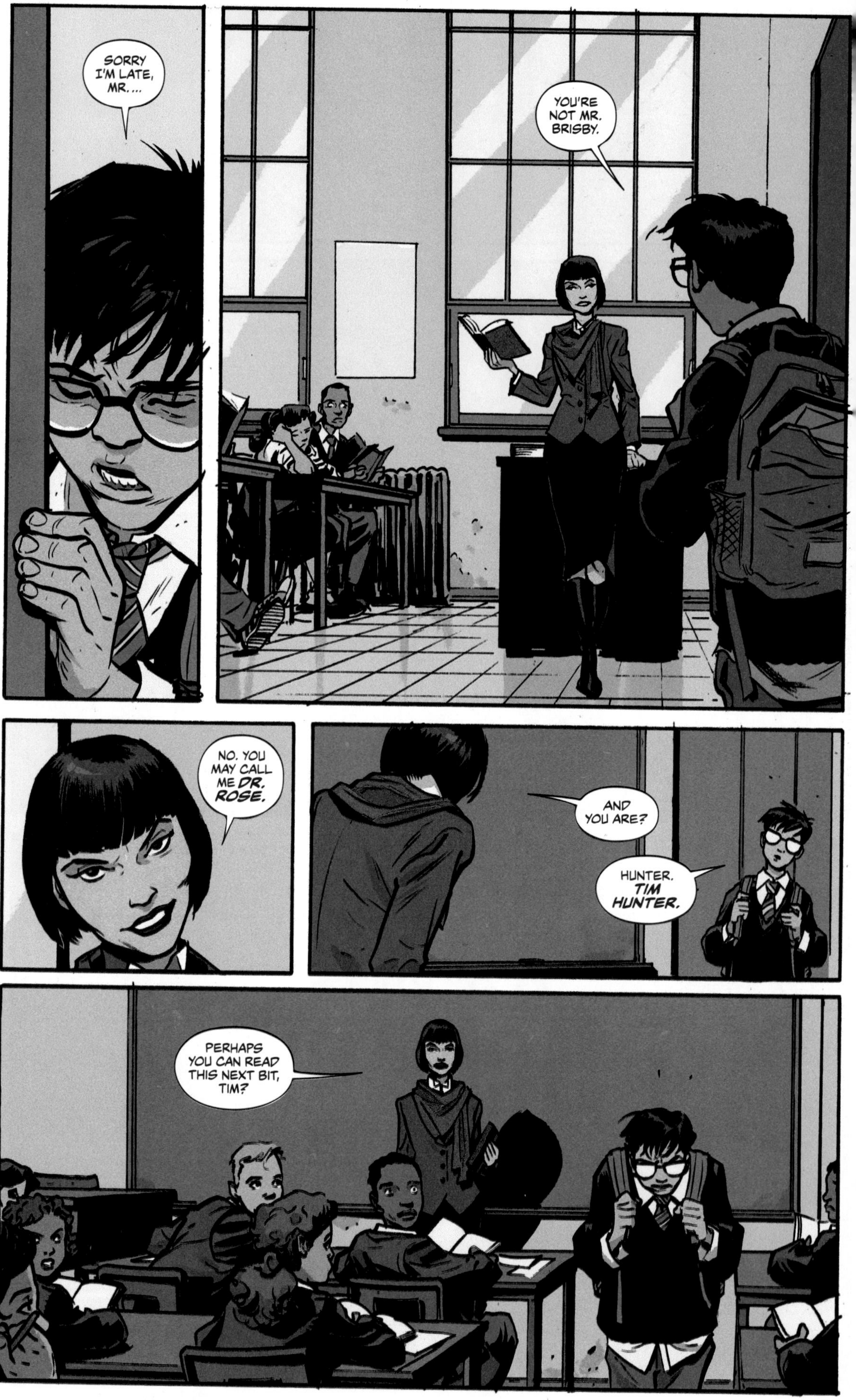
SORRY I'M LATE, MR....
YOU'RE NOT MR. BRISBY.
NO. YOU MAY CALL ME DR. ROSE.
AND YOU ARE?
HUNTER. TIM HUNTER.
PERHAPS YOU CAN READ THIS NEXT BIT, TIM?

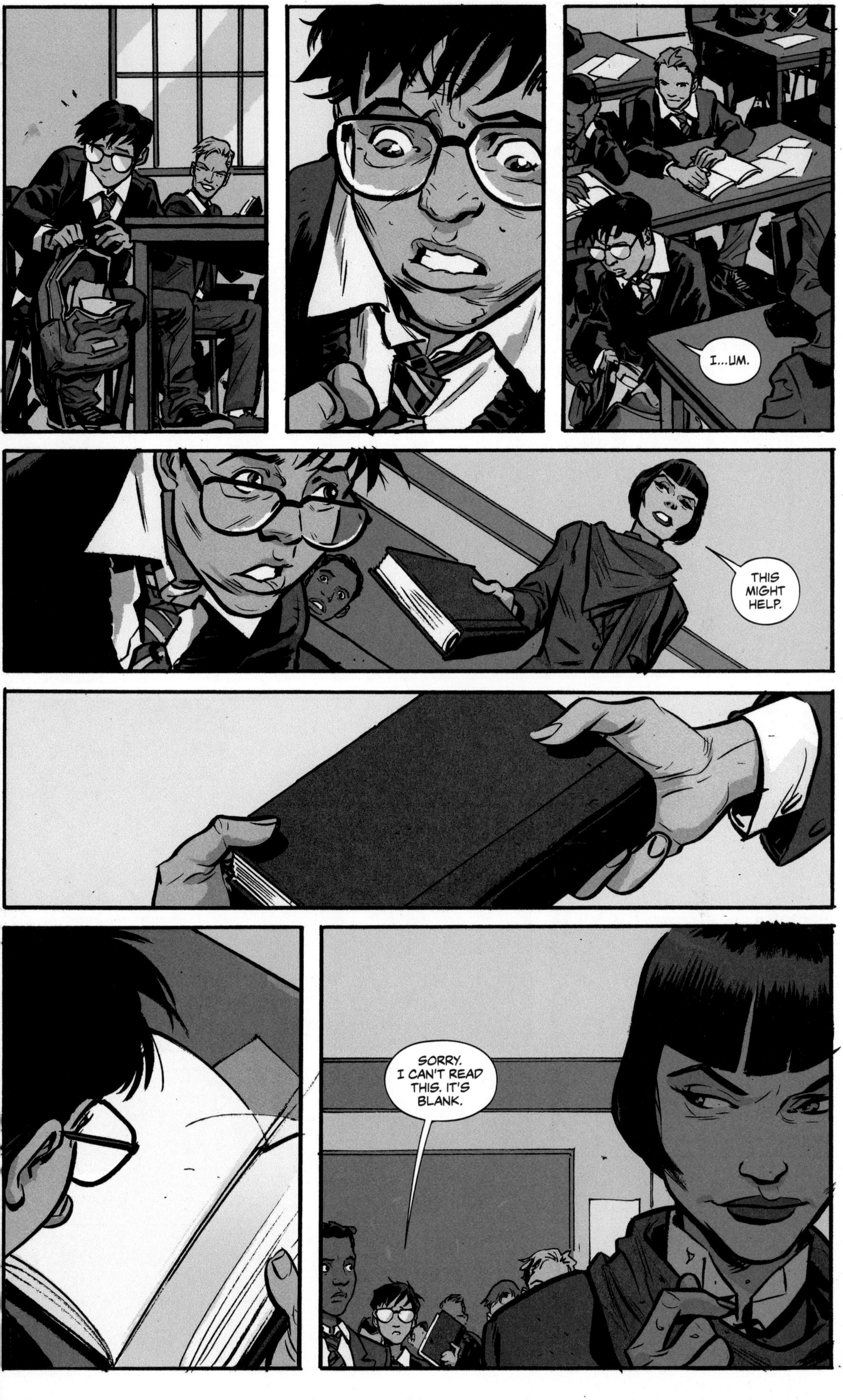
I...UM.
THIS MIGHT HELP.
SORRY. I CAN'T READ THIS. IT'S BLANK.

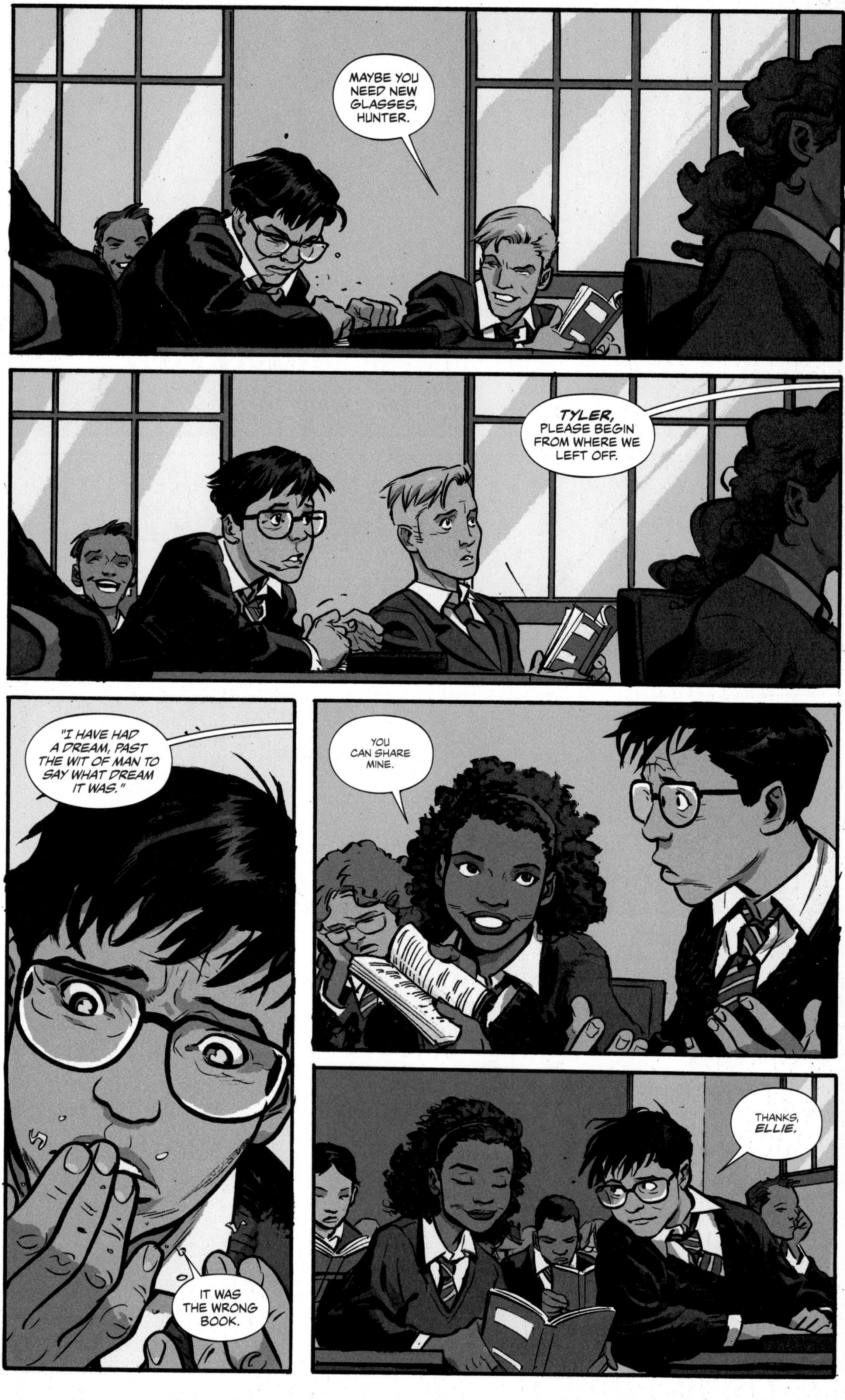
MAYBE YOU NEED NEW GLASSES, HUNTER.
TYLER, PLEASE BEGIN FROM WHERE WE LEFT OFF.
"I HAVE HAD A DREAM, PAST THE WIT OF MAN TO SAY WHAT DREAM IT WAS."
IT WAS THE WRONG BOOK.
YOU CAN SHARE MINE.
THANKS, ELLIE.

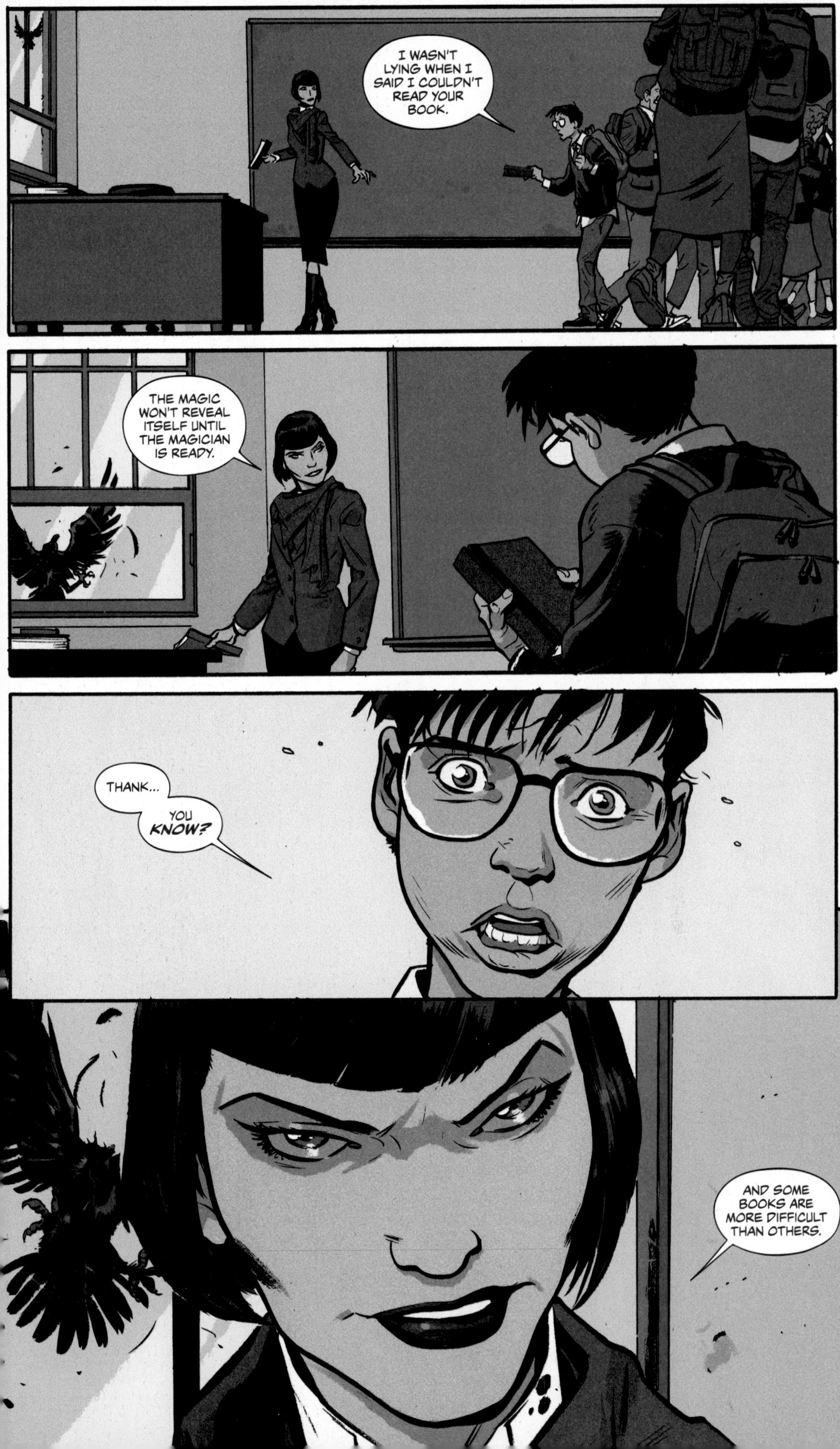
I WASN'T LYING WHEN I SAID I COULDN'T READ YOUR BOOK.
THE MAGIC WON'T REVEAL ITSELF UNTIL THE MAGICIAN IS READY.
THANK...
YOU *KNOW?*
AND SOME BOOKS ARE MORE DIFFICULT THAN OTHERS.

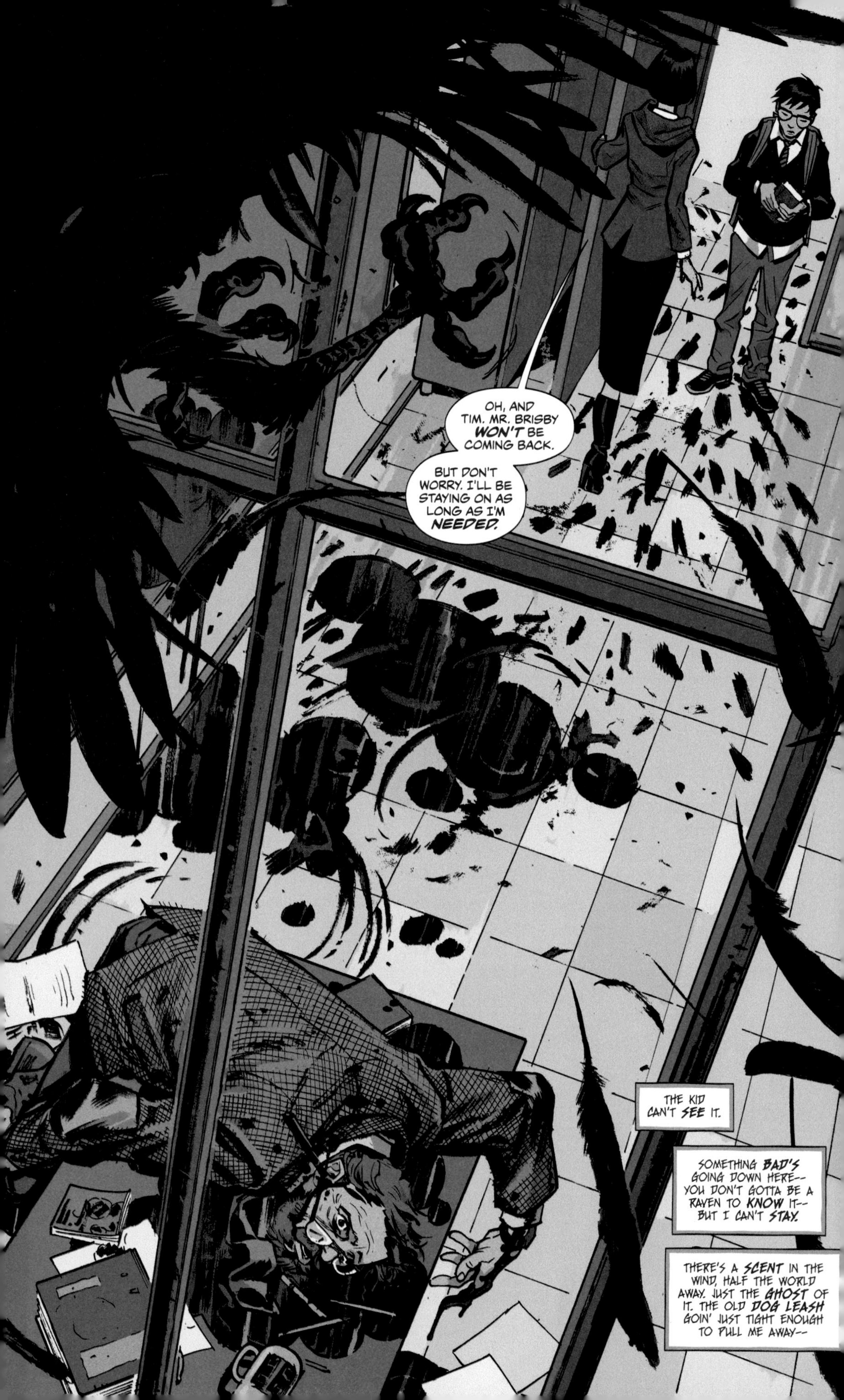
OH, AND TIM. MR. BRISBY **WON'T** BE COMING BACK.
BUT DON'T WORRY. I'LL BE STAYING ON AS LONG AS I'M **NEEDED.**
THE KID CAN'T **SEE** IT.
SOMETHING **BAD'S** GOING DOWN HERE-- YOU DON'T GOTTA BE A RAVEN TO **KNOW** IT-- BUT I CAN'T **STAY.**
THERE'S A **SCENT** IN THE WIND, HALF THE WORLD AWAY. JUST THE **GHOST** OF IT. THE OLD **DOG LEASH** GOIN' JUST TIGHT ENOUGH TO PULL ME AWAY--

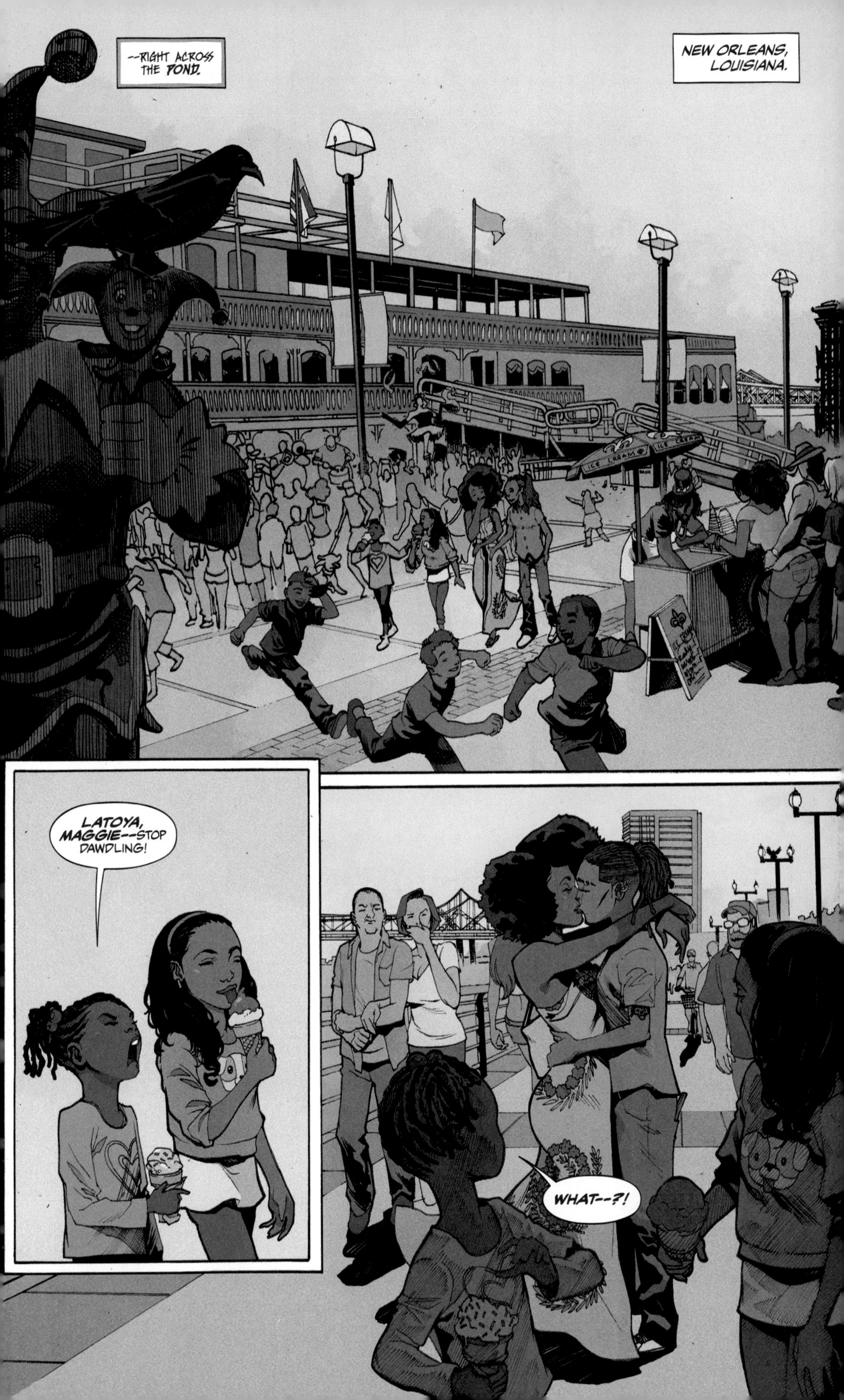
--RIGHT ACROSS THE POND.
NEW ORLEANS, LOUISIANA.
LATOYA, MAGGIE--STOP DAWDLING!
WHAT--?!

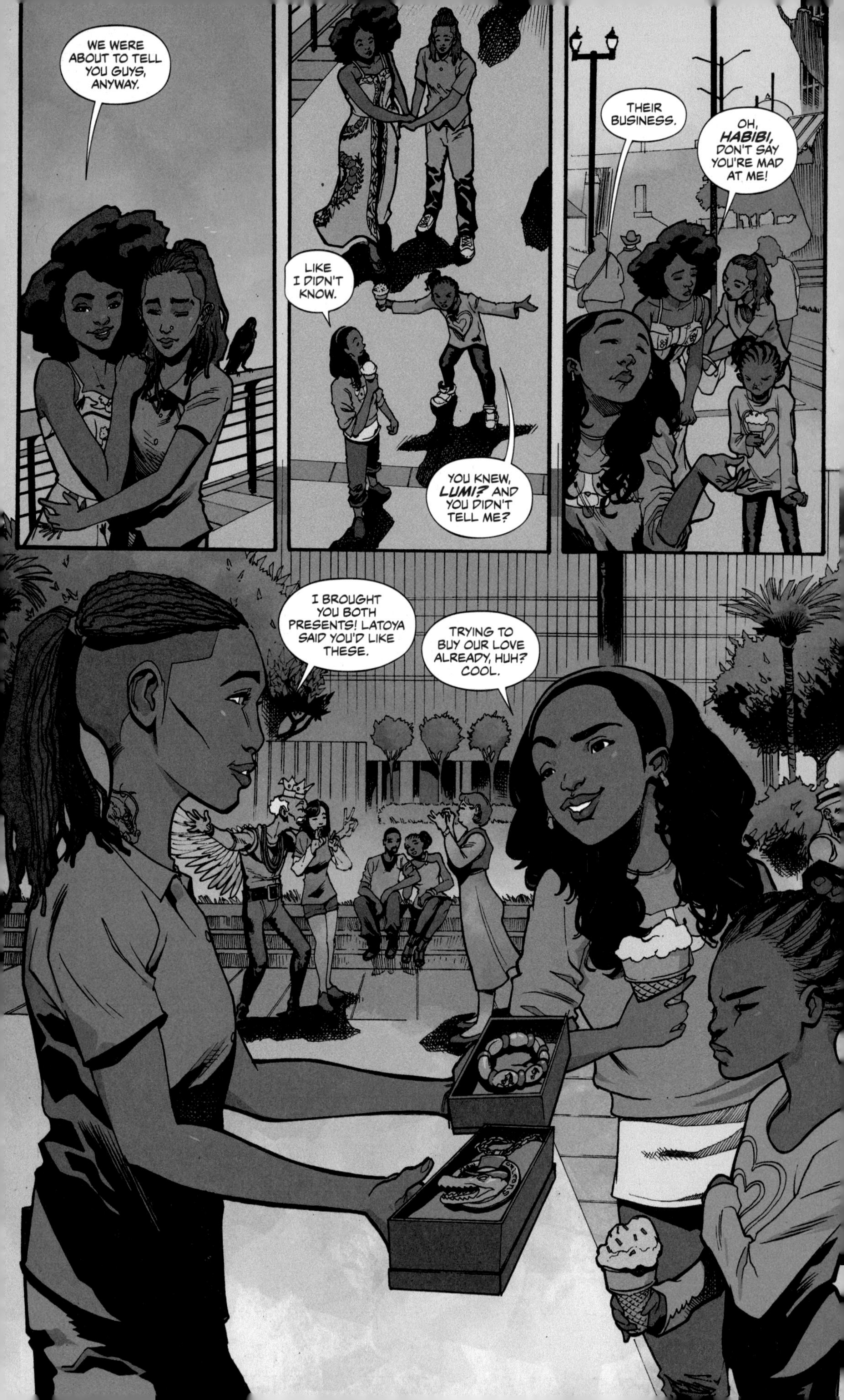
WE WERE ABOUT TO TELL YOU GUYS, ANYWAY.
LIKE I DIDN'T KNOW.
YOU KNEW, LUMI? AND YOU DIDN'T TELL ME?
THEIR BUSINESS.
OH, HABIBI, DON'T SAY YOU'RE MAD AT ME!
I BROUGHT YOU BOTH PRESENTS! LATOYA SAID YOU'D LIKE THESE.
TRYING TO BUY OUR LOVE ALREADY, HUH? COOL.

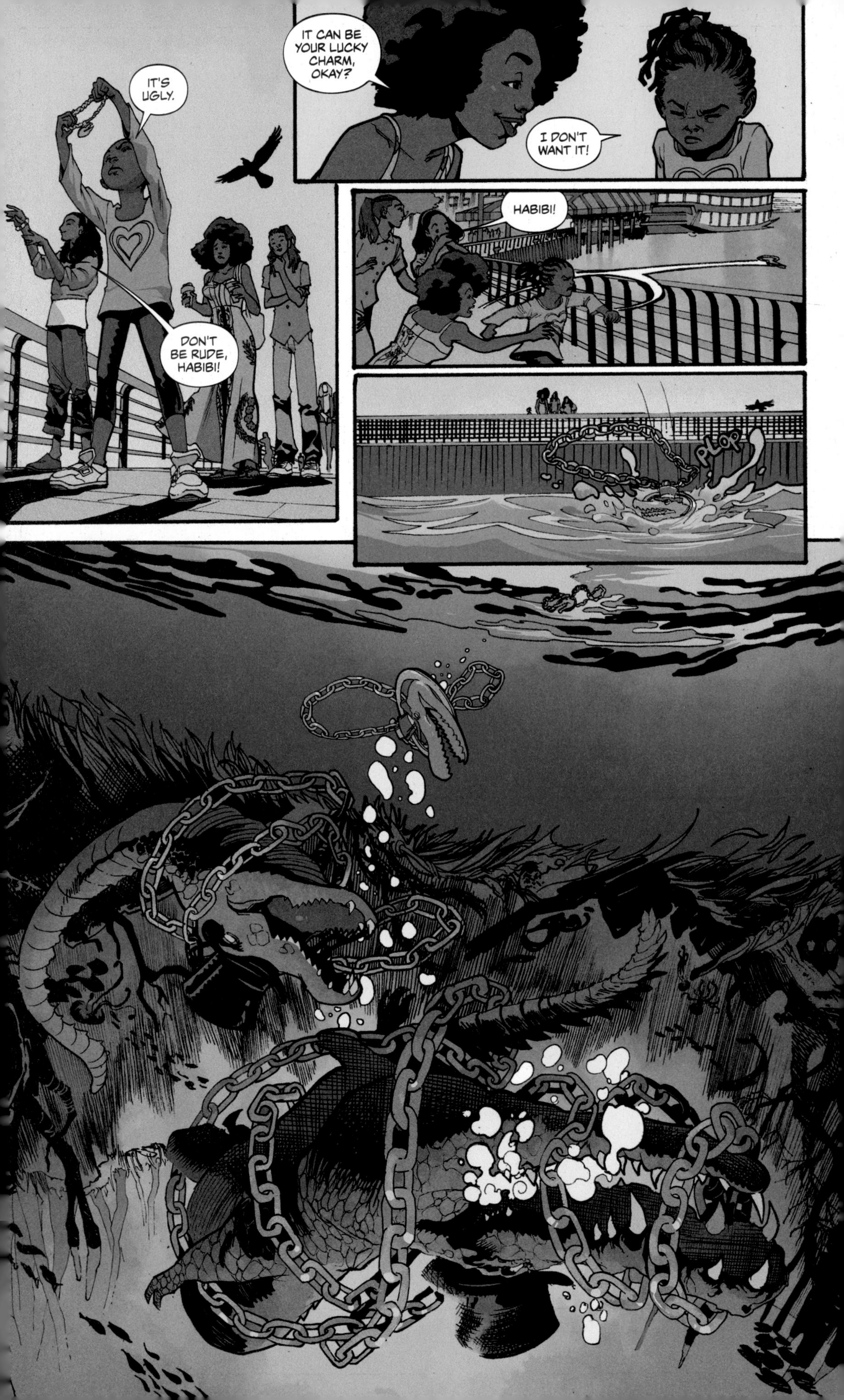
IT'S UGLY.
DON'T BE RUDE, HABIBI!
IT CAN BE YOUR LUCKY CHARM, OKAY?
I DON'T WANT IT!
HABIBI!
PLOP

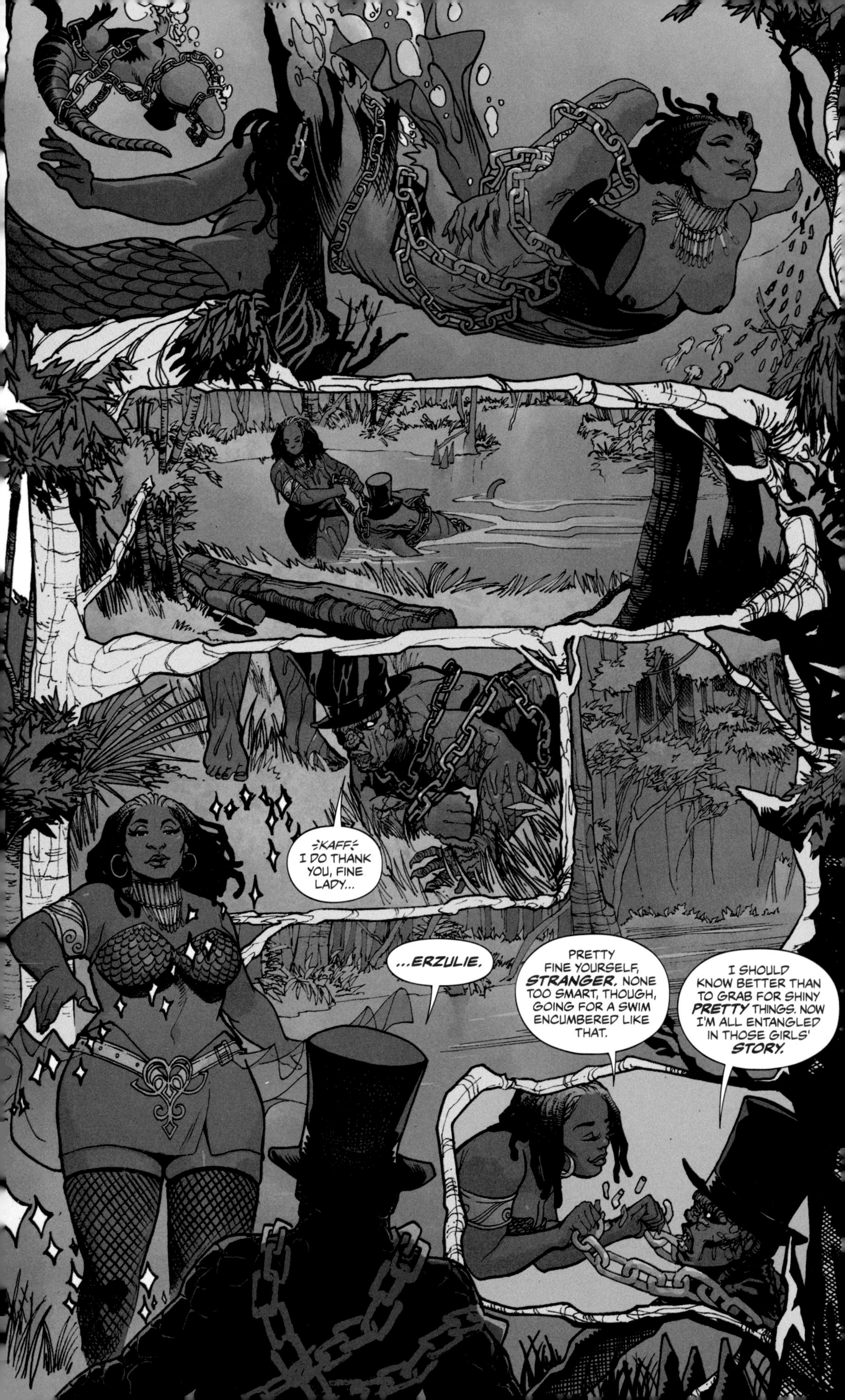

KAFF I DO THANK YOU, FINE LADY...
...ERZULIE.
PRETTY FINE YOURSELF, STRANGER. NONE TOO SMART, THOUGH, GOING FOR A SWIM ENCUMBERED LIKE THAT.
I SHOULD KNOW BETTER THAN TO GRAB FOR SHINY PRETTY THINGS. NOW I'M ALL ENTANGLED IN THOSE GIRLS' STORY.

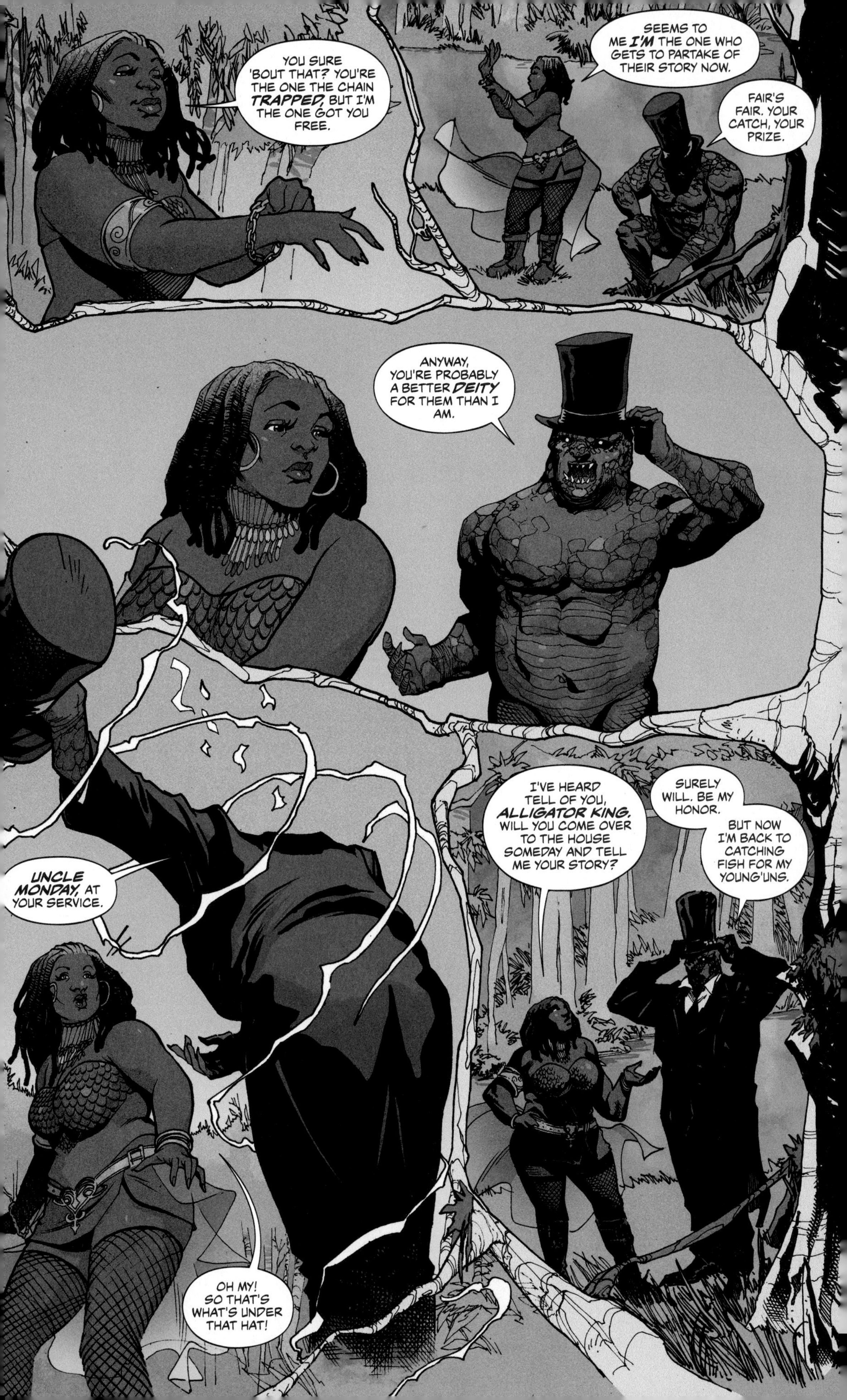

YOU SURE 'BOUT THAT? YOU'RE THE ONE THE CHAIN TRAPPED, BUT I'M THE ONE GOT YOU FREE.
SEEMS TO ME I'M THE ONE WHO GETS TO PARTAKE OF THEIR STORY NOW.
FAIR'S FAIR. YOUR CATCH, YOUR PRIZE.
ANYWAY, YOU'RE PROBABLY A BETTER DEITY FOR THEM THAN I AM.
UNCLE MONDAY, AT YOUR SERVICE.
OH MY! SO THAT'S WHAT'S UNDER THAT HAT!
I'VE HEARD TELL OF YOU, ALLIGATOR KING. WILL YOU COME OVER TO THE HOUSE SOMEDAY AND TELL ME YOUR STORY?
SURELY WILL. BE MY HONOR.
BUT NOW I'M BACK TO CATCHING FISH FOR MY YOUNG'UNS.

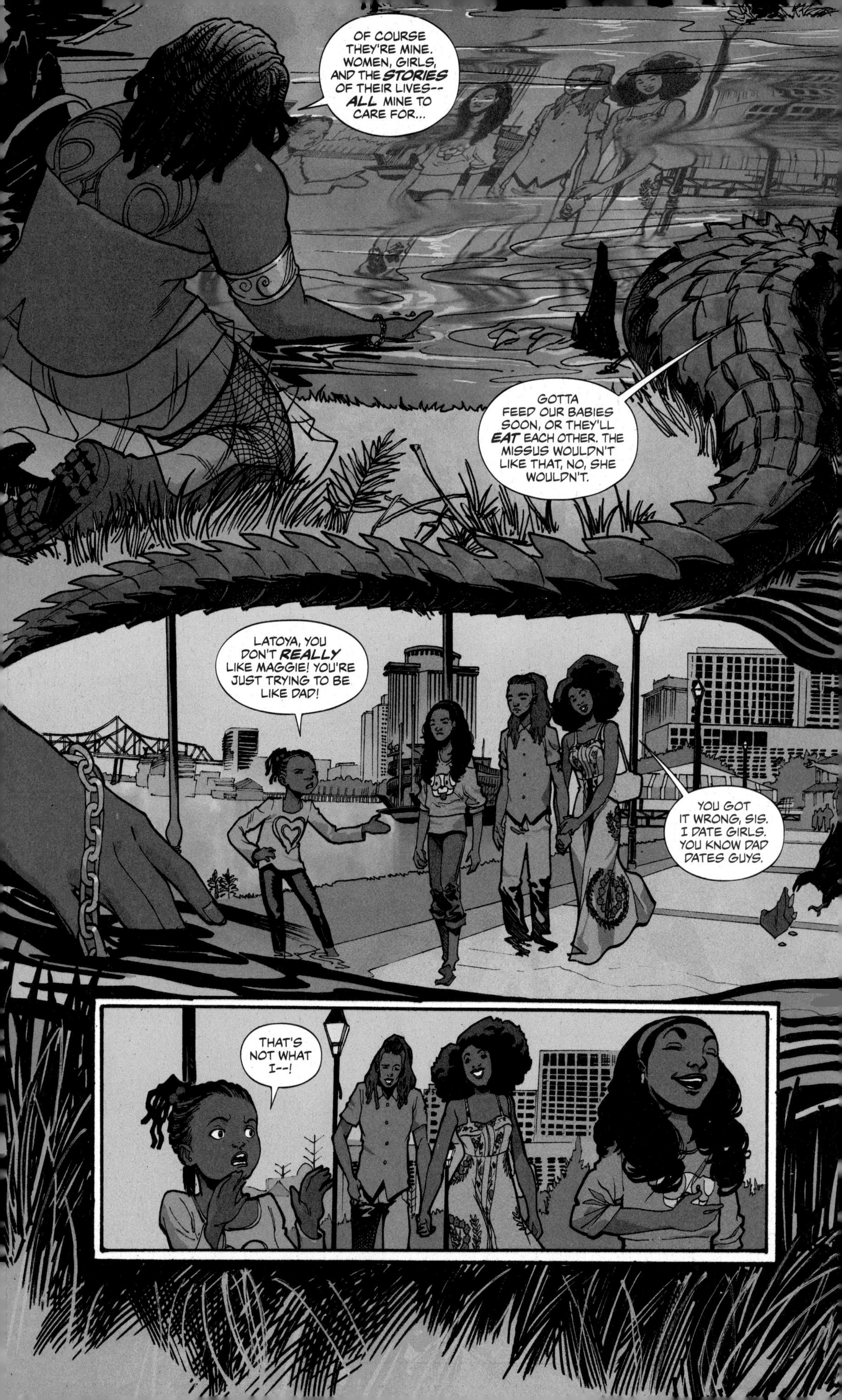
OF COURSE THEY'RE MINE. WOMEN, GIRLS, AND THE STORIES OF THEIR LIVES--ALL MINE TO CARE FOR...
GOTTA FEED OUR BABIES SOON, OR THEY'LL EAT EACH OTHER. THE MISSUS WOULDN'T LIKE THAT, NO, SHE WOULDN'T.
LATOYA, YOU DON'T REALLY LIKE MAGGIE! YOU'RE JUST TRYING TO BE LIKE DAD!
YOU GOT IT WRONG, SIS. I DATE GIRLS. YOU KNOW DAD DATES GUYS.
THAT'S NOT WHAT I--!

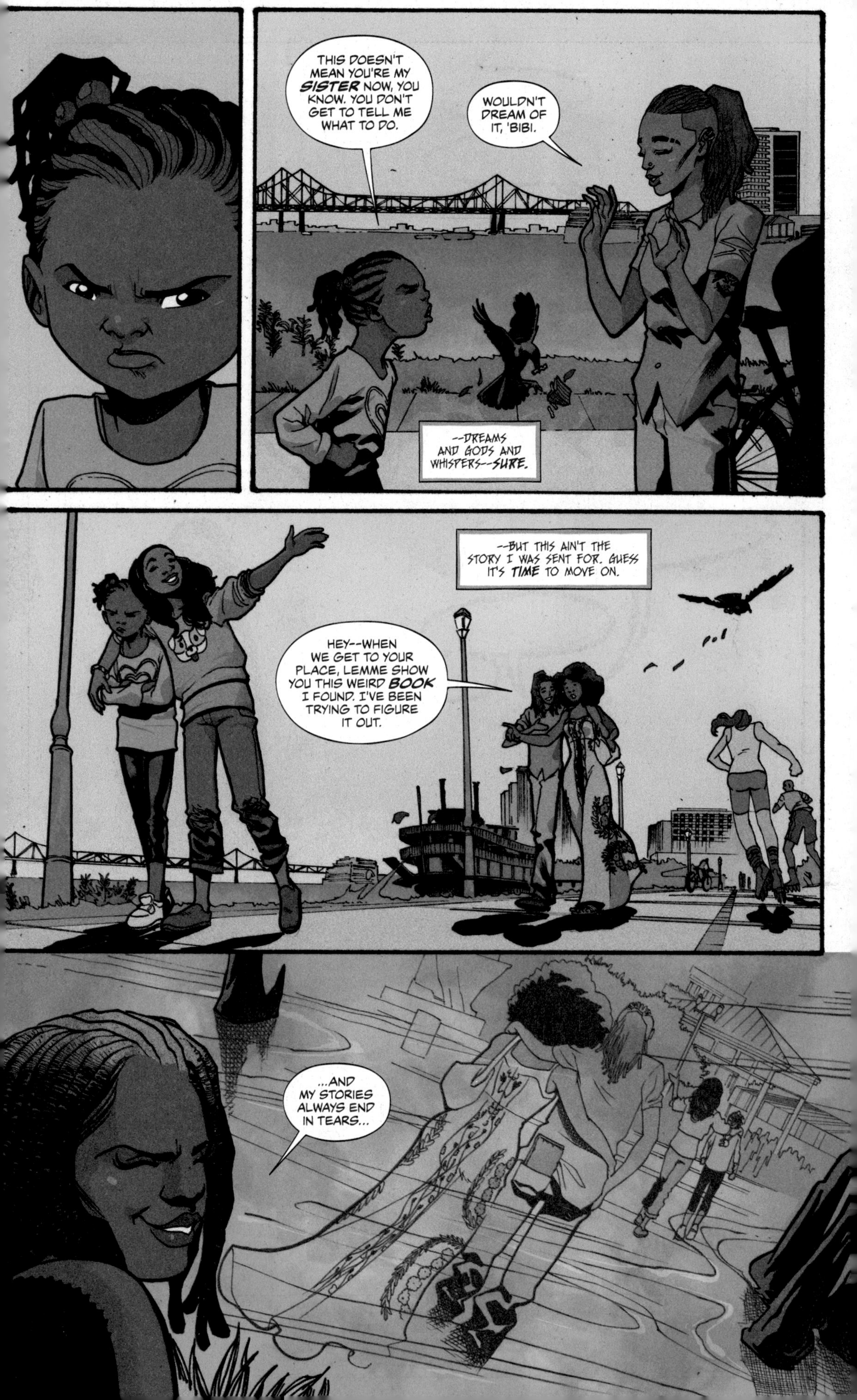
THIS DOESN'T MEAN YOU'RE MY SISTER NOW, YOU KNOW. YOU DON'T GET TO TELL ME WHAT TO DO.
WOULDN'T DREAM OF IT, 'BIBI.
--DREAMS AND GODS AND WHISPERS--SURE.
--BUT THIS AIN'T THE STORY I WAS SENT FOR. GUESS IT'S TIME TO MOVE ON.
HEY--WHEN WE GET TO YOUR PLACE, LEMME SHOW YOU THIS WEIRD BOOK I FOUND. I'VE BEEN TRYING TO FIGURE IT OUT.
...AND MY STORIES ALWAYS END IN TEARS...

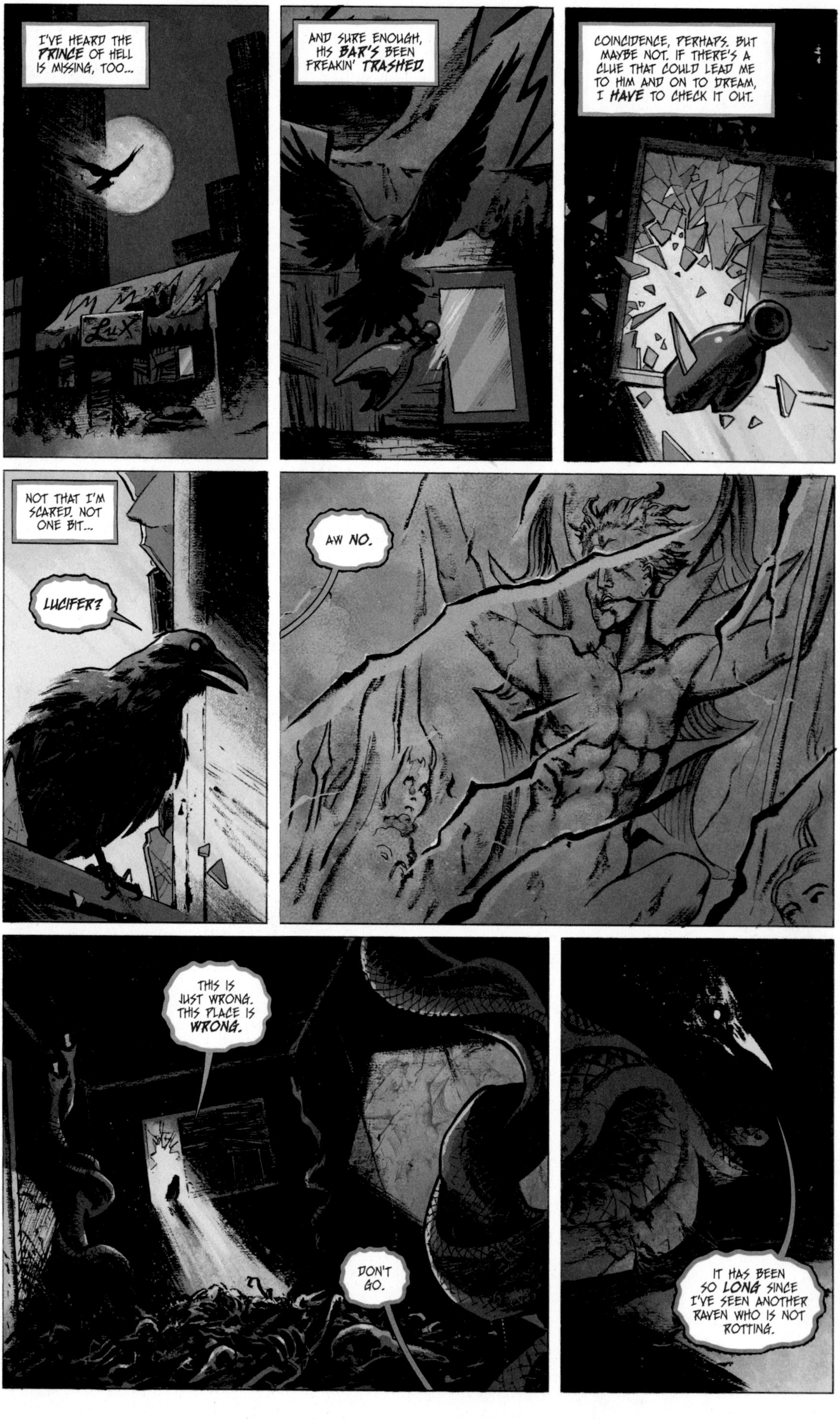
I'VE HEARD THE PRINCE OF HELL IS MISSING, TOO...
AND SURE ENOUGH, HIS BAR'S BEEN FREAKIN' TRASHED.
COINCIDENCE, PERHAPS. BUT MAYBE NOT. IF THERE'S A CLUE THAT COULD LEAD ME TO HIM AND ON TO DREAM, I HAVE TO CHECK IT OUT.
NOT THAT I'M SCARED. NOT ONE BIT...
LUCIFER?
AW NO.
THIS IS JUST WRONG. THIS PLACE IS WRONG.
DON'T GO.
IT HAS BEEN SO LONG SINCE I'VE SEEN ANOTHER RAVEN WHO IS NOT ROTTING.

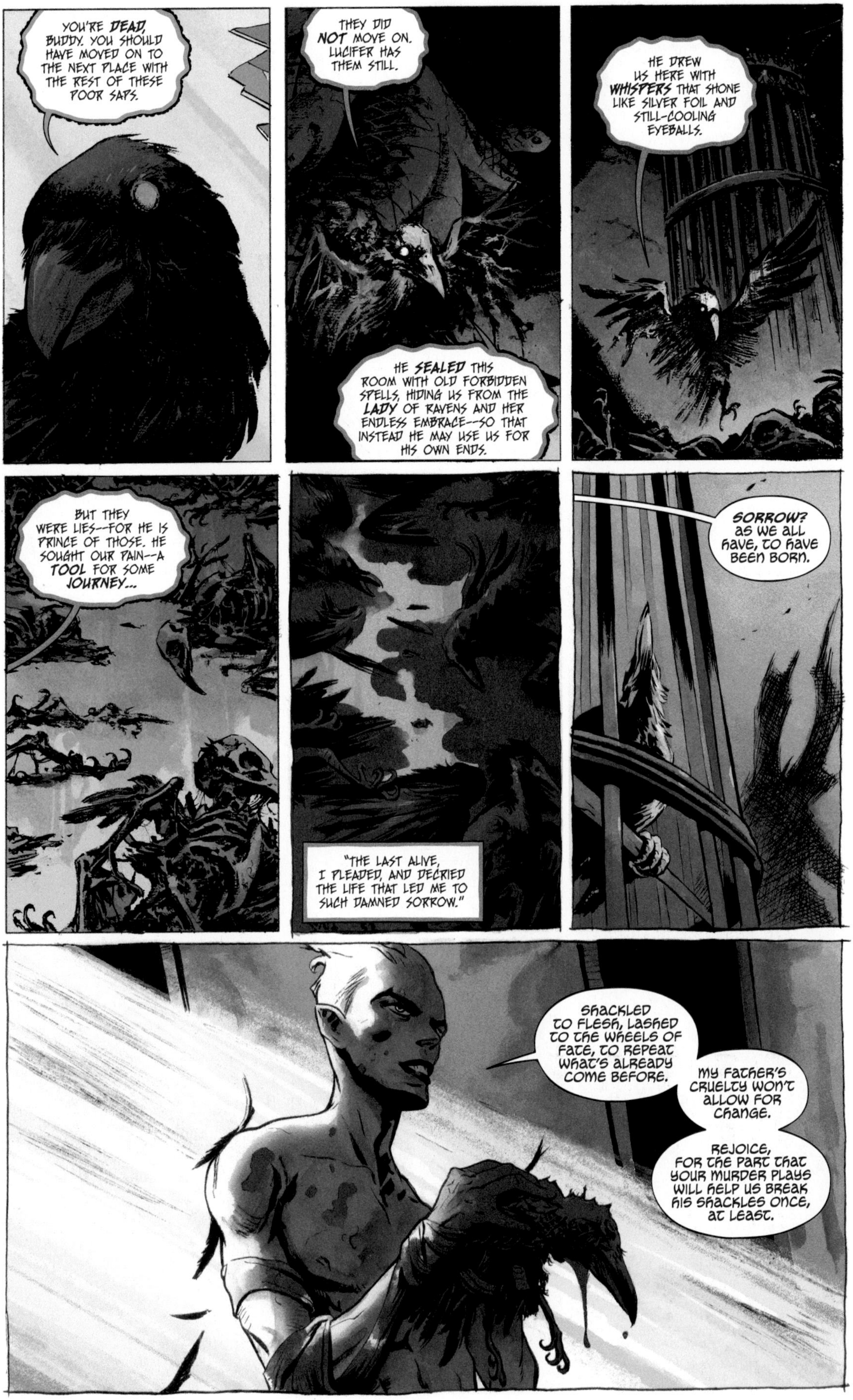
YOU'RE DEAD, BUDDY. YOU SHOULD HAVE MOVED ON TO THE NEXT PLACE WITH THE REST OF THESE POOR SAPS.
THEY DID NOT MOVE ON. LUCIFER HAS THEM STILL.
HE SEALED THIS ROOM WITH OLD FORBIDDEN SPELLS, HIDING US FROM THE LADY OF RAVENS AND HER ENDLESS EMBRACE--SO THAT INSTEAD HE MAY USE US FOR HIS OWN ENDS.
HE DREW US HERE WITH WHISPERS THAT SHONE LIKE SILVER FOIL AND STILL-COOLING EYEBALLS.
BUT THEY WERE LIES--FOR HE IS PRINCE OF THOSE. HE SOUGHT OUR PAIN--A TOOL FOR SOME JOURNEY...
"THE LAST ALIVE, I PLEADED, AND DECRIED THE LIFE THAT LED ME TO SUCH DAMNED SORROW."
SORROW? AS WE ALL HAVE, TO HAVE BEEN BORN.
SHACKLED TO FLESH, LASHED TO THE WHEELS OF FATE, TO REPEAT WHAT'S ALREADY COME BEFORE.
MY FATHER'S CRUELTY WON'T ALLOW FOR CHANGE.
REJOICE, FOR THE PART THAT YOUR MURDER PLAYS WILL HELP US BREAK HIS SHACKLES ONCE, AT LEAST.

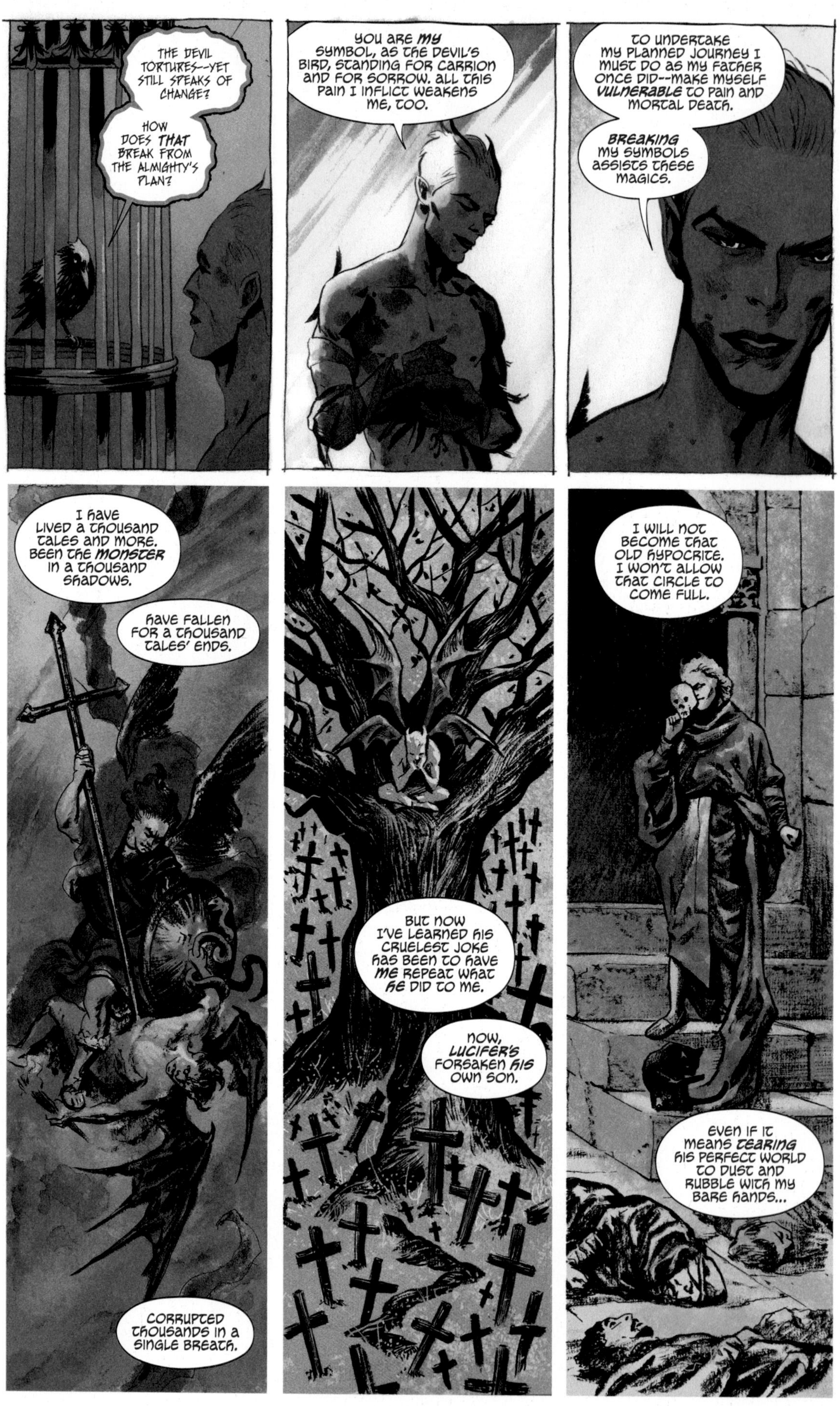
THE DEVIL TORTURES--YET STILL SPEAKS OF CHANGE?
HOW DOES THAT BREAK FROM THE ALMIGHTY'S PLAN?
YOU ARE MY SYMBOL, AS THE DEVIL'S BIRD, STANDING FOR CARRION AND FOR SORROW. ALL THIS PAIN I INFLICT WEAKENS ME, TOO.
TO UNDERTAKE MY PLANNED JOURNEY I MUST DO AS MY FATHER ONCE DID--MAKE MYSELF VULNERABLE TO PAIN AND MORTAL DEATH.
BREAKING MY SYMBOLS ASSISTS THESE MAGICS.
I HAVE LIVED A THOUSAND TALES AND MORE. BEEN THE MONSTER IN A THOUSAND SHADOWS.
HAVE FALLEN FOR A THOUSAND TALES' ENDS.
CORRUPTED THOUSANDS IN A SINGLE BREATH.
BUT NOW I'VE LEARNED HIS CRUELEST JOKE HAS BEEN TO HAVE ME REPEAT WHAT HE DID TO ME.
NOW, LUCIFER'S FORSAKEN HIS OWN SON.
I WILL NOT BECOME THAT OLD HYPOCRITE. I WON'T ALLOW THAT CIRCLE TO COME FULL.
EVEN IF IT MEANS TEARING HIS PERFECT WORLD TO DUST AND RUBBLE WITH MY BARE HANDS...

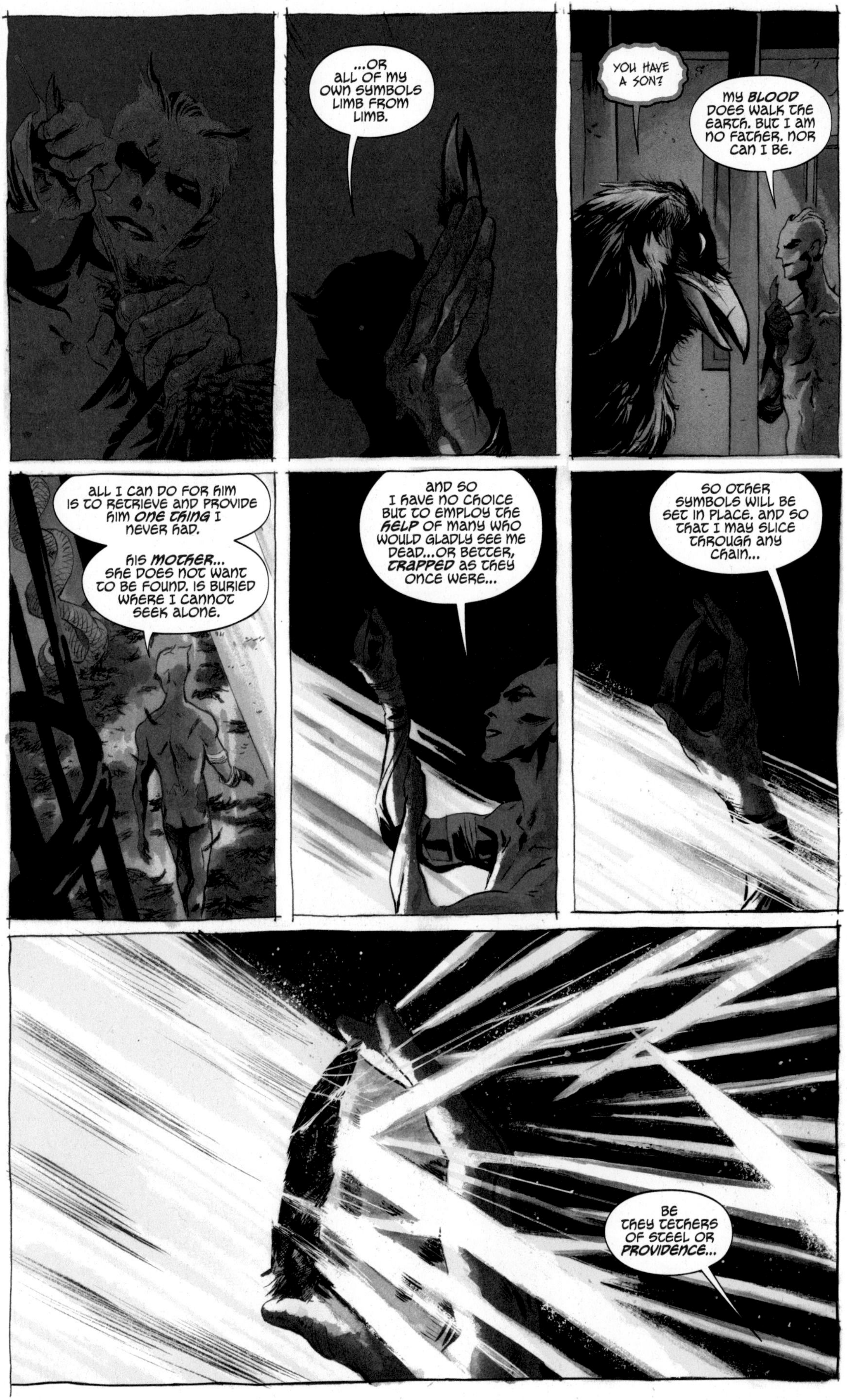
...OR ALL OF MY OWN SYMBOLS LIMB FROM LIMB.
YOU HAVE A SON?
MY BLOOD DOES WALK THE EARTH. BUT I AM NO FATHER. NOR CAN I BE.
ALL I CAN DO FOR HIM IS TO RETRIEVE AND PROVIDE HIM ONE THING I NEVER HAD.
HIS MOTHER... SHE DOES NOT WANT TO BE FOUND. IS BURIED WHERE I CANNOT SEEK ALONE.
AND SO I HAVE NO CHOICE BUT TO EMPLOY THE HELP OF MANY WHO WOULD GLADLY SEE ME DEAD...OR BETTER, TRAPPED AS THEY ONCE WERE...
SO OTHER SYMBOLS WILL BE SET IN PLACE. AND SO THAT I MAY SLICE THROUGH ANY CHAIN...
BE THEY TETHERS OF STEEL OR PROVIDENCE...

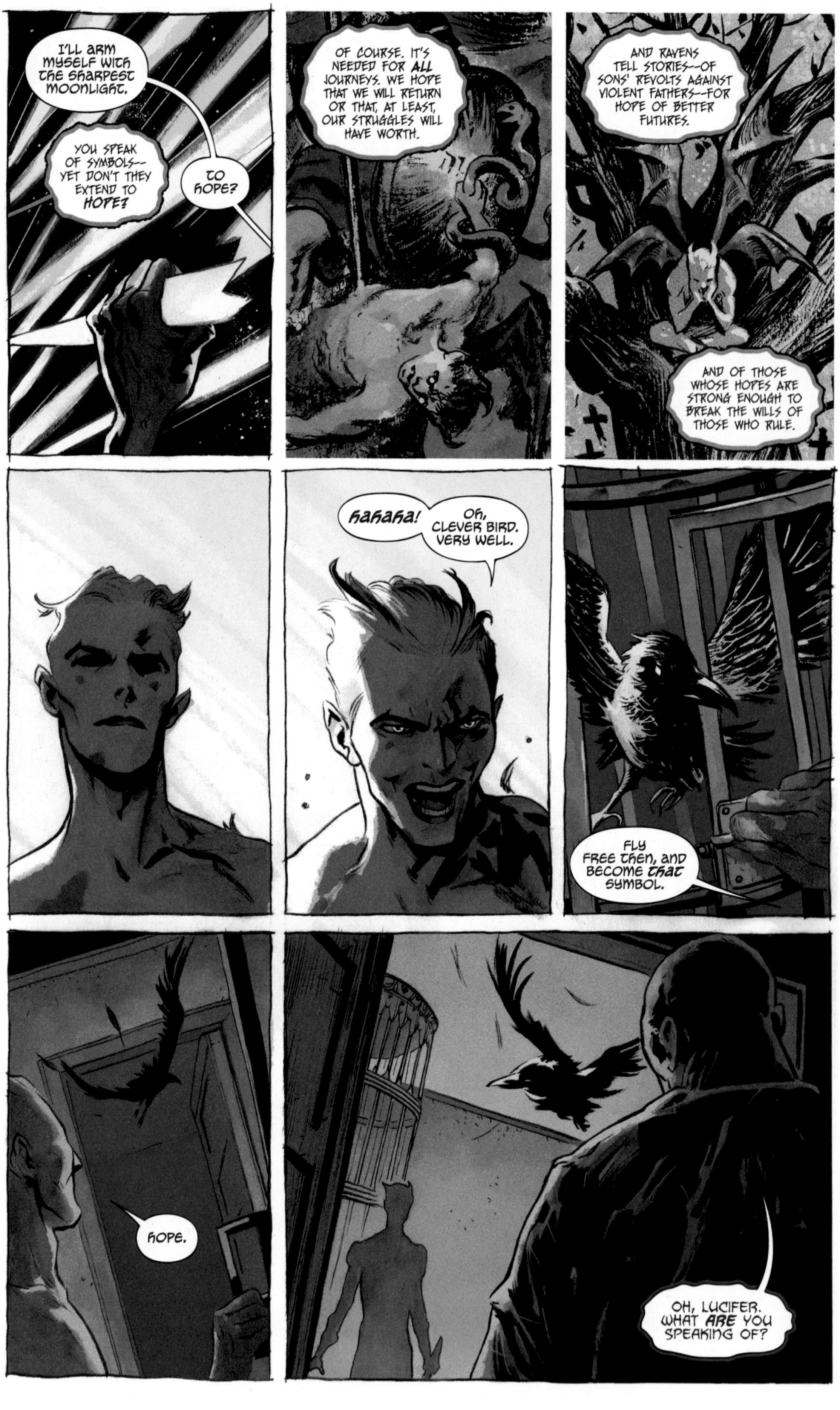
I'LL ARM MYSELF WITH THE SHARPEST MOONLIGHT.
YOU SPEAK OF SYMBOLS--YET DON'T THEY EXTEND TO HOPE?
TO HOPE?
OF COURSE. IT'S NEEDED FOR ALL JOURNEYS. WE HOPE THAT WE WILL RETURN OR THAT, AT LEAST, OUR STRUGGLES WILL HAVE WORTH.
AND RAVENS TELL STORIES--OF SONS' REVOLTS AGAINST VIOLENT FATHERS--FOR HOPE OF BETTER FUTURES.
AND OF THOSE WHOSE HOPES ARE STRONG ENOUGH TO BREAK THE WILLS OF THOSE WHO RULE.
HAHAHA!
OH, CLEVER BIRD. VERY WELL.
FLY FREE THEN, AND BECOME THAT SYMBOL.
HOPE.
OH, LUCIFER. WHAT ARE YOU SPEAKING OF?

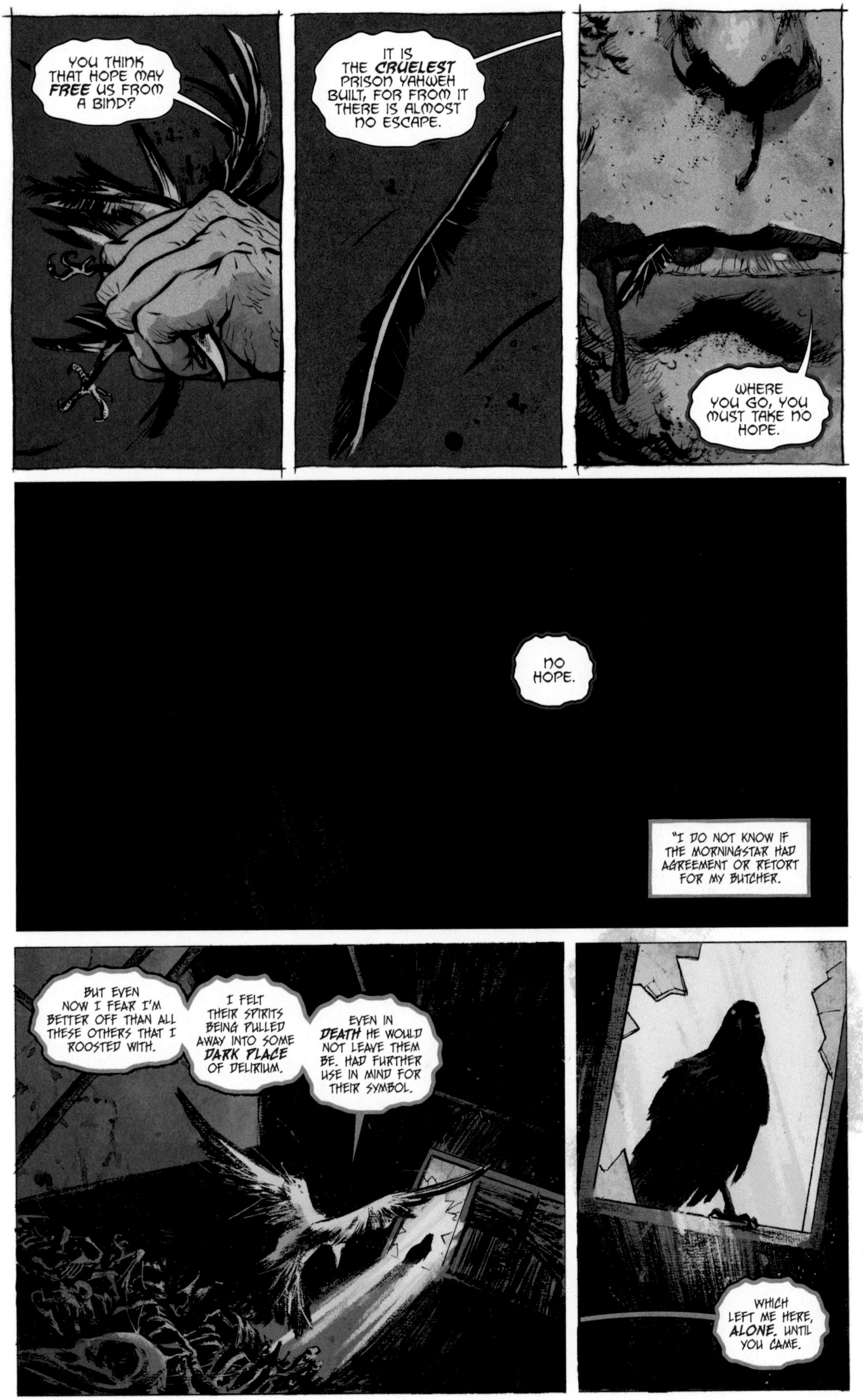
YOU THINK THAT HOPE MAY FREE US FROM A BIND?
IT IS THE CRUELEST PRISON YAHWEH BUILT, FOR FROM IT THERE IS ALMOST NO ESCAPE.
WHERE YOU GO, YOU MUST TAKE NO HOPE.
NO HOPE.
"I DO NOT KNOW IF THE MORNINGSTAR HAD AGREEMENT OR RETORT FOR MY BUTCHER.
BUT EVEN NOW I FEAR I'M BETTER OFF THAN ALL THESE OTHERS THAT I ROOSTED WITH.
I FELT THEIR SPIRITS BEING PULLED AWAY INTO SOME DARK PLACE OF DELIRIUM.
EVEN IN DEATH HE WOULD NOT LEAVE THEM BE. HAD FURTHER USE IN MIND FOR THEIR SYMBOL.
WHICH LEFT ME HERE, ALONE. UNTIL YOU CAME.

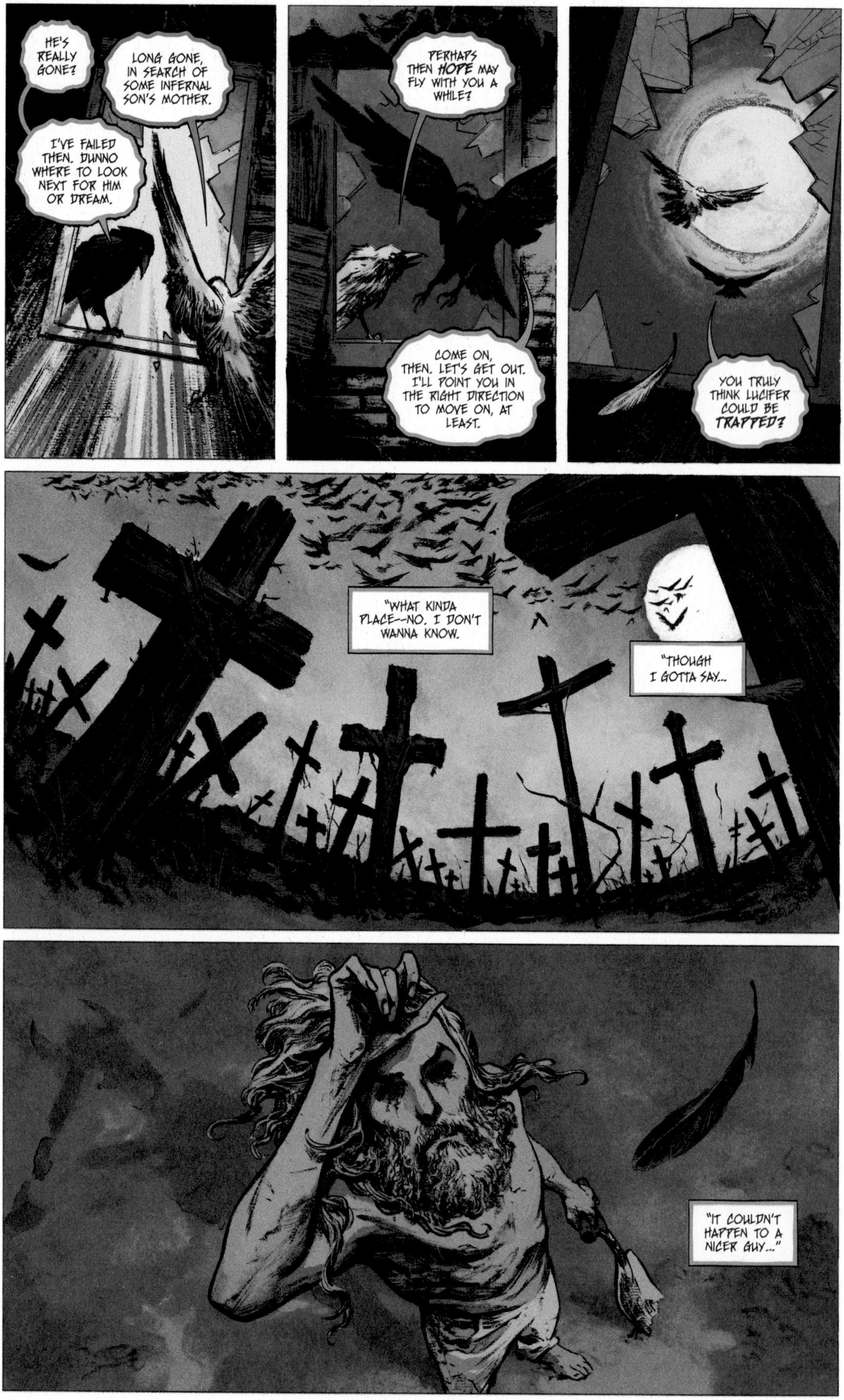
HE'S REALLY GONE?
LONG GONE, IN SEARCH OF SOME INFERNAL SON'S MOTHER.
I'VE FAILED THEN. DUNNO WHERE TO LOOK NEXT FOR HIM OR DREAM.
PERHAPS THEN HOPE MAY FLY WITH YOU A WHILE?
COME ON, THEN. LET'S GET OUT. I'LL POINT YOU IN THE RIGHT DIRECTION TO MOVE ON, AT LEAST.
YOU TRULY THINK LUCIFER COULD BE TRAPPED?
"WHAT KINDA PLACE--NO. I DON'T WANNA KNOW.
"THOUGH I GOTTA SAY...
"IT COULDN'T HAPPEN TO A NICER GUY..."

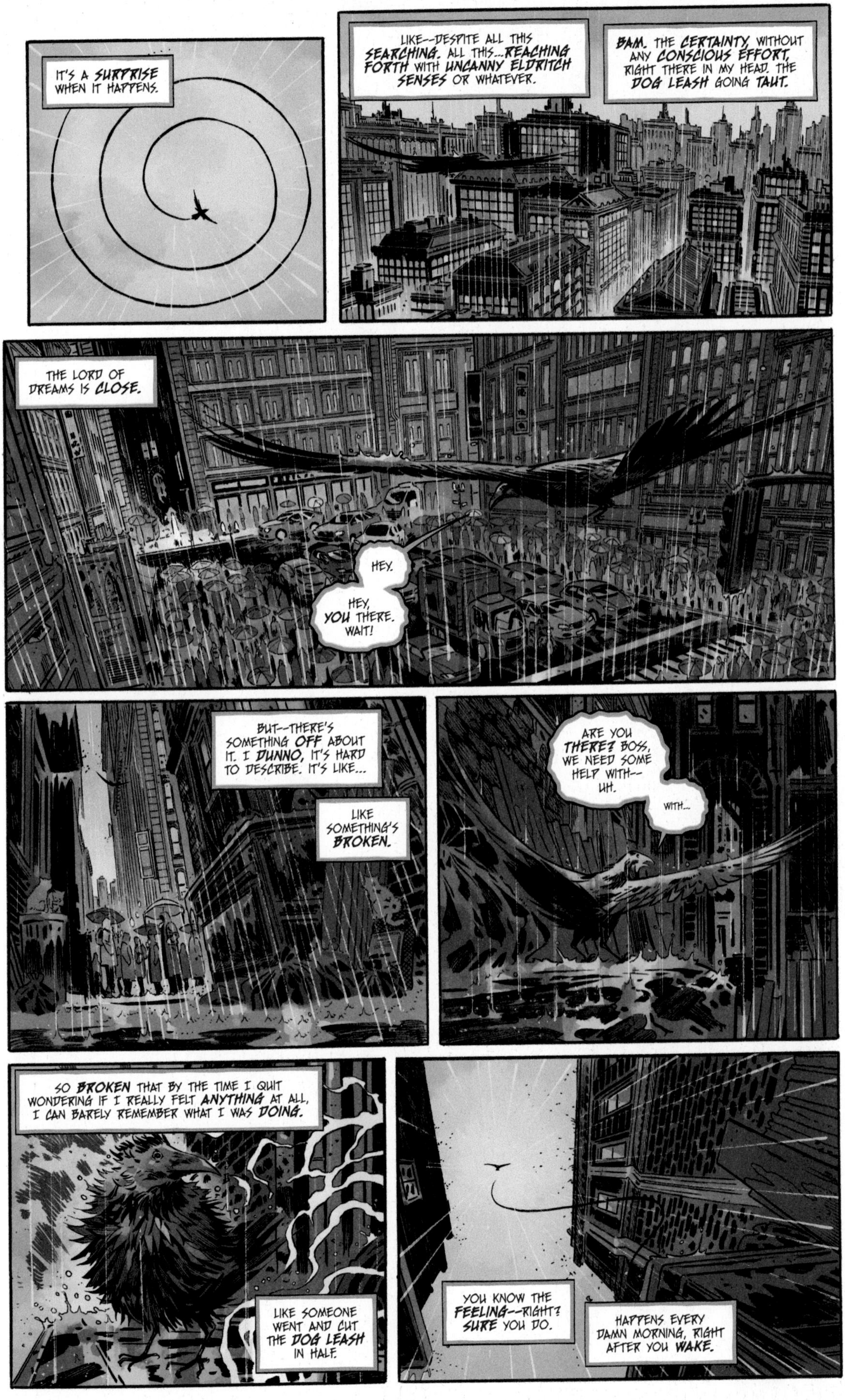

IT'S A SURPRISE WHEN IT HAPPENS.
LIKE--DESPITE ALL THIS SEARCHING. ALL THIS...REACHING FORTH WITH UNCANNY ELDRITCH SENSES OR WHATEVER.
BAM. THE CERTAINTY, WITHOUT ANY CONSCIOUS EFFORT, RIGHT THERE IN MY HEAD. THE DOG LEASH GOING TAUT.
THE LORD OF DREAMS IS CLOSE.
HEY.
HEY, YOU THERE. WAIT!
BUT--THERE'S SOMETHING OFF ABOUT IT. I DUNNO, IT'S HARD TO DESCRIBE. IT'S LIKE...
LIKE SOMETHING'S BROKEN.
ARE YOU THERE? BOSS, WE NEED SOME HELP WITH-- UH.
WITH...
SO BROKEN THAT BY THE TIME I QUIT WONDERING IF I REALLY FELT ANYTHING AT ALL, I CAN BARELY REMEMBER WHAT I WAS DOING.
LIKE SOMEONE WENT AND CUT THE DOG LEASH IN HALF.
YOU KNOW THE FEELING--RIGHT? SURE YOU DO.
HAPPENS EVERY DAMN MORNING, RIGHT AFTER YOU WAKE.

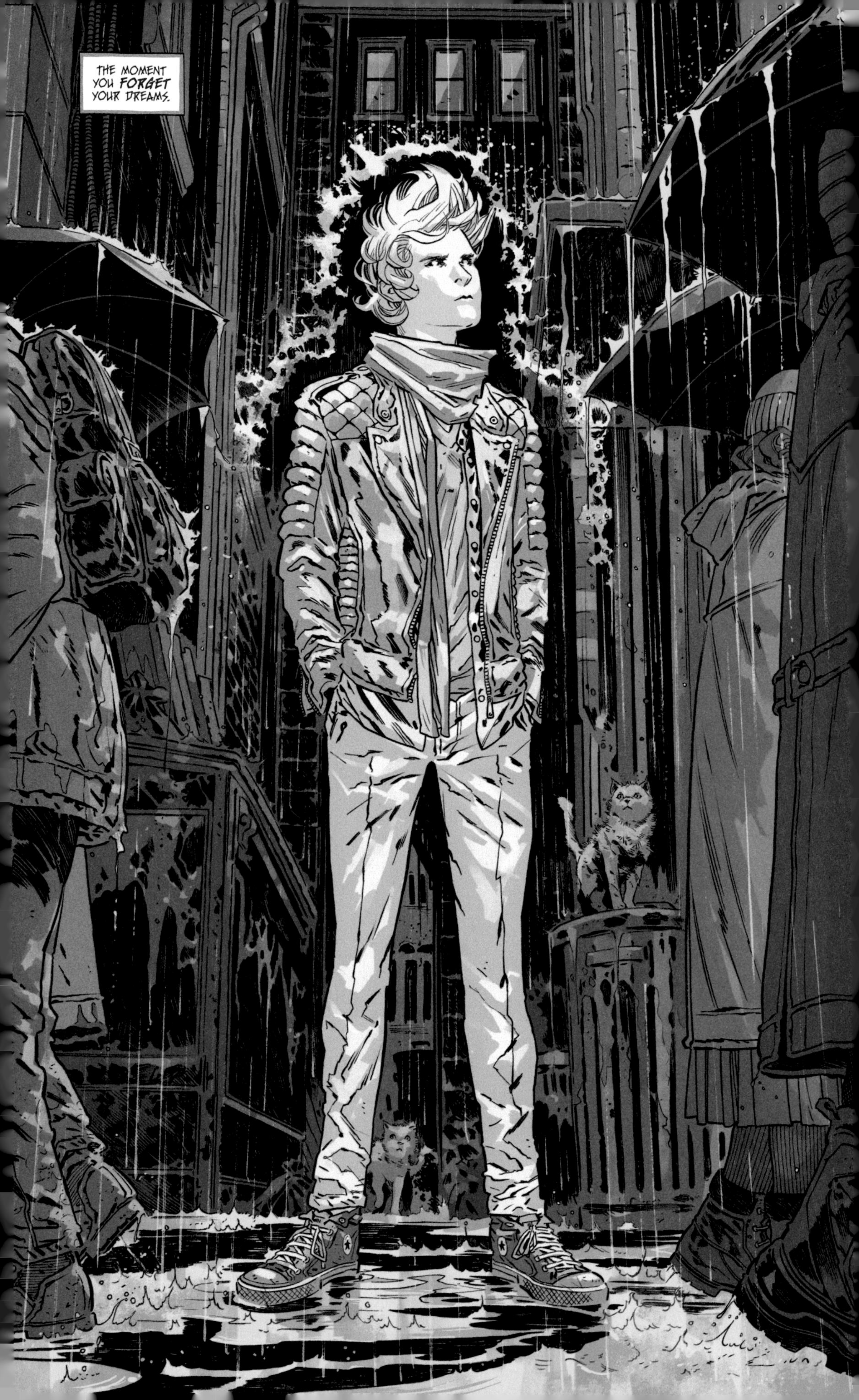
THE MOMENT YOU FORGET YOUR DREAMS.

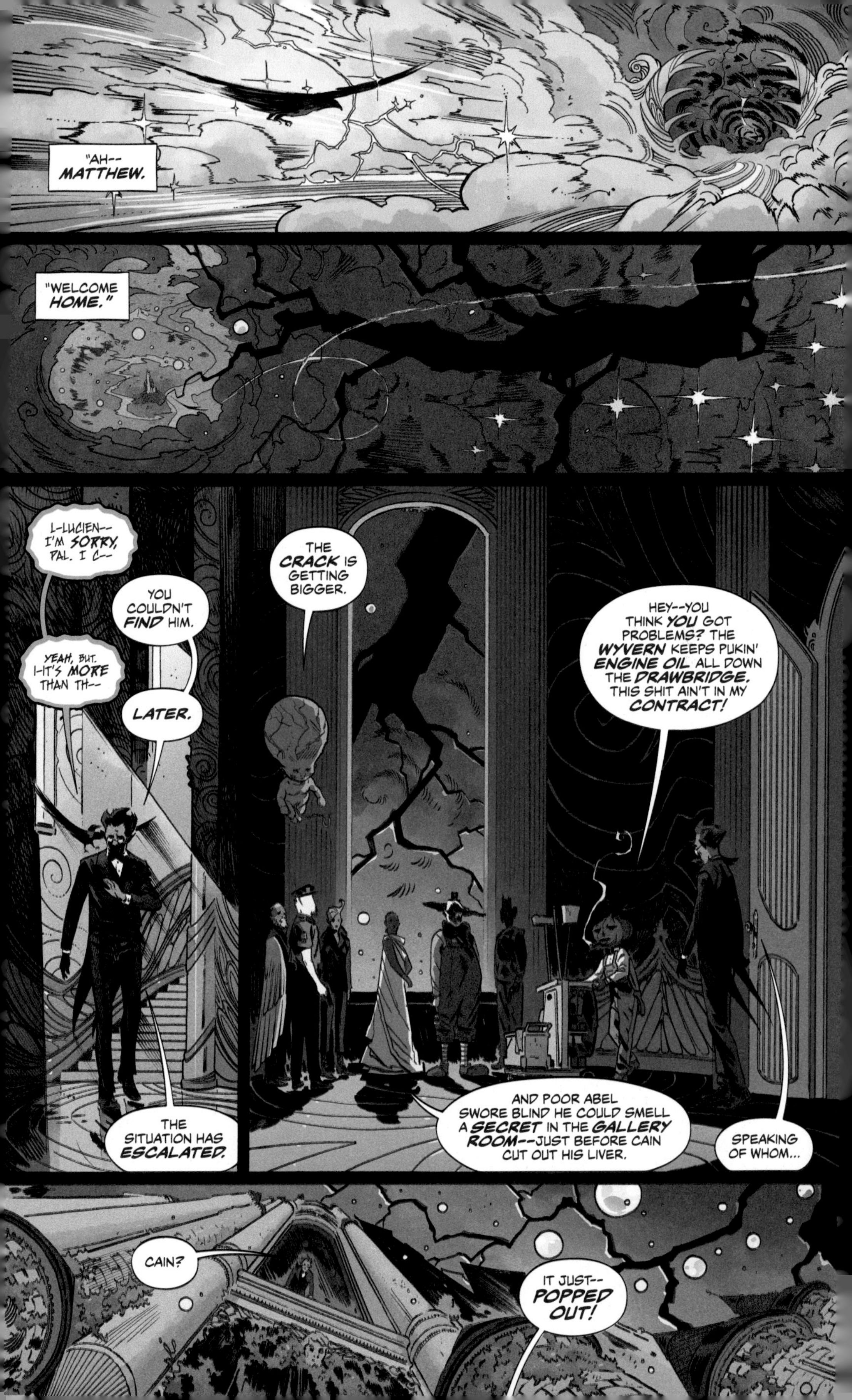
"AH--
MATTHEW.
"WELCOME
HOME."
L-LUCIEN--
I'M SORRY,
PAL. I C--
YOU
COULDN'T
FIND HIM.
YEAH, BUT.
I-IT'S MORE
THAN TH--
LATER.
THE
SITUATION HAS
ESCALATED.
THE
CRACK IS
GETTING
BIGGER.
HEY--YOU
THINK YOU GOT
PROBLEMS? THE
WYVERN KEEPS PUKIN'
ENGINE OIL ALL DOWN
THE DRAWBRIDGE.
THIS SHIT AIN'T IN MY
CONTRACT!
AND POOR ABEL
SWORE BLIND HE COULD SMELL
A SECRET IN THE GALLERY
ROOM--JUST BEFORE CAIN
CUT OUT HIS LIVER.
SPEAKING
OF WHOM...
CAIN?
IT JUST--
POPPED
OUT!

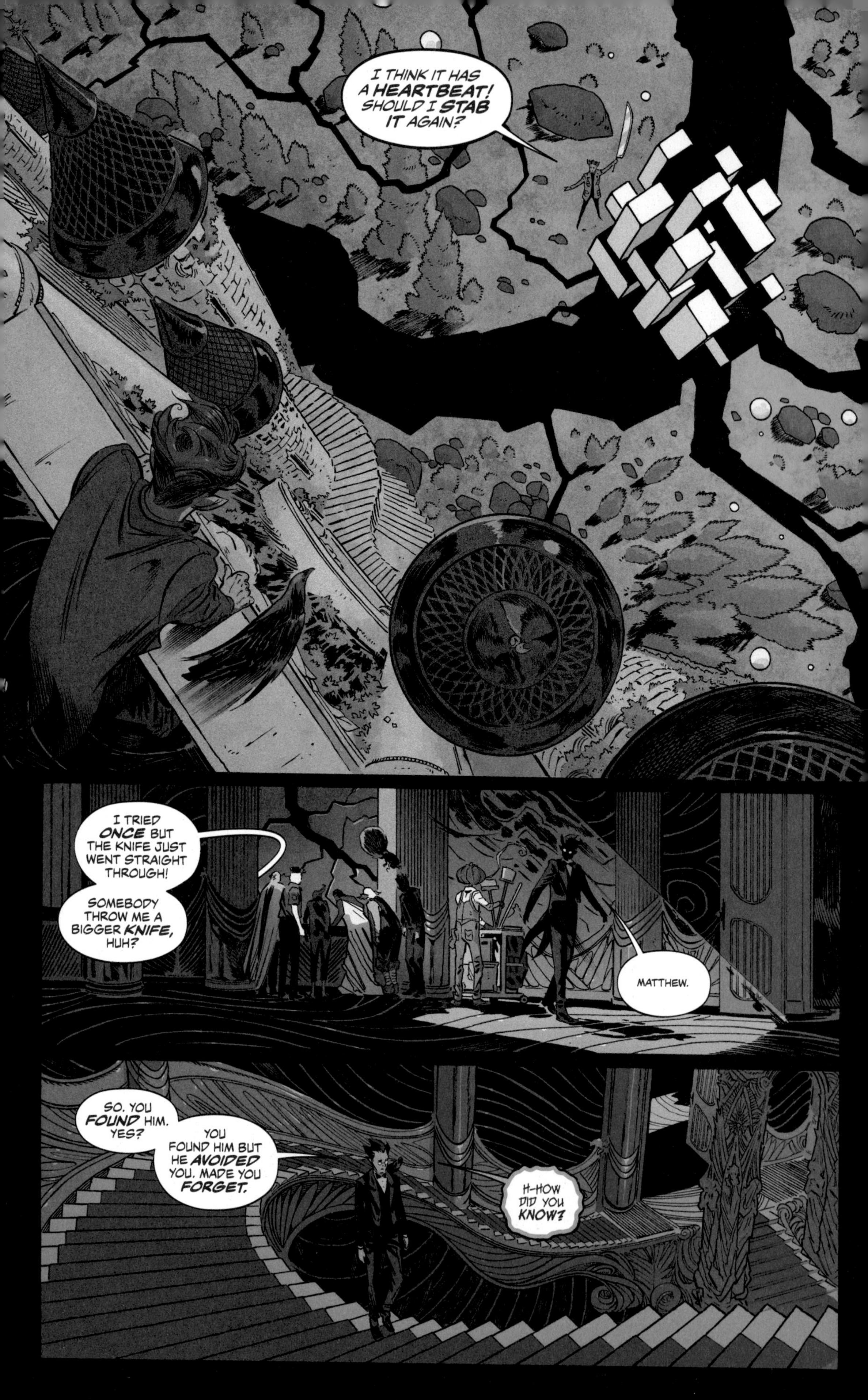
I THINK IT HAS A HEARTBEAT! SHOULD I STAB IT AGAIN?
I TRIED ONCE BUT THE KNIFE JUST WENT STRAIGHT THROUGH!
SOMEBODY THROW ME A BIGGER KNIFE, HUH?
MATTHEW.
SO. YOU FOUND HIM. YES?
YOU FOUND HIM BUT HE AVOIDED YOU. MADE YOU FORGET.
H-HOW DID YOU KNOW?

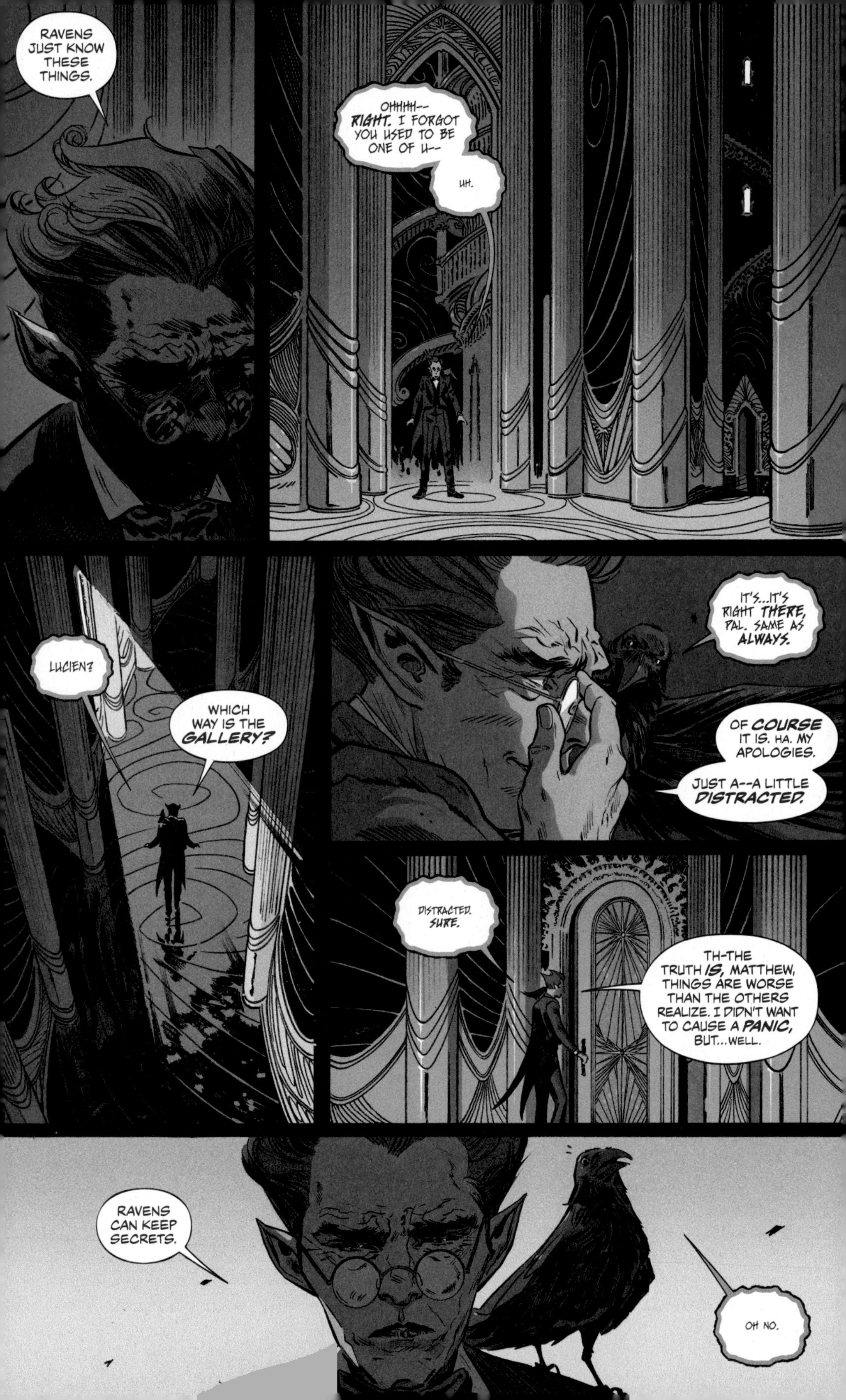
RAVENS JUST KNOW THESE THINGS.
OHHHH-- RIGHT. I FORGOT YOU USED TO BE ONE OF U--
UH.
LUCIEN?
WHICH WAY IS THE GALLERY?
IT'S...IT'S RIGHT THERE, PAL. SAME AS ALWAYS.
OF COURSE IT IS. HA. MY APOLOGIES.
JUST A--A LITTLE DISTRACTED.
DISTRACTED. SURE.
TH-THE TRUTH IS, MATTHEW, THINGS ARE WORSE THAN THE OTHERS REALIZE. I DIDN'T WANT TO CAUSE A PANIC, BUT...WELL.
RAVENS CAN KEEP SECRETS.
OH NO.

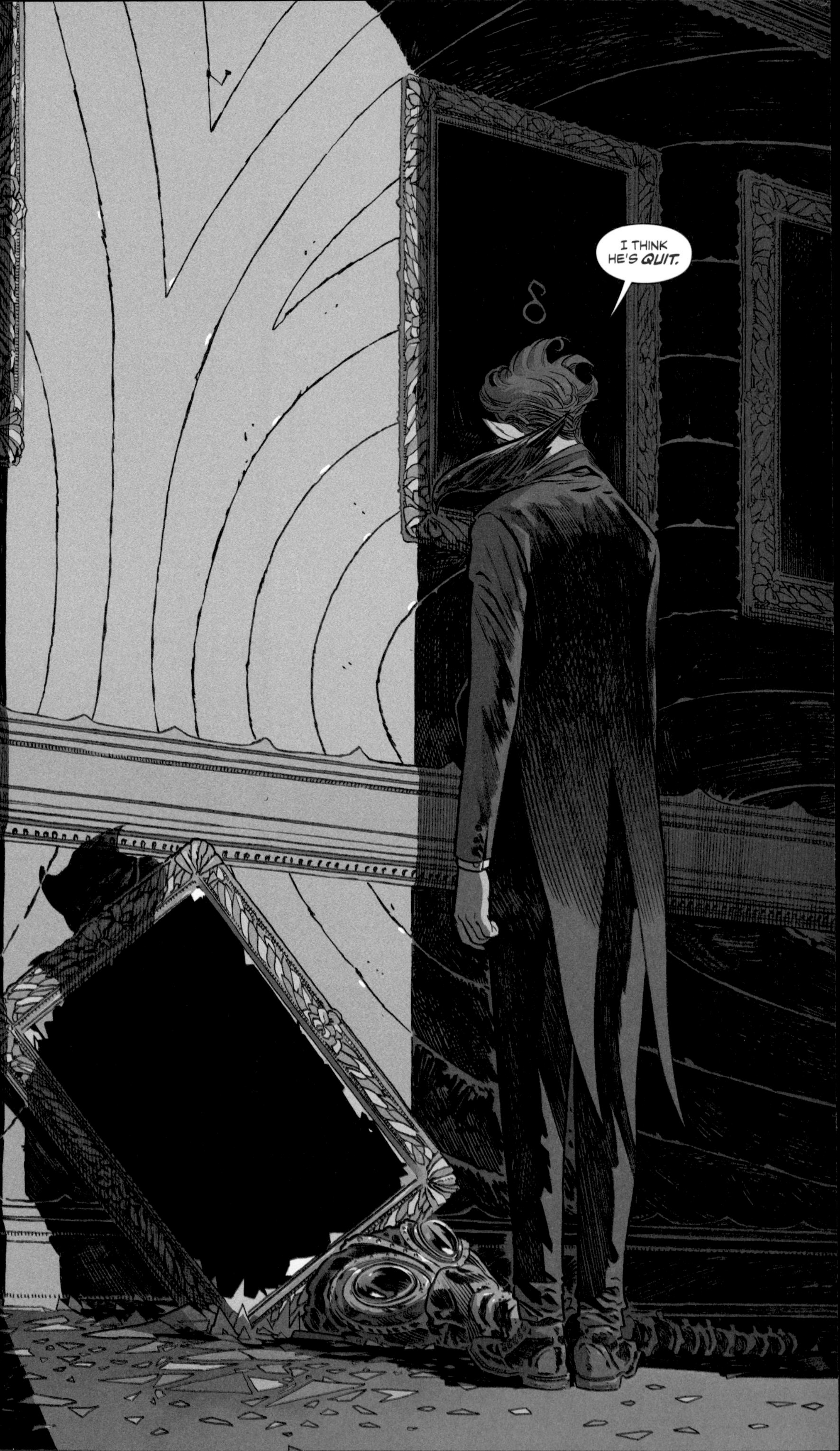
I THINK HE'S QUIT.

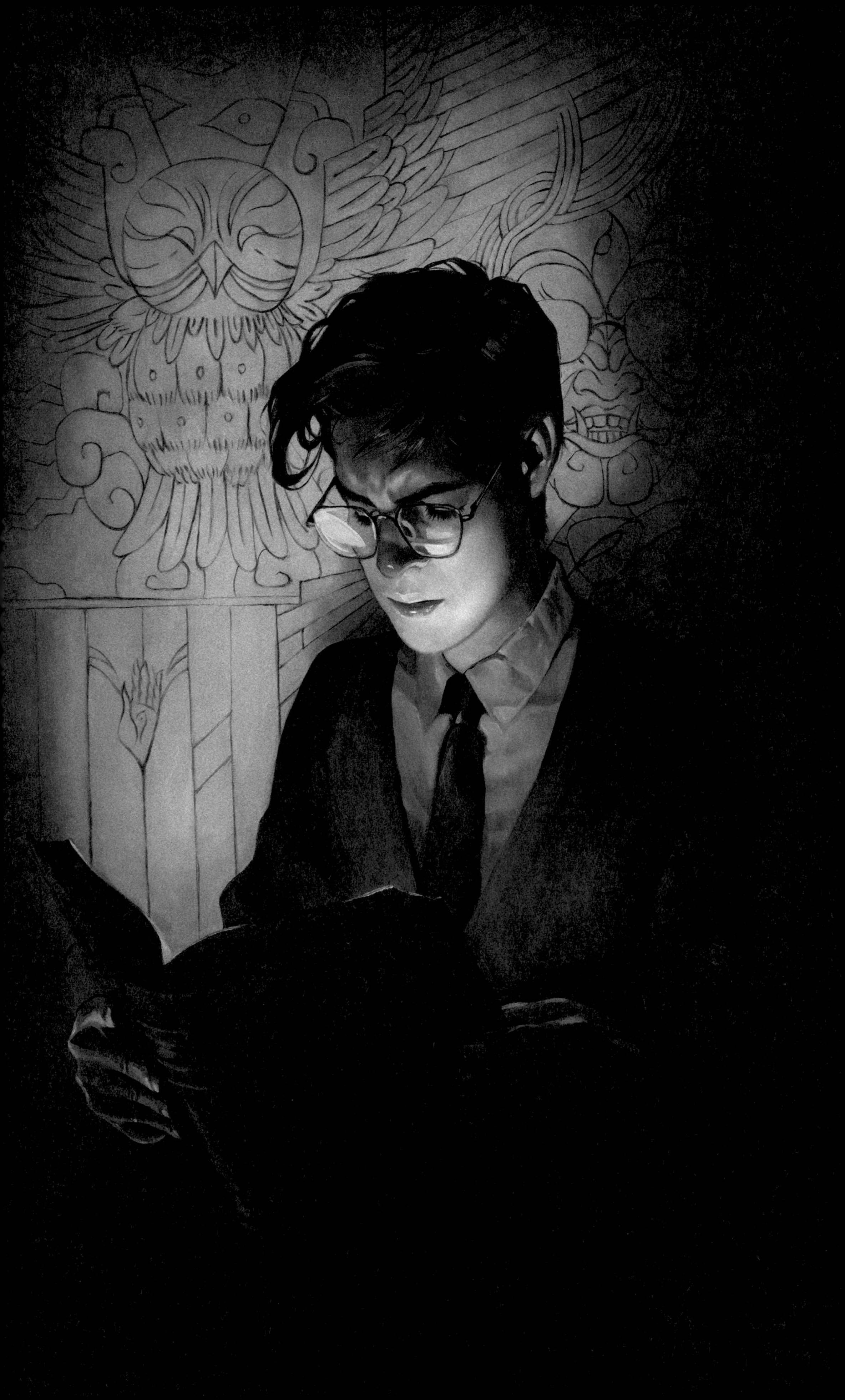

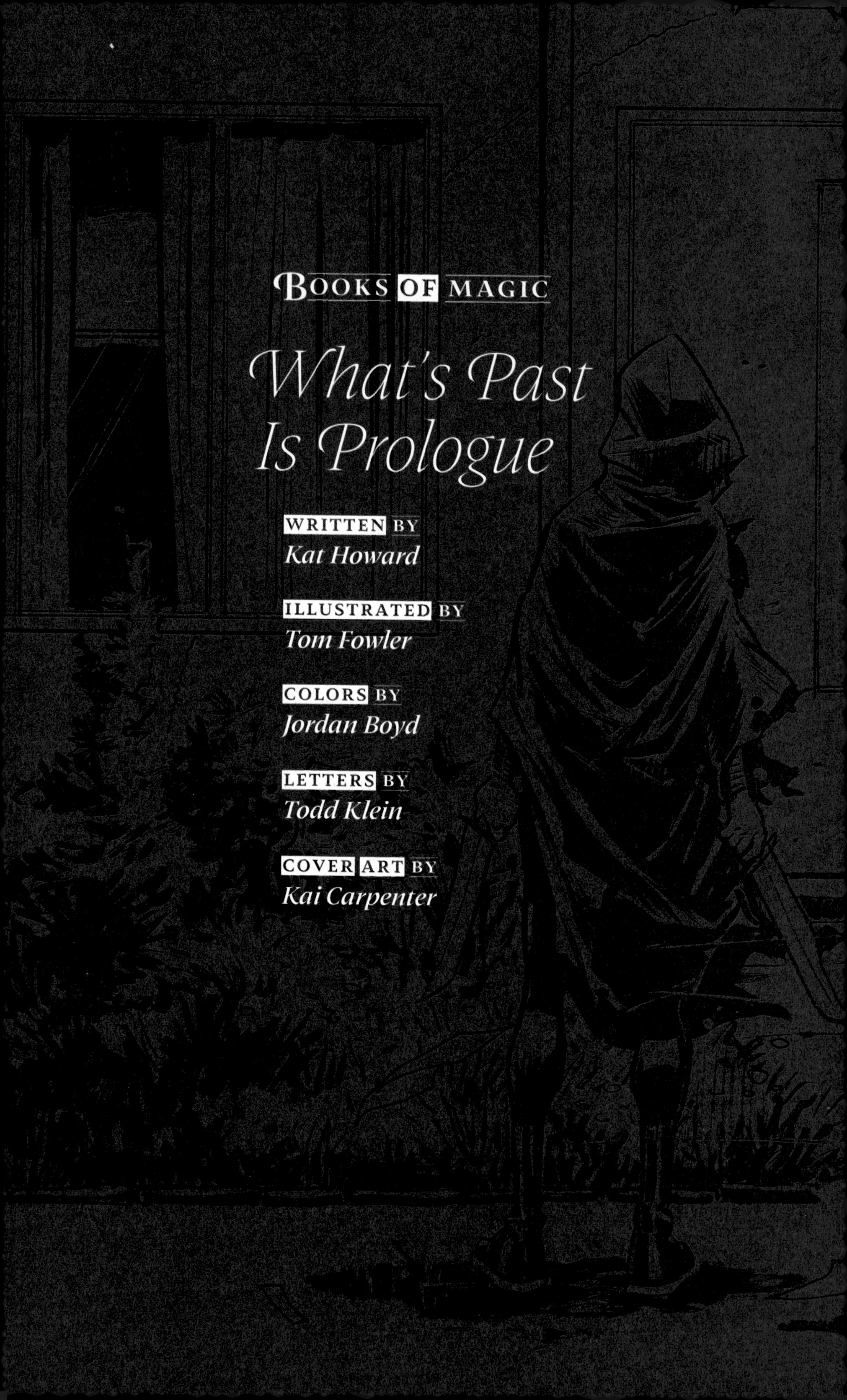

BOOKS OF MAGIC

What's Past Is Prologue

WRITTEN BY
Kat Howard

ILLUSTRATED BY
Tom Fowler

COLORS BY
Jordan Boyd

LETTERS BY
Todd Klein

COVER ART BY
Kai Carpenter

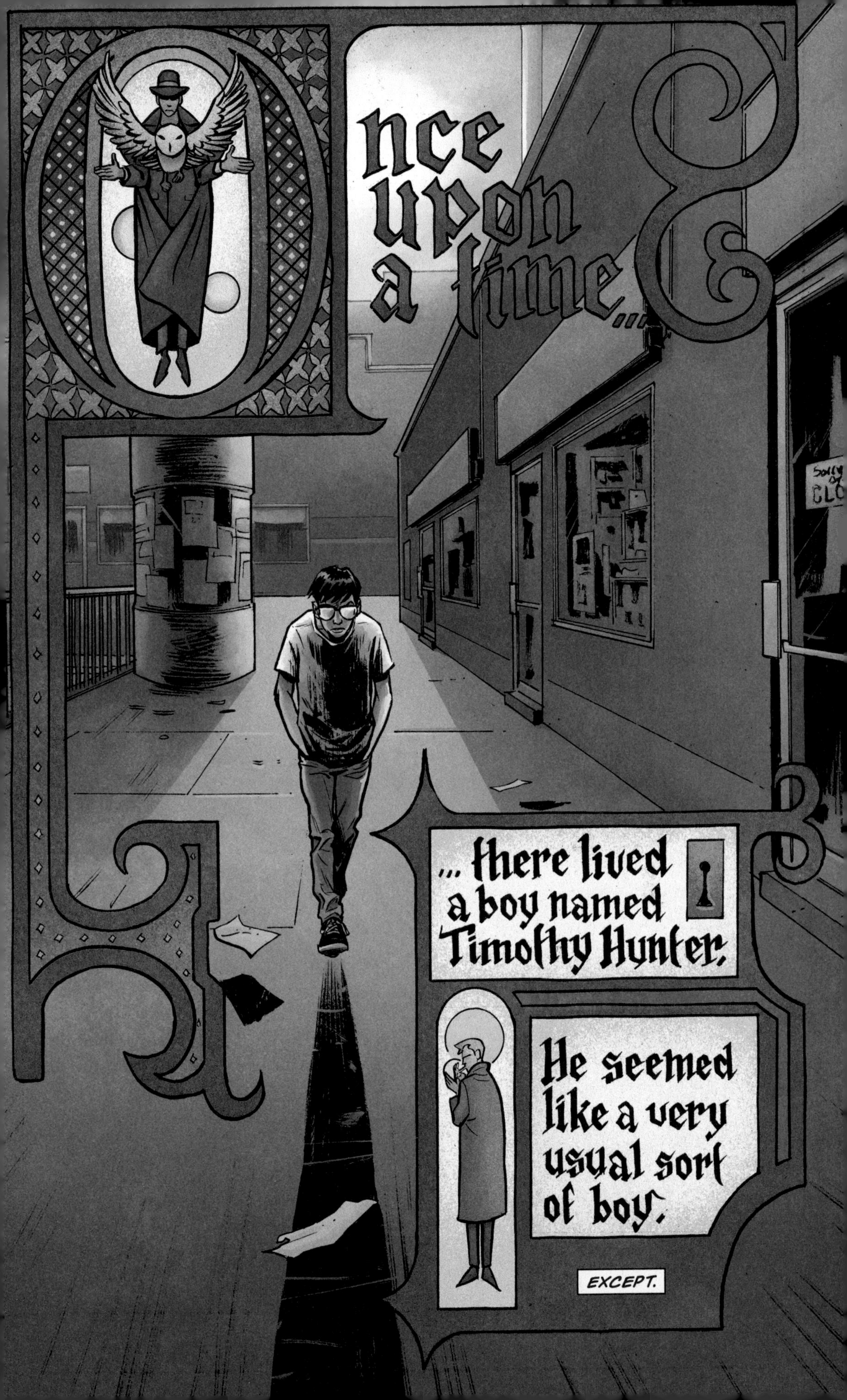
Once upon a time...
... there lived a boy named Timothy Hunter.
He seemed like a very usual sort of boy.
EXCEPT.

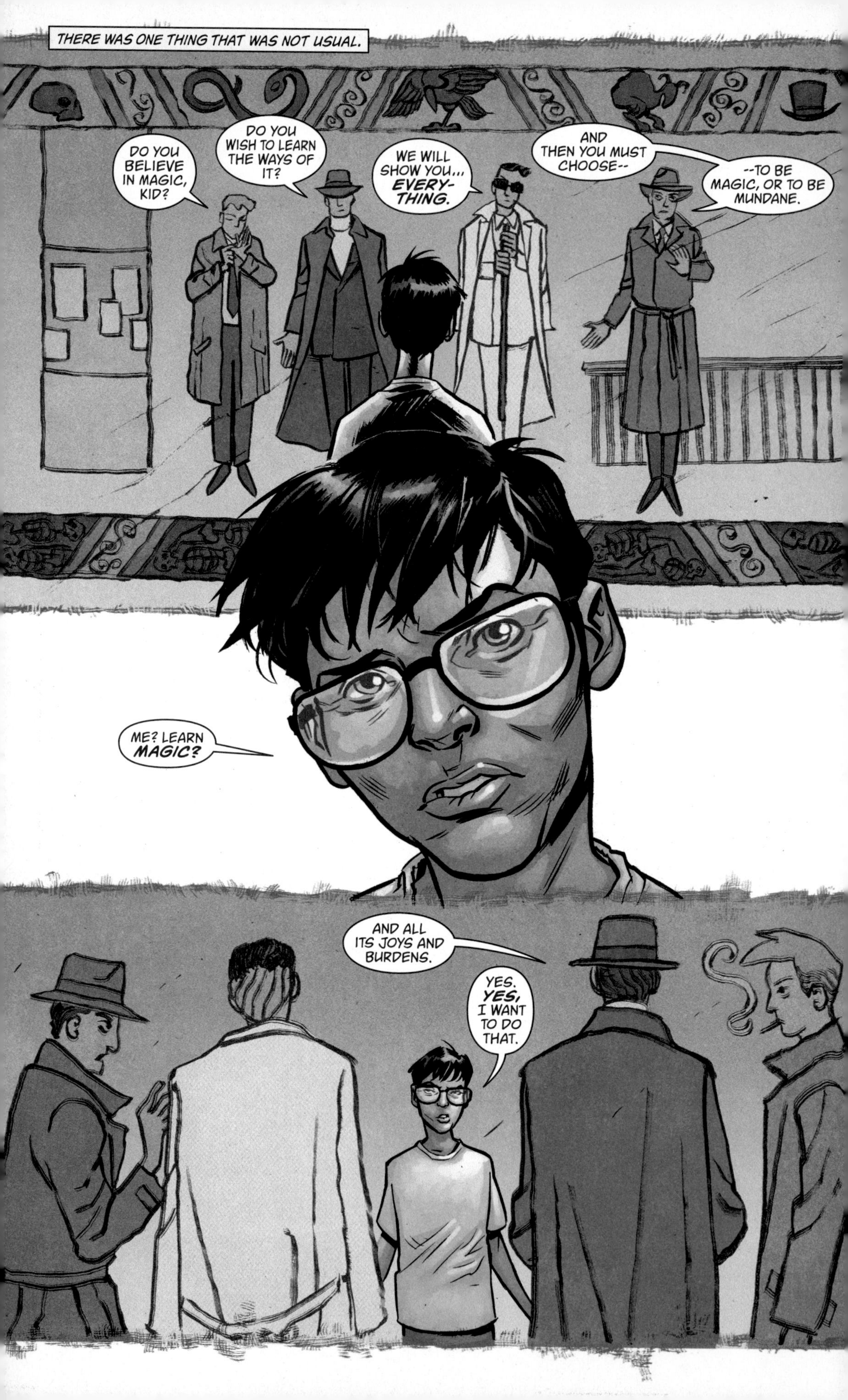
THERE WAS ONE THING THAT WAS NOT USUAL.
DO YOU BELIEVE IN MAGIC, KID?
DO YOU WISH TO LEARN THE WAYS OF IT?
WE WILL SHOW YOU... EVERYTHING.
AND THEN YOU MUST CHOOSE--
--TO BE MAGIC, OR TO BE MUNDANE.
ME? LEARN MAGIC?
AND ALL ITS JOYS AND BURDENS.
YES. YES, I WANT TO DO THAT.

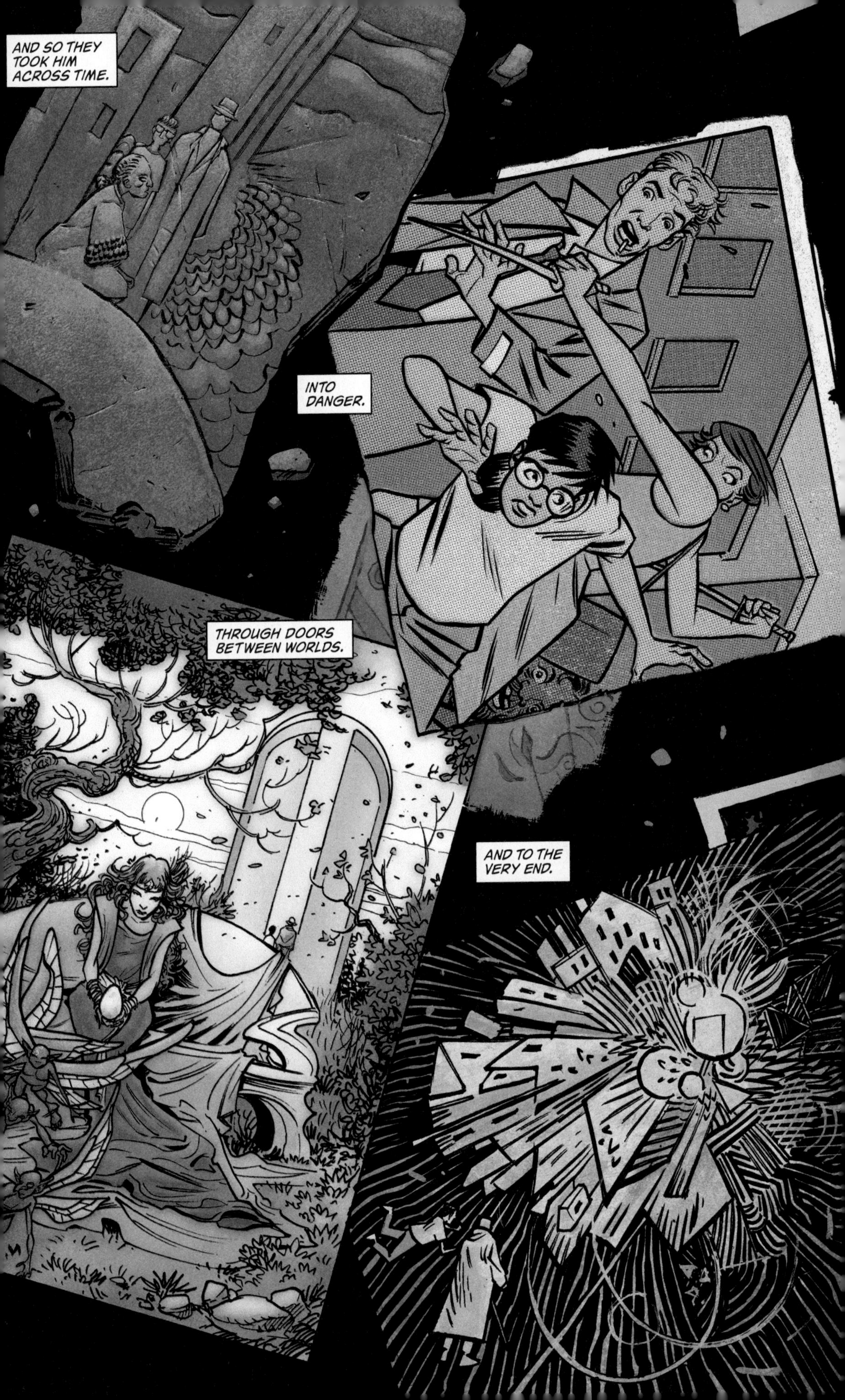
AND SO THEY TOOK HIM ACROSS TIME.
INTO DANGER.
THROUGH DOORS BETWEEN WORLDS.
AND TO THE VERY END.

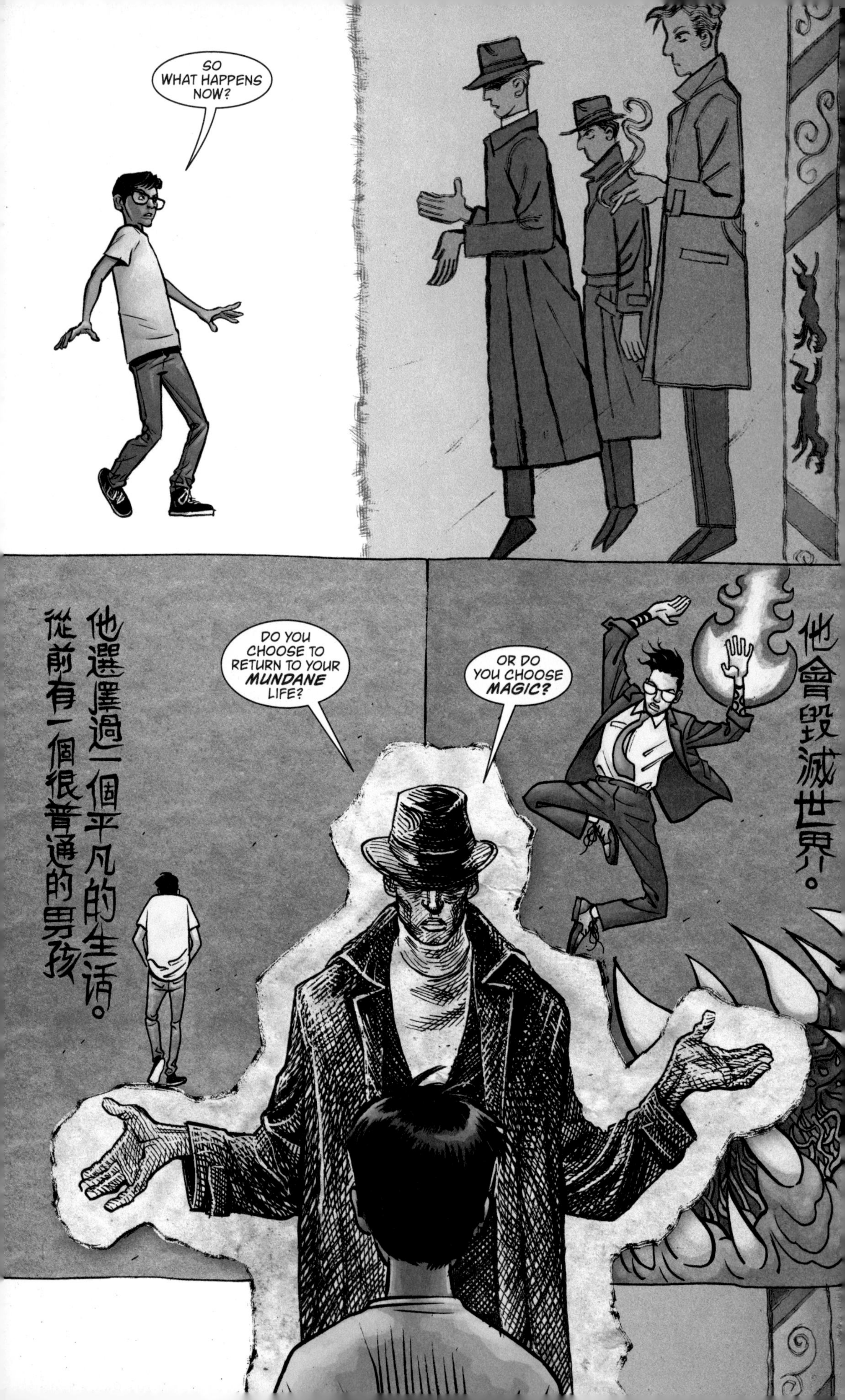
SO WHAT HAPPENS NOW?
從前有一個很普通的男孩
他選擇過一個平凡的生活。
DO YOU CHOOSE TO RETURN TO YOUR *MUNDANE* LIFE?
OR DO YOU CHOOSE *MAGIC?*
他會毀滅世界。

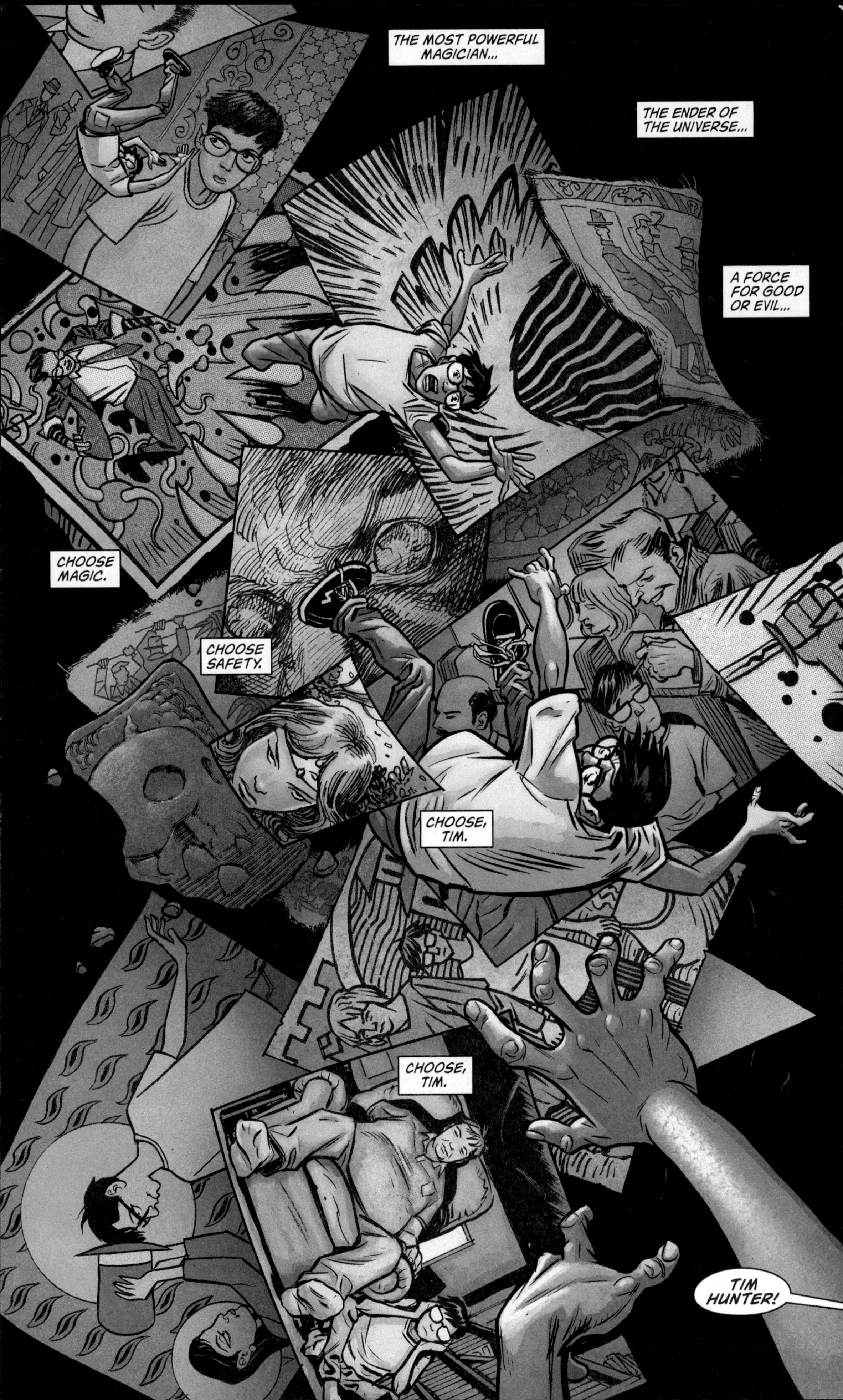
THE MOST POWERFUL MAGICIAN...
THE ENDER OF THE UNIVERSE...
A FORCE FOR GOOD OR EVIL...
CHOOSE MAGIC.
CHOOSE SAFETY.
CHOOSE, TIM.
CHOOSE, TIM.
TIM HUNTER!

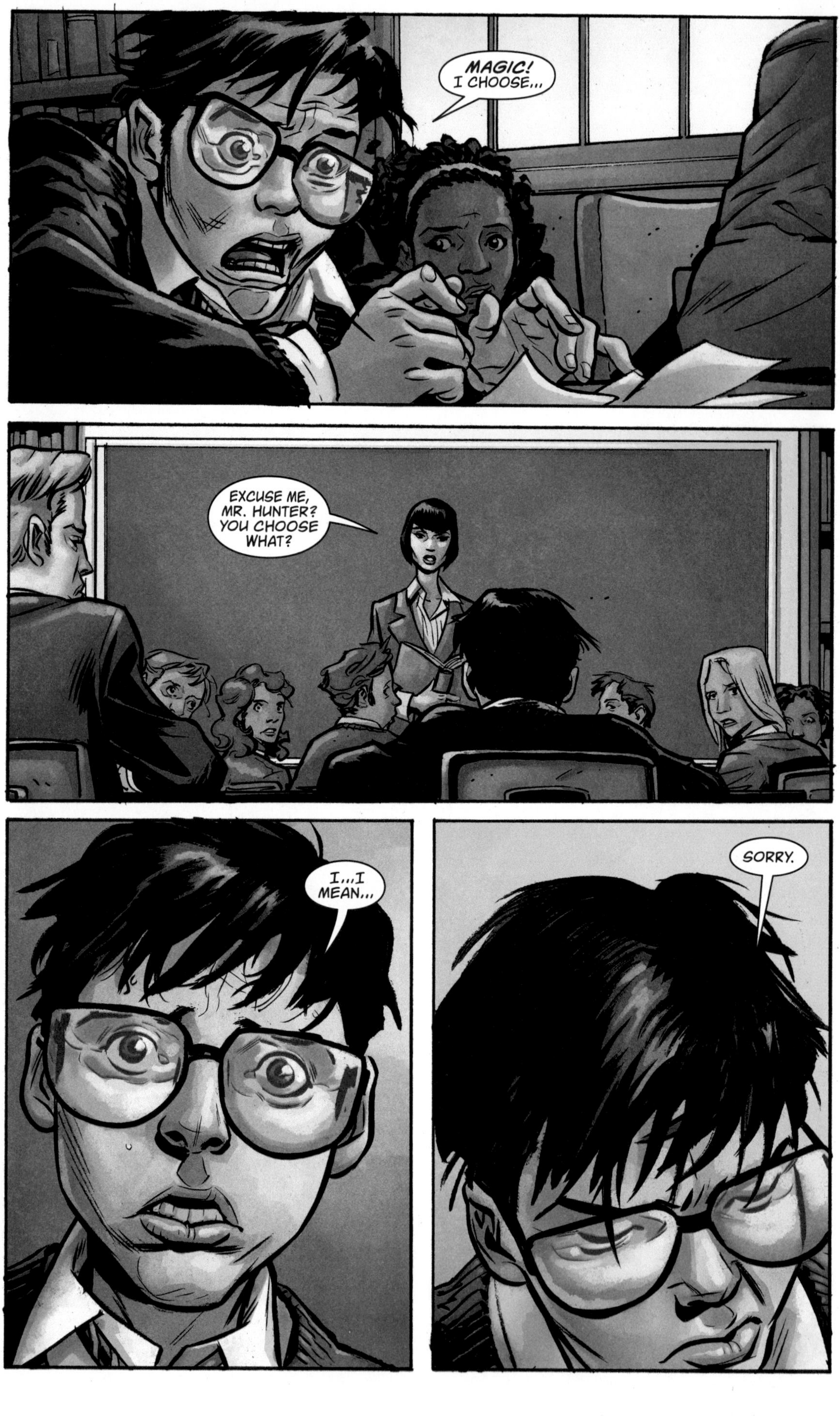
MAGIC! I CHOOSE...
EXCUSE ME, MR. HUNTER? YOU CHOOSE WHAT?
I...I MEAN...
SORRY.

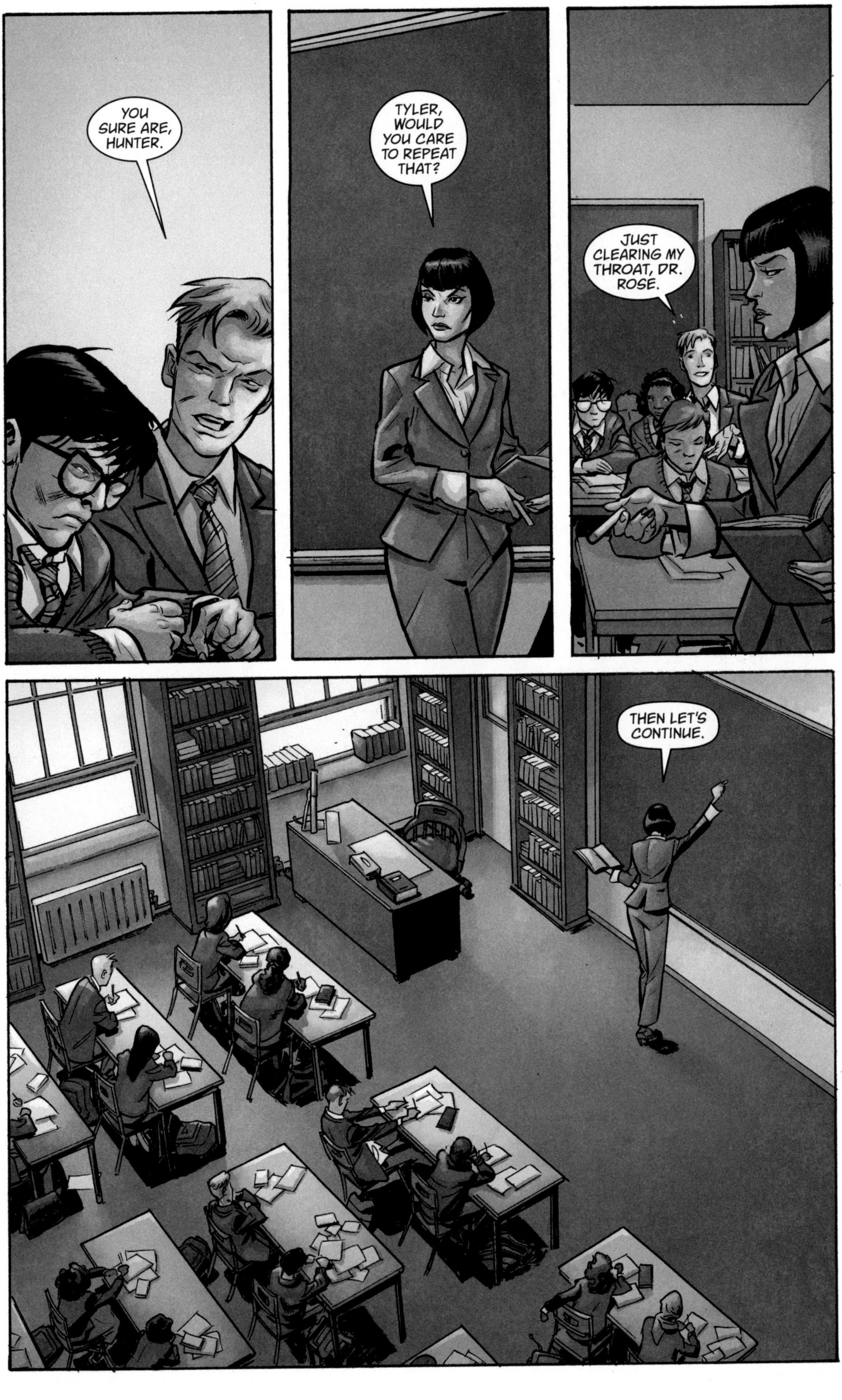

YOU SURE ARE, HUNTER.
TYLER, WOULD YOU CARE TO REPEAT THAT?
JUST CLEARING MY THROAT, DR. ROSE.
THEN LET'S CONTINUE.

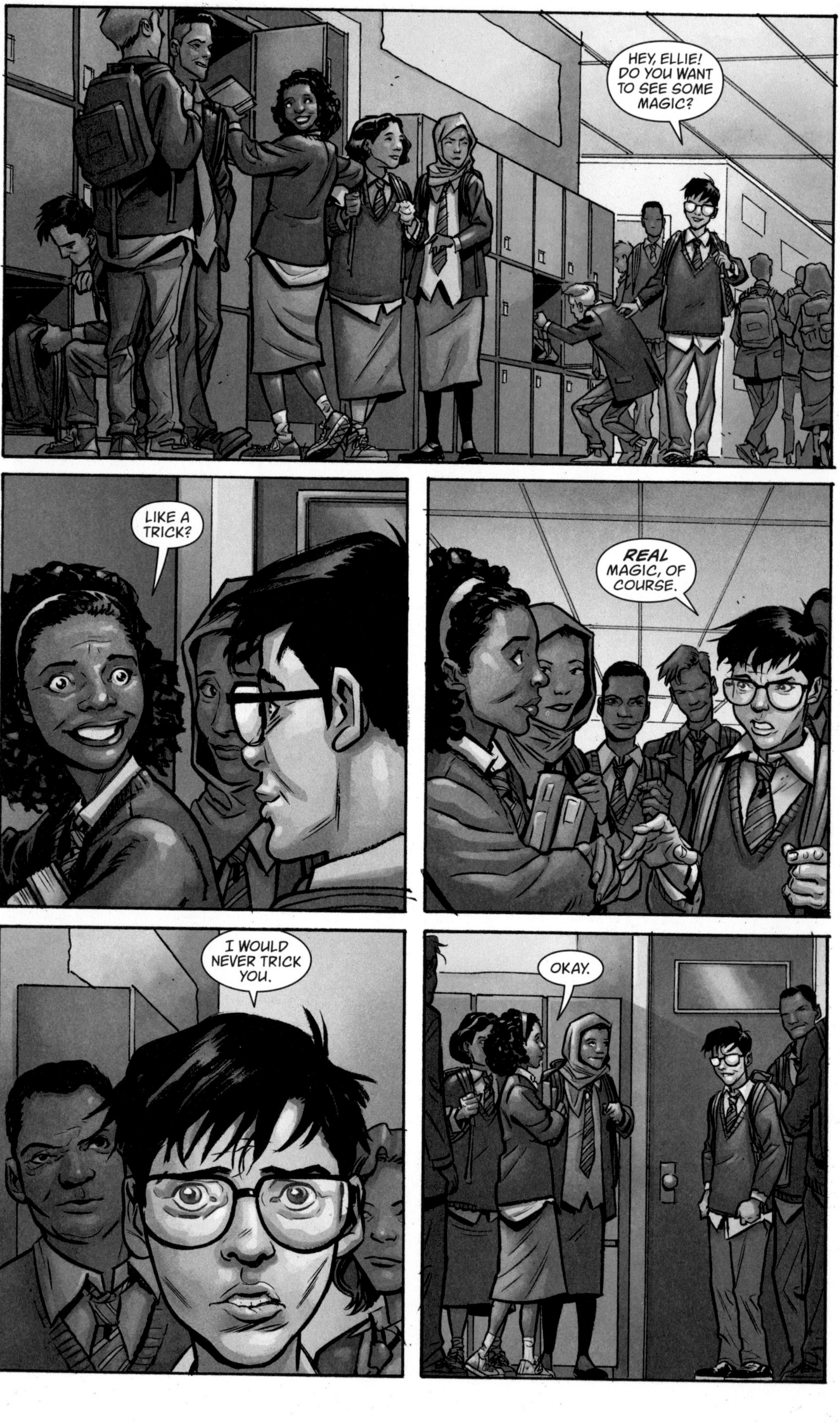
HEY, ELLIE! DO YOU WANT TO SEE SOME MAGIC?
LIKE A TRICK?
REAL MAGIC, OF COURSE.
I WOULD NEVER TRICK YOU.
OKAY.

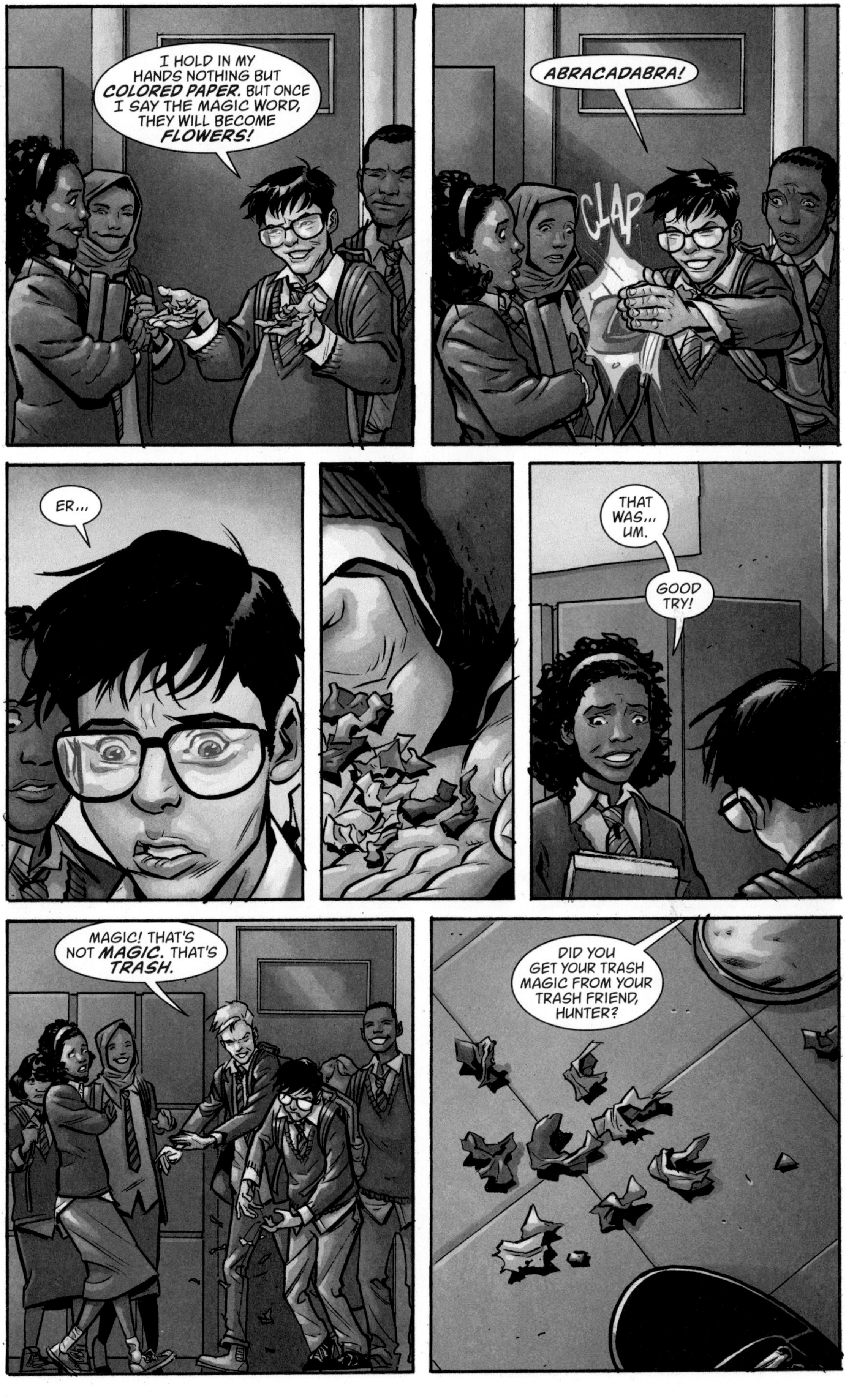
I HOLD IN MY HANDS NOTHING BUT COLORED PAPER. BUT ONCE I SAY THE MAGIC WORD, THEY WILL BECOME FLOWERS!
ABRACADABRA!
CLAP
ER...
THAT WAS... UM.
GOOD TRY!
MAGIC! THAT'S NOT MAGIC. THAT'S TRASH.
DID YOU GET YOUR TRASH MAGIC FROM YOUR TRASH FRIEND, HUNTER?

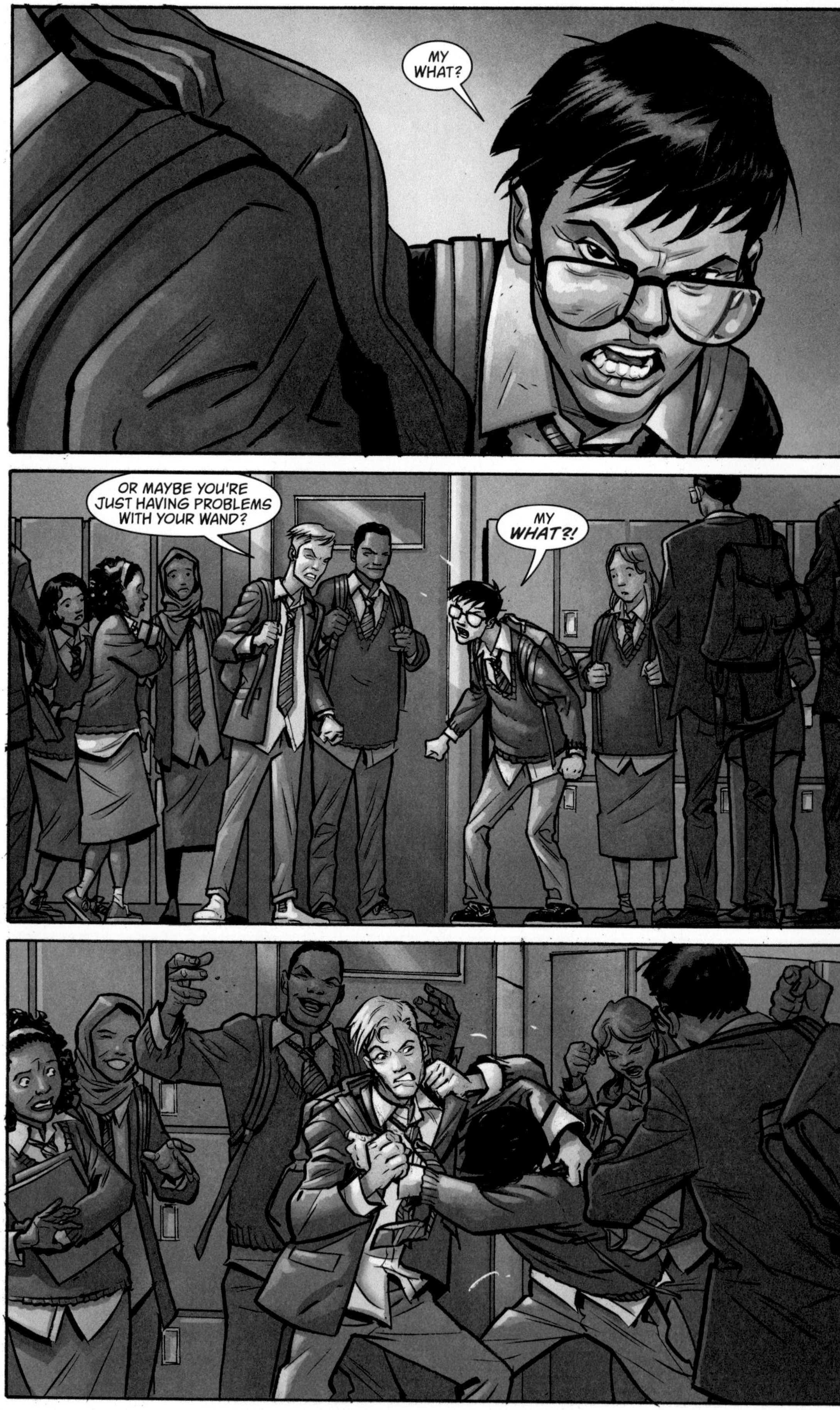
MY WHAT?
OR MAYBE YOU'RE JUST HAVING PROBLEMS WITH YOUR WAND?
MY WHAT?!

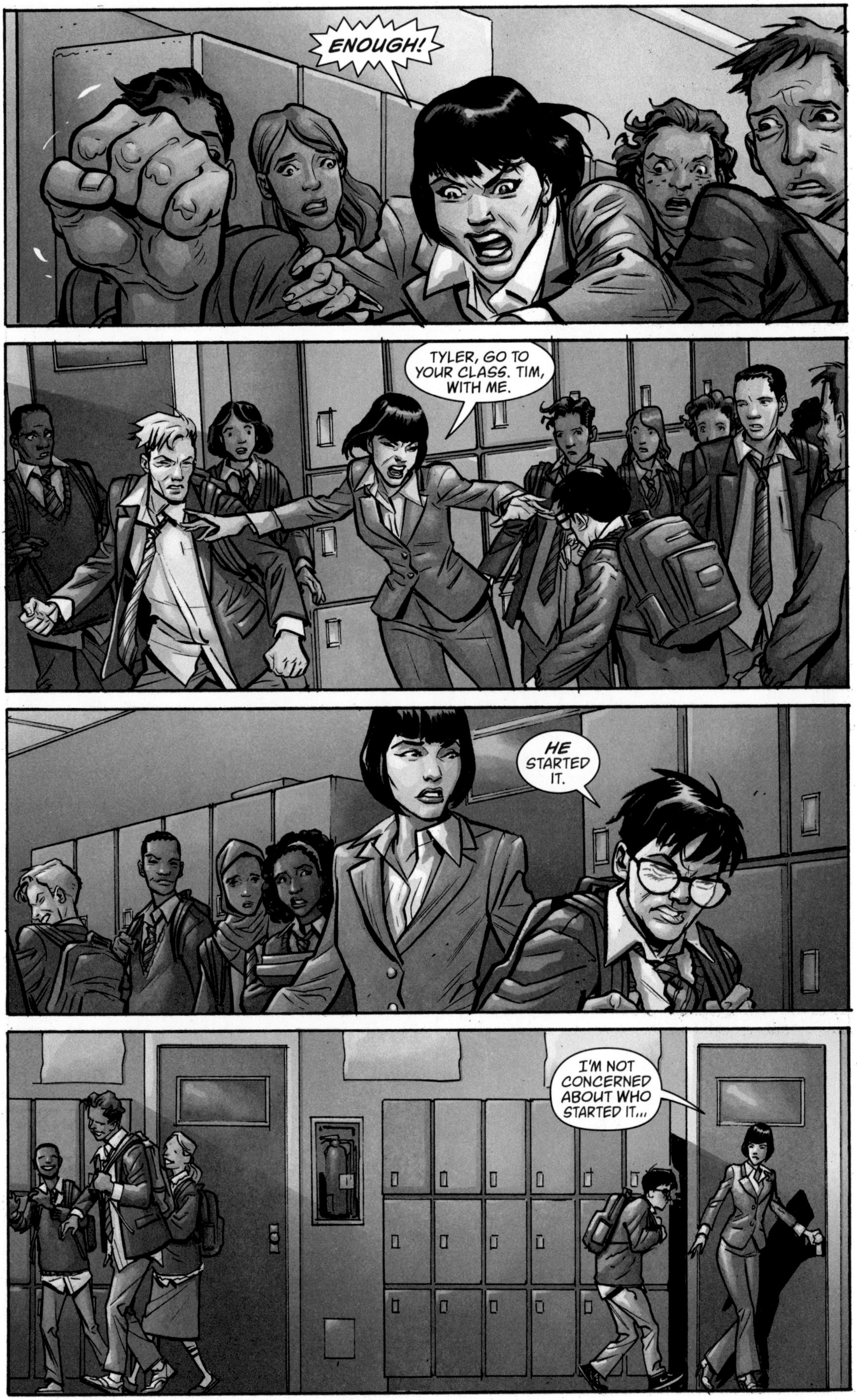
ENOUGH!
TYLER, GO TO YOUR CLASS. TIM, WITH ME.
HE STARTED IT.
I'M NOT CONCERNED ABOUT WHO STARTED IT...

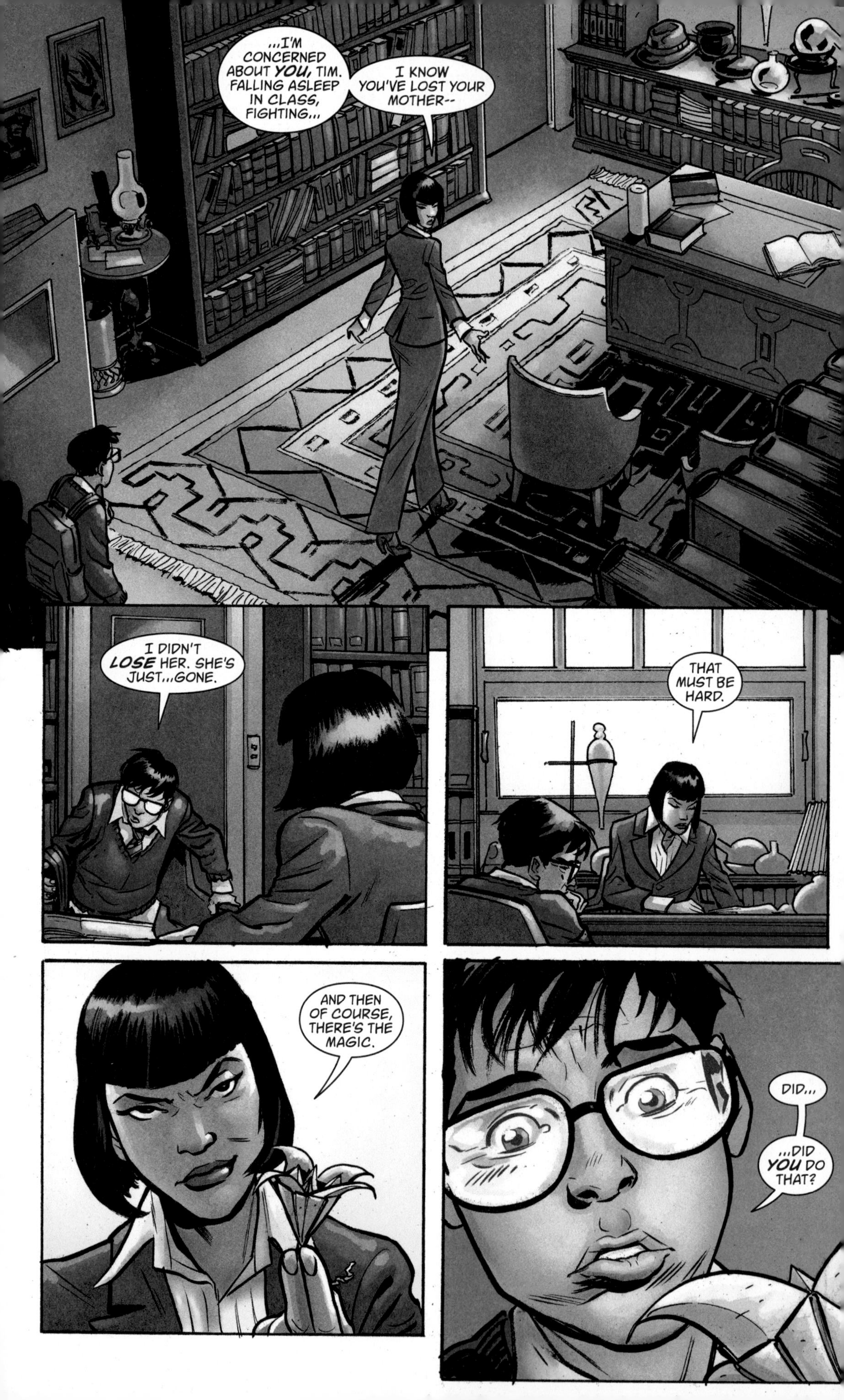
...I'M CONCERNED ABOUT YOU, TIM. FALLING ASLEEP IN CLASS, FIGHTING...
I KNOW YOU'VE LOST YOUR MOTHER--
I DIDN'T LOSE HER. SHE'S JUST...GONE.
THAT MUST BE HARD.
AND THEN OF COURSE, THERE'S THE MAGIC.
DID...
...DID YOU DO THAT?

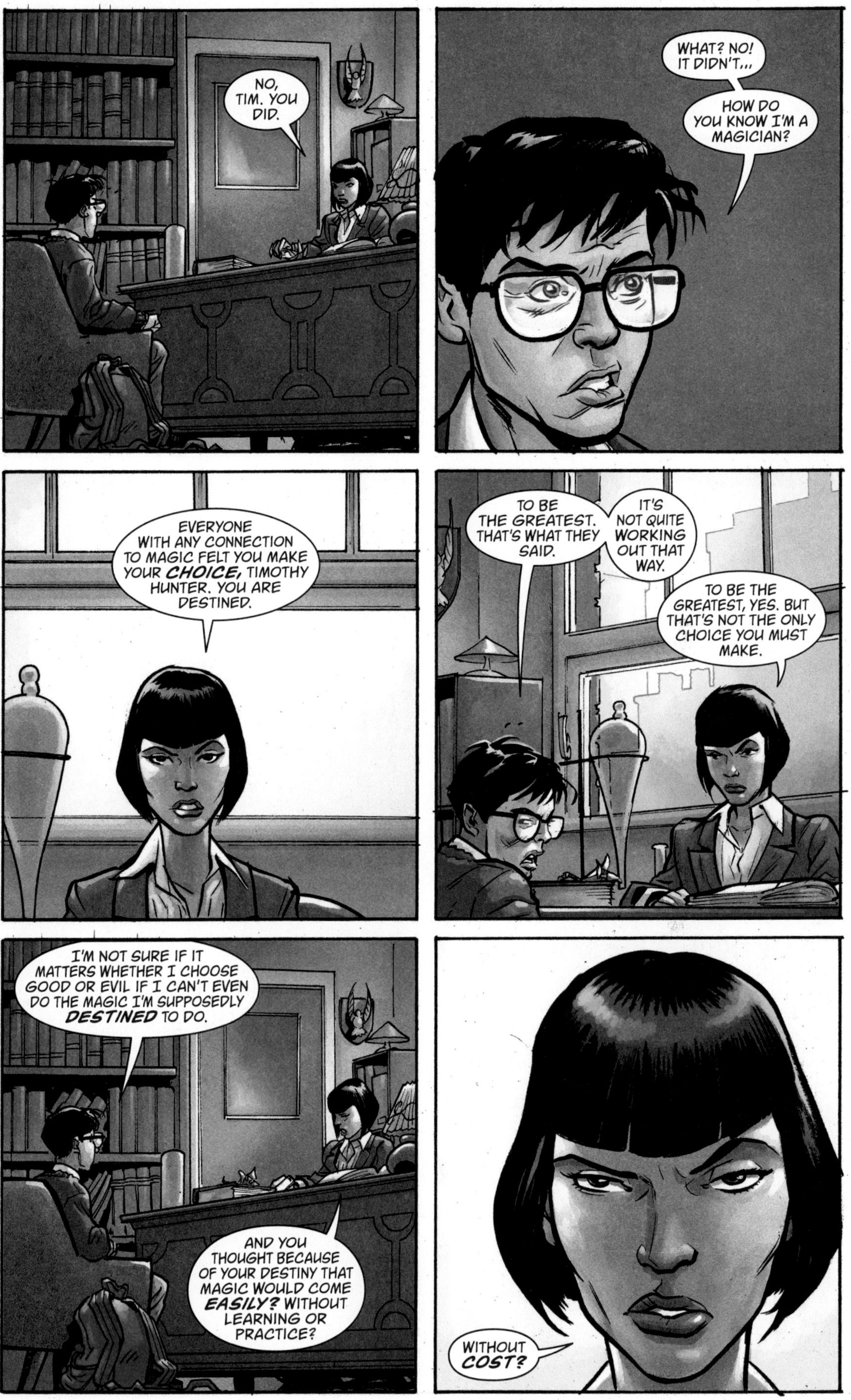
NO, TIM. YOU DID.
WHAT? NO! IT DIDN'T...
HOW DO YOU KNOW I'M A MAGICIAN?
EVERYONE WITH ANY CONNECTION TO MAGIC FELT YOU MAKE YOUR **CHOICE,** TIMOTHY HUNTER. YOU ARE DESTINED.
TO BE THE GREATEST. THAT'S WHAT THEY SAID.
IT'S NOT QUITE WORKING OUT THAT WAY.
TO BE THE GREATEST, YES. BUT THAT'S NOT THE ONLY CHOICE YOU MUST MAKE.
I'M NOT SURE IF IT MATTERS WHETHER I CHOOSE GOOD OR EVIL IF I CAN'T EVEN DO THE MAGIC I'M SUPPOSEDLY ***DESTINED*** TO DO.
AND YOU THOUGHT BECAUSE OF YOUR DESTINY THAT MAGIC WOULD COME ***EASILY?*** WITHOUT LEARNING OR PRACTICE?
WITHOUT ***COST?***

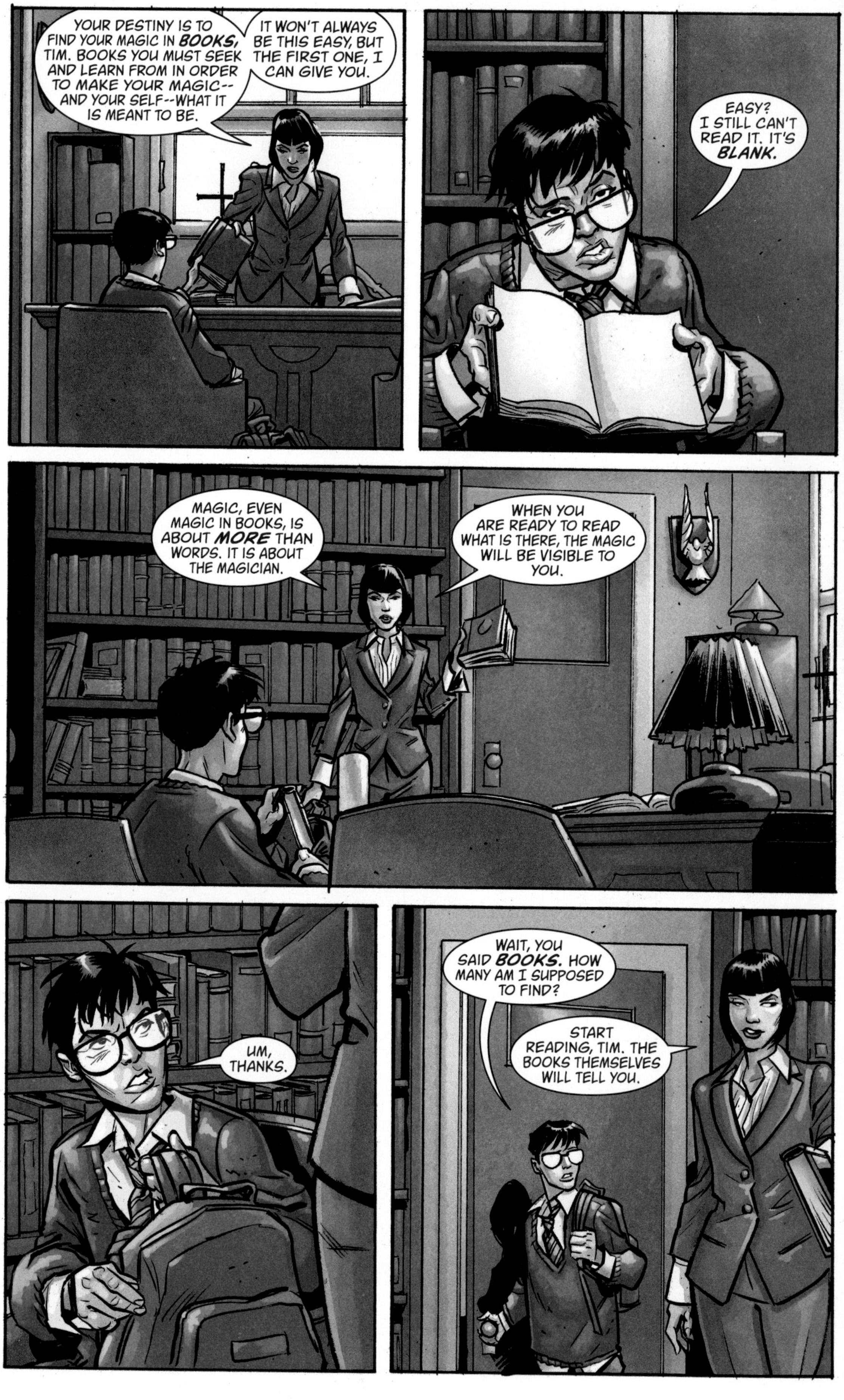
YOUR DESTINY IS TO FIND YOUR MAGIC IN BOOKS, TIM. BOOKS YOU MUST SEEK AND LEARN FROM IN ORDER TO MAKE YOUR MAGIC-- AND YOUR SELF--WHAT IT IS MEANT TO BE.
IT WON'T ALWAYS BE THIS EASY, BUT THE FIRST ONE, I CAN GIVE YOU.
EASY? I STILL CAN'T READ IT. IT'S BLANK.
MAGIC, EVEN MAGIC IN BOOKS, IS ABOUT MORE THAN WORDS. IT IS ABOUT THE MAGICIAN.
WHEN YOU ARE READY TO READ WHAT IS THERE, THE MAGIC WILL BE VISIBLE TO YOU.
UM, THANKS.
WAIT, YOU SAID BOOKS. HOW MANY AM I SUPPOSED TO FIND?
START READING, TIM. THE BOOKS THEMSELVES WILL TELL YOU.

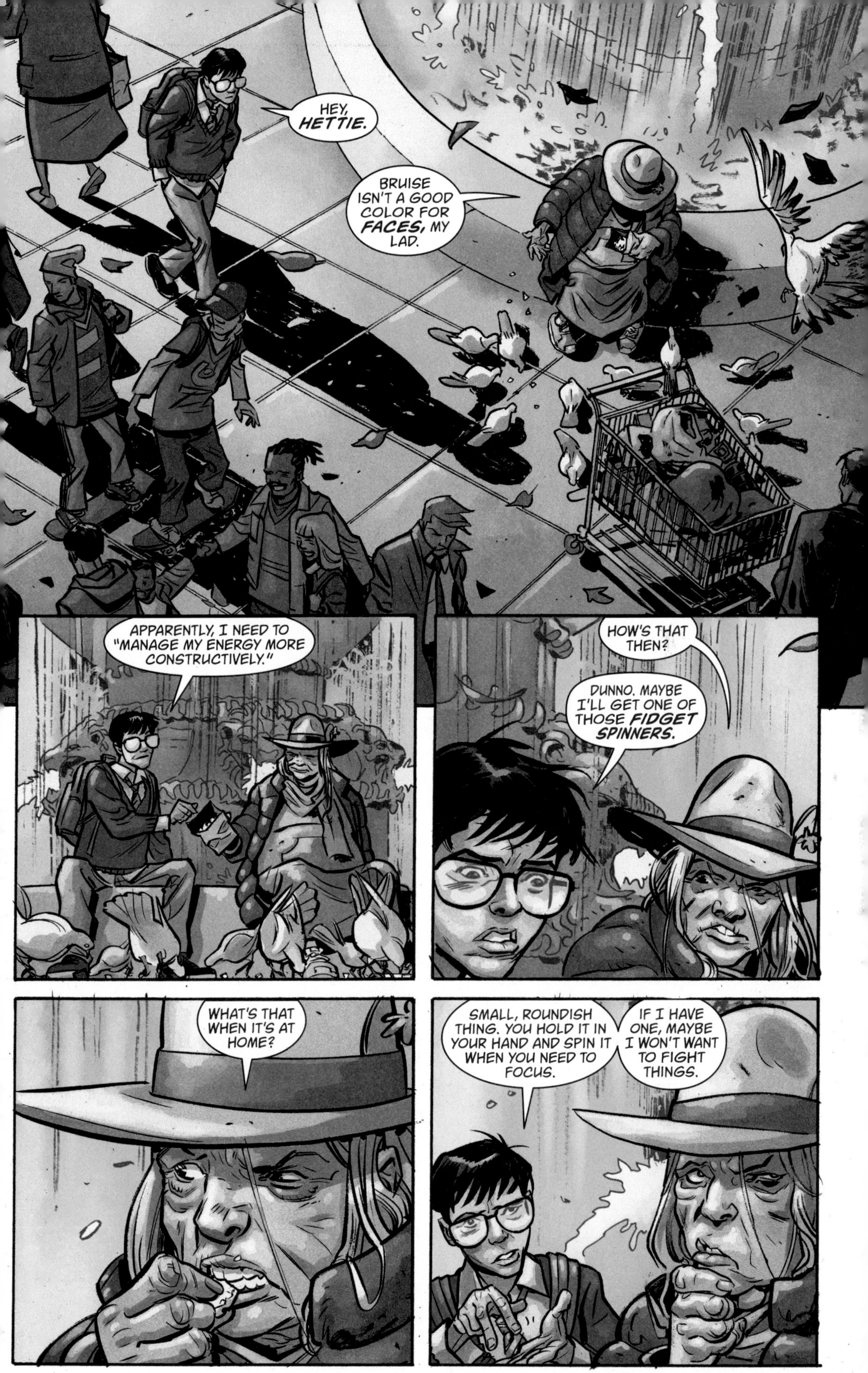
HEY, HETTIE.
BRUISE ISN'T A GOOD COLOR FOR FACES, MY LAD.
APPARENTLY, I NEED TO "MANAGE MY ENERGY MORE CONSTRUCTIVELY."
HOW'S THAT THEN?
DUNNO. MAYBE I'LL GET ONE OF THOSE FIDGET SPINNERS.
WHAT'S THAT WHEN IT'S AT HOME?
SMALL, ROUNDISH THING. YOU HOLD IT IN YOUR HAND AND SPIN IT WHEN YOU NEED TO FOCUS.
IF I HAVE ONE, MAYBE I WON'T WANT TO FIGHT THINGS.

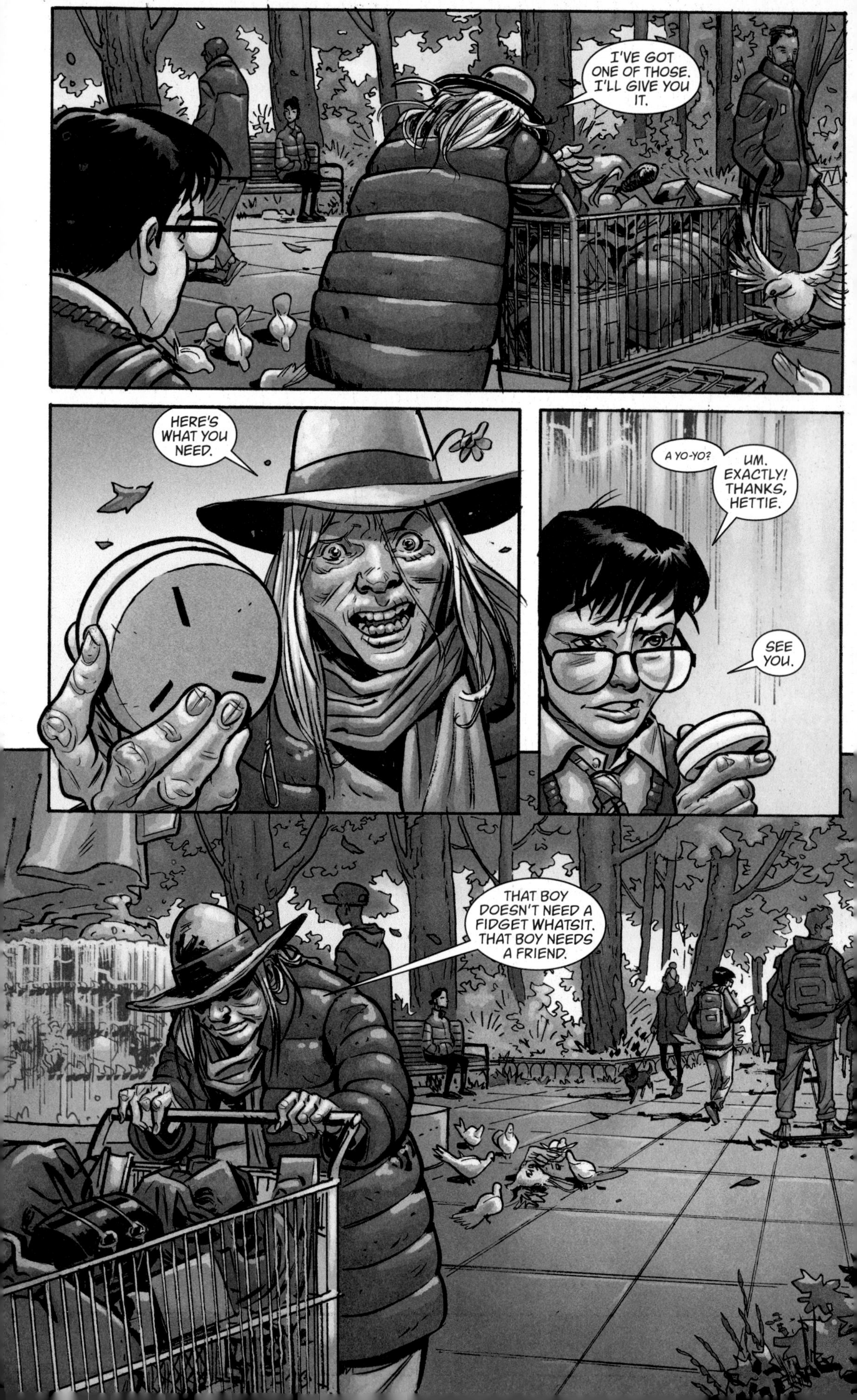
I'VE GOT ONE OF THOSE. I'LL GIVE YOU IT.
HERE'S WHAT YOU NEED.
A YO-YO?
UM. EXACTLY! THANKS, HETTIE.
SEE YOU.
THAT BOY DOESN'T NEED A FIDGET WHATSIT. THAT BOY NEEDS A FRIEND.

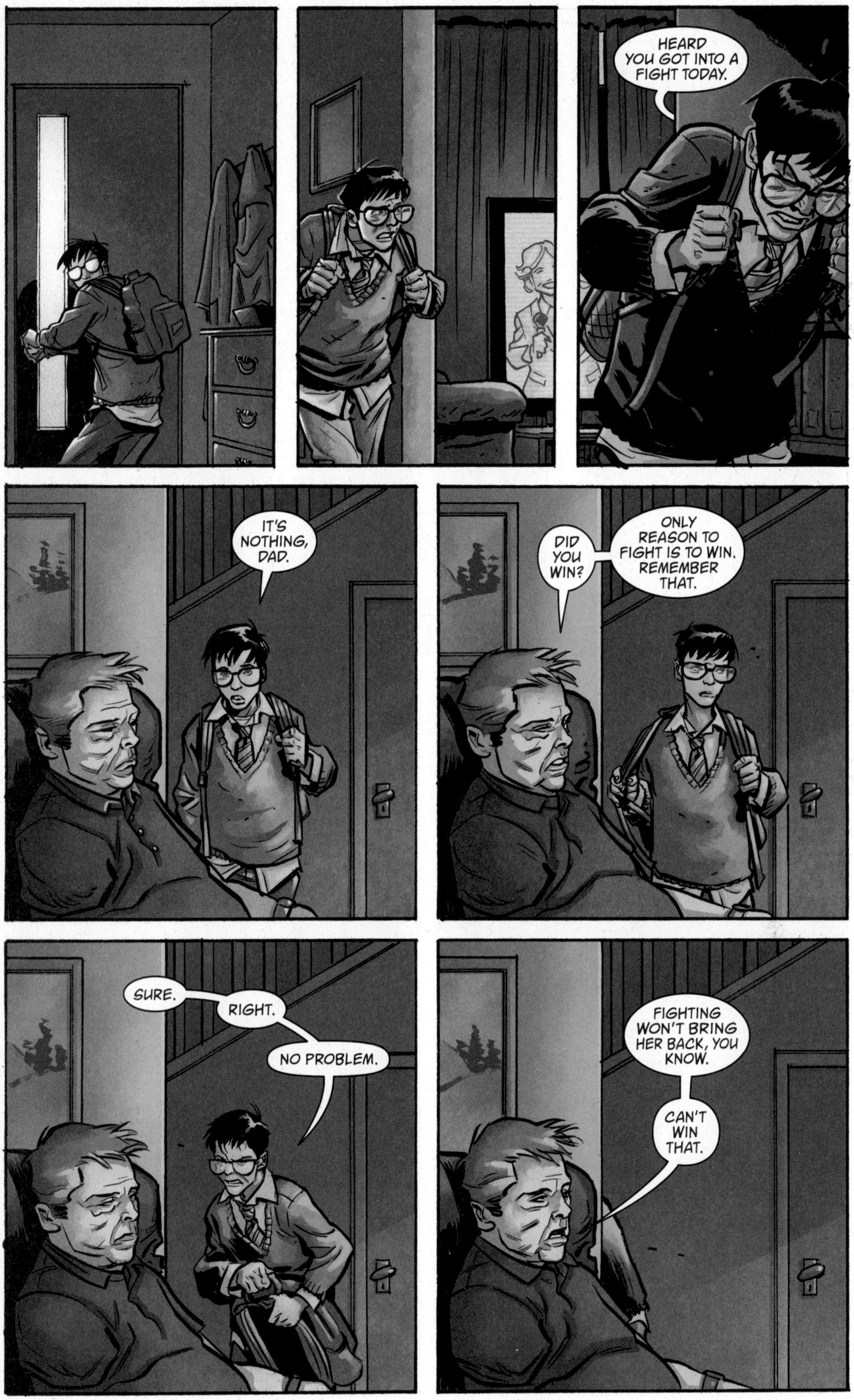
HEARD YOU GOT INTO A FIGHT TODAY.
IT'S NOTHING, DAD.
DID YOU WIN?
ONLY REASON TO FIGHT IS TO WIN. REMEMBER THAT.
SURE.
RIGHT.
NO PROBLEM.
FIGHTING WON'T BRING HER BACK, YOU KNOW.
CAN'T WIN THAT.

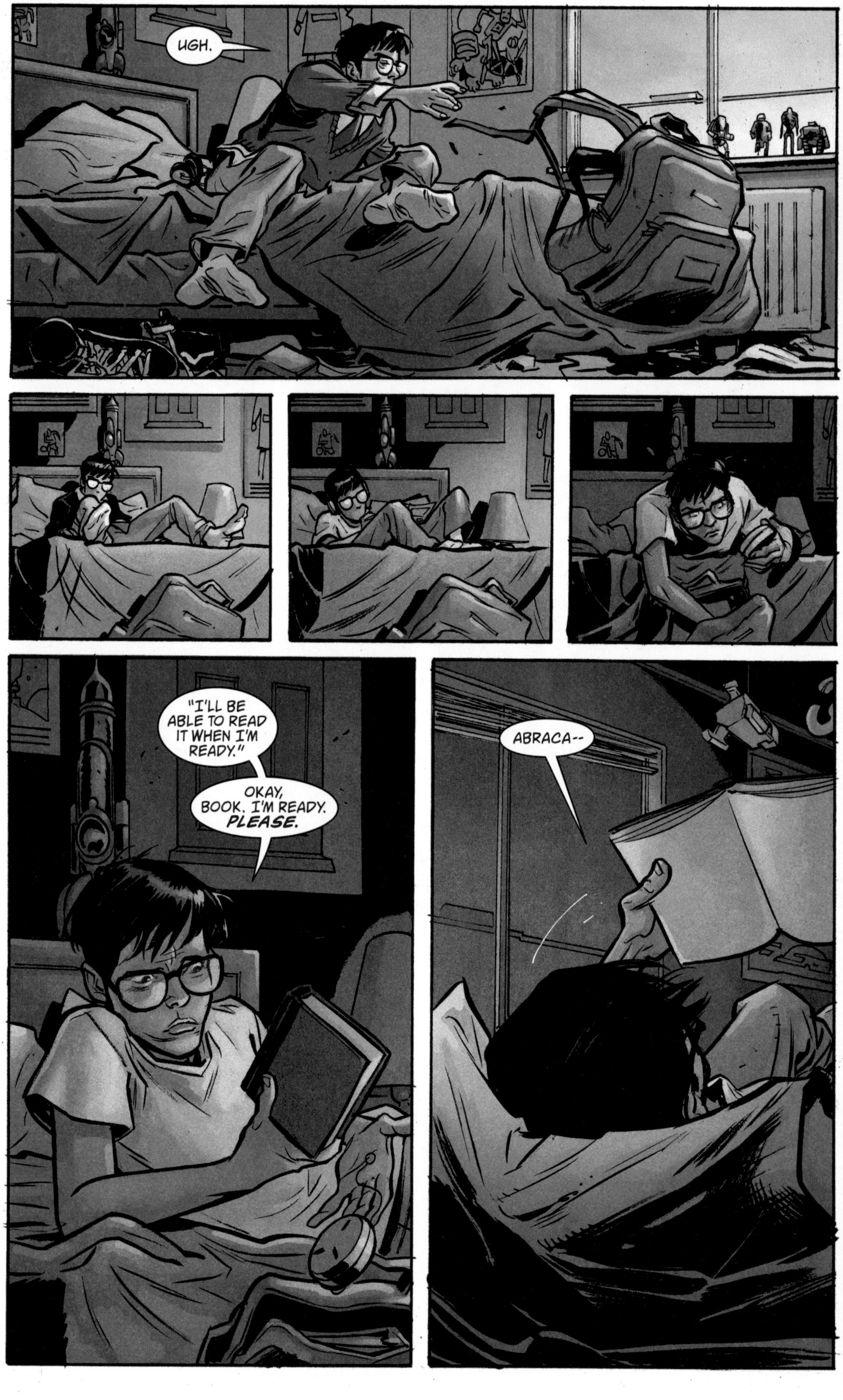
UGH.
"I'LL BE ABLE TO READ IT WHEN I'M READY."
OKAY, BOOK. I'M READY. *PLEASE.*
ABRACA--

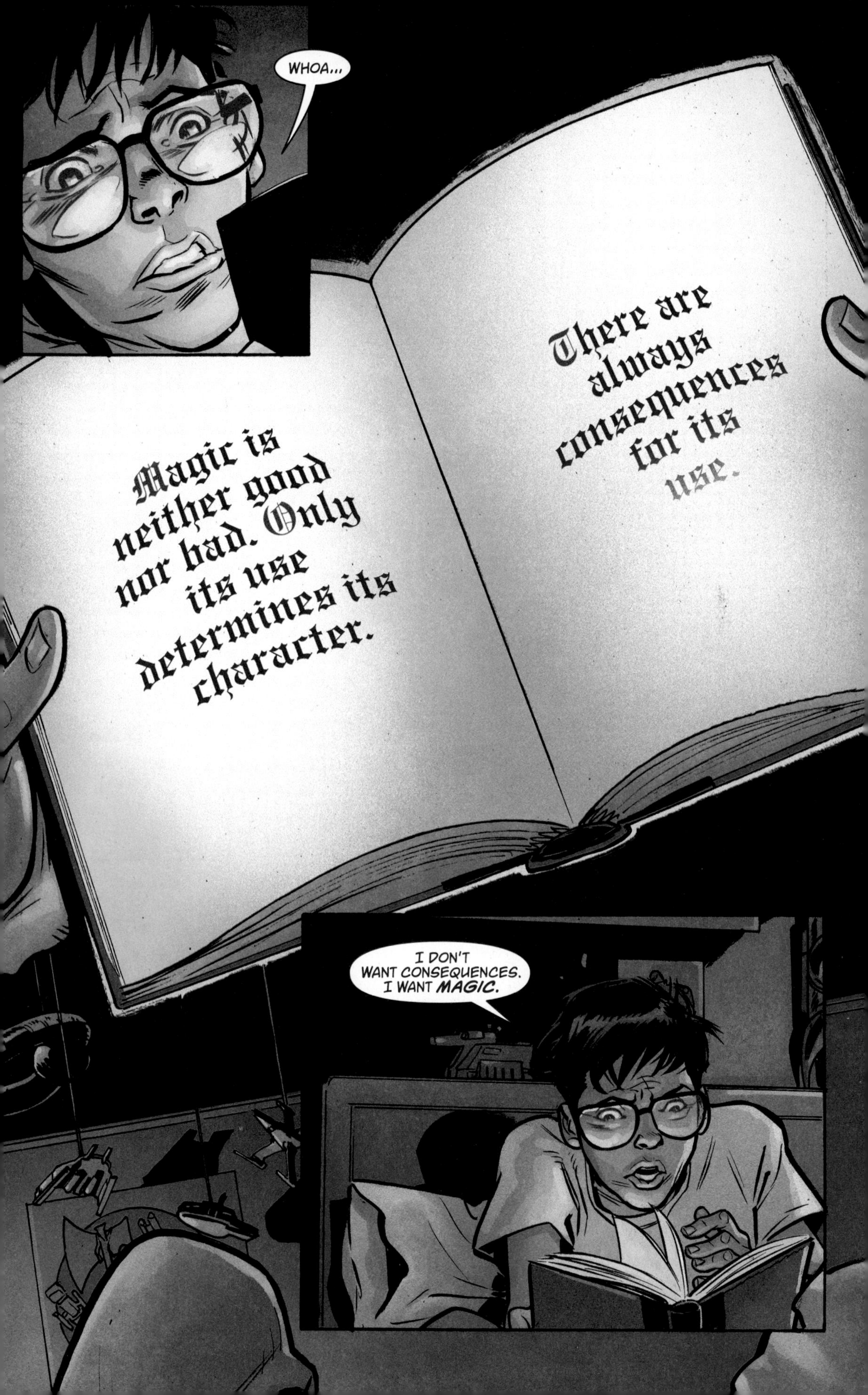
WHOA...
Magic is neither good nor bad. Only its use determines its character.
There are always consequences for its use.
I DON'T WANT CONSEQUENCES. I WANT *MAGIC*.

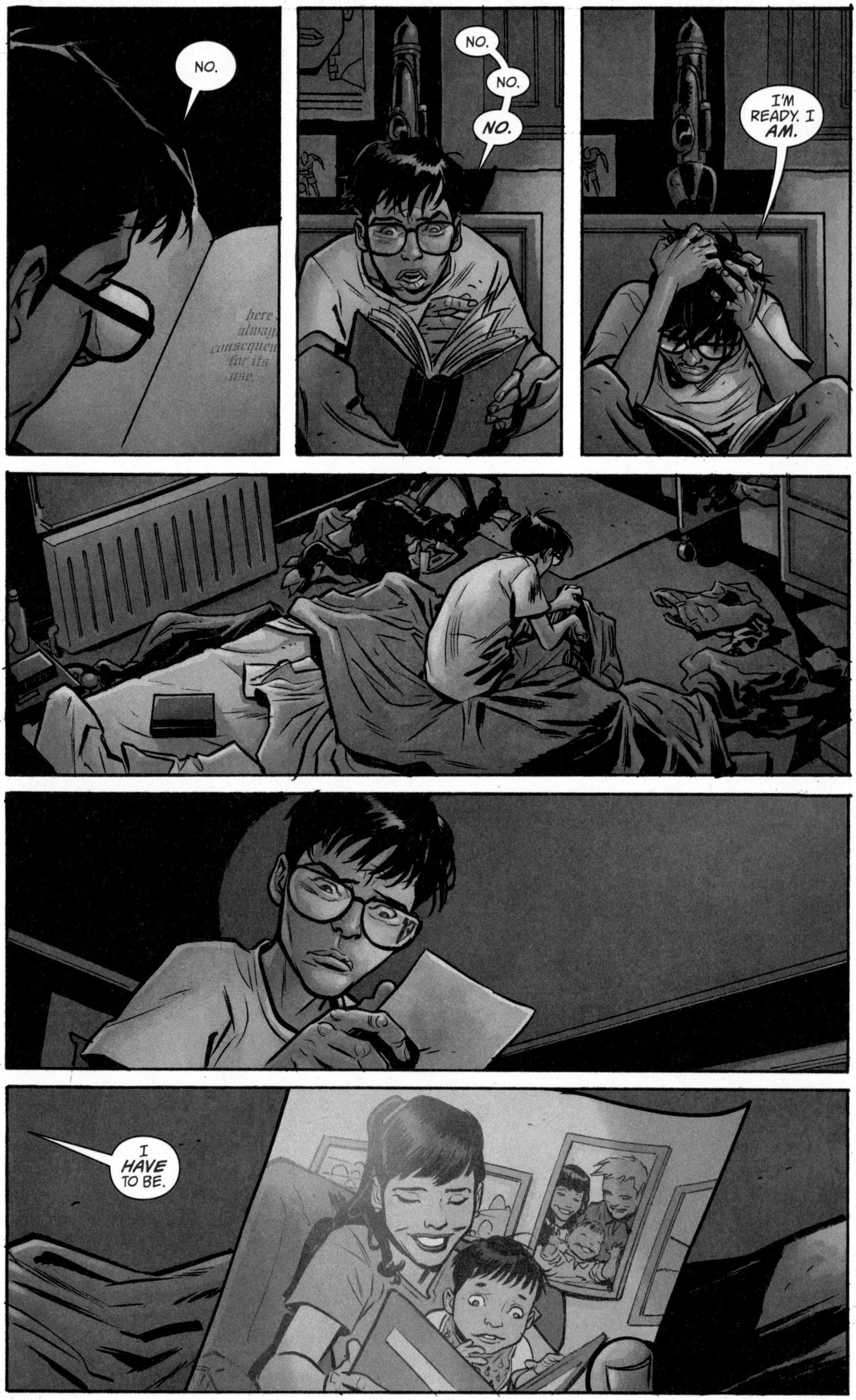

NO.
NO.
NO.
NO.
I'M READY. I AM.
I HAVE TO BE.

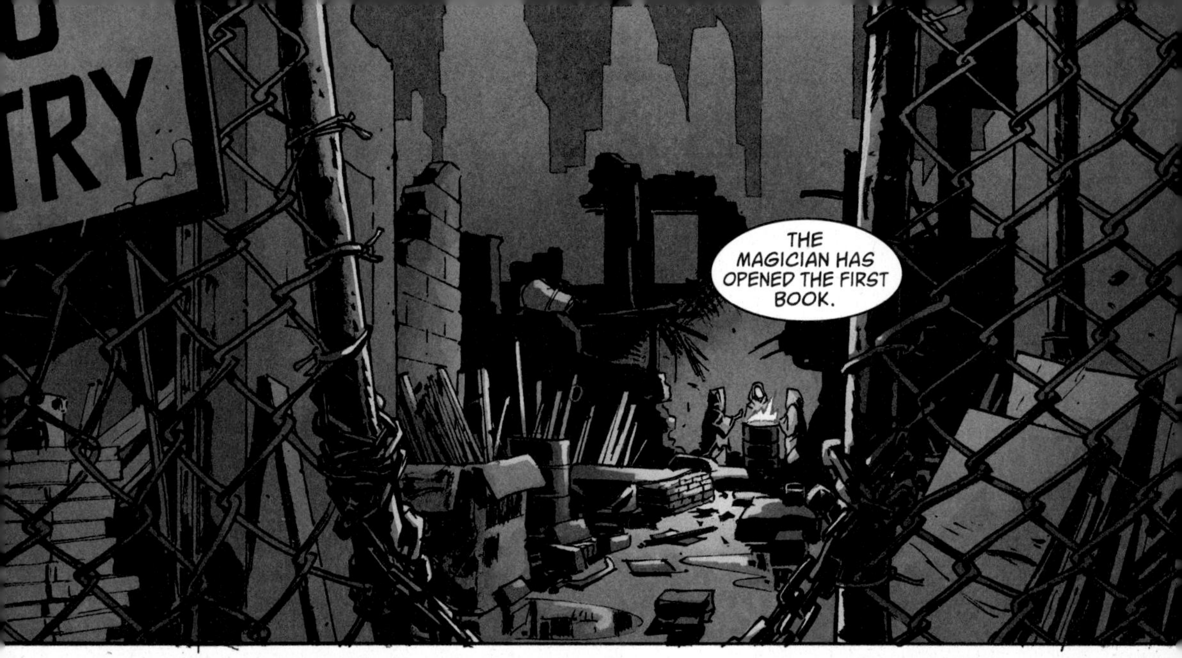
THE MAGICIAN HAS OPENED THE FIRST BOOK.

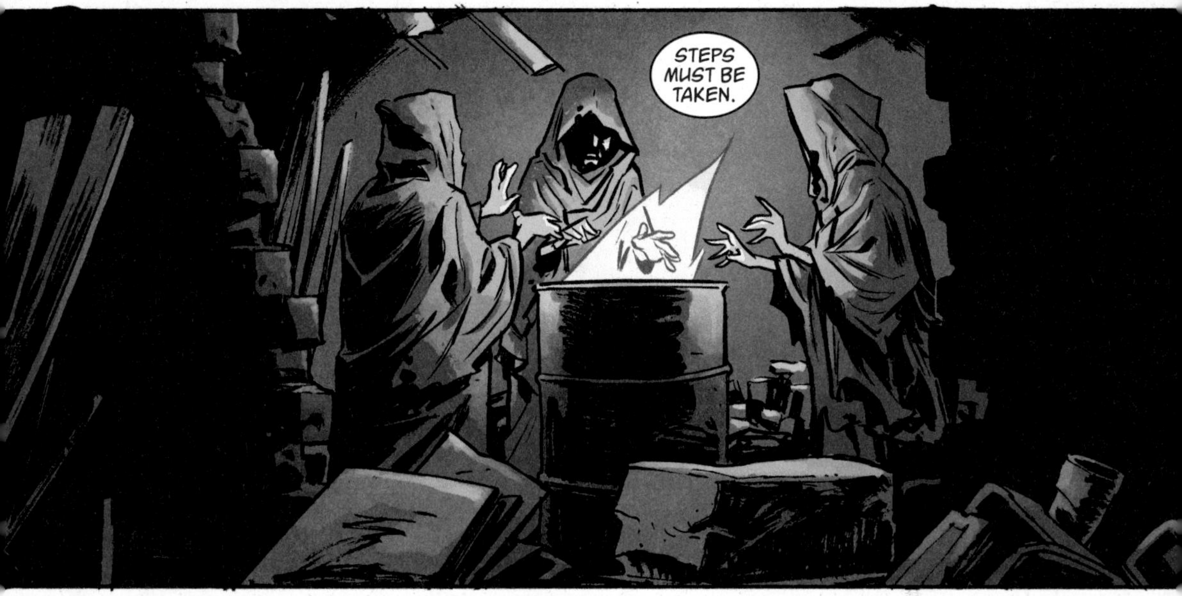
STEPS MUST BE TAKEN.

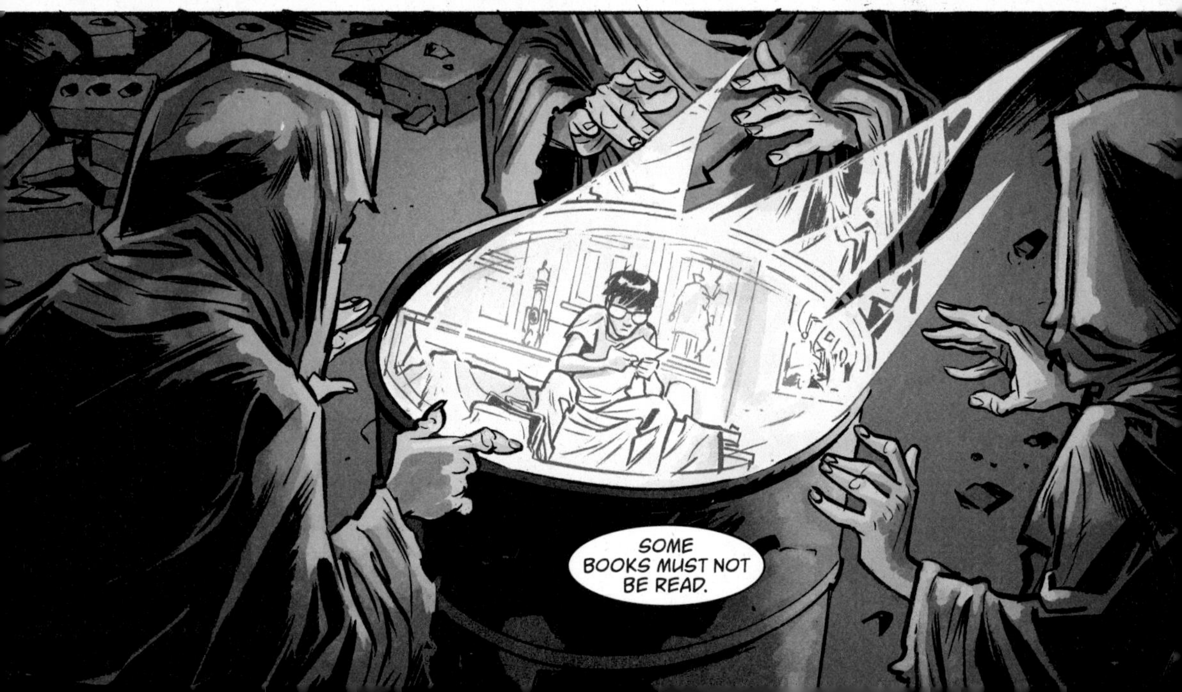
SOME BOOKS MUST NOT BE READ.

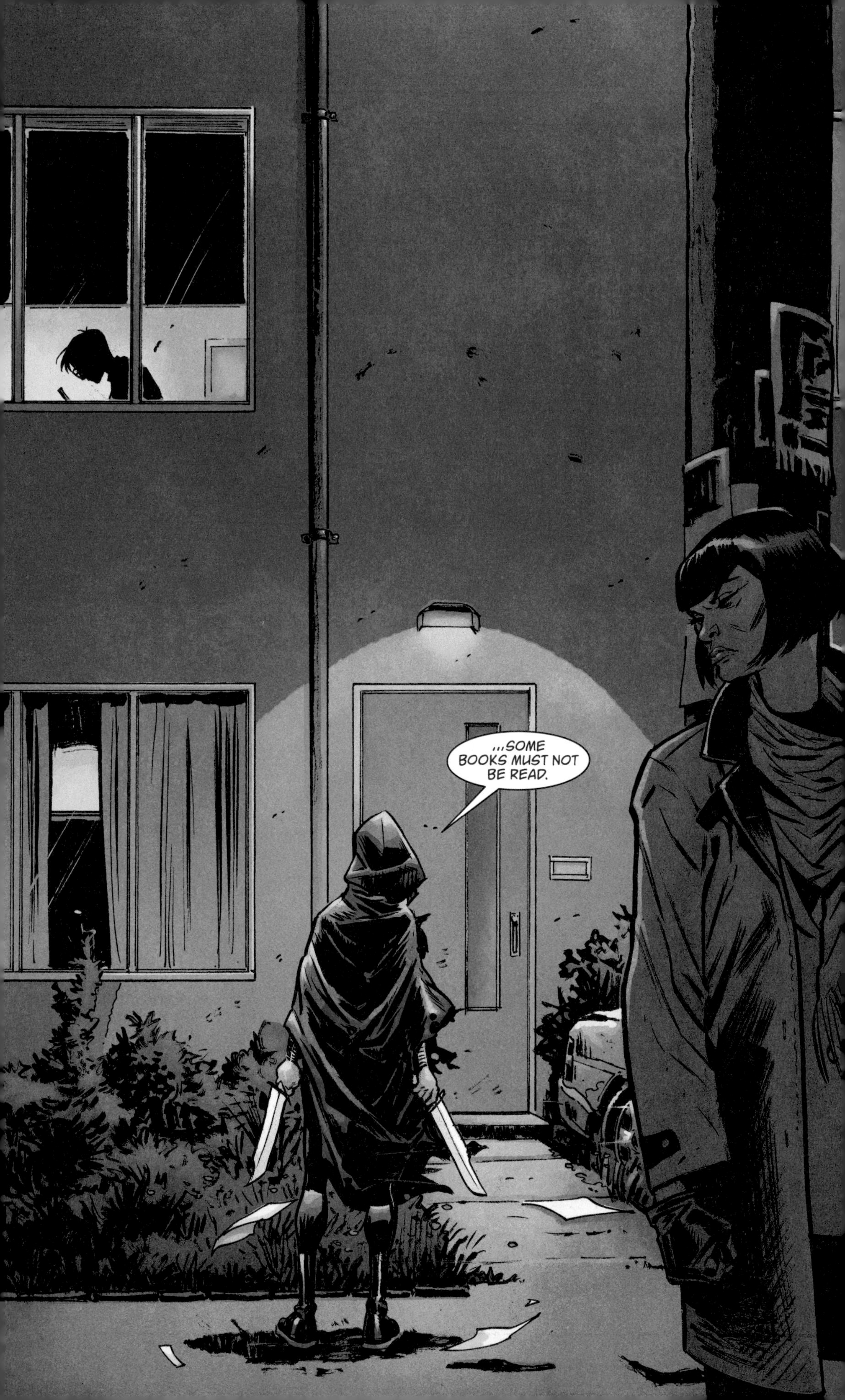
...SOME BOOKS MUST NOT BE READ.

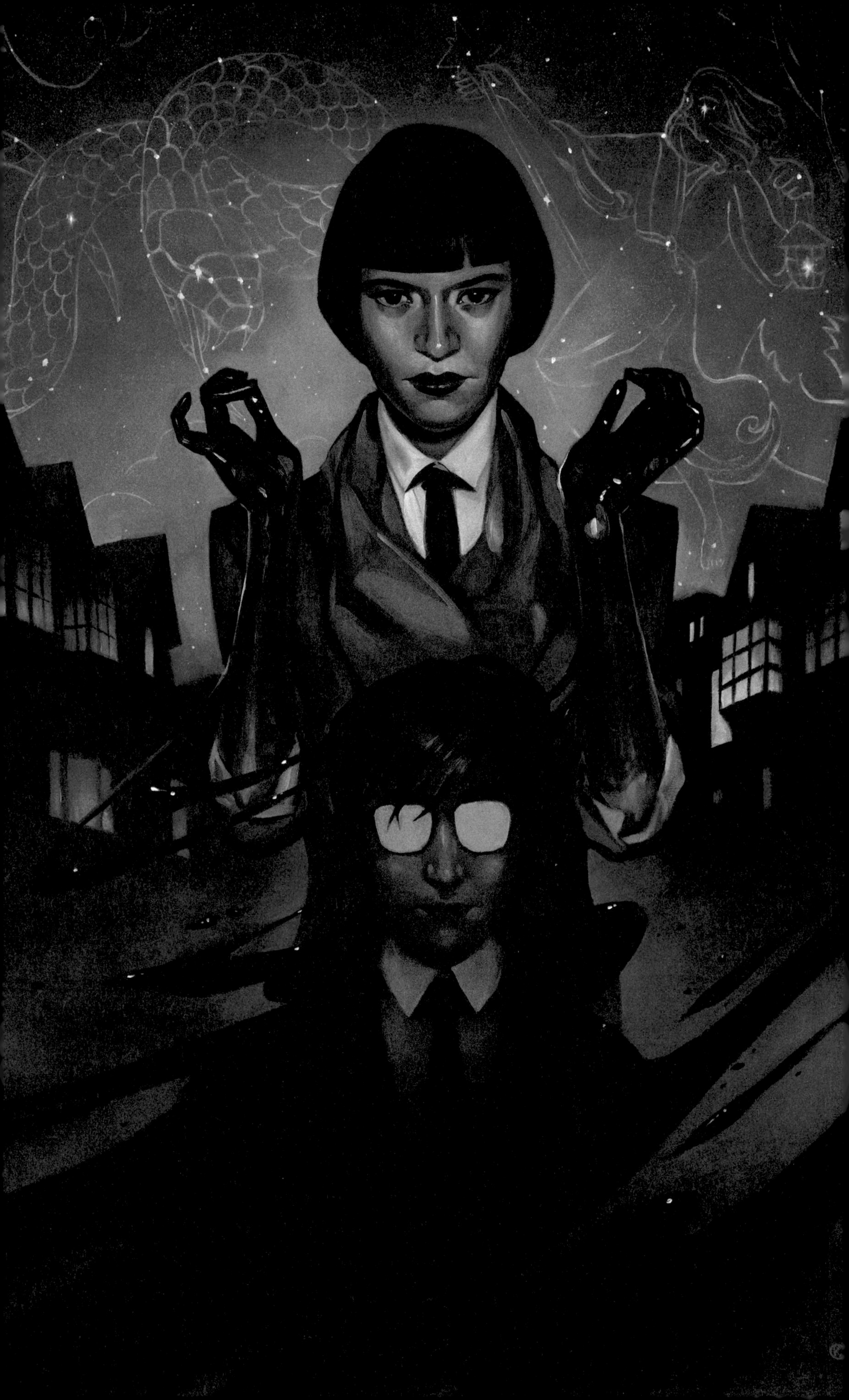

BOOKS OF MAGIC

Unreliable Narrators

WRITTEN BY
Kat Howard

ILLUSTRATED BY
Tom Fowler

COLORS BY
Jordan Boyd

LETTERS BY
Todd Klein

COVER ART BY
Kai Carpenter

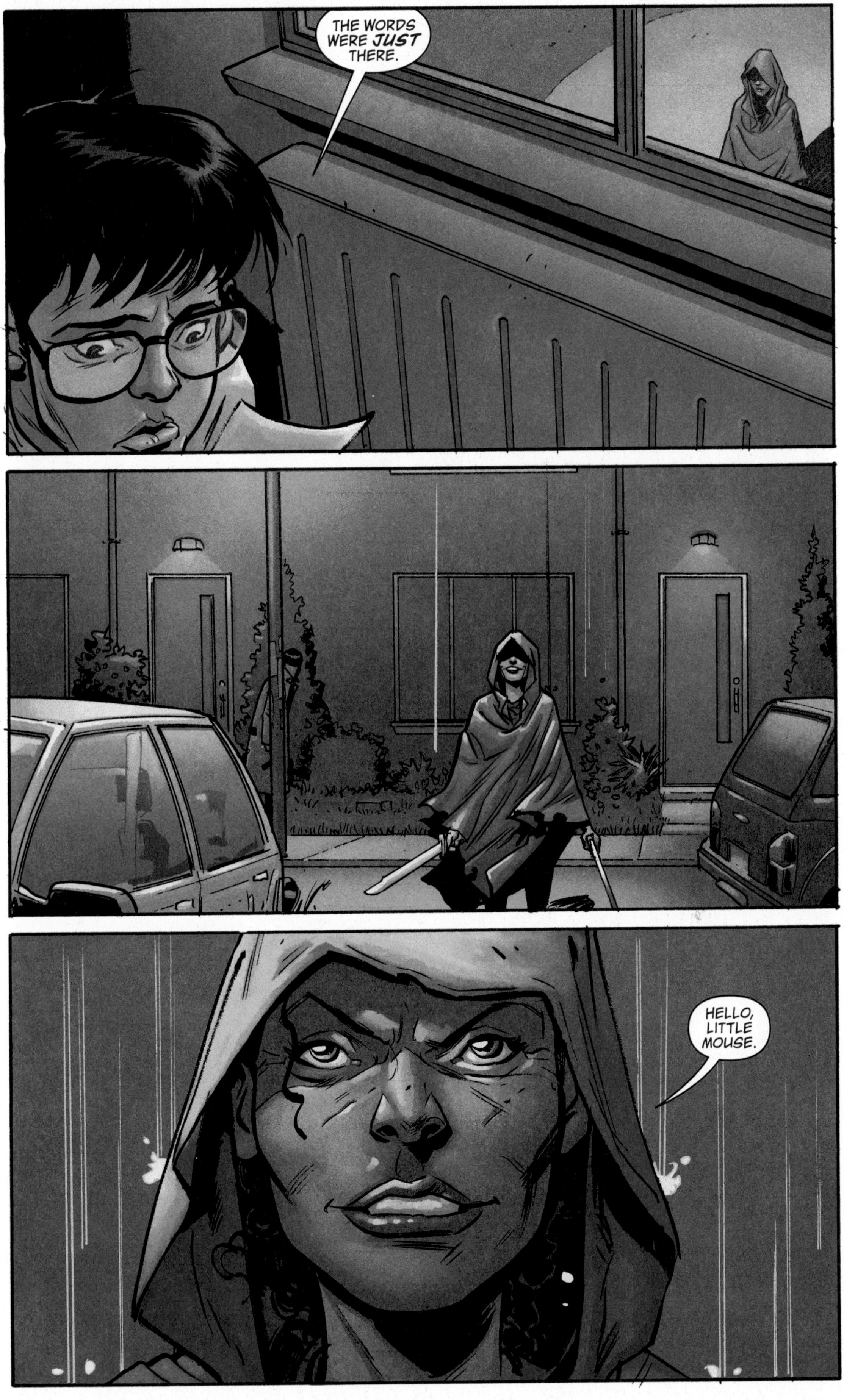
THE WORDS WERE JUST THERE.
HELLO, LITTLE MOUSE.

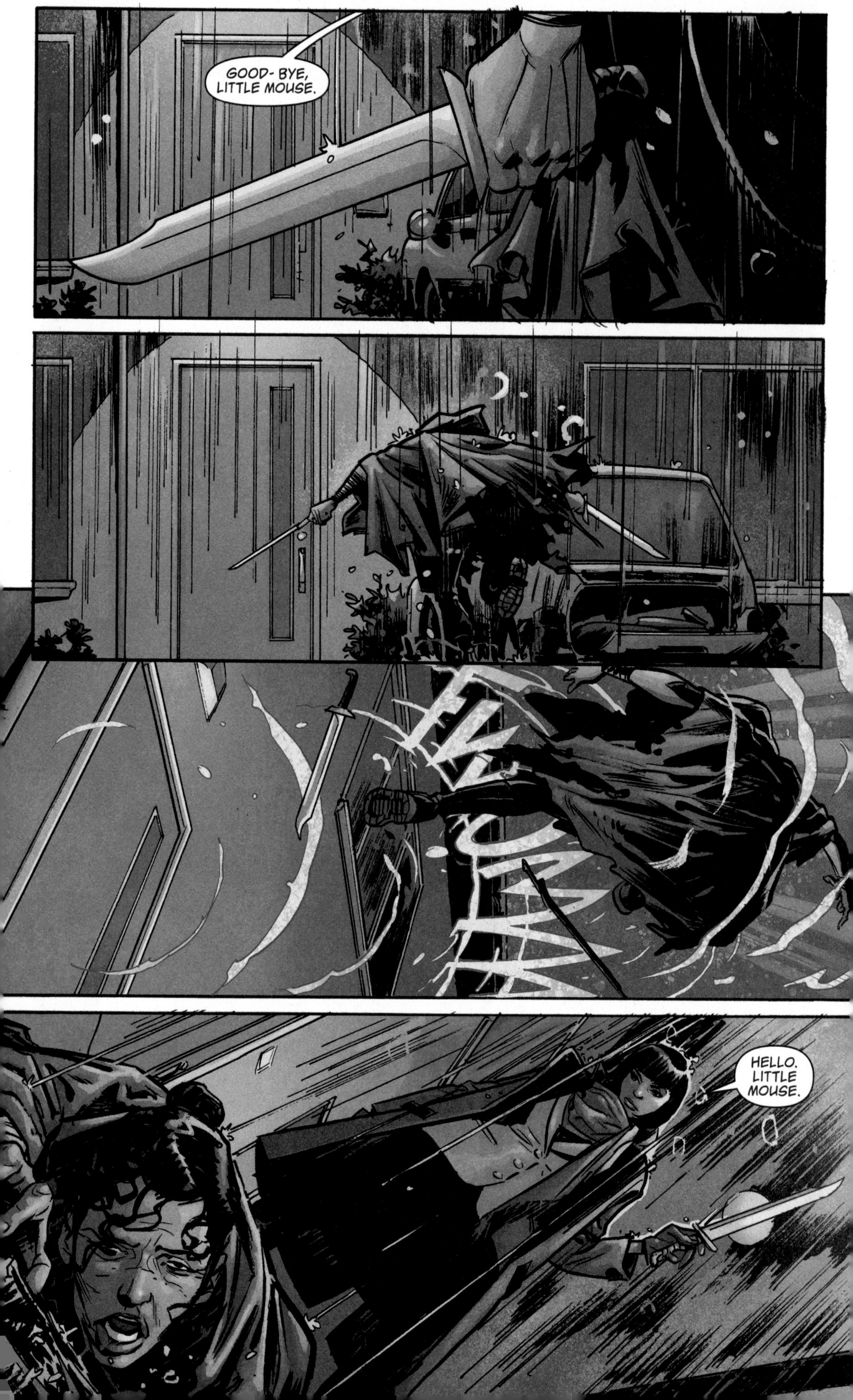
GOOD- BYE, LITTLE MOUSE.
HELLO. LITTLE MOUSE.

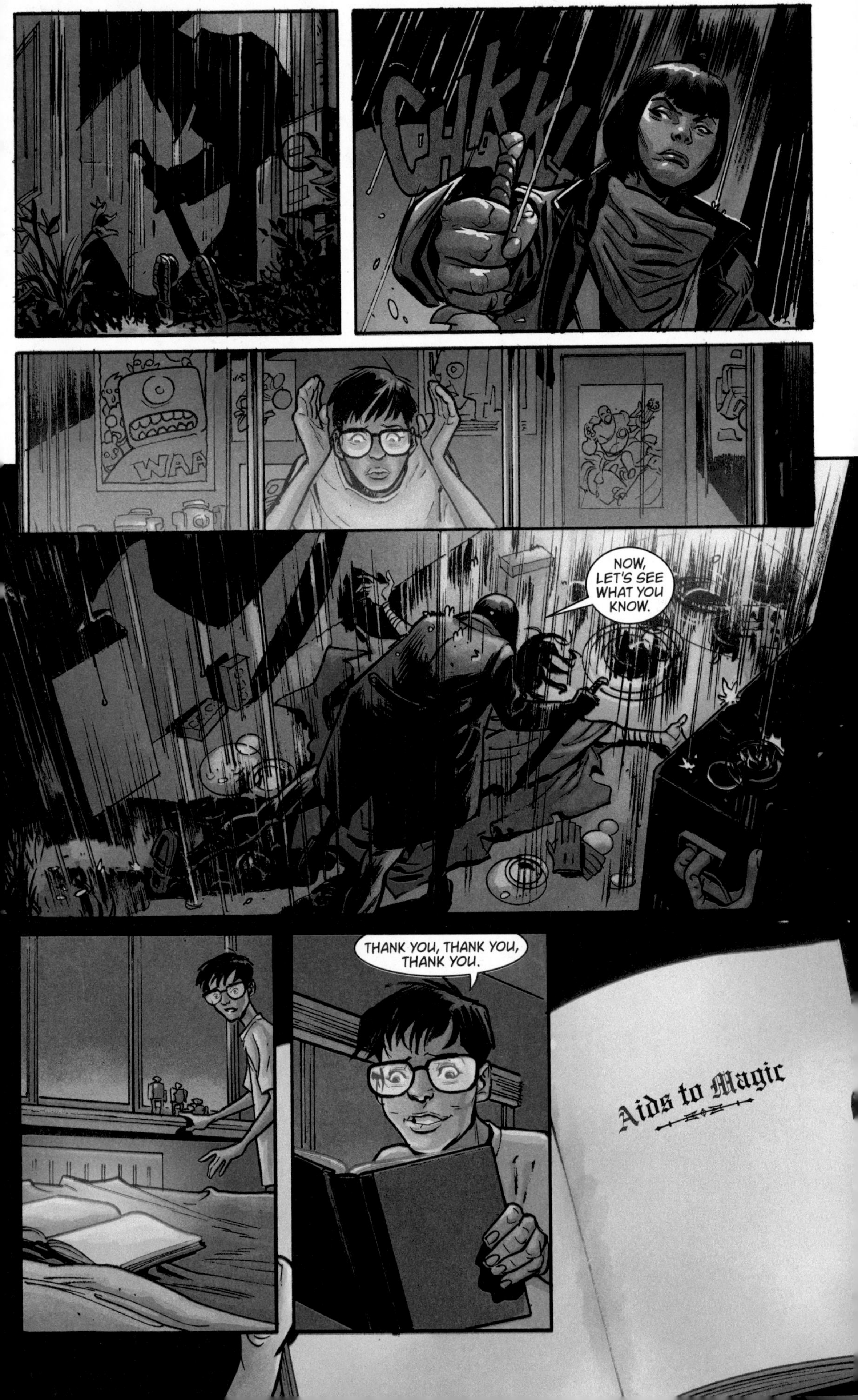
CHKK!
WAA
NOW, LET'S SEE WHAT YOU KNOW.
THANK YOU, THANK YOU, THANK YOU.
Aids to Magic

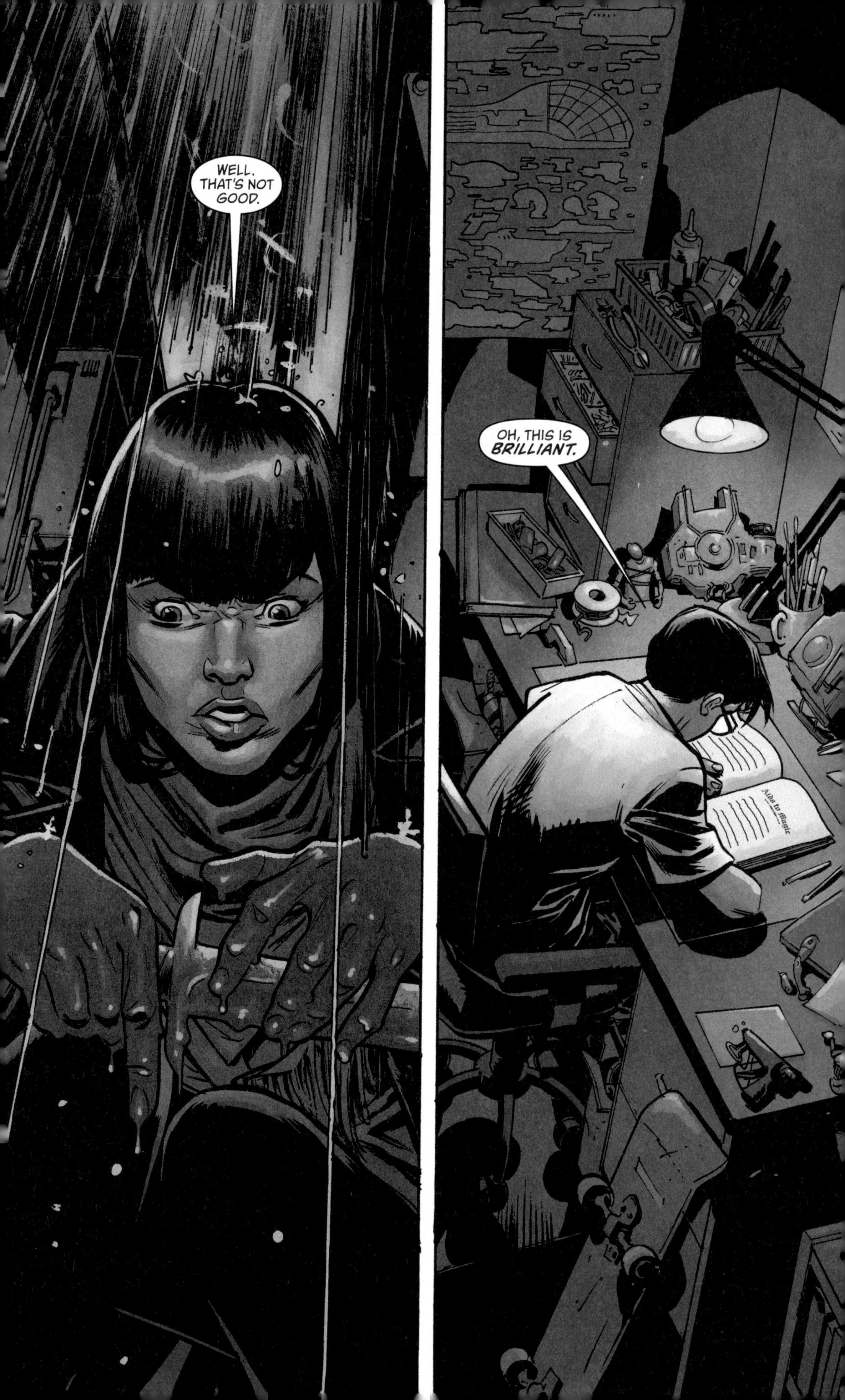
WELL. THAT'S NOT GOOD.
OH, THIS IS BRILLIANT.

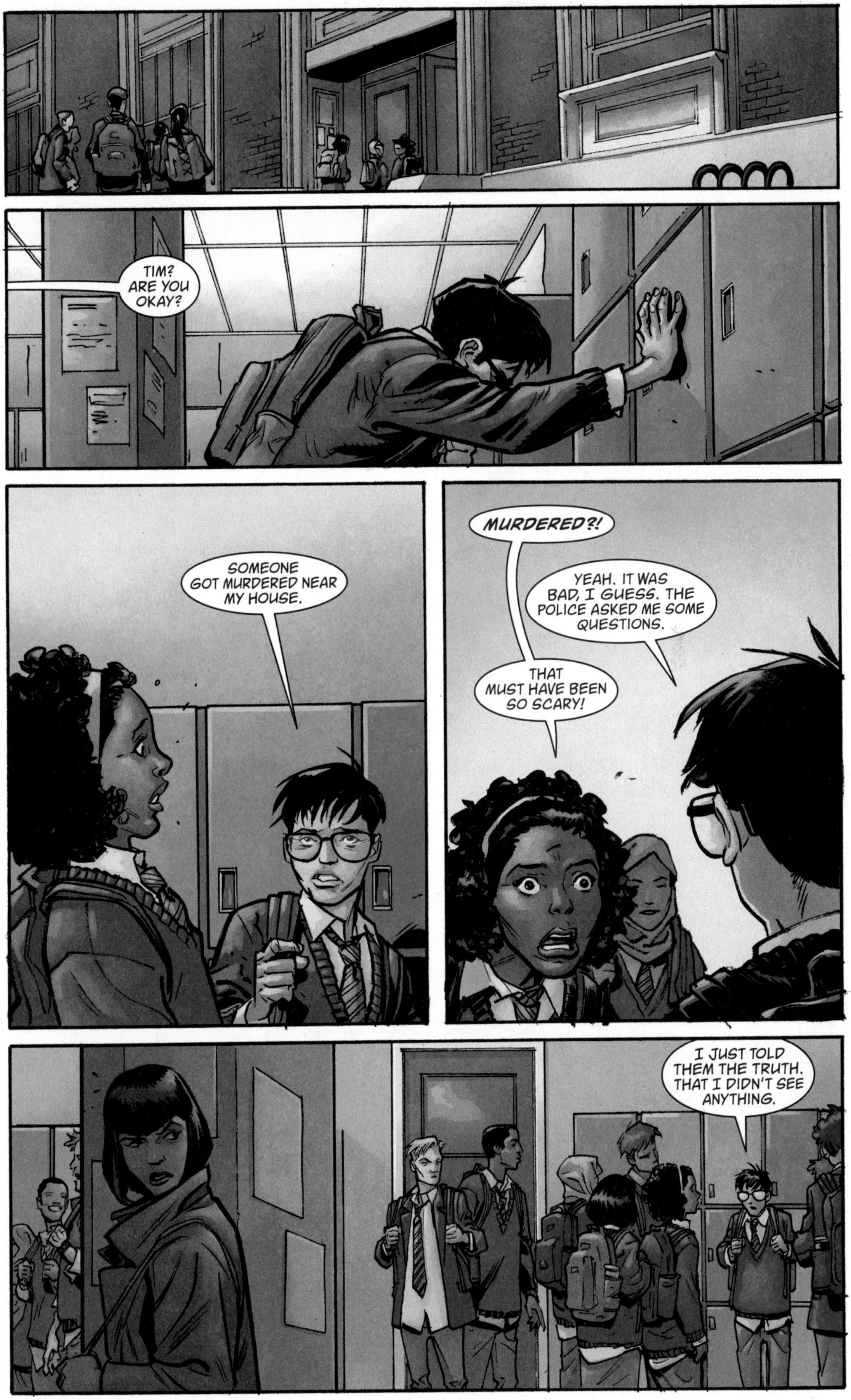
TIM? ARE YOU OKAY?
SOMEONE GOT MURDERED NEAR MY HOUSE.
MURDERED?!
YEAH. IT WAS BAD, I GUESS. THE POLICE ASKED ME SOME QUESTIONS.
THAT MUST HAVE BEEN SO SCARY!
I JUST TOLD THEM THE TRUTH. THAT I DIDN'T SEE ANYTHING.

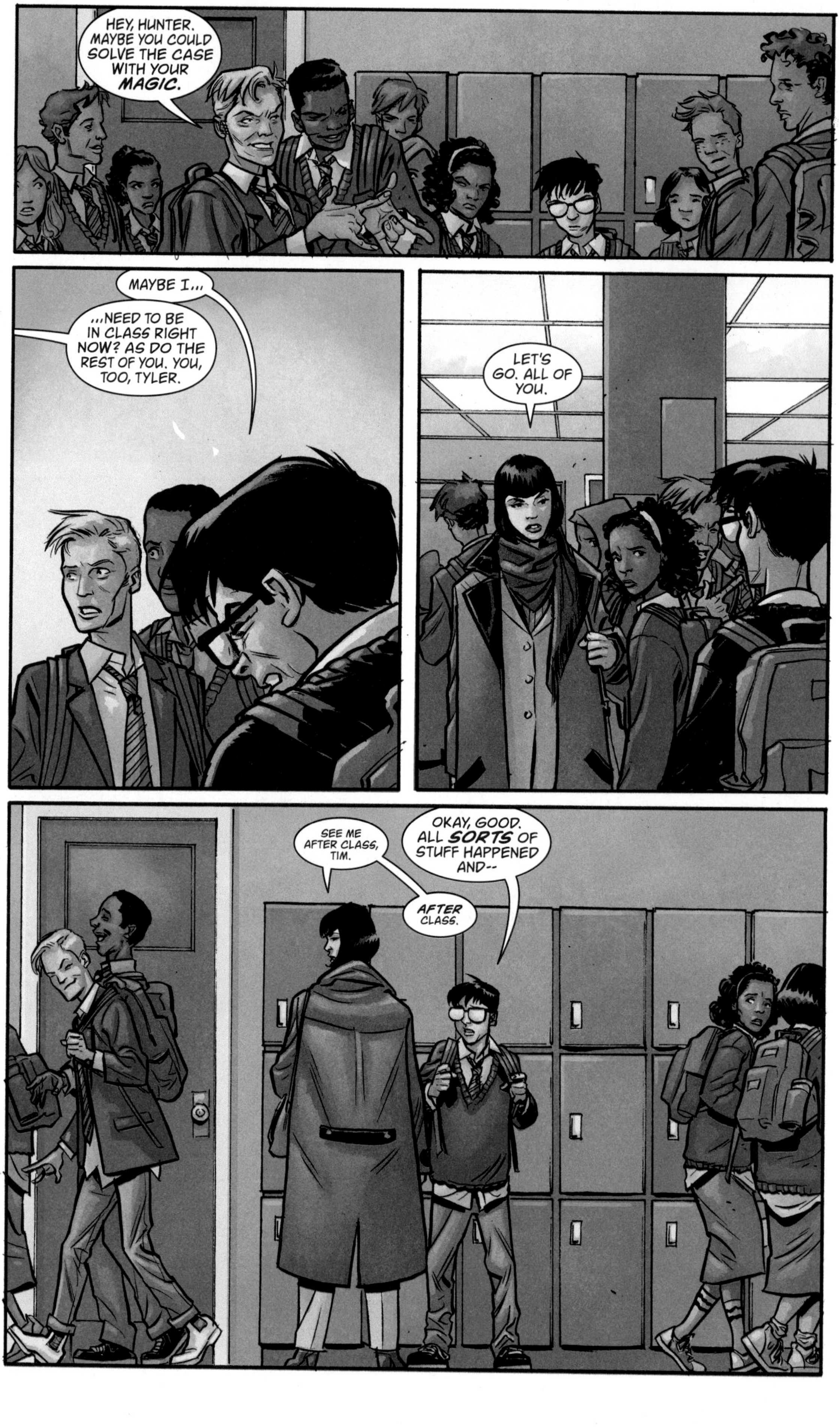
HEY, HUNTER. MAYBE YOU COULD SOLVE THE CASE WITH YOUR MAGIC.
MAYBE I...
...NEED TO BE IN CLASS RIGHT NOW? AS DO THE REST OF YOU. YOU, TOO, TYLER.
LET'S GO. ALL OF YOU.
SEE ME AFTER CLASS, TIM.
OKAY, GOOD. ALL SORTS OF STUFF HAPPENED AND--
AFTER CLASS.

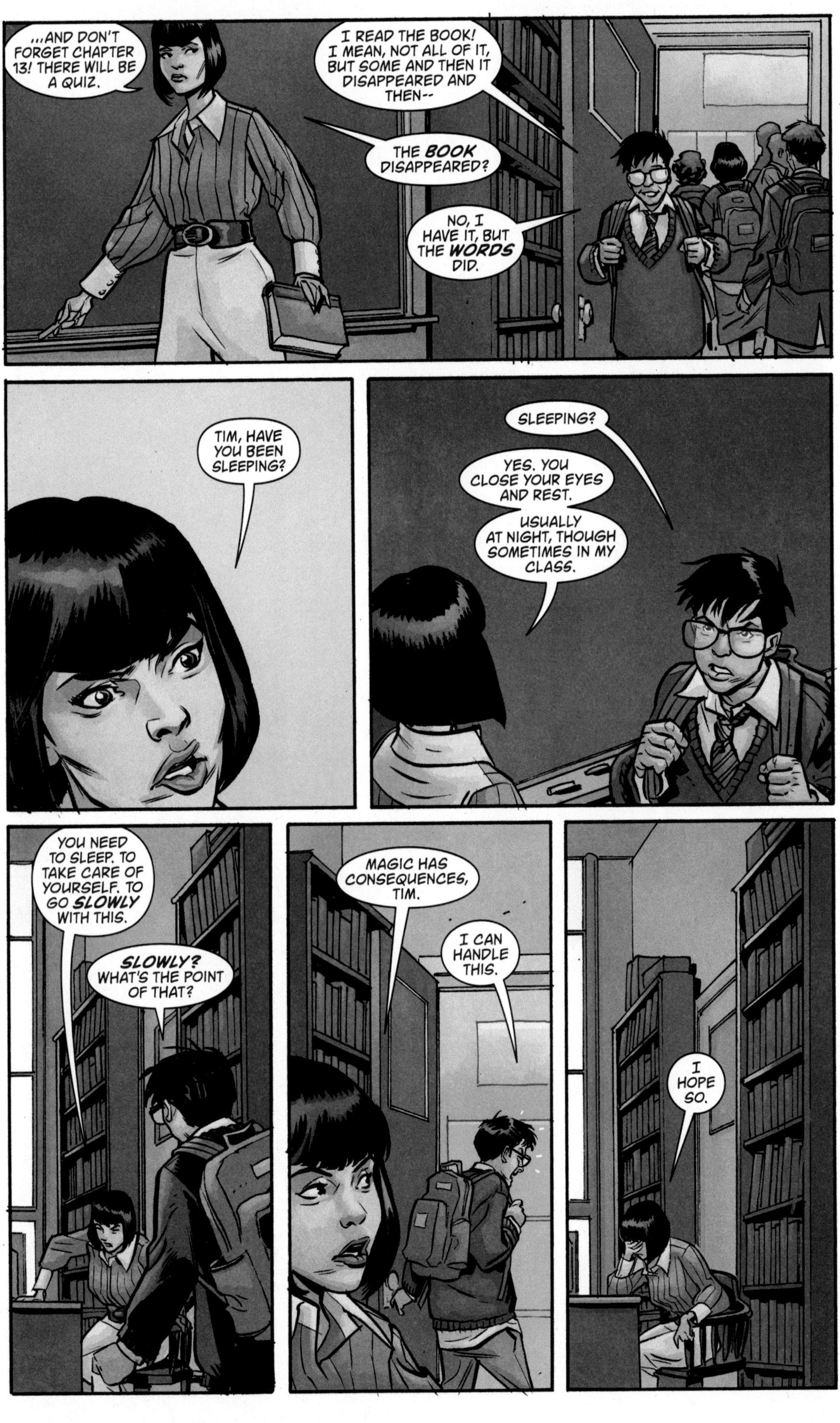
...AND DON'T FORGET CHAPTER 13! THERE WILL BE A QUIZ.
I READ THE BOOK! I MEAN, NOT ALL OF IT, BUT SOME AND THEN IT DISAPPEARED AND THEN--
THE BOOK DISAPPEARED?
NO, I HAVE IT, BUT THE WORDS DID.
TIM, HAVE YOU BEEN SLEEPING?
SLEEPING?
YES. YOU CLOSE YOUR EYES AND REST.
USUALLY AT NIGHT, THOUGH SOMETIMES IN MY CLASS.
YOU NEED TO SLEEP. TO TAKE CARE OF YOURSELF. TO GO SLOWLY WITH THIS.
SLOWLY? WHAT'S THE POINT OF THAT?
MAGIC HAS CONSEQUENCES, TIM.
I CAN HANDLE THIS.
I HOPE SO.

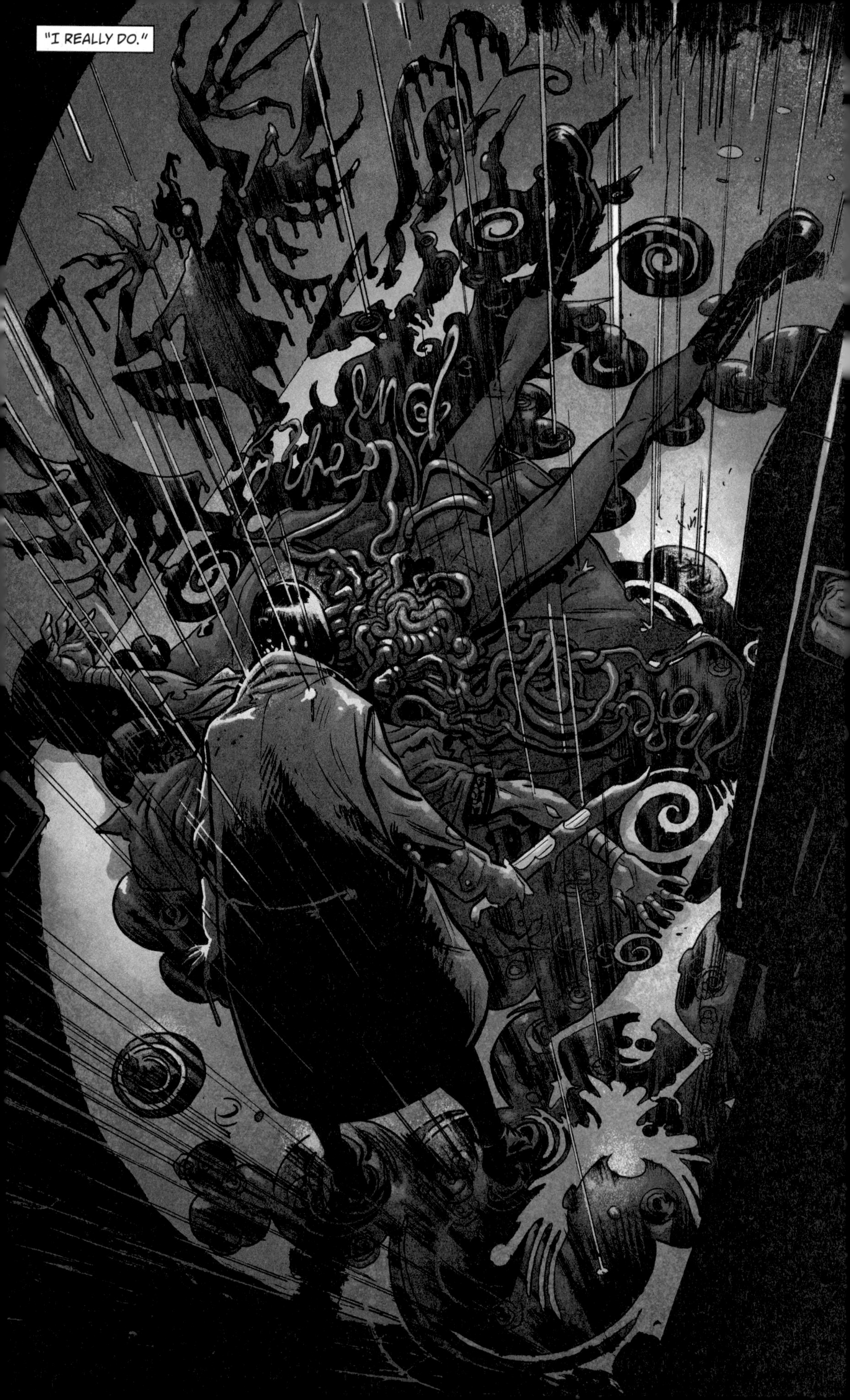
"I REALLY DO."

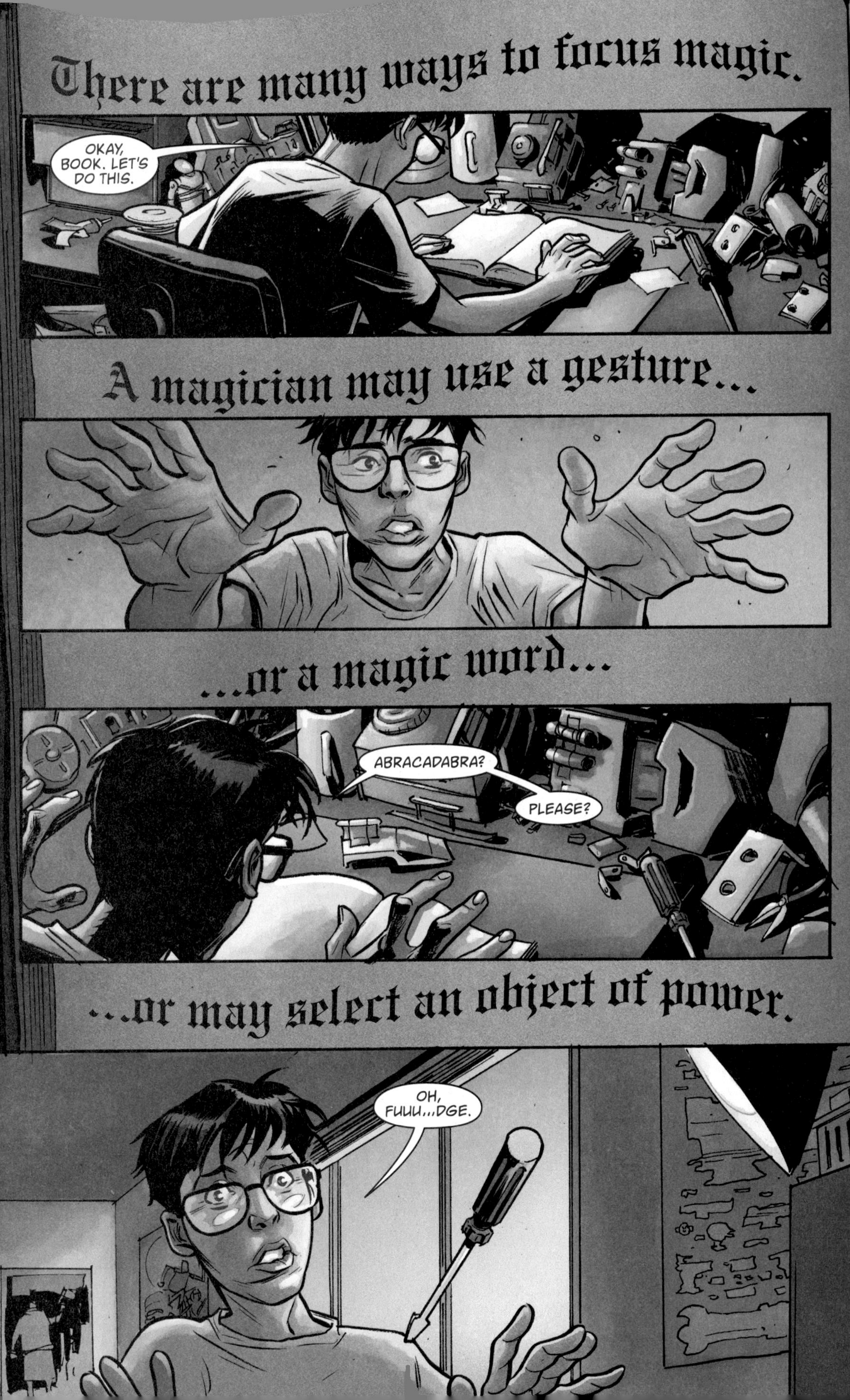
There are many ways to focus magic.
OKAY, BOOK. LET'S DO THIS.
A magician may use a gesture...
...or a magic word...
ABRACADABRA?
PLEASE?
...or may select an object of power.
OH, FUUU...DGE.

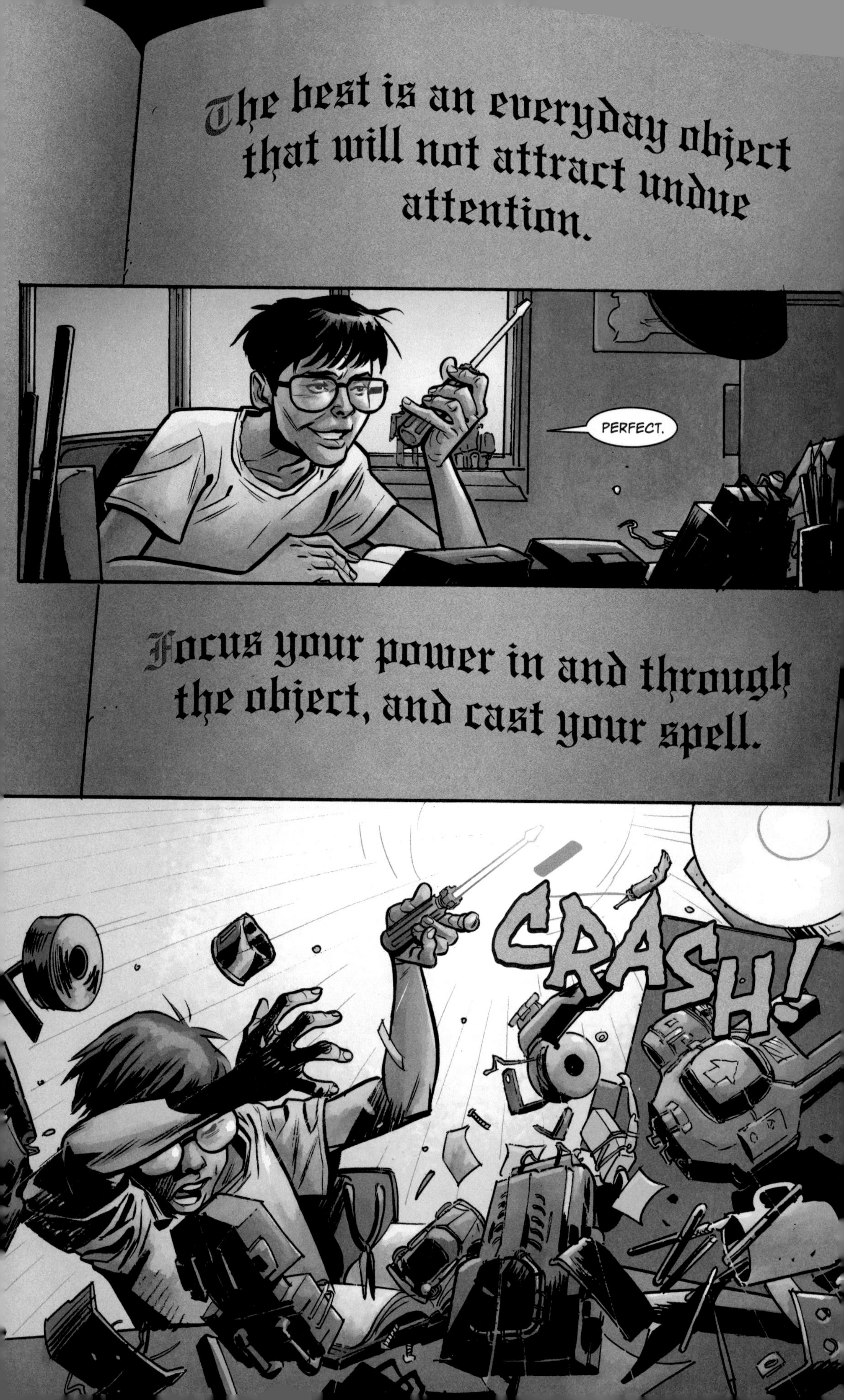
The best is an everyday object that will not attract undue attention.
PERFECT.
Focus your power in and through the object, and cast your spell.
CRASH!

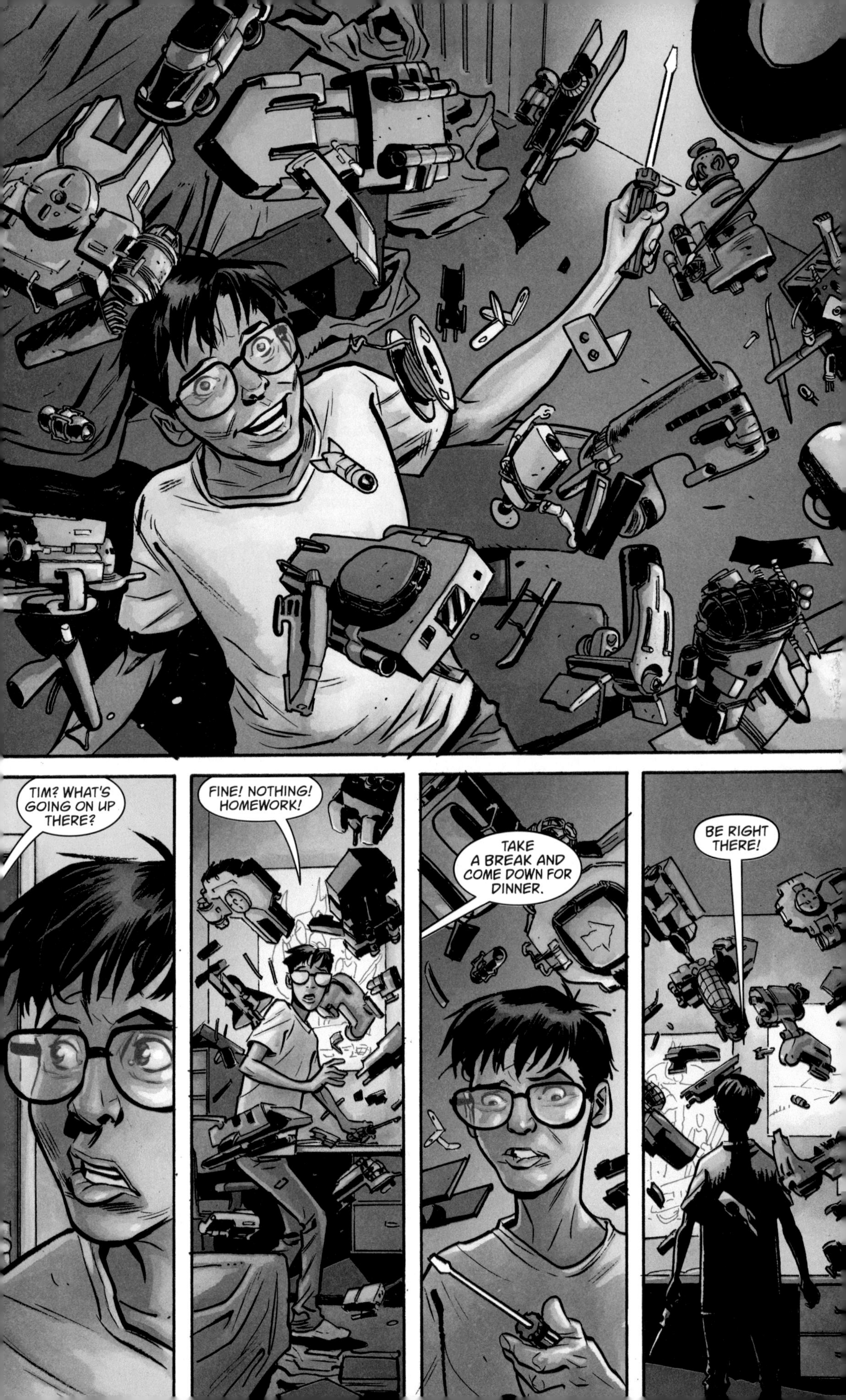
TIM? WHAT'S GOING ON UP THERE?
FINE! NOTHING! HOMEWORK!
TAKE A BREAK AND COME DOWN FOR DINNER.
BE RIGHT THERE!

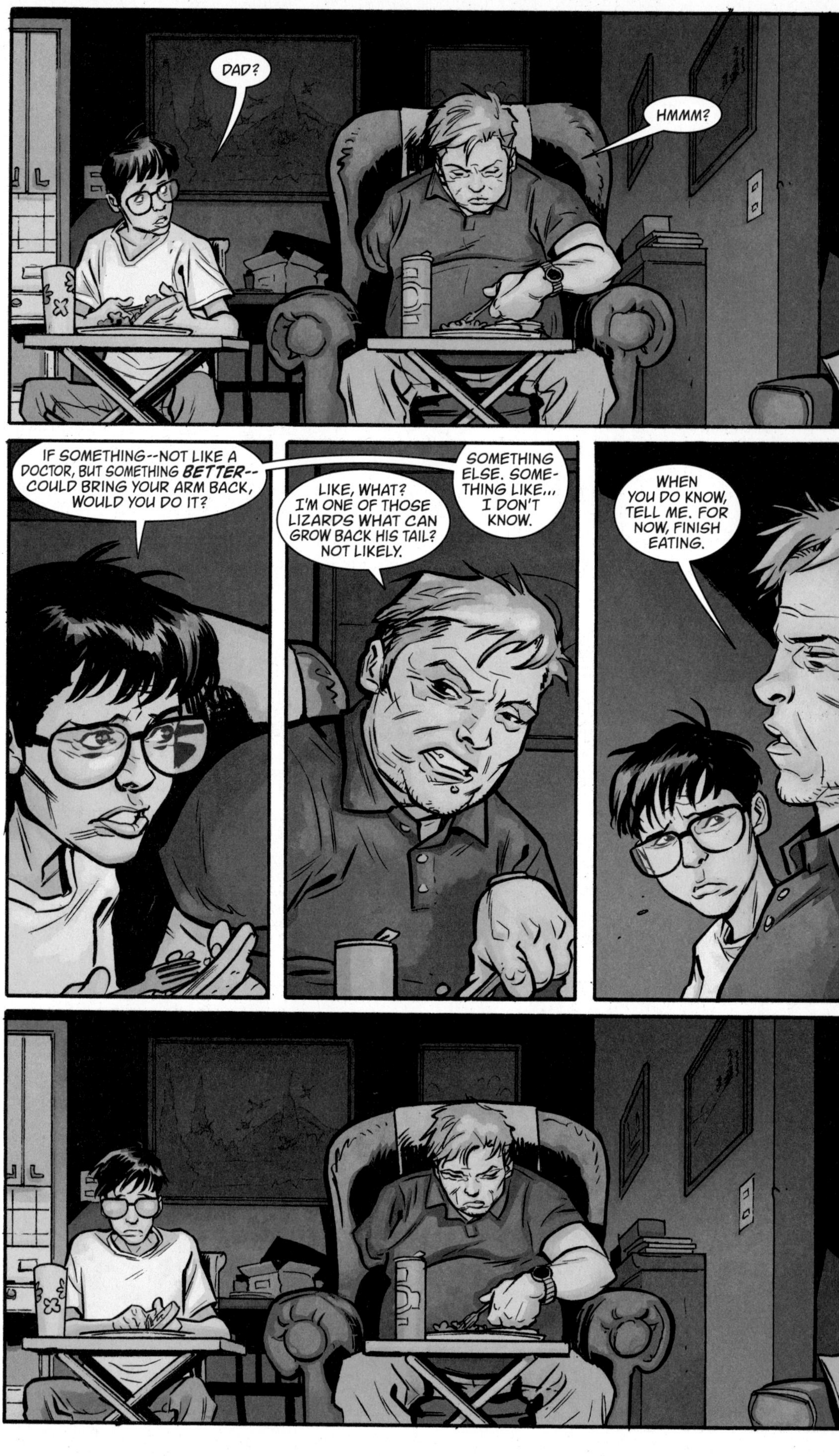
DAD?
HMMM?
IF SOMETHING--NOT LIKE A DOCTOR, BUT SOMETHING BETTER--COULD BRING YOUR ARM BACK, WOULD YOU DO IT?
LIKE, WHAT? I'M ONE OF THOSE LIZARDS WHAT CAN GROW BACK HIS TAIL? NOT LIKELY.
SOMETHING ELSE. SOMETHING LIKE... I DON'T KNOW.
WHEN YOU DO KNOW, TELL ME. FOR NOW, FINISH EATING.

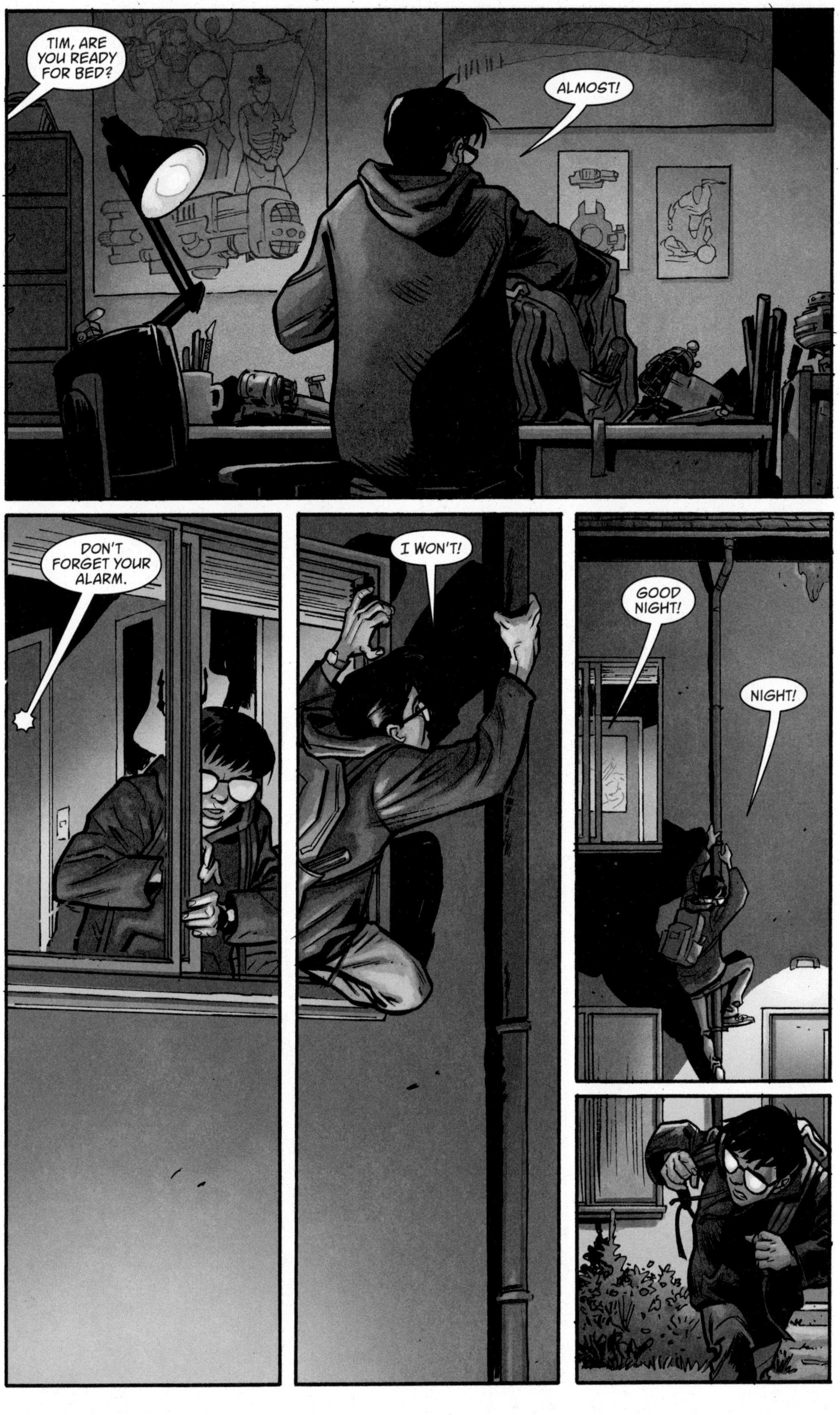
TIM, ARE YOU READY FOR BED?
ALMOST!
DON'T FORGET YOUR ALARM.
I WON'T!
GOOD NIGHT!
NIGHT!

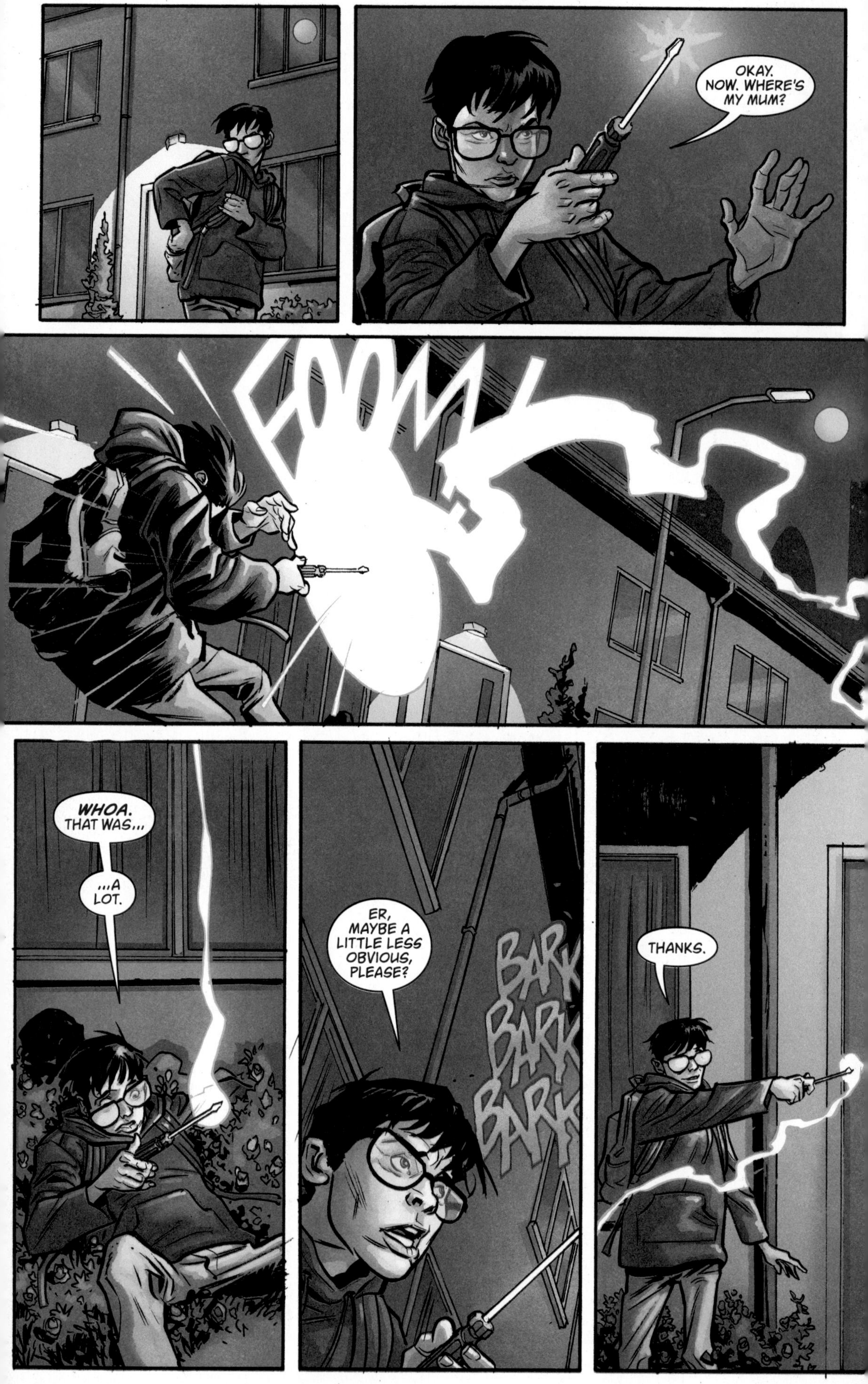

OKAY. NOW. WHERE'S MY MUM?
FOOM
WHOA. THAT WAS...
...A LOT.
ER, MAYBE A LITTLE LESS OBVIOUS, PLEASE?
BARK BARK BARK
THANKS.

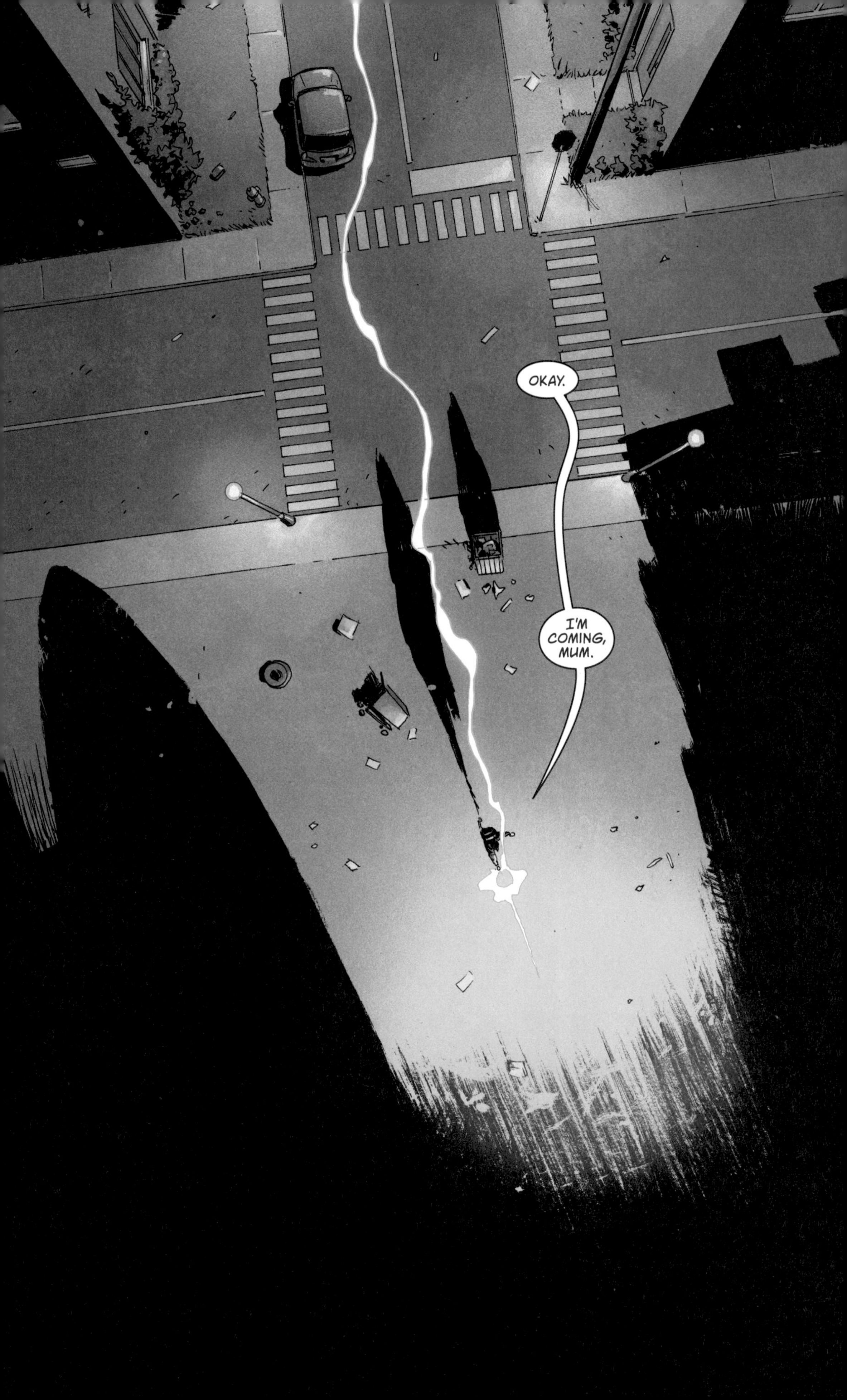
OKAY.
I'M COMING, MUM.

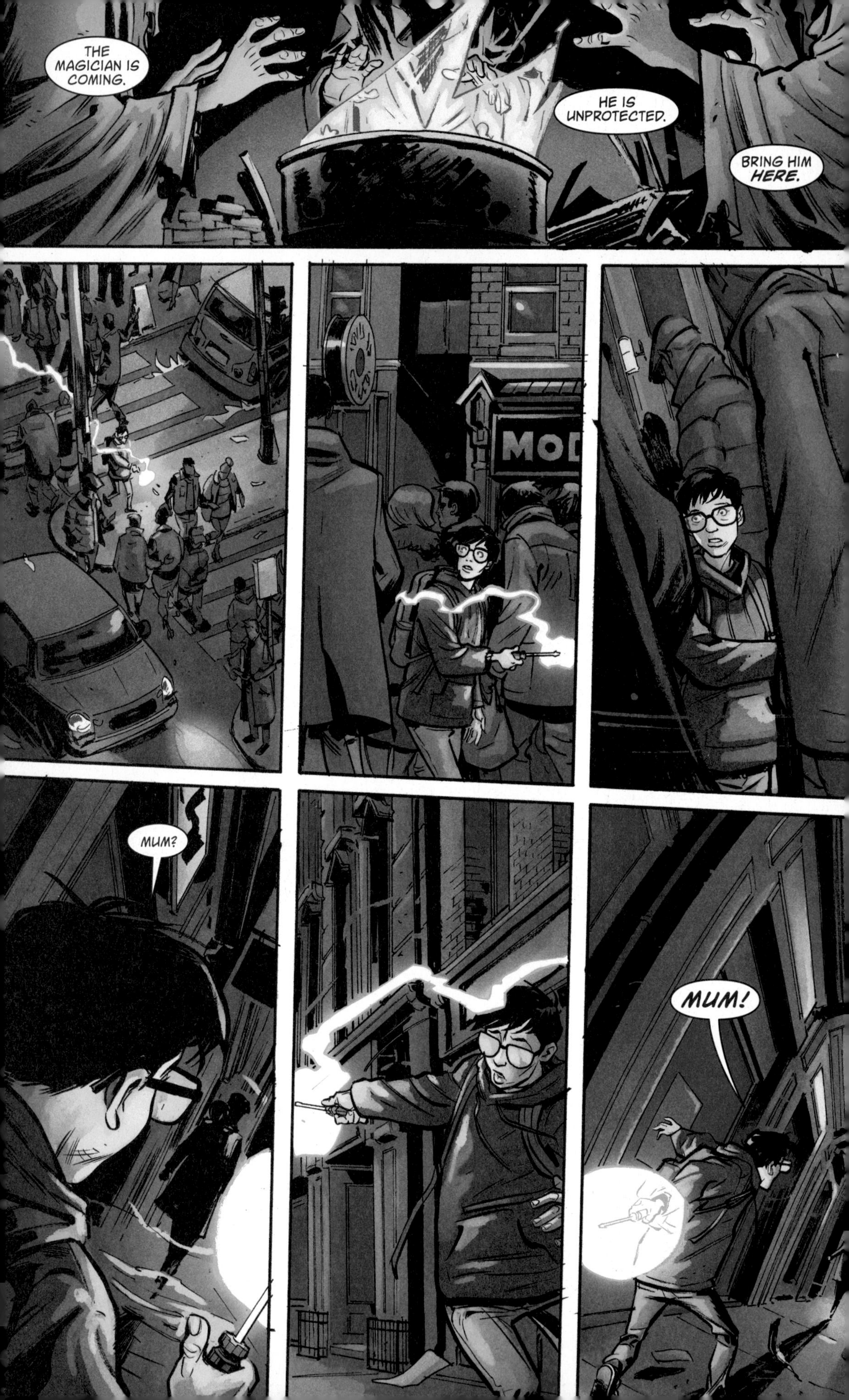
THE MAGICIAN IS COMING.
HE IS UNPROTECTED.
BRING HIM HERE.
MOD
MUM?
MUM!

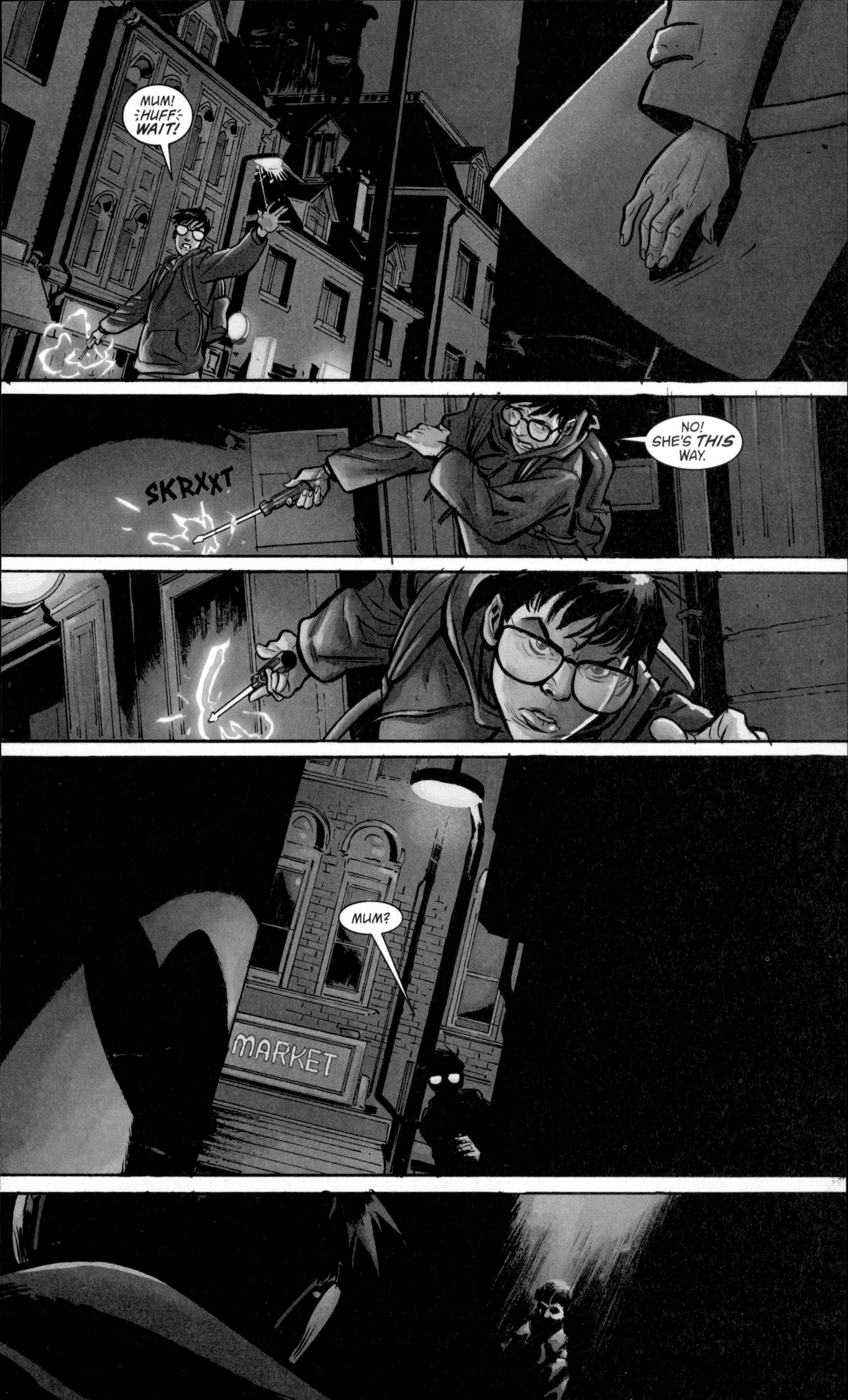
MUM! HUFF WAIT!
NO! SHE'S THIS WAY.
SKRXXT
MUM?
MARKET

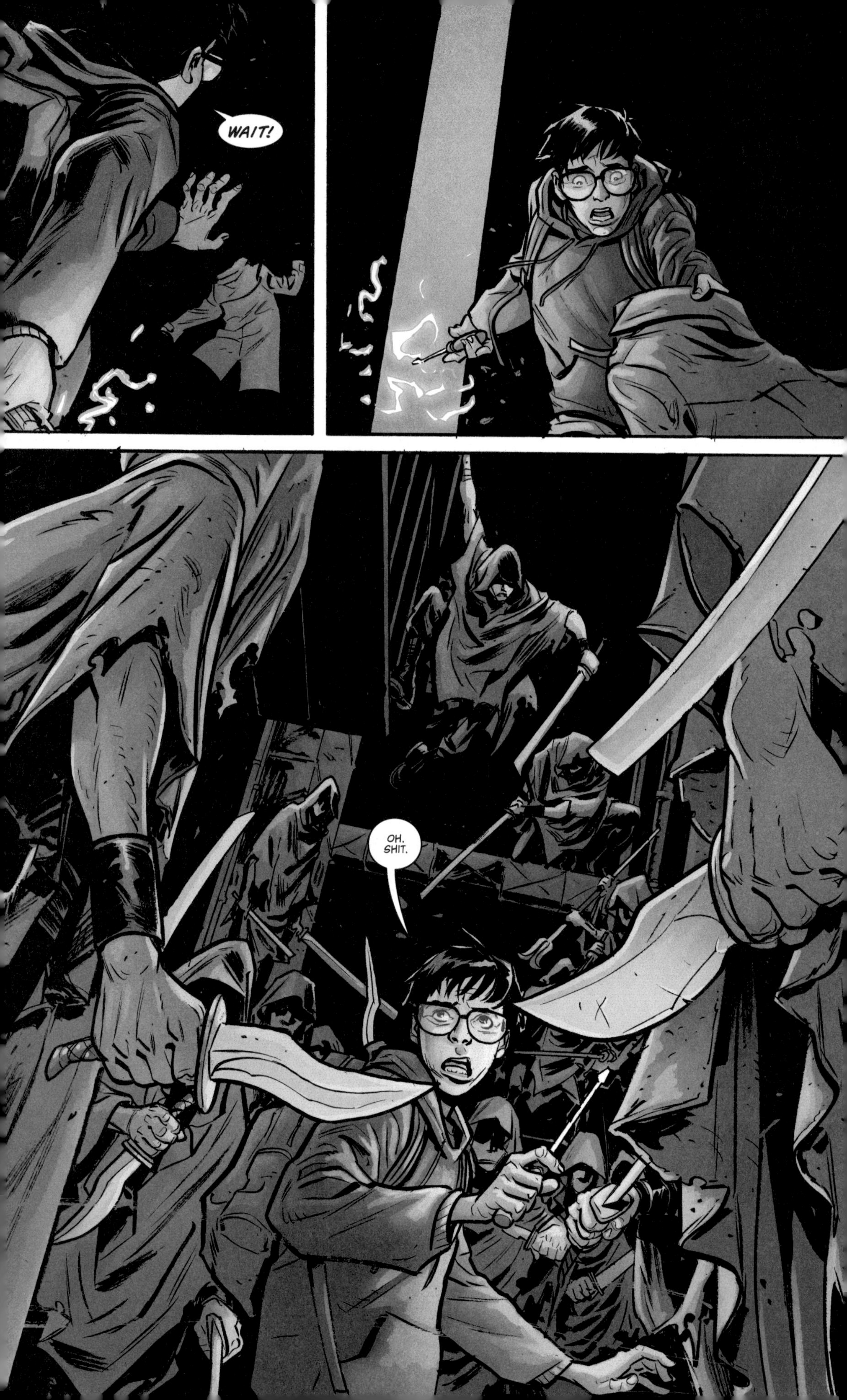
WAIT!
OH. SHIT.

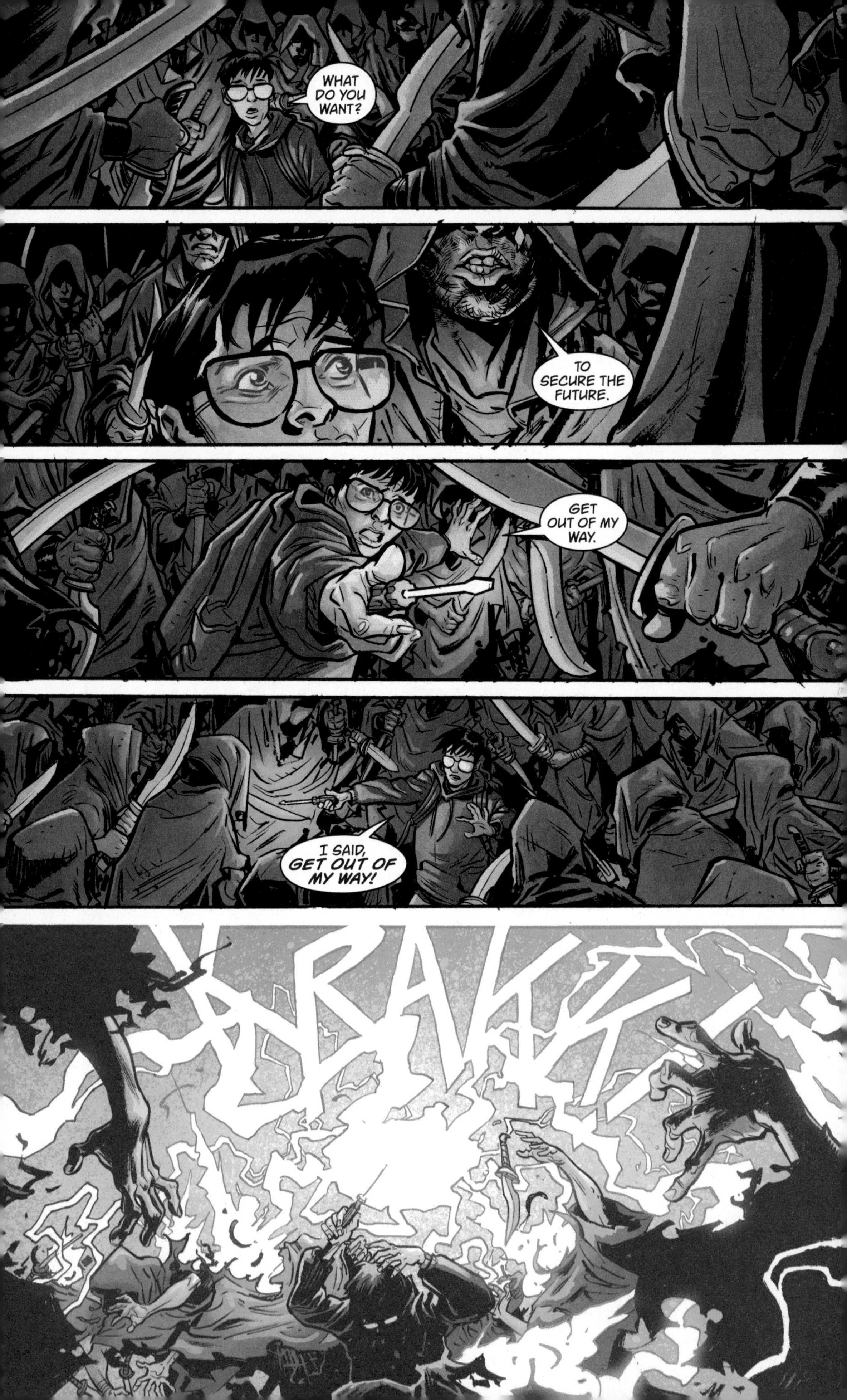

WHAT DO YOU WANT?
TO SECURE THE FUTURE.
GET OUT OF MY WAY.
I SAID, ***GET OUT OF MY WAY!***

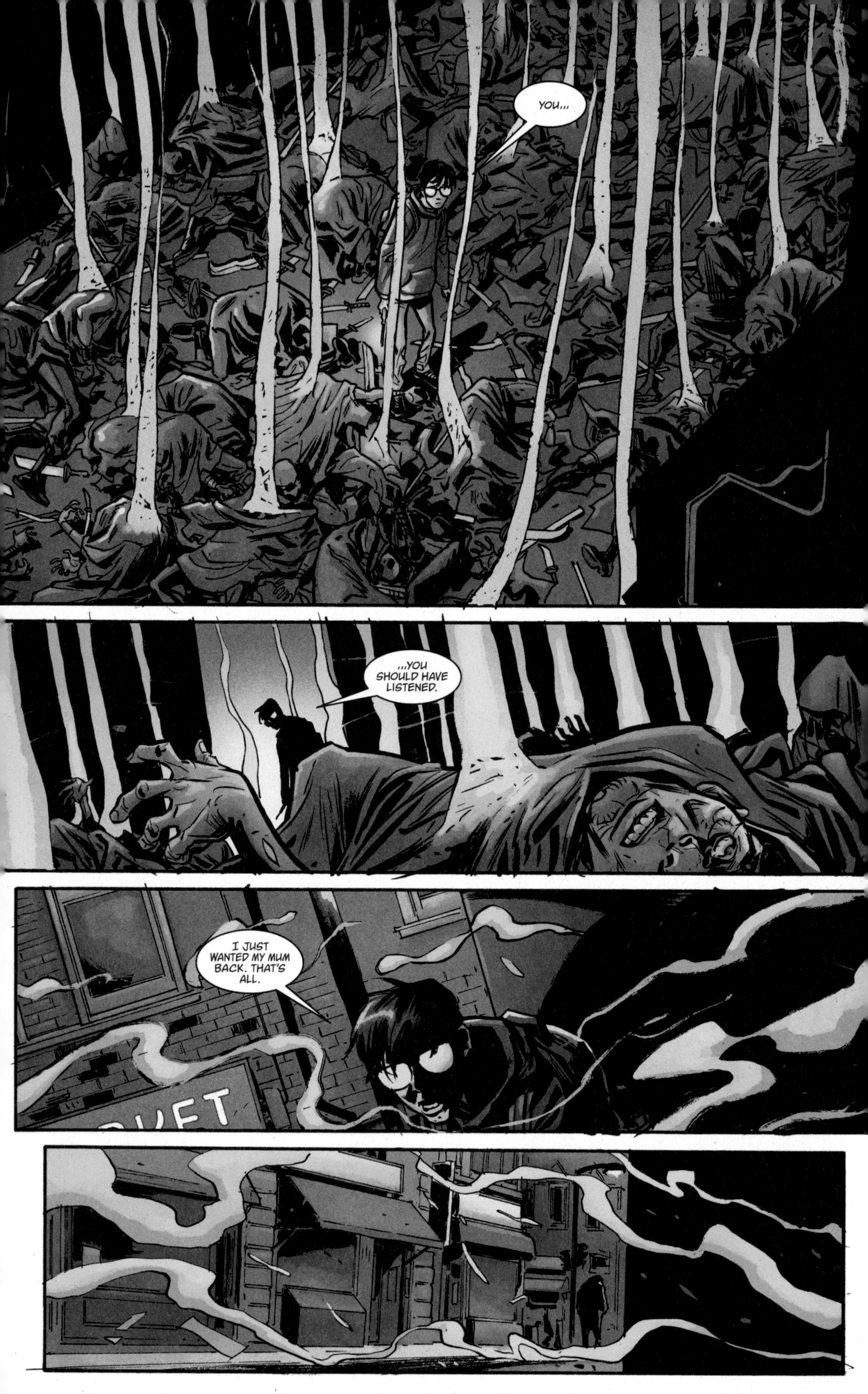
YOU...
...YOU SHOULD HAVE LISTENED.
I JUST WANTED MY MUM BACK. THAT'S ALL.

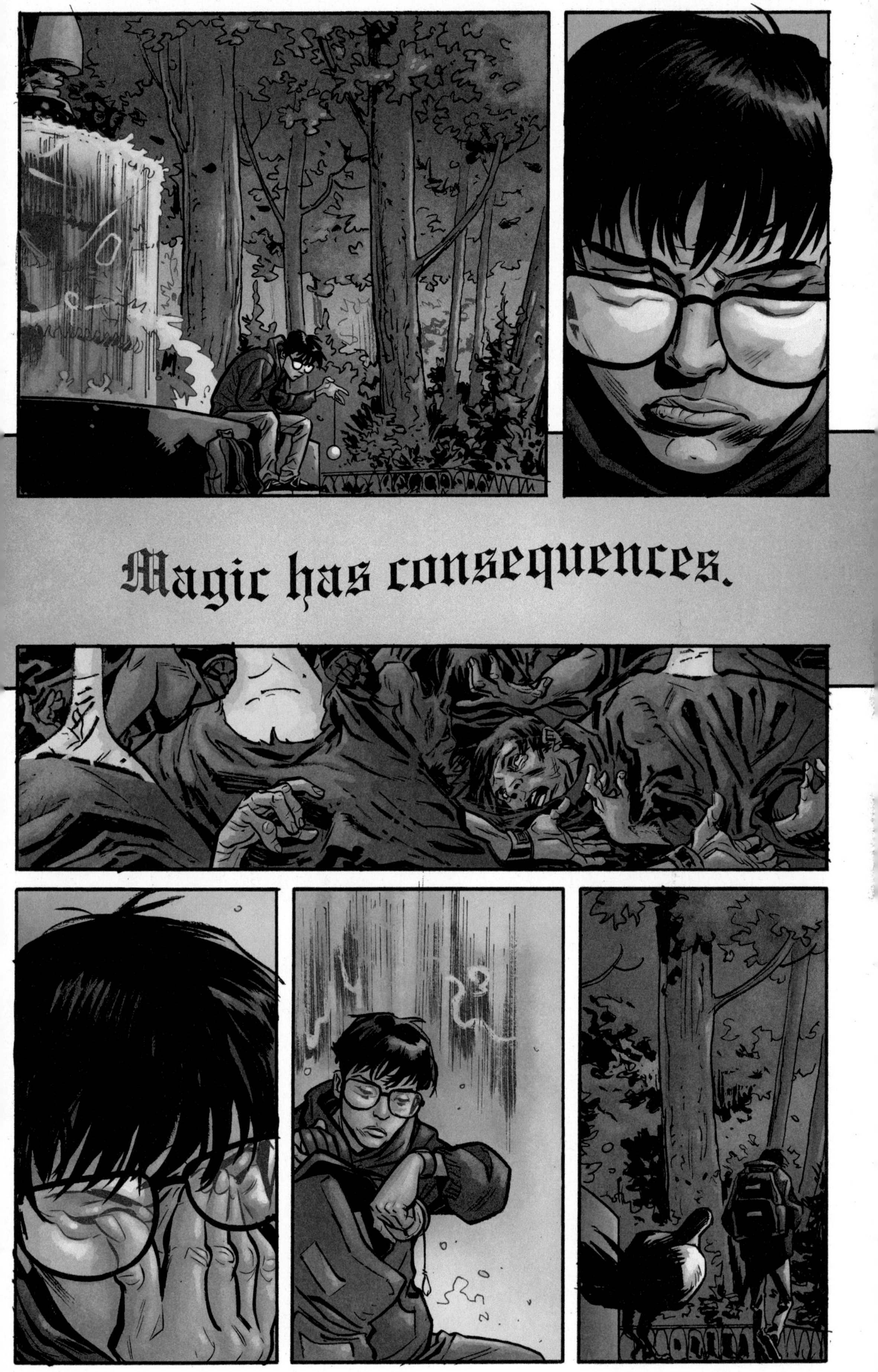
Magic has consequences.

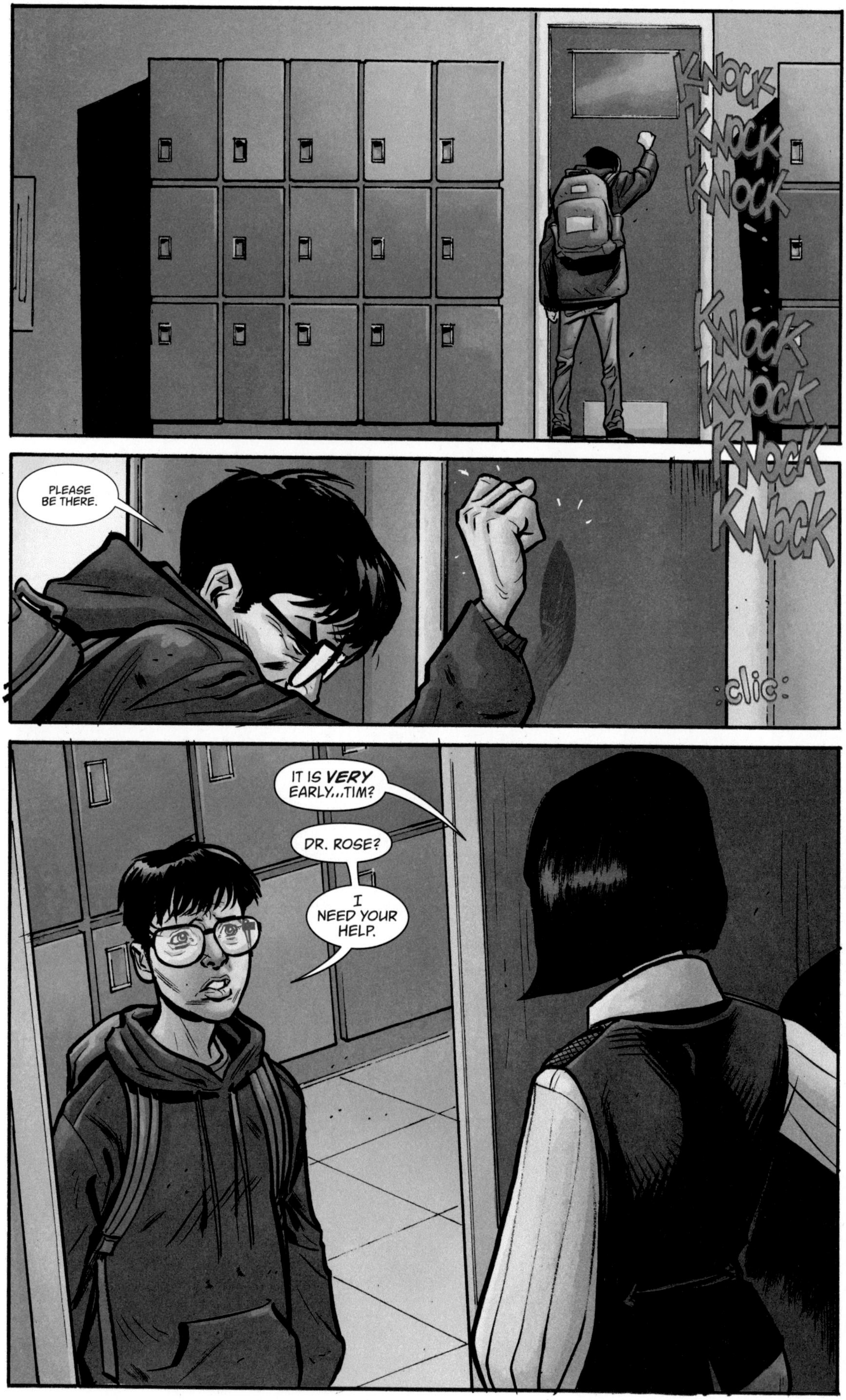
KNOCK KNOCK KNOCK
KNOCK KNOCK KNOCK KNOCK
PLEASE BE THERE.
clic
IT IS VERY EARLY...TIM?
DR. ROSE?
I NEED YOUR HELP.

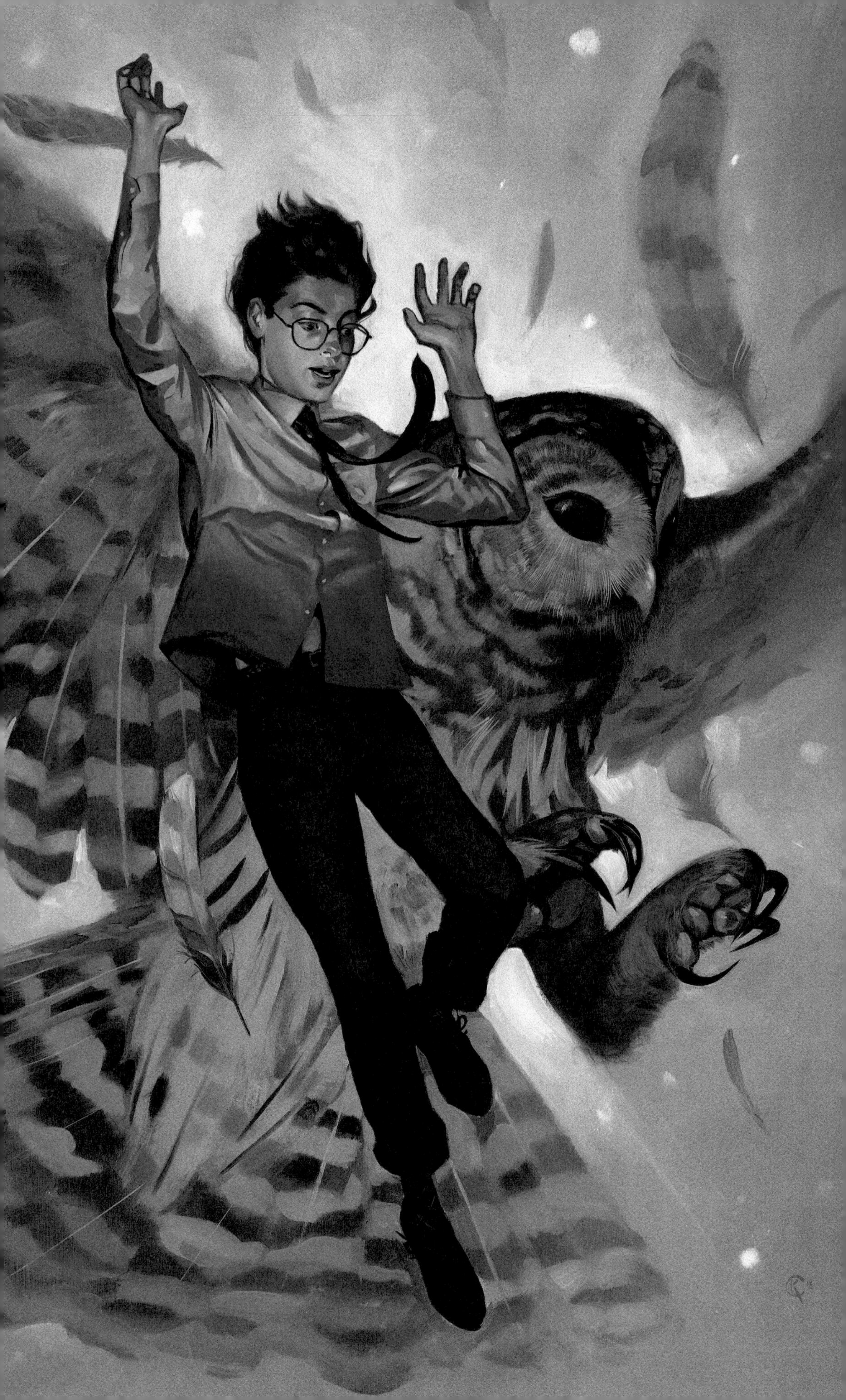

Books of Magic

In Memoriam

WRITTEN BY
Kat Howard

ILLUSTRATED BY
Tom Fowler

COLORS BY
Jordan Boyd

LETTERS BY
Todd Klein

COVER ART BY
Kai Carpenter

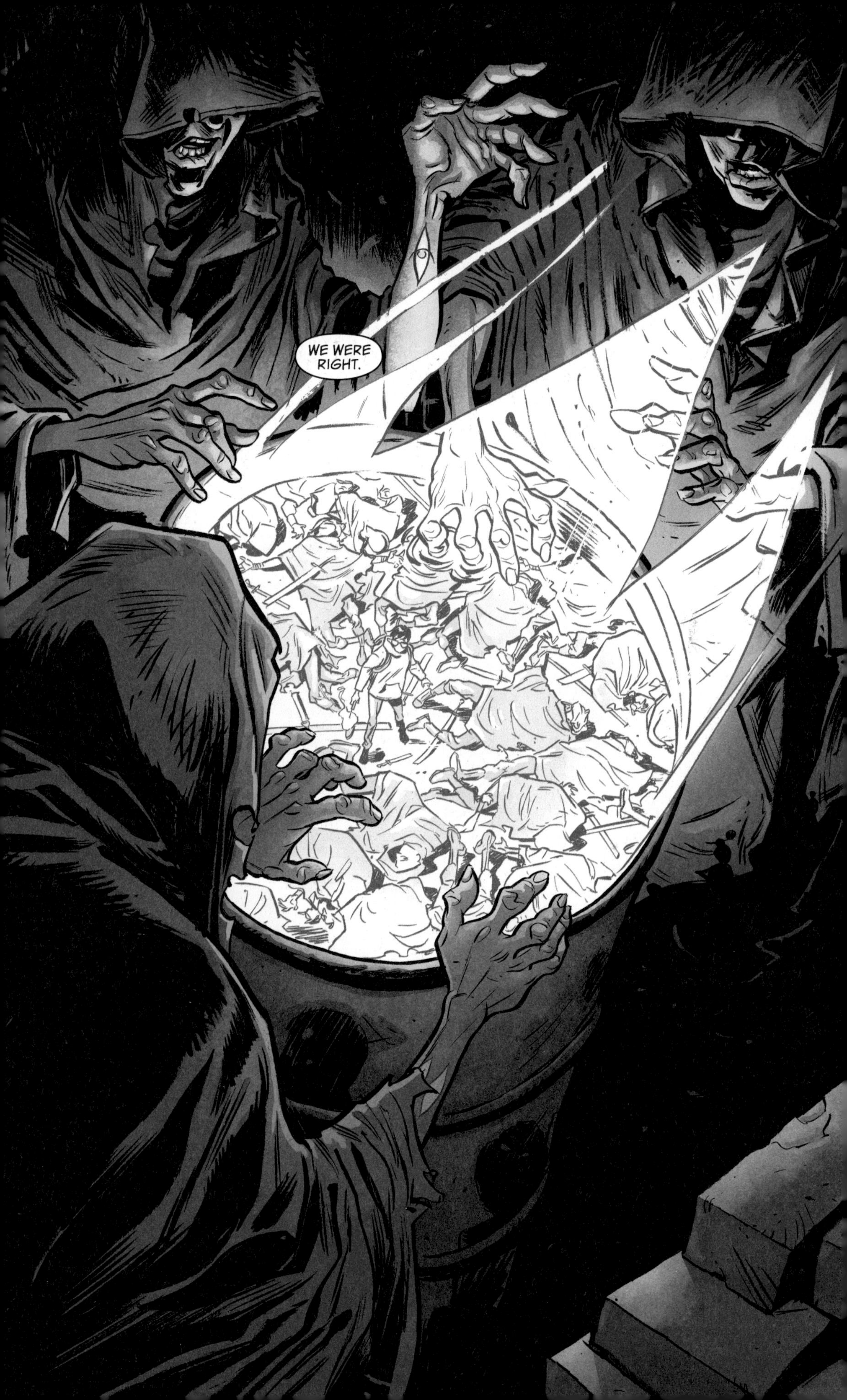
WE WERE RIGHT.

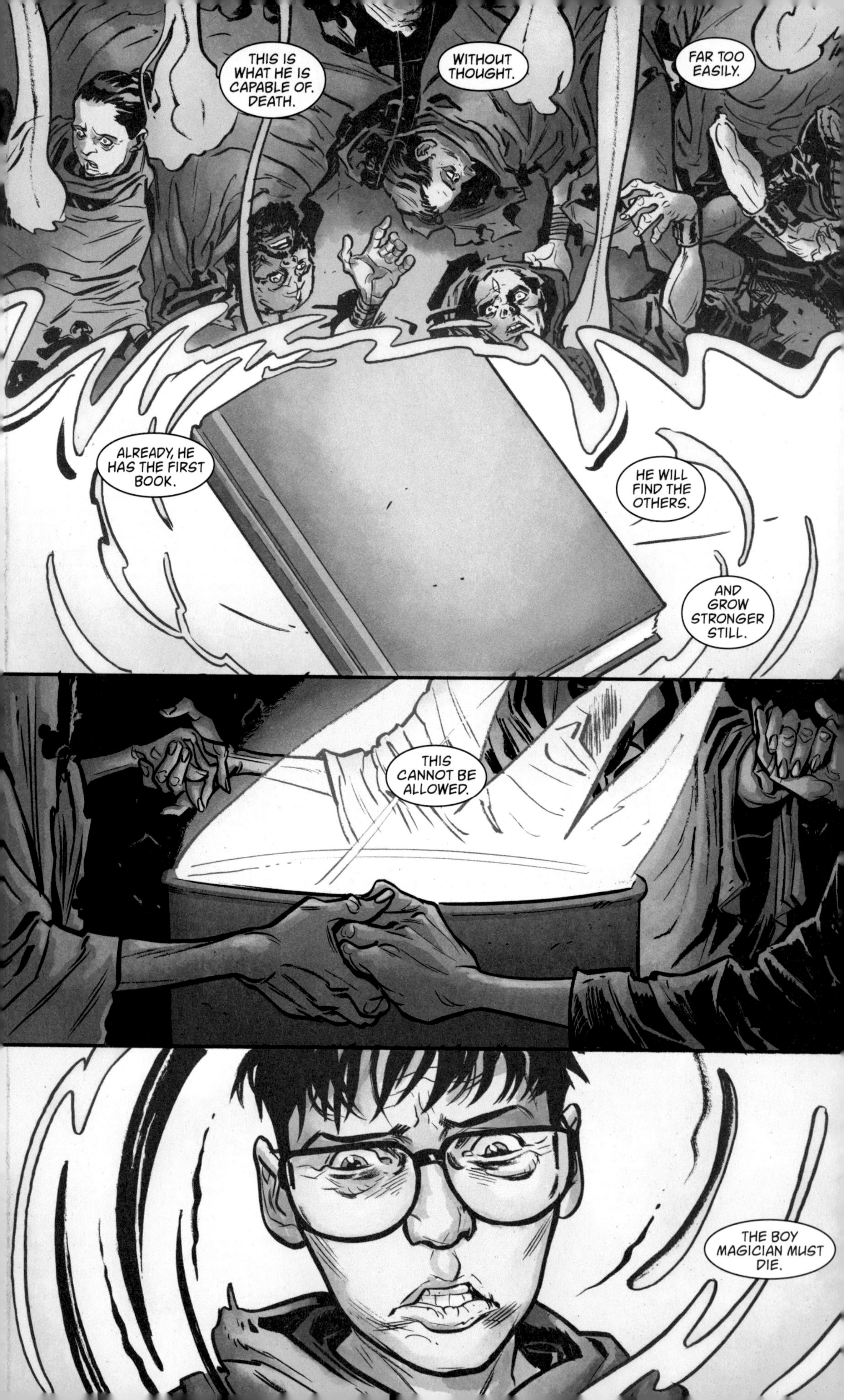
THIS IS WHAT HE IS CAPABLE OF. DEATH.
WITHOUT THOUGHT.
FAR TOO EASILY.
ALREADY, HE HAS THE FIRST BOOK.
HE WILL FIND THE OTHERS.
AND GROW STRONGER STILL.
THIS CANNOT BE ALLOWED.
THE BOY MAGICIAN MUST DIE.

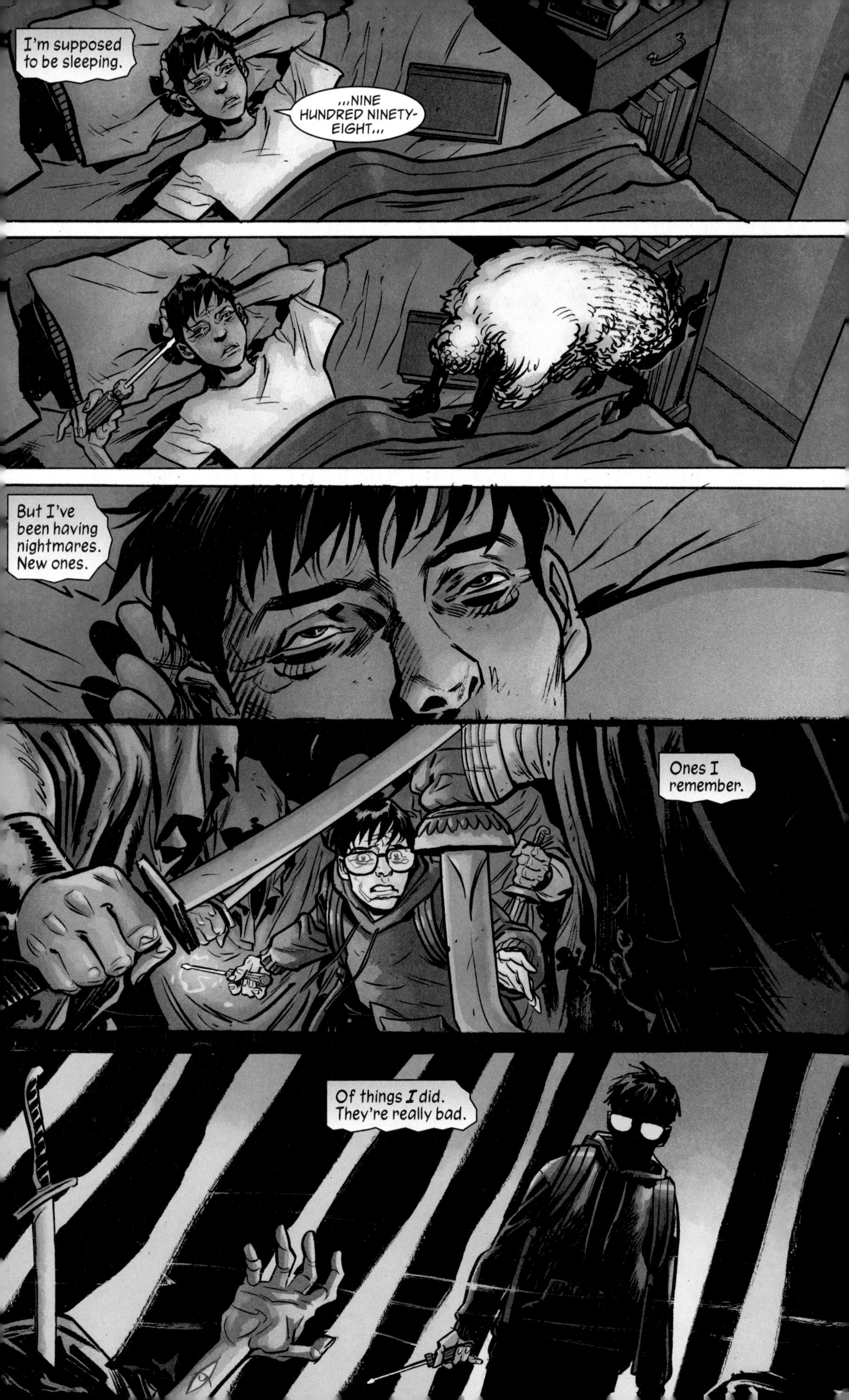
I'm supposed to be sleeping.
...NINE HUNDRED NINETY-EIGHT...
But I've been having nightmares. New ones.
Ones I remember.
Of things I did. They're really bad.

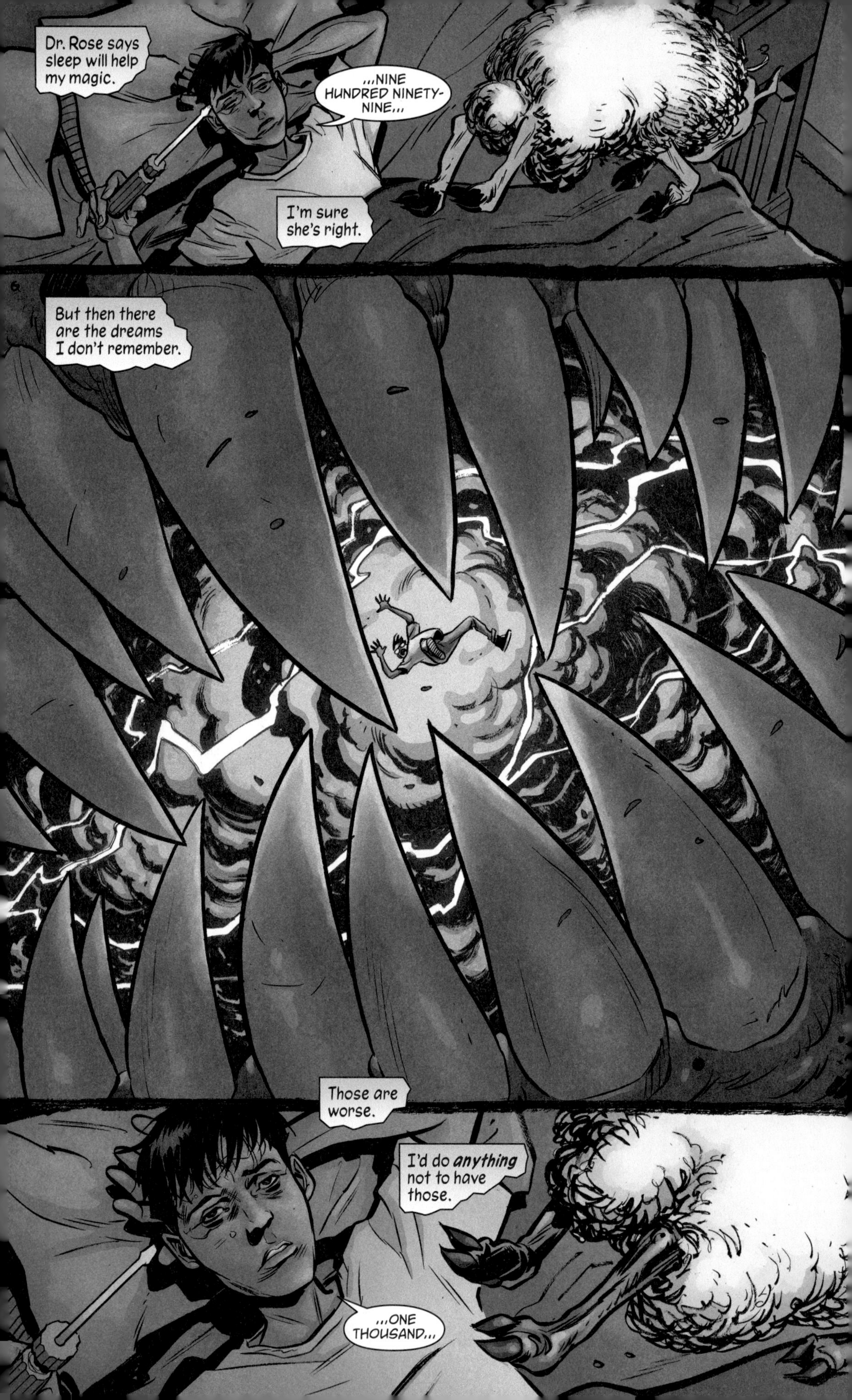
Dr. Rose says sleep will help my magic.
...NINE HUNDRED NINETY-NINE...
I'm sure she's right.
But then there are the dreams I don't remember.
Those are worse.
I'd do *anything* not to have those.
...ONE THOUSAND...

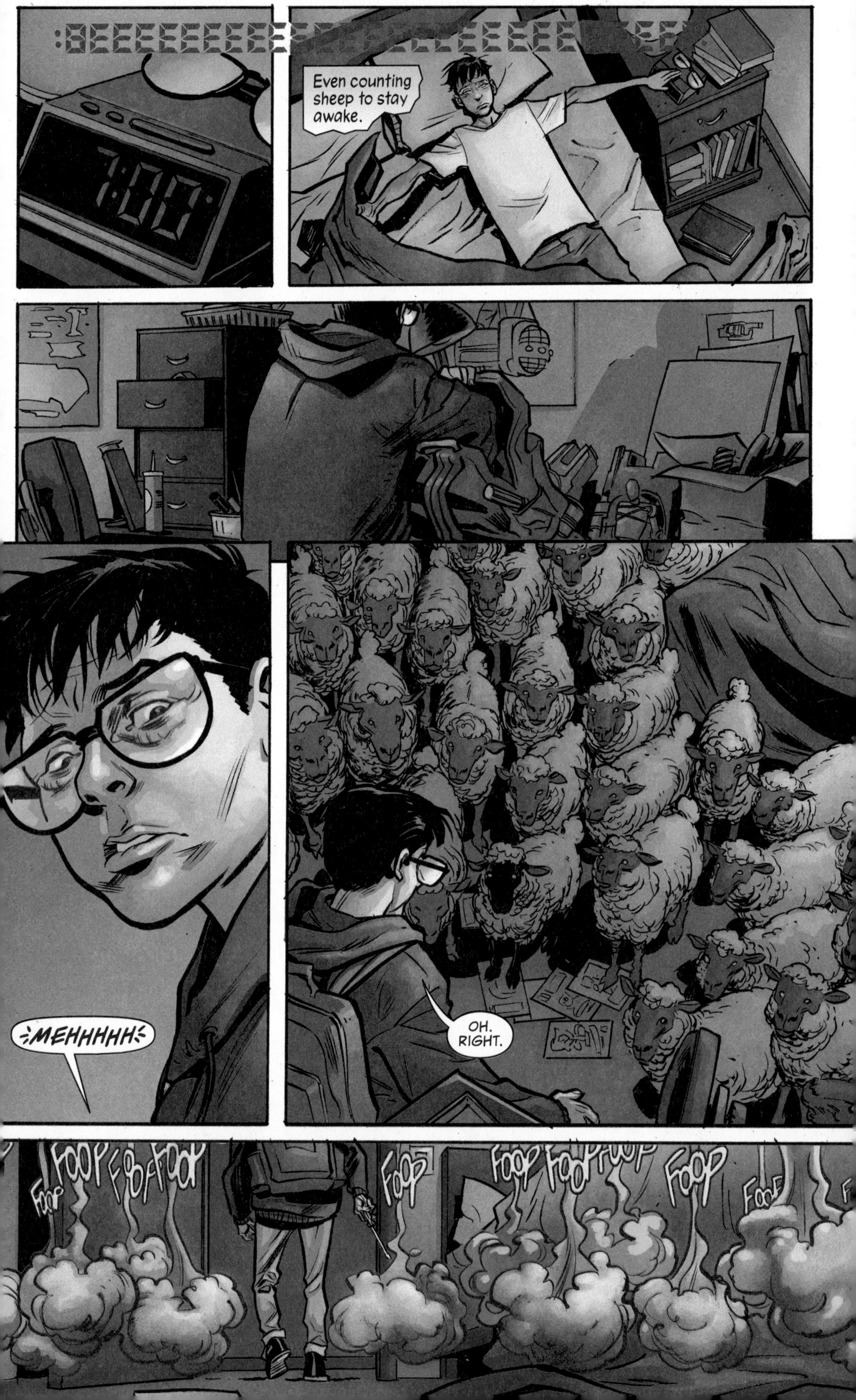
BEEEEEEEEEEEEEEEEEEEEP
Even counting sheep to stay awake.
MEHHHHH
OH. RIGHT.
FOOP FOOP FOOP FOOP FOOP
FOOP FOOP FOOP FOOP
FOOP

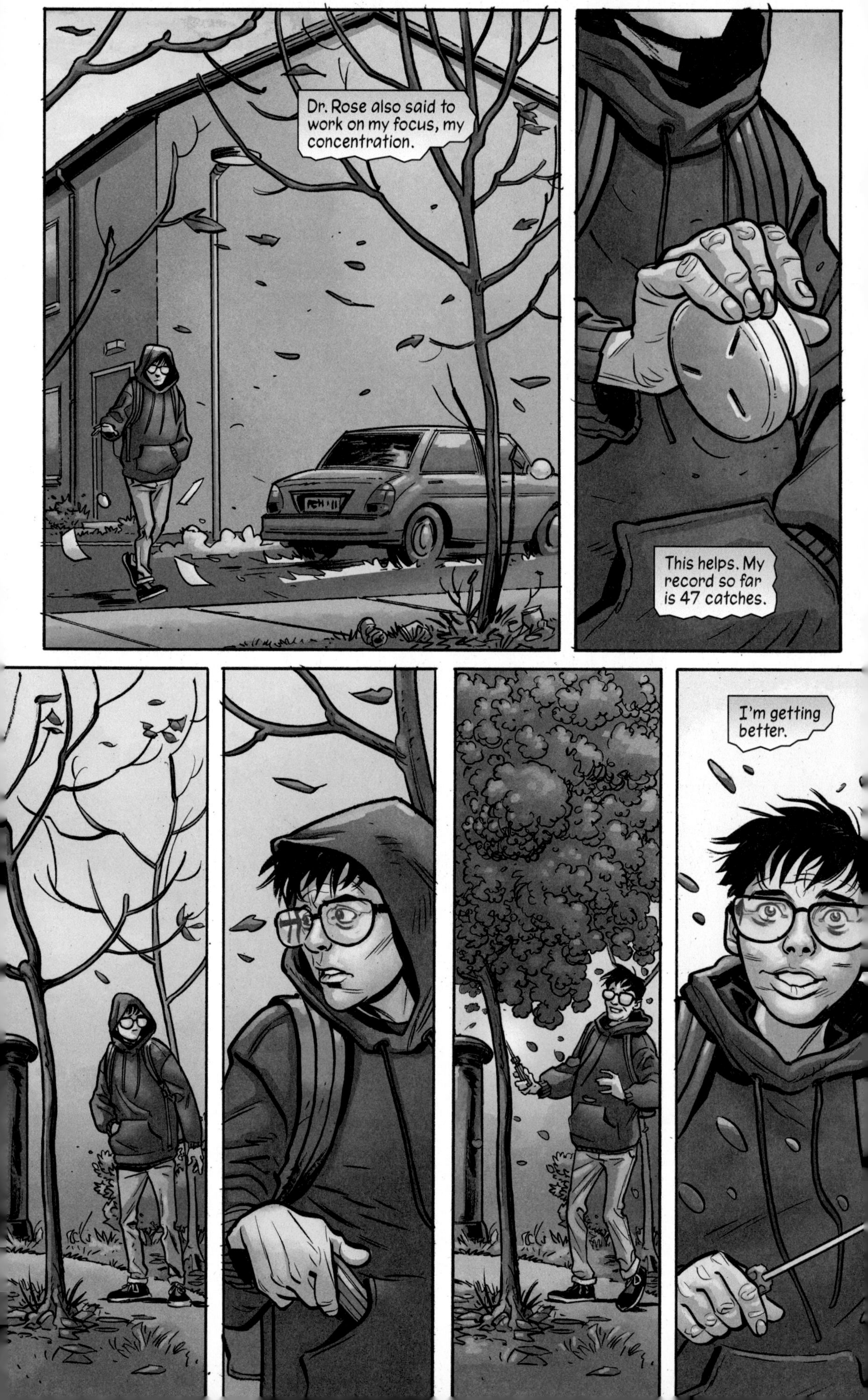
Dr. Rose also said to work on my focus, my concentration.
This helps. My record so far is 47 catches.
I'm getting better.

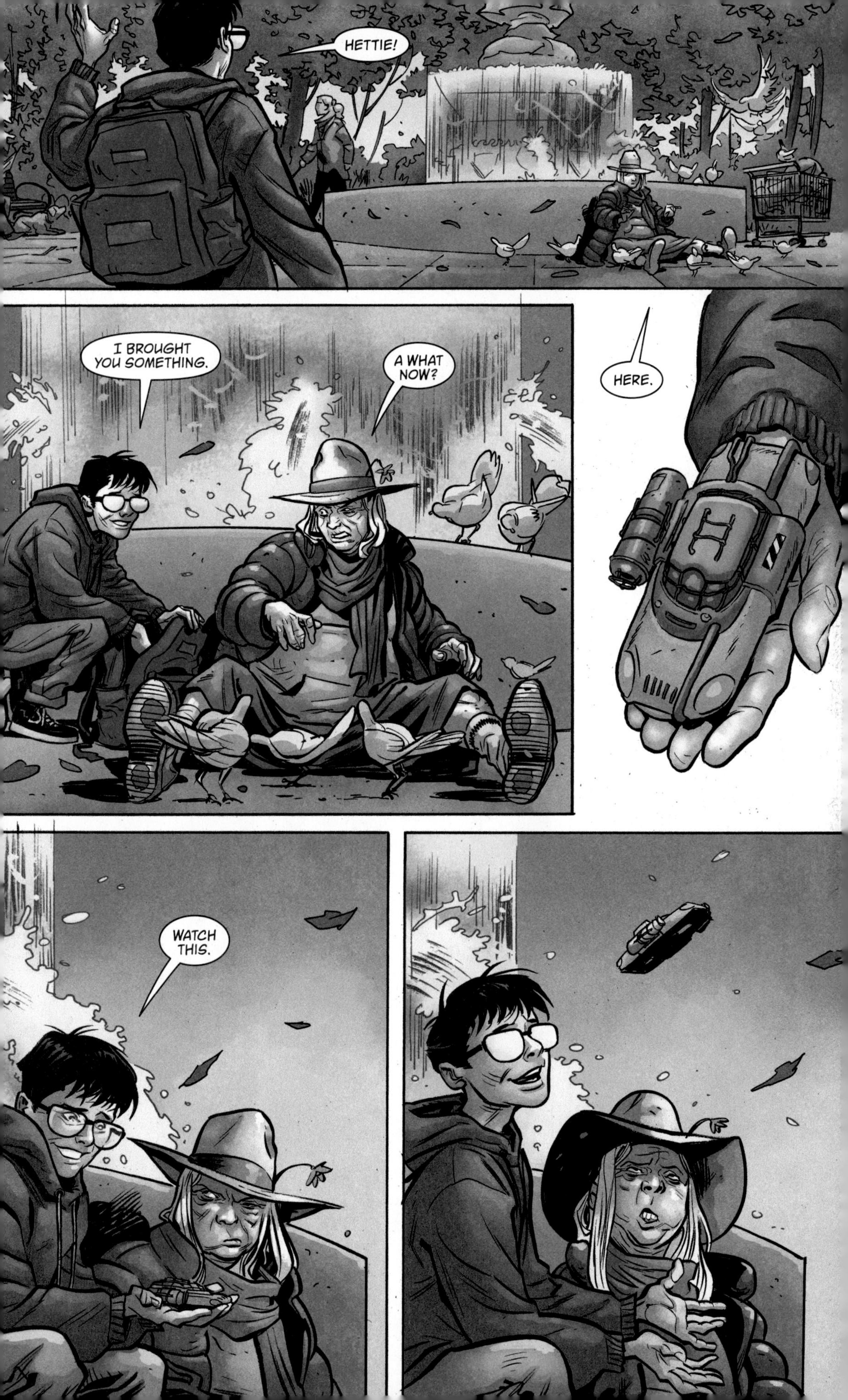
HETTIE!
I BROUGHT YOU SOMETHING.
A WHAT NOW?
HERE.
WATCH THIS.

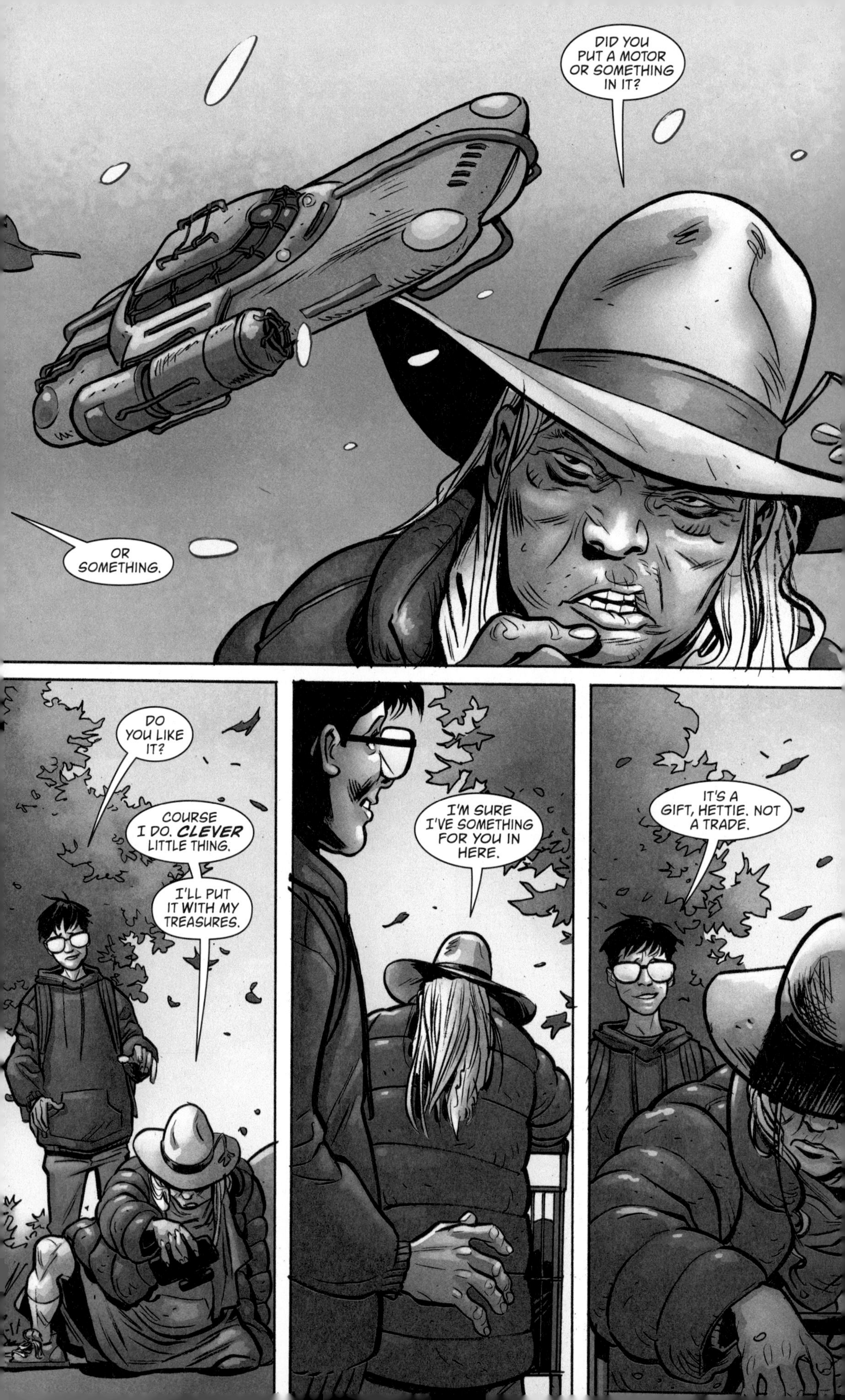
DID YOU PUT A MOTOR OR SOMETHING IN IT?
OR SOMETHING.
DO YOU LIKE IT?
COURSE I DO. CLEVER LITTLE THING.
I'LL PUT IT WITH MY TREASURES.
I'M SURE I'VE SOMETHING FOR YOU IN HERE.
IT'S A GIFT, HETTIE. NOT A TRADE.

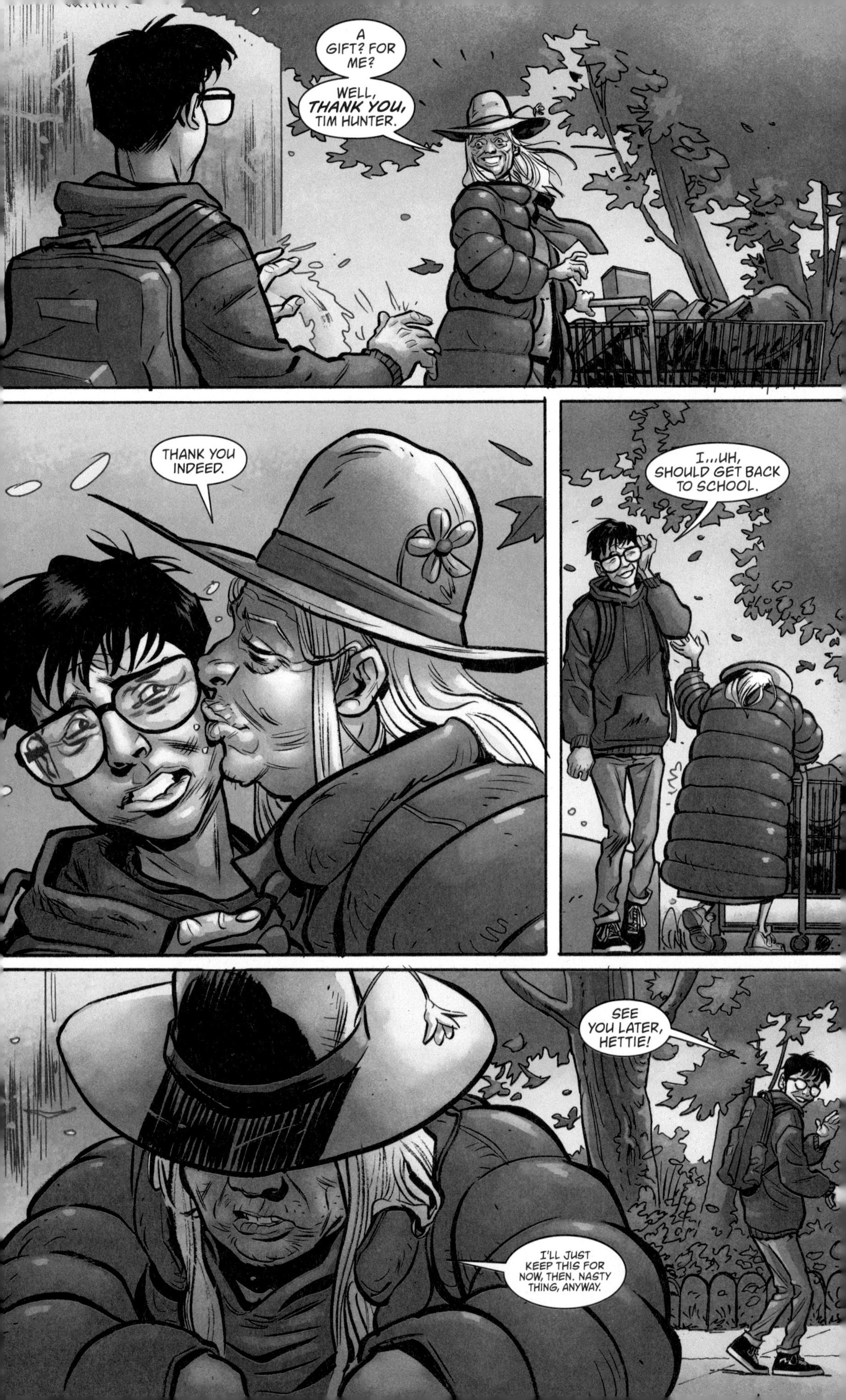
A GIFT? FOR ME?
WELL, THANK YOU, TIM HUNTER.
THANK YOU INDEED.
I...UH, SHOULD GET BACK TO SCHOOL.
SEE YOU LATER, HETTIE!
I'LL JUST KEEP THIS FOR NOW, THEN. NASTY THING, ANYWAY.

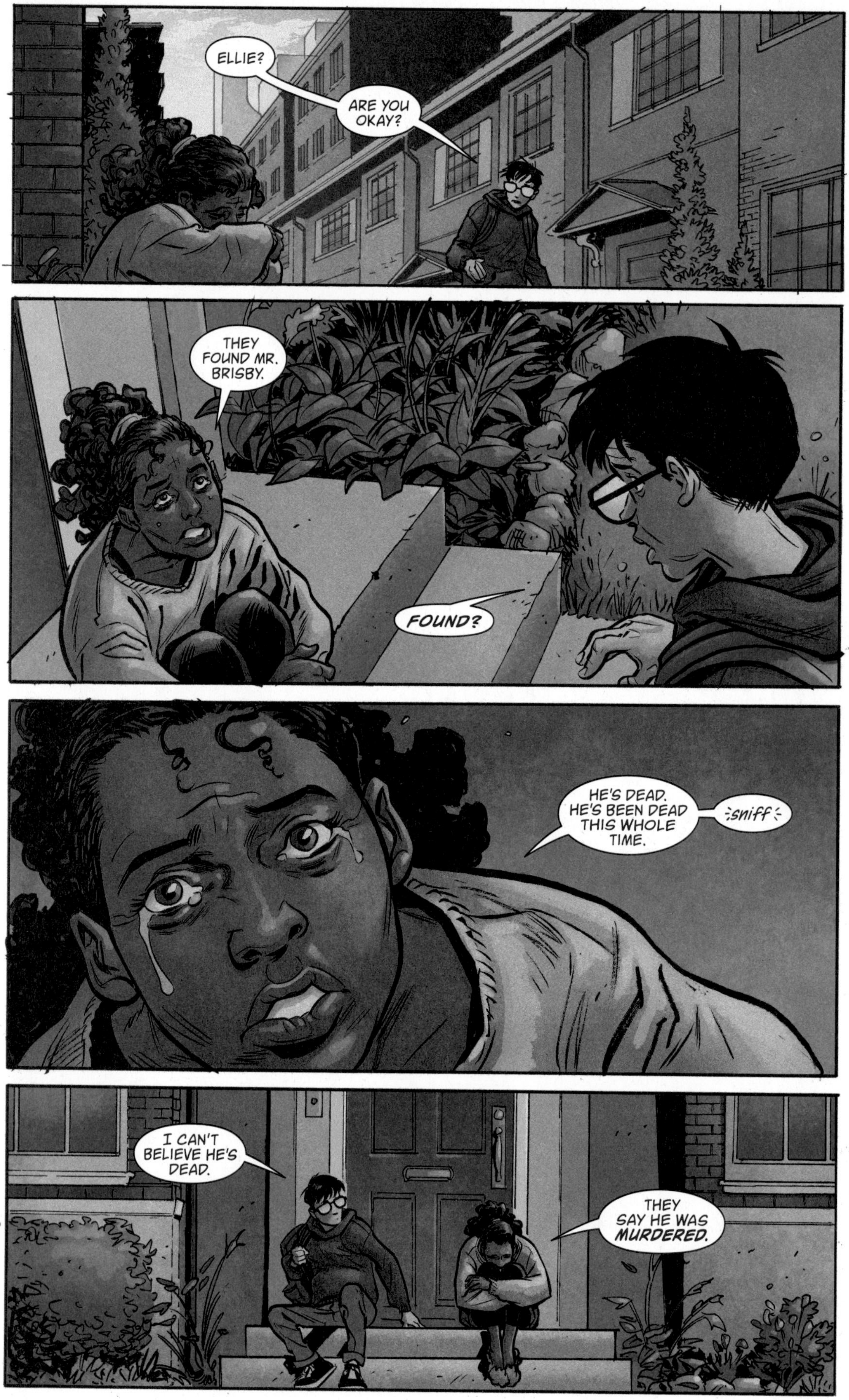
ELLIE?
ARE YOU OKAY?
THEY FOUND MR. BRISBY.
FOUND?
HE'S DEAD. HE'S BEEN DEAD THIS WHOLE TIME.
sniff
I CAN'T BELIEVE HE'S DEAD.
THEY SAY HE WAS MURDERED.

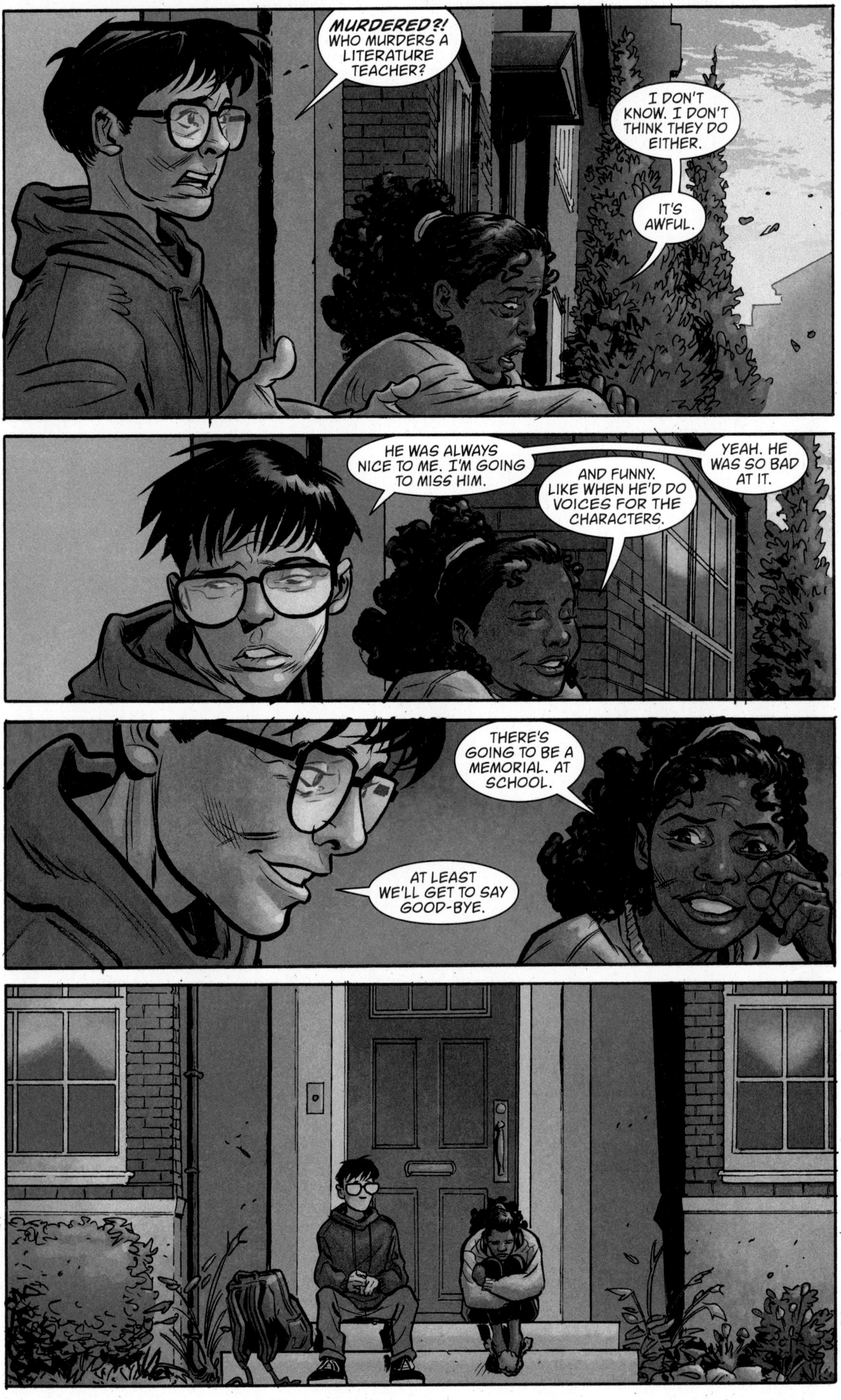
MURDERED?! WHO MURDERS A LITERATURE TEACHER?
I DON'T KNOW. I DON'T THINK THEY DO EITHER.
IT'S AWFUL.
HE WAS ALWAYS NICE TO ME. I'M GOING TO MISS HIM.
AND FUNNY. LIKE WHEN HE'D DO VOICES FOR THE CHARACTERS.
YEAH. HE WAS SO BAD AT IT.
THERE'S GOING TO BE A MEMORIAL. AT SCHOOL.
AT LEAST WE'LL GET TO SAY GOOD-BYE.

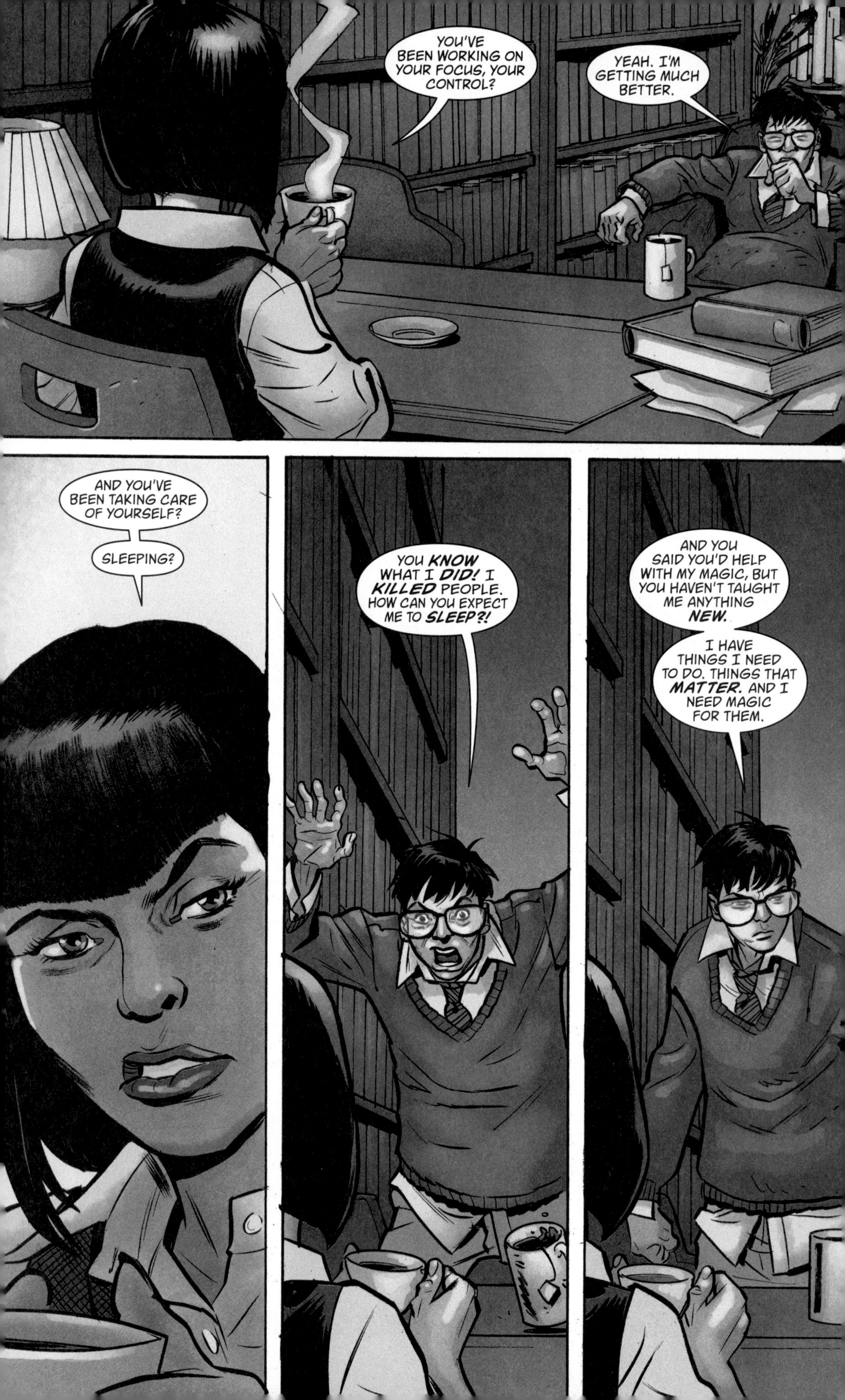

YOU'VE BEEN WORKING ON YOUR FOCUS, YOUR CONTROL?
YEAH. I'M GETTING MUCH BETTER.
AND YOU'VE BEEN TAKING CARE OF YOURSELF?
SLEEPING?
YOU KNOW WHAT I DID! I KILLED PEOPLE. HOW CAN YOU EXPECT ME TO SLEEP?!
AND YOU SAID YOU'D HELP WITH MY MAGIC, BUT YOU HAVEN'T TAUGHT ME ANYTHING NEW.
I HAVE THINGS I NEED TO DO. THINGS THAT MATTER. AND I NEED MAGIC FOR THEM.

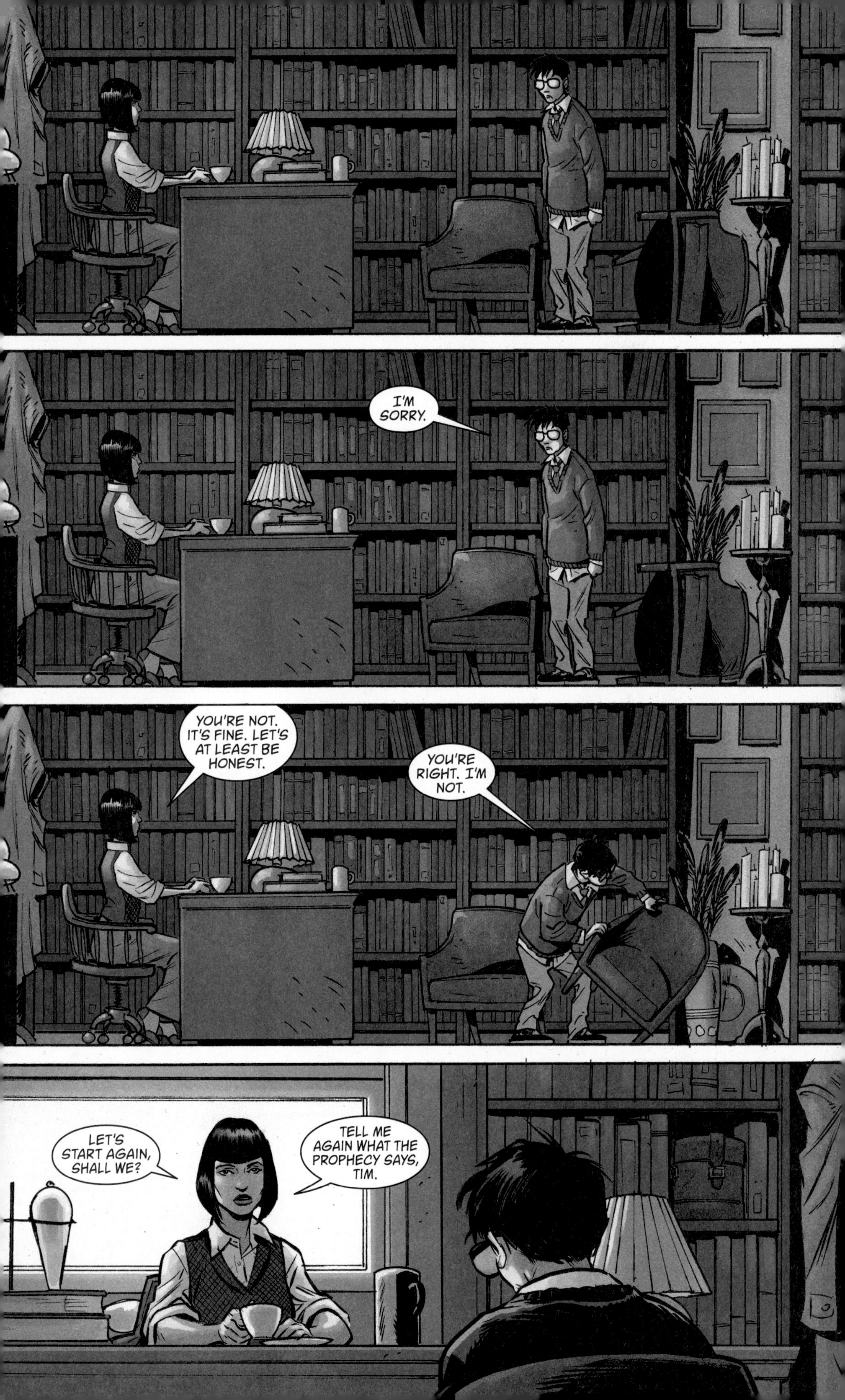
I'M SORRY.
YOU'RE NOT. IT'S FINE. LET'S AT LEAST BE HONEST.
YOU'RE RIGHT. I'M NOT.
LET'S START AGAIN, SHALL WE?
TELL ME AGAIN WHAT THE PROPHECY SAYS, TIM.

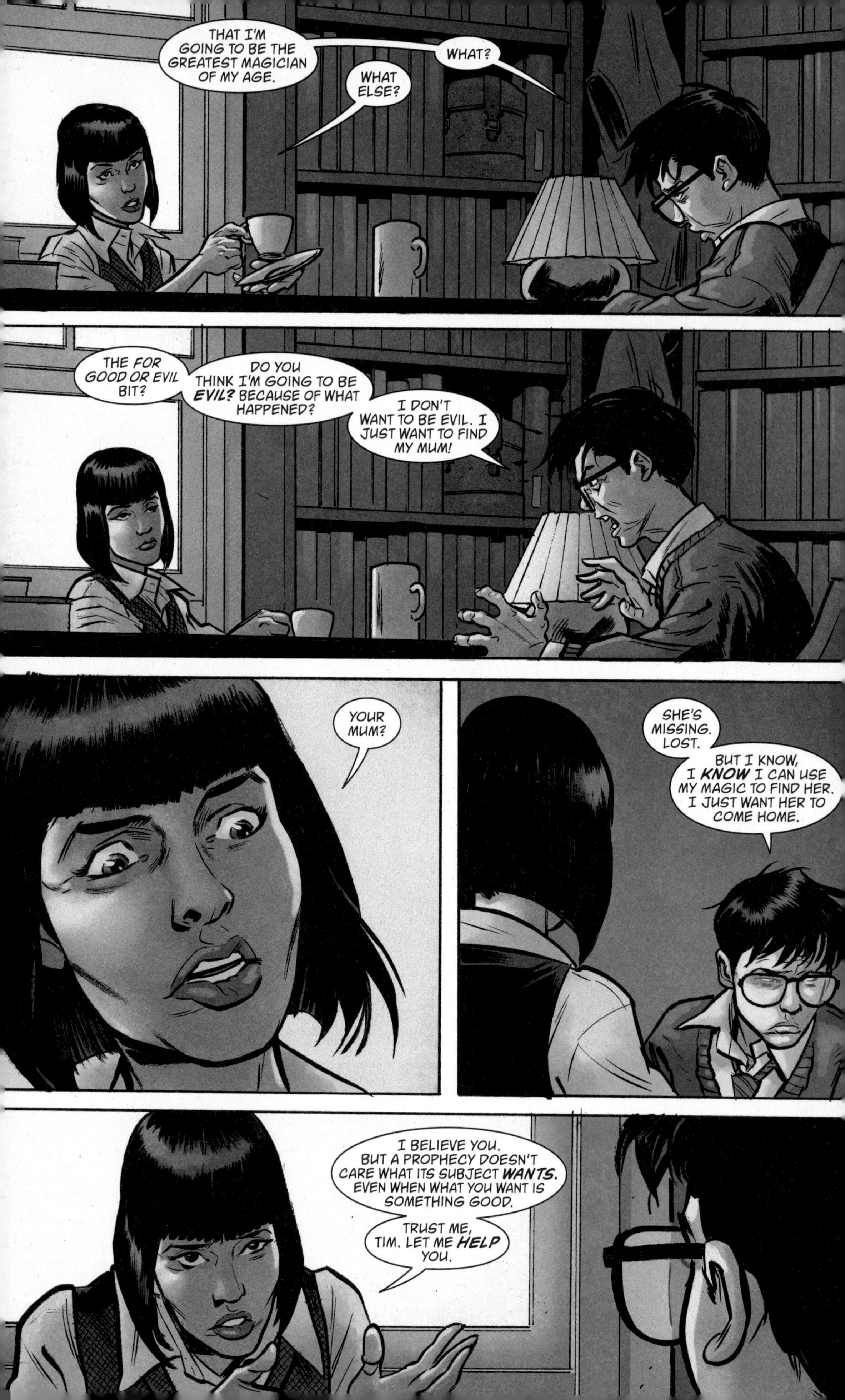
THAT I'M GOING TO BE THE GREATEST MAGICIAN OF MY AGE.
WHAT?
WHAT ELSE?
THE FOR GOOD OR EVIL BIT?
DO YOU THINK I'M GOING TO BE EVIL? BECAUSE OF WHAT HAPPENED?
I DON'T WANT TO BE EVIL. I JUST WANT TO FIND MY MUM!
YOUR MUM?
SHE'S MISSING. LOST.
BUT I KNOW, I KNOW I CAN USE MY MAGIC TO FIND HER. I JUST WANT HER TO COME HOME.
I BELIEVE YOU. BUT A PROPHECY DOESN'T CARE WHAT ITS SUBJECT WANTS. EVEN WHEN WHAT YOU WANT IS SOMETHING GOOD.
TRUST ME, TIM. LET ME HELP YOU.

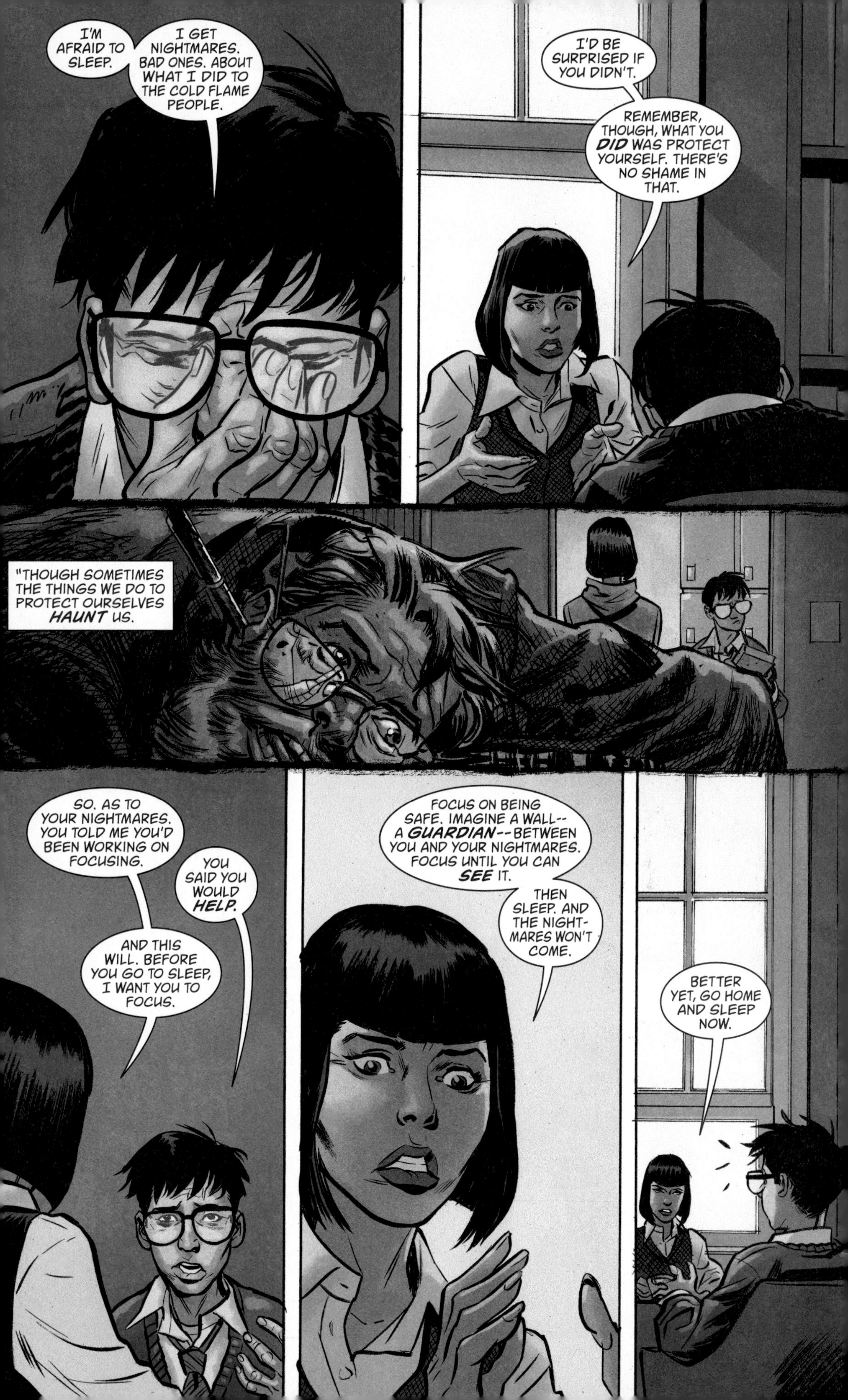
I'M AFRAID TO SLEEP.
I GET NIGHTMARES. BAD ONES. ABOUT WHAT I DID TO THE COLD FLAME PEOPLE.
I'D BE SURPRISED IF YOU DIDN'T.
REMEMBER, THOUGH, WHAT YOU DID WAS PROTECT YOURSELF. THERE'S NO SHAME IN THAT.
"THOUGH SOMETIMES THE THINGS WE DO TO PROTECT OURSELVES HAUNT US.
SO. AS TO YOUR NIGHTMARES. YOU TOLD ME YOU'D BEEN WORKING ON FOCUSING.
YOU SAID YOU WOULD HELP.
AND THIS WILL. BEFORE YOU GO TO SLEEP, I WANT YOU TO FOCUS.
FOCUS ON BEING SAFE. IMAGINE A WALL-- A GUARDIAN--BETWEEN YOU AND YOUR NIGHTMARES. FOCUS UNTIL YOU CAN SEE IT.
THEN SLEEP. AND THE NIGHT-MARES WON'T COME.
BETTER YET, GO HOME AND SLEEP NOW.

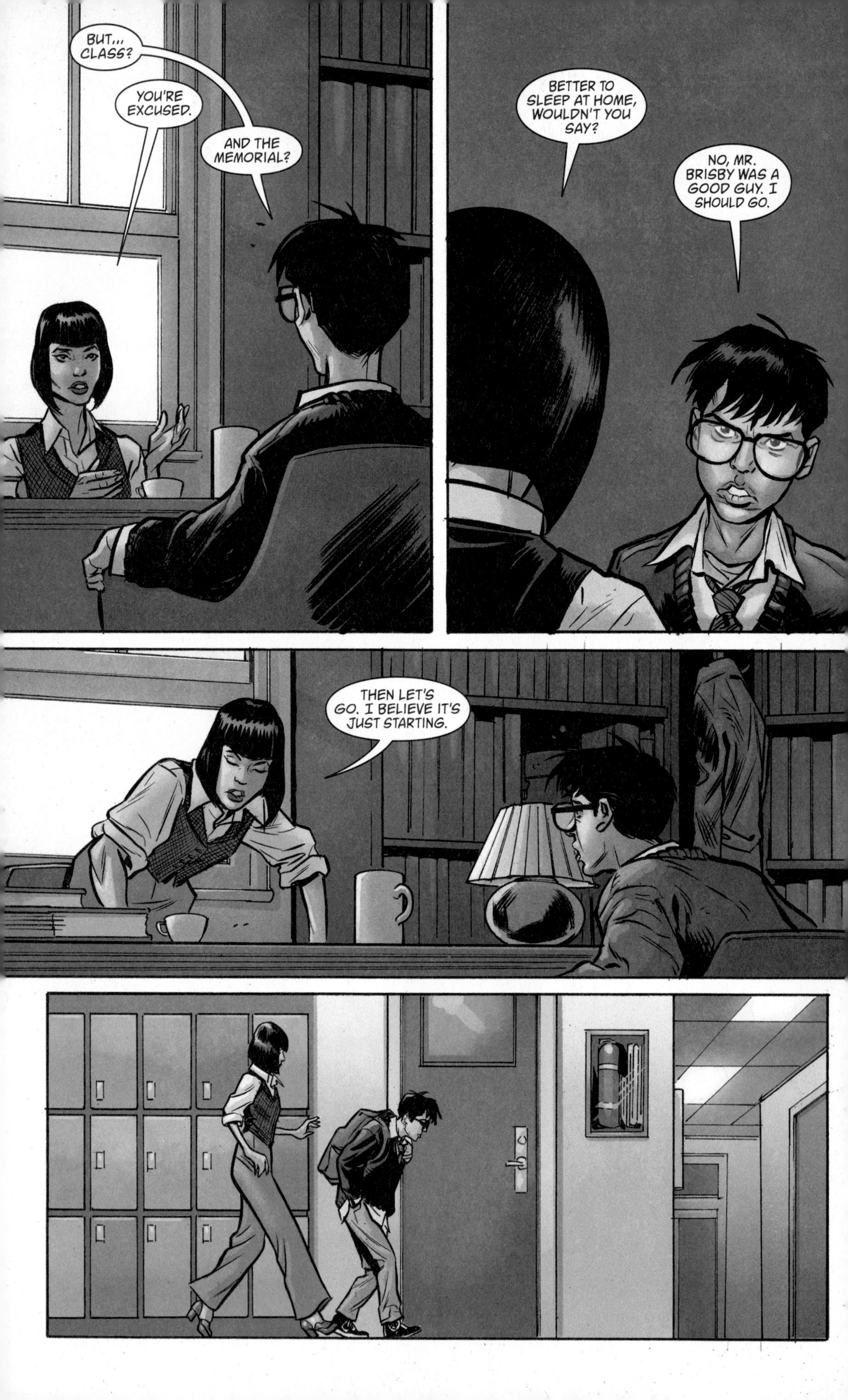
BUT... CLASS?
YOU'RE EXCUSED.
AND THE MEMORIAL?
BETTER TO SLEEP AT HOME, WOULDN'T YOU SAY?
NO, MR. BRISBY WAS A GOOD GUY. I SHOULD GO.
THEN LET'S GO. I BELIEVE IT'S JUST STARTING.

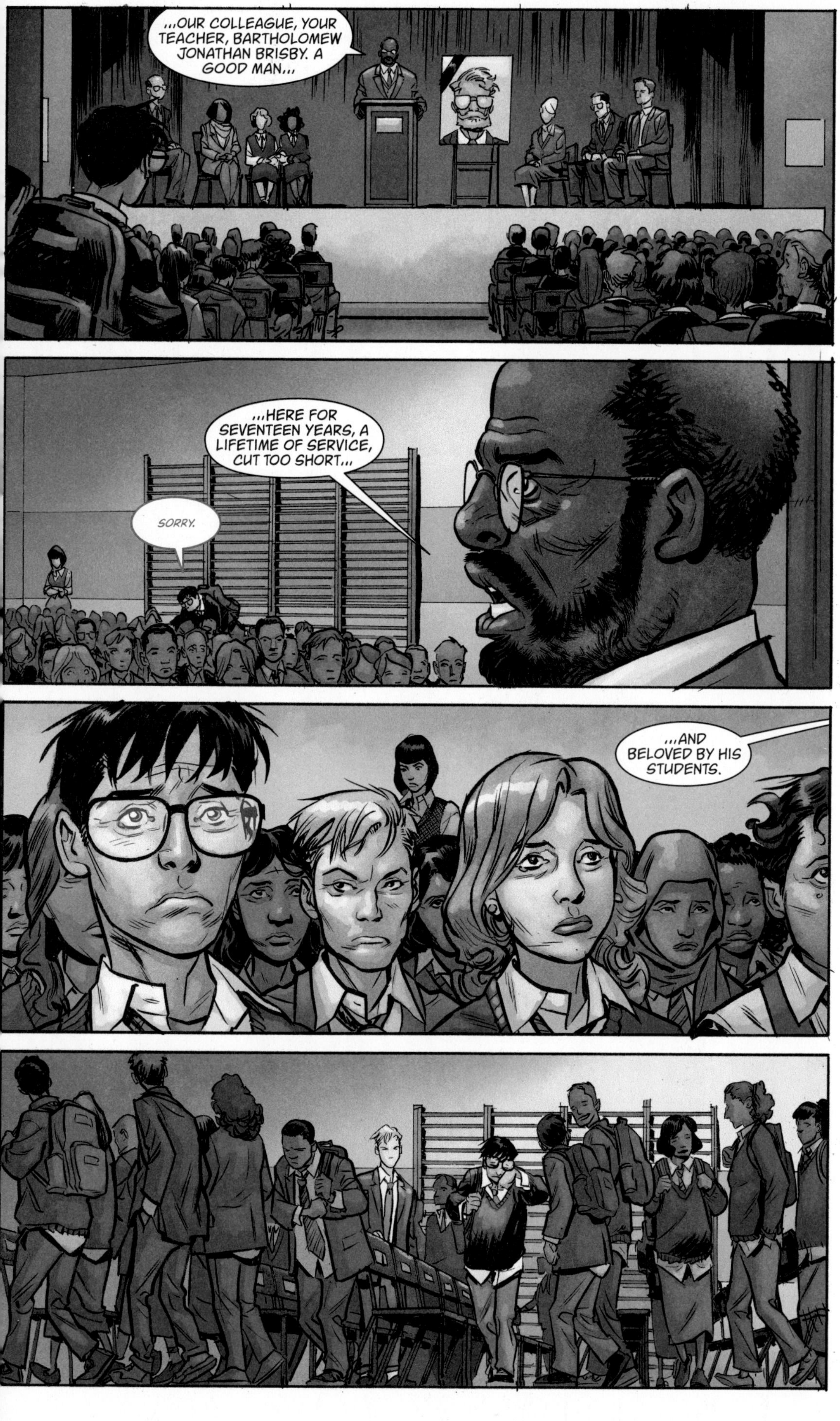
...OUR COLLEAGUE, YOUR TEACHER, BARTHOLOMEW JONATHAN BRISBY. A GOOD MAN...
...HERE FOR SEVENTEEN YEARS, A LIFETIME OF SERVICE, CUT TOO SHORT...
SORRY.
...AND BELOVED BY HIS STUDENTS.

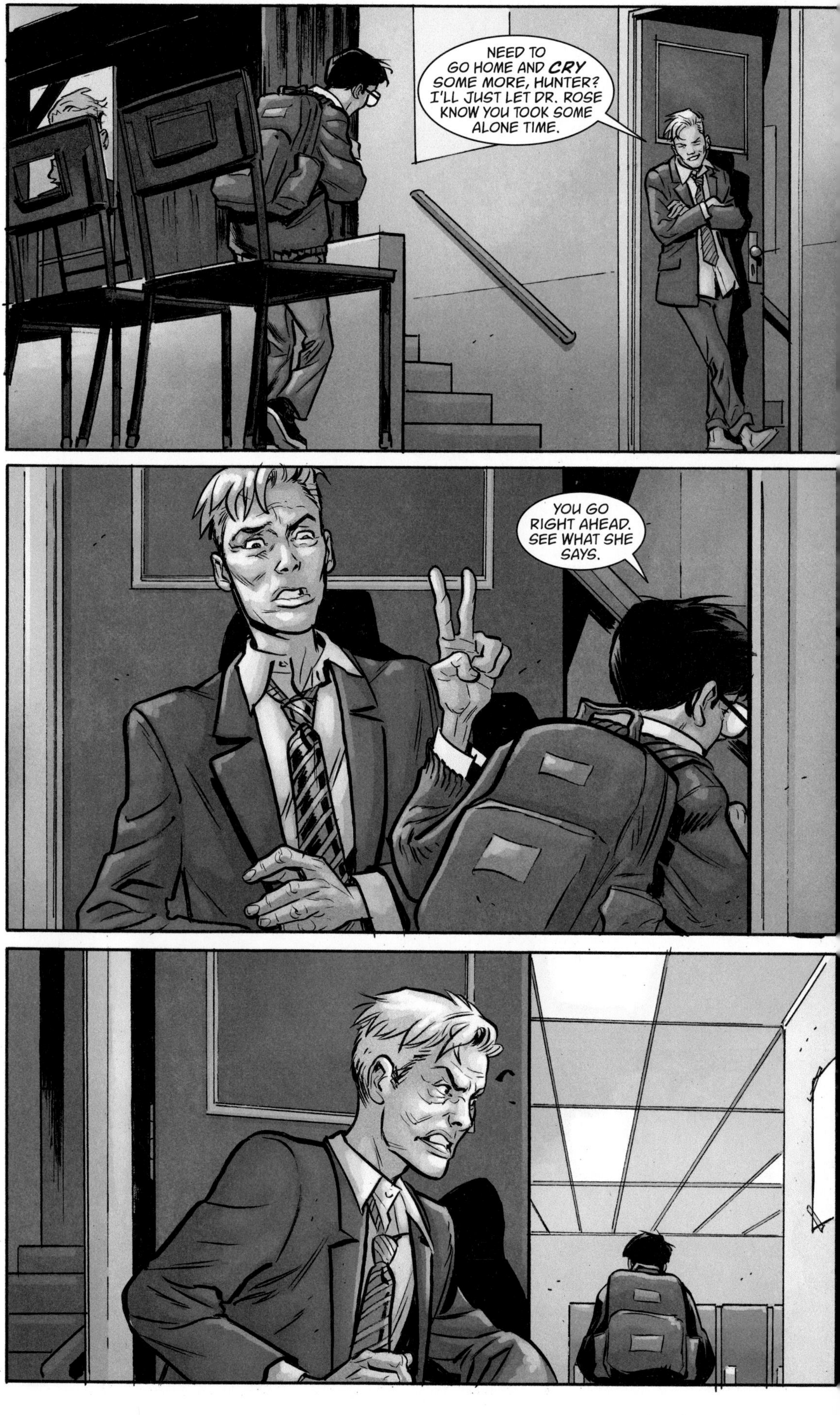
NEED TO GO HOME AND CRY SOME MORE, HUNTER? I'LL JUST LET DR. ROSE KNOW YOU TOOK SOME ALONE TIME.
YOU GO RIGHT AHEAD. SEE WHAT SHE SAYS.

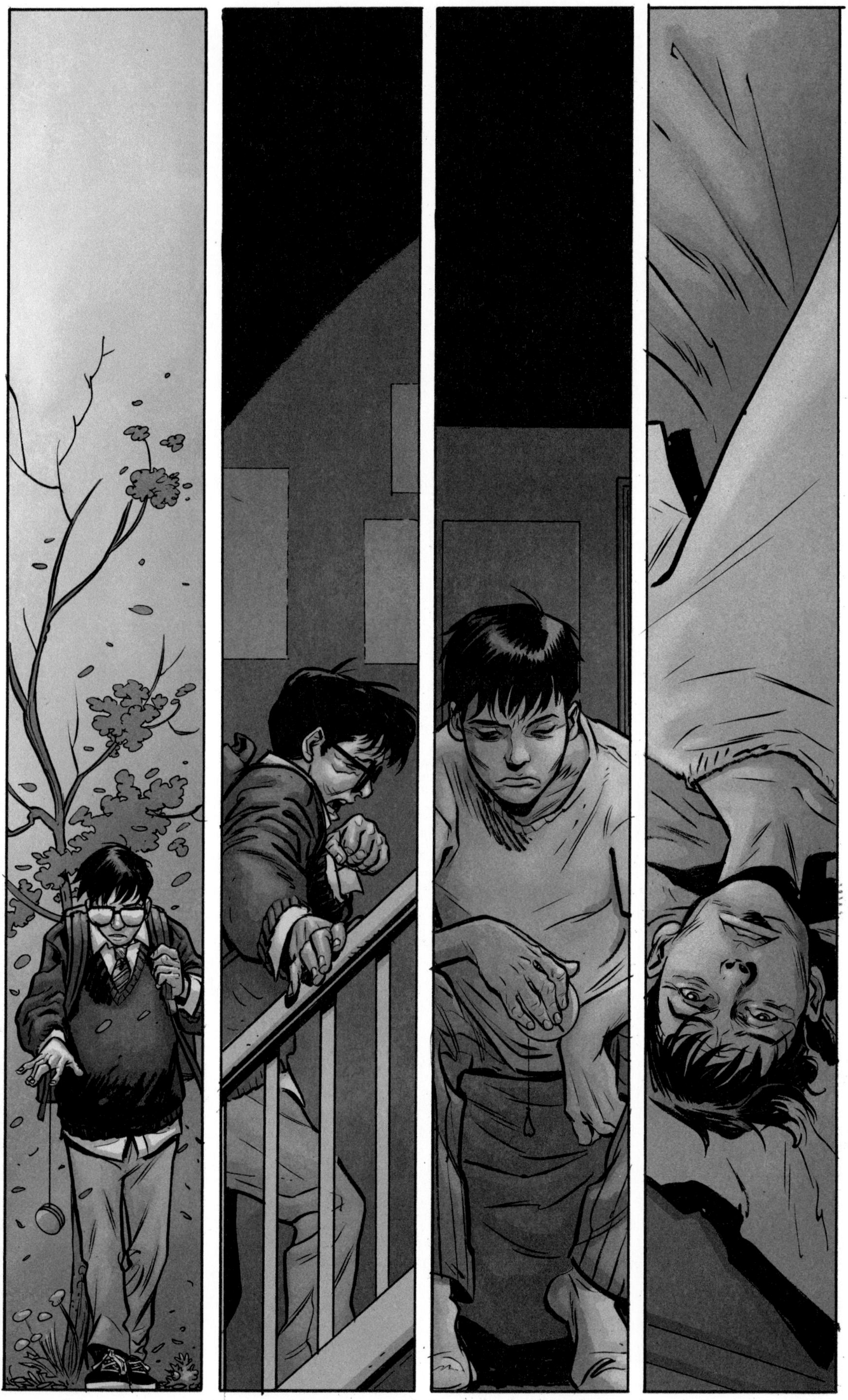

Focus on a wall between you and your nightmares.

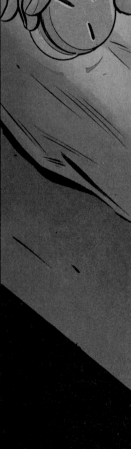

OKAY, MAGIC.

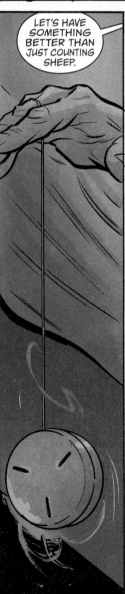

LET'S HAVE SOMETHING BETTER THAN JUST COUNTING SHEEP.

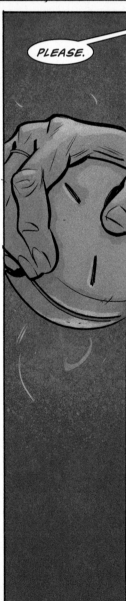

PLEASE.

Focus on a *guardian.*

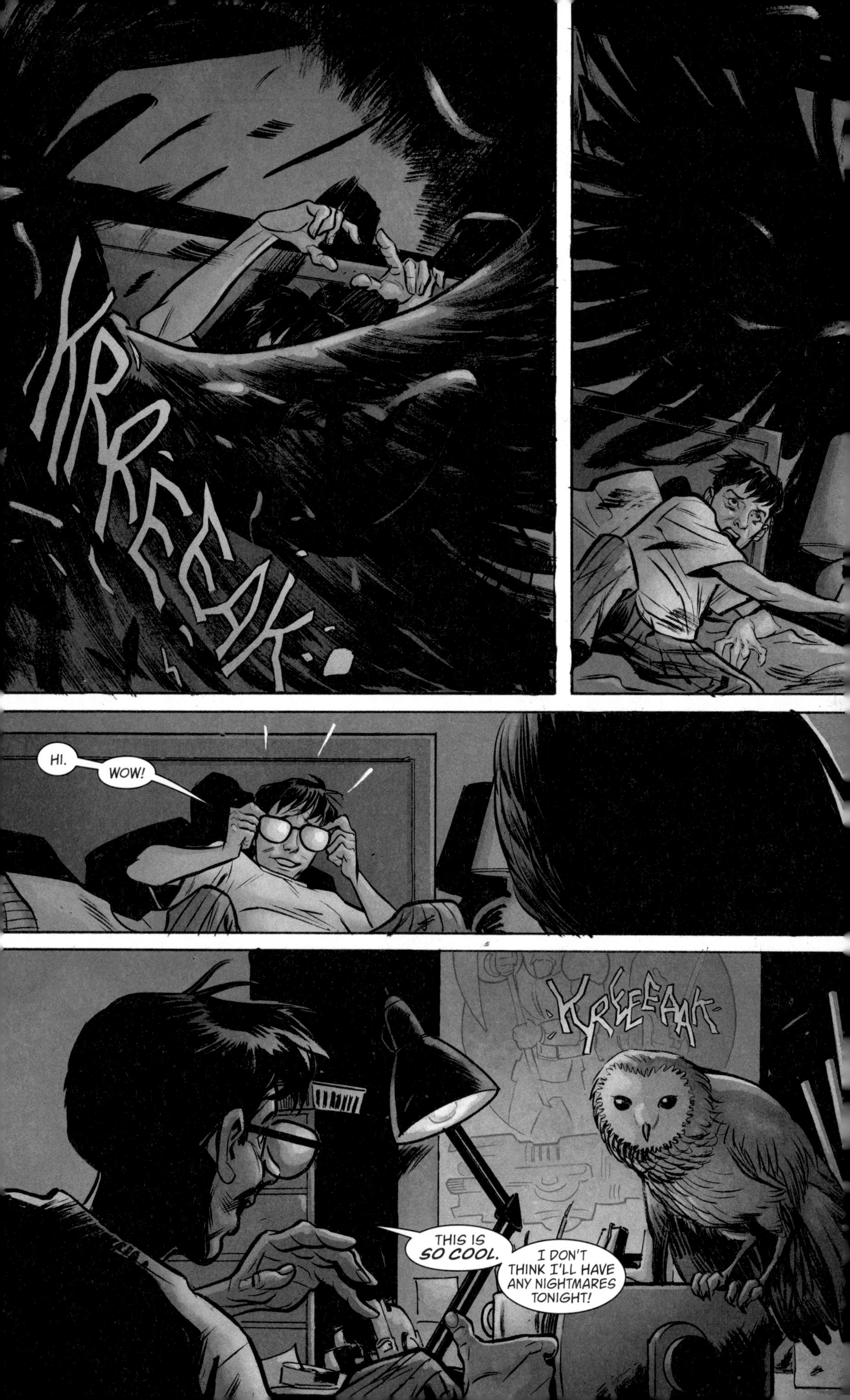
KRREEAK
HI.
WOW!
KREEEAAK
THIS IS *SO COOL.*
I DON'T THINK I'LL HAVE ANY NIGHTMARES TONIGHT!

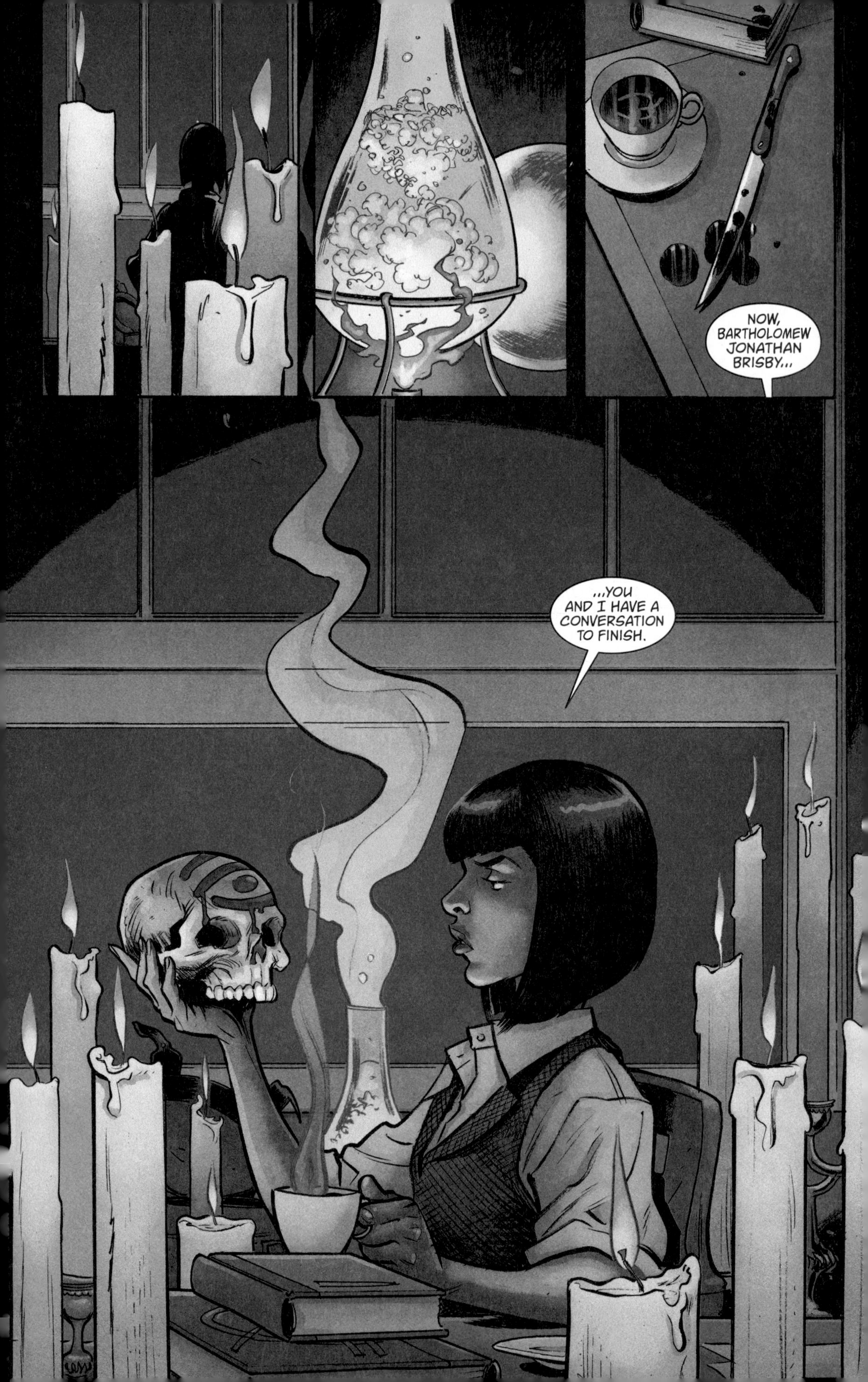
NOW, BARTHOLOMEW JONATHAN BRISBY...
...YOU AND I HAVE A CONVERSATION TO FINISH.

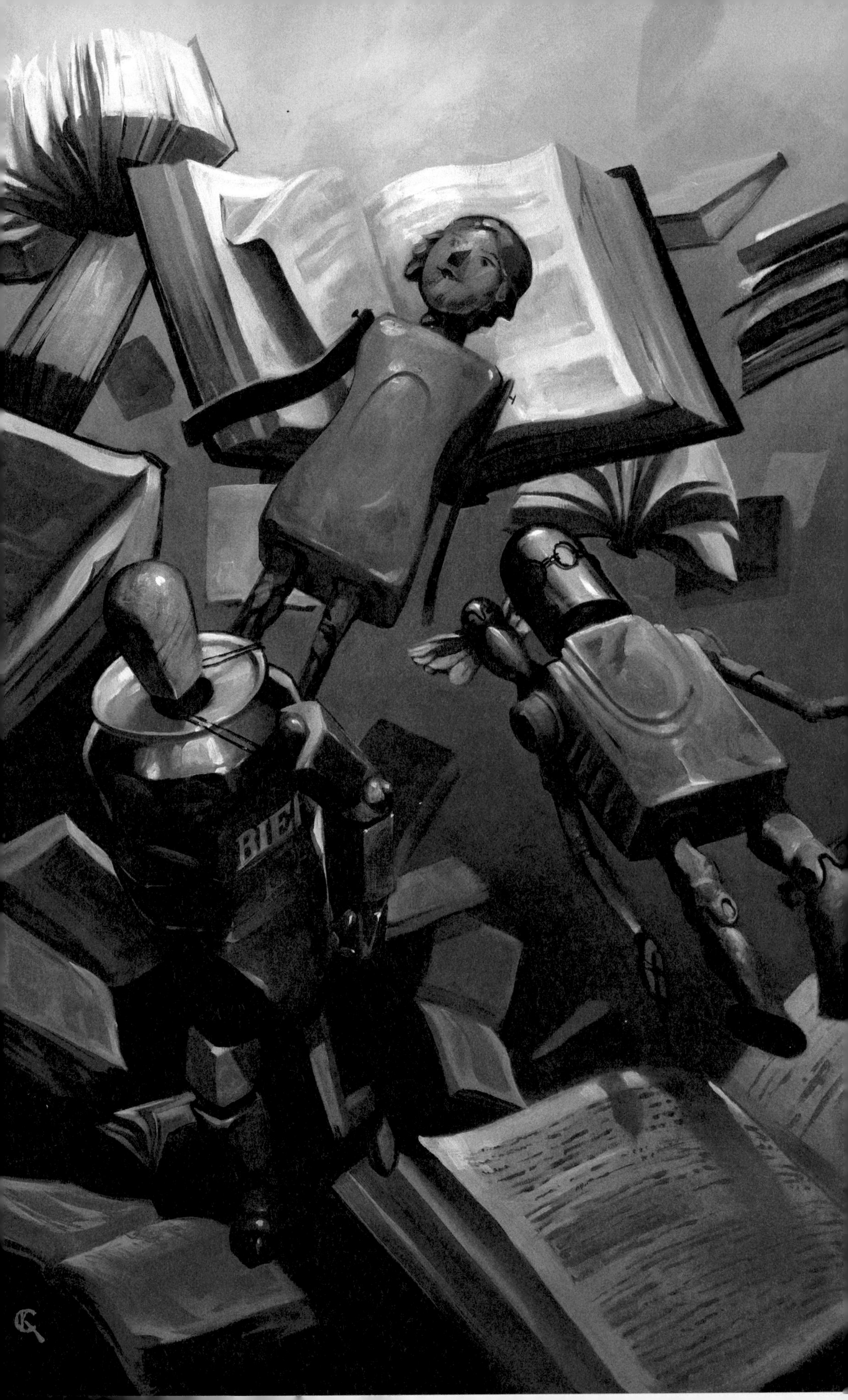
BIE

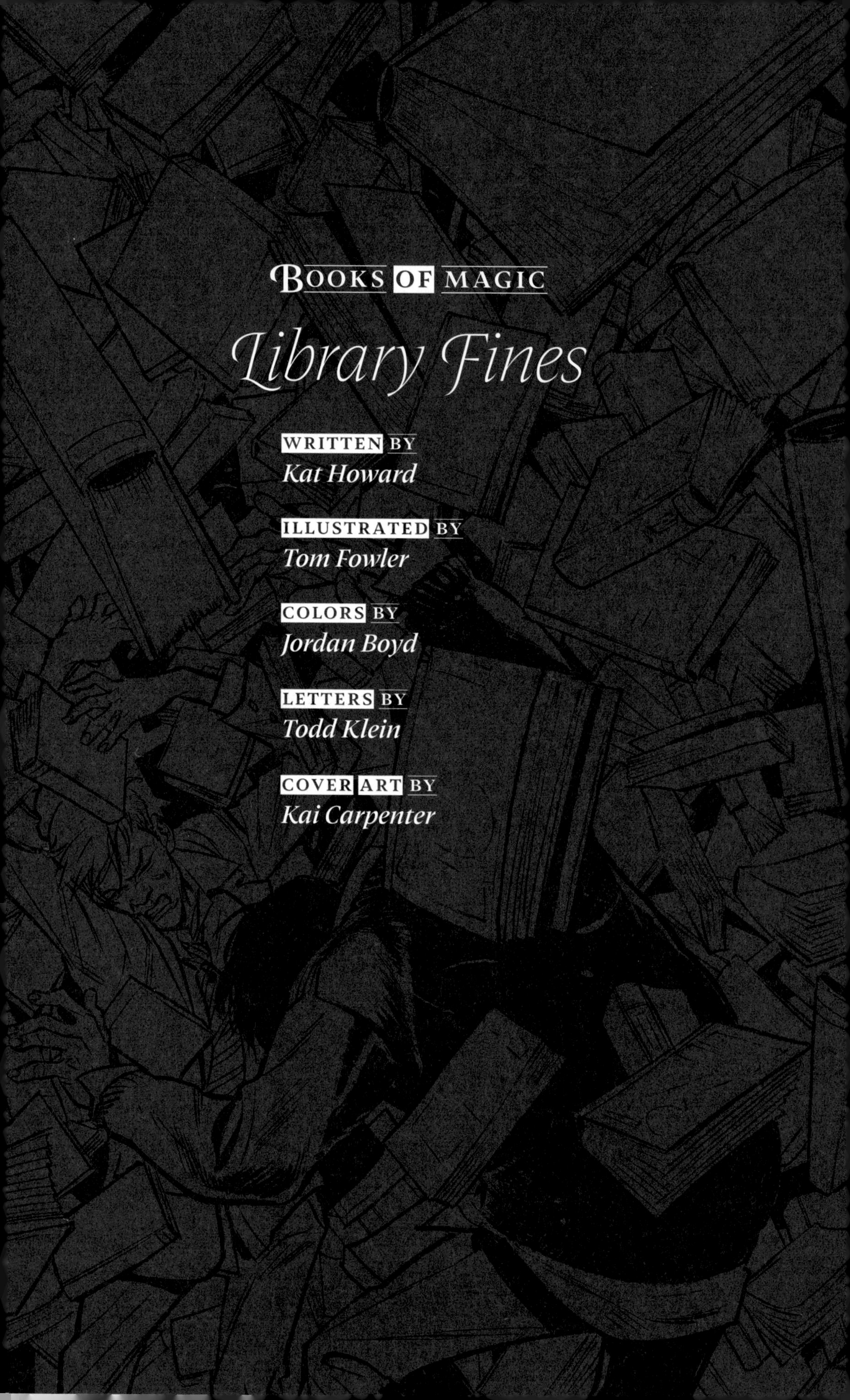

BOOKS OF MAGIC

Library Fines

WRITTEN BY
Kat Howard

ILLUSTRATED BY
Tom Fowler

COLORS BY
Jordan Boyd

LETTERS BY
Todd Klein

COVER ART BY
Kai Carpenter

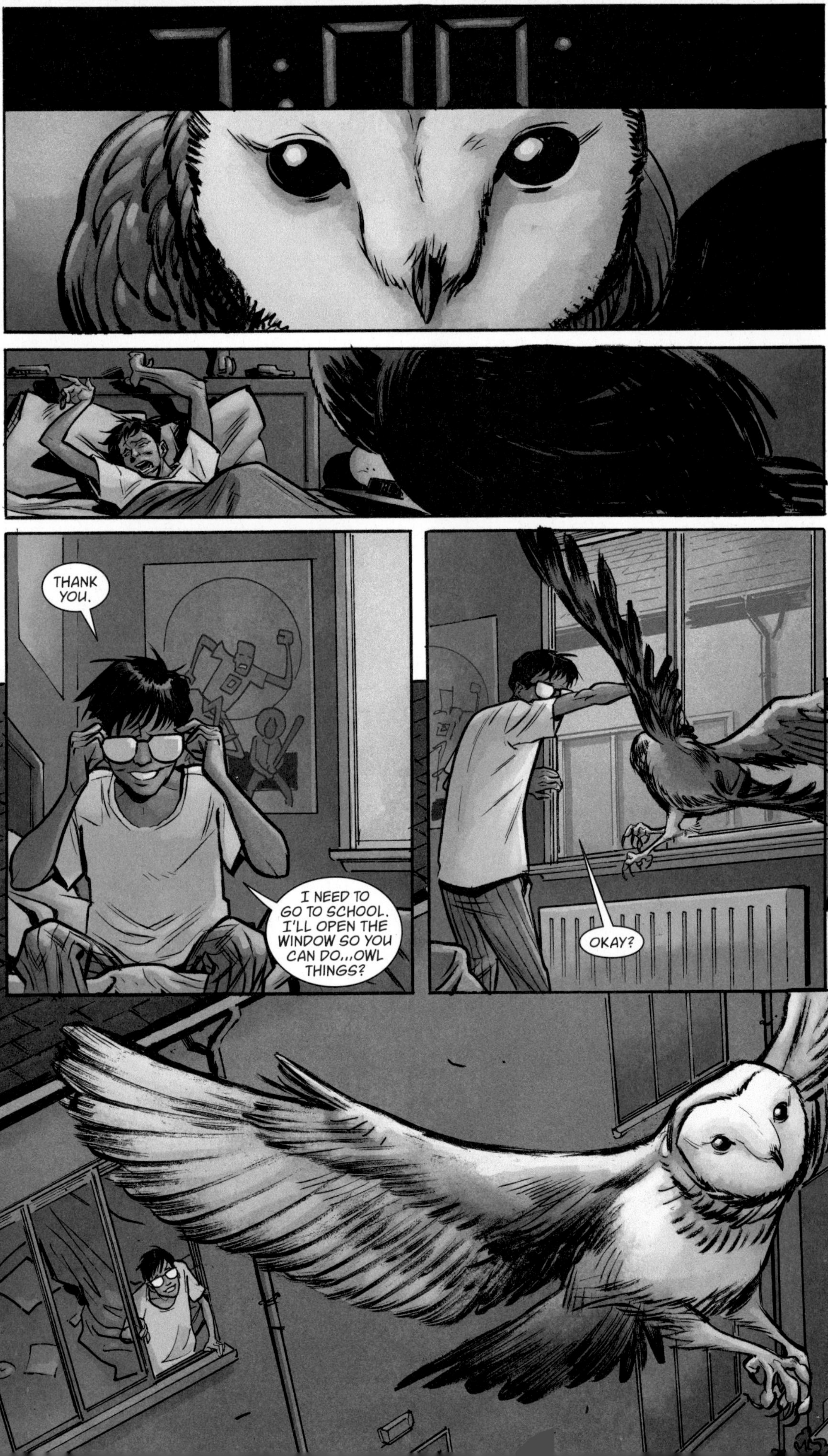
THANK YOU.
I NEED TO GO TO SCHOOL. I'LL OPEN THE WINDOW SO YOU CAN DO...OWL THINGS?
OKAY?

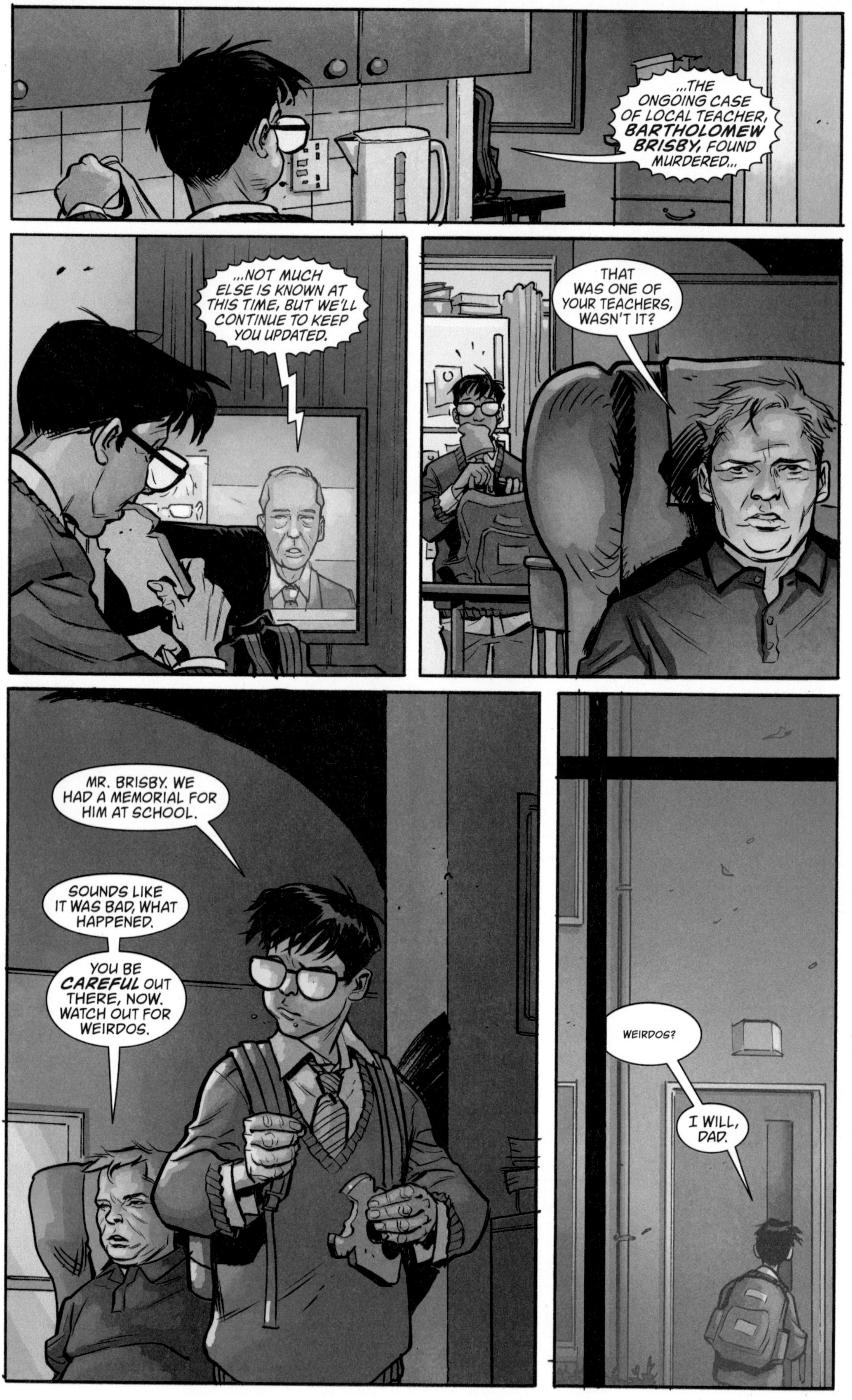
...THE ONGOING CASE OF LOCAL TEACHER, BARTHOLOMEW BRISBY, FOUND MURDERED...
...NOT MUCH ELSE IS KNOWN AT THIS TIME, BUT WE'LL CONTINUE TO KEEP YOU UPDATED.
THAT WAS ONE OF YOUR TEACHERS, WASN'T IT?
MR. BRISBY. WE HAD A MEMORIAL FOR HIM AT SCHOOL.
SOUNDS LIKE IT WAS BAD, WHAT HAPPENED.
YOU BE CAREFUL OUT THERE, NOW. WATCH OUT FOR WEIRDOS.
WEIRDOS?
I WILL, DAD.

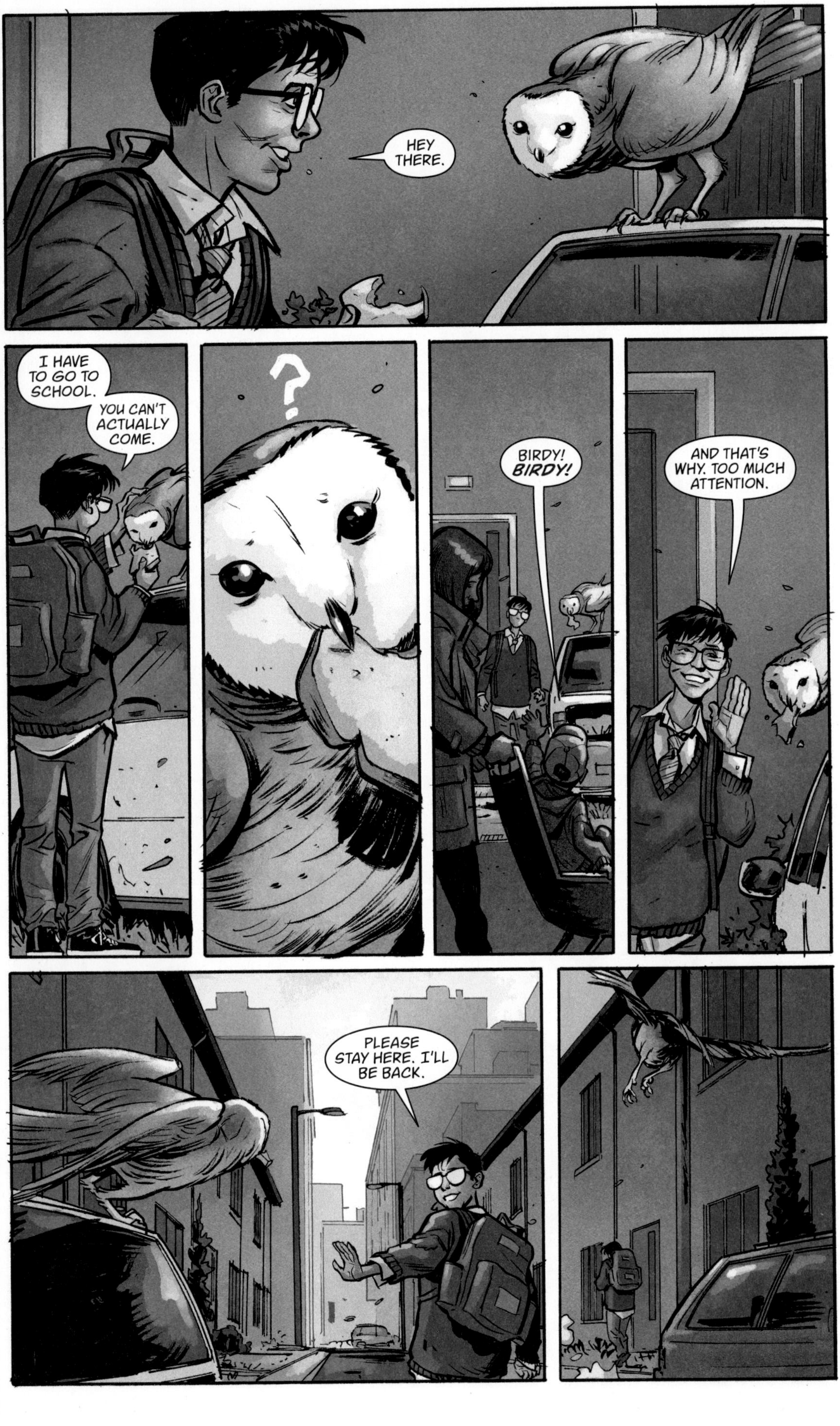
HEY THERE.
I HAVE TO GO TO SCHOOL.
YOU CAN'T ACTUALLY COME.
?
BIRDY! BIRDY!
AND THAT'S WHY. TOO MUCH ATTENTION.
PLEASE STAY HERE. I'LL BE BACK.

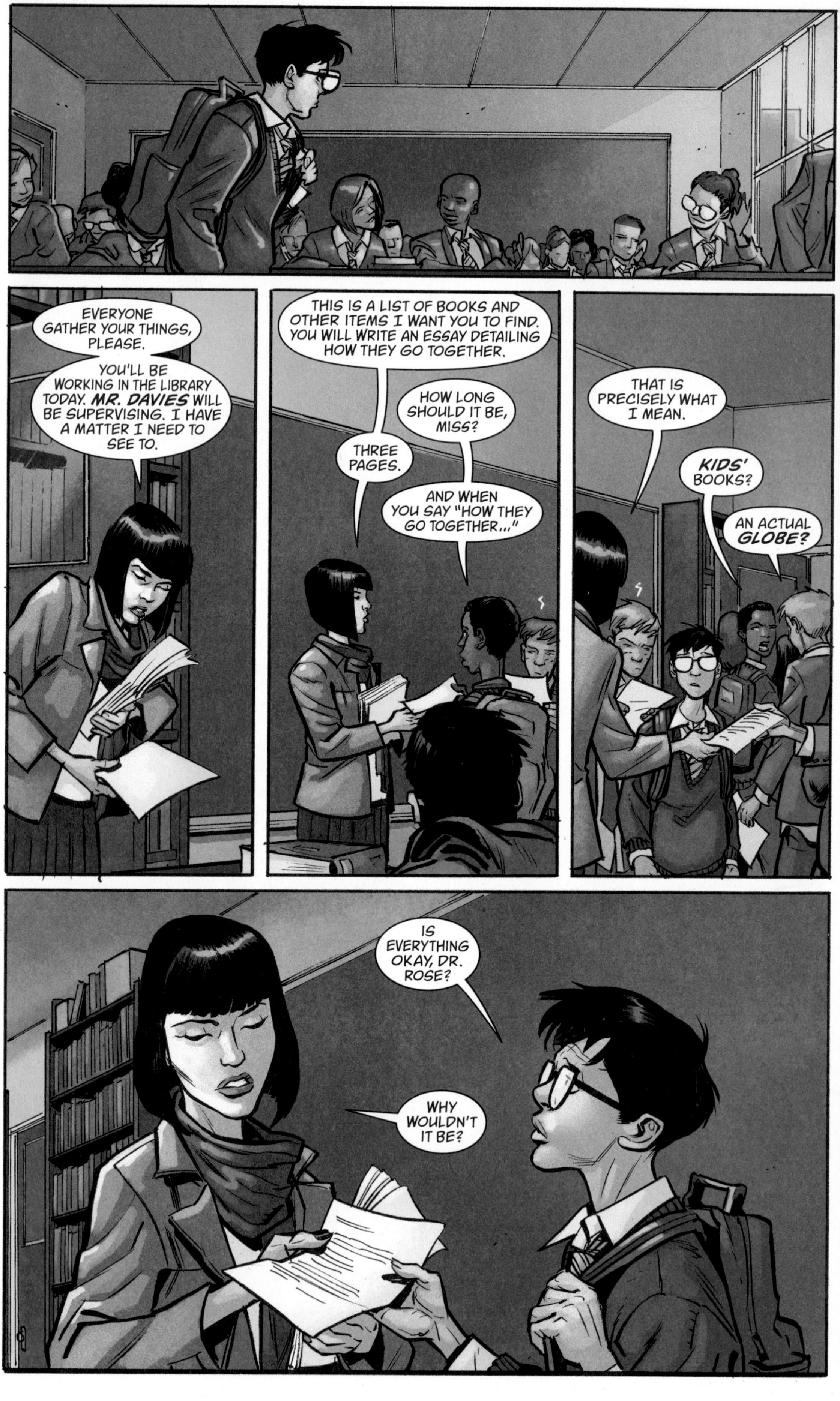

EVERYONE GATHER YOUR THINGS, PLEASE.
YOU'LL BE WORKING IN THE LIBRARY TODAY. MR. DAVIES WILL BE SUPERVISING. I HAVE A MATTER I NEED TO SEE TO.
THIS IS A LIST OF BOOKS AND OTHER ITEMS I WANT YOU TO FIND. YOU WILL WRITE AN ESSAY DETAILING HOW THEY GO TOGETHER.
HOW LONG SHOULD IT BE, MISS?
THREE PAGES.
AND WHEN YOU SAY "HOW THEY GO TOGETHER..."
THAT IS PRECISELY WHAT I MEAN.
KIDS' BOOKS?
AN ACTUAL GLOBE?
IS EVERYTHING OKAY, DR. ROSE?
WHY WOULDN'T IT BE?

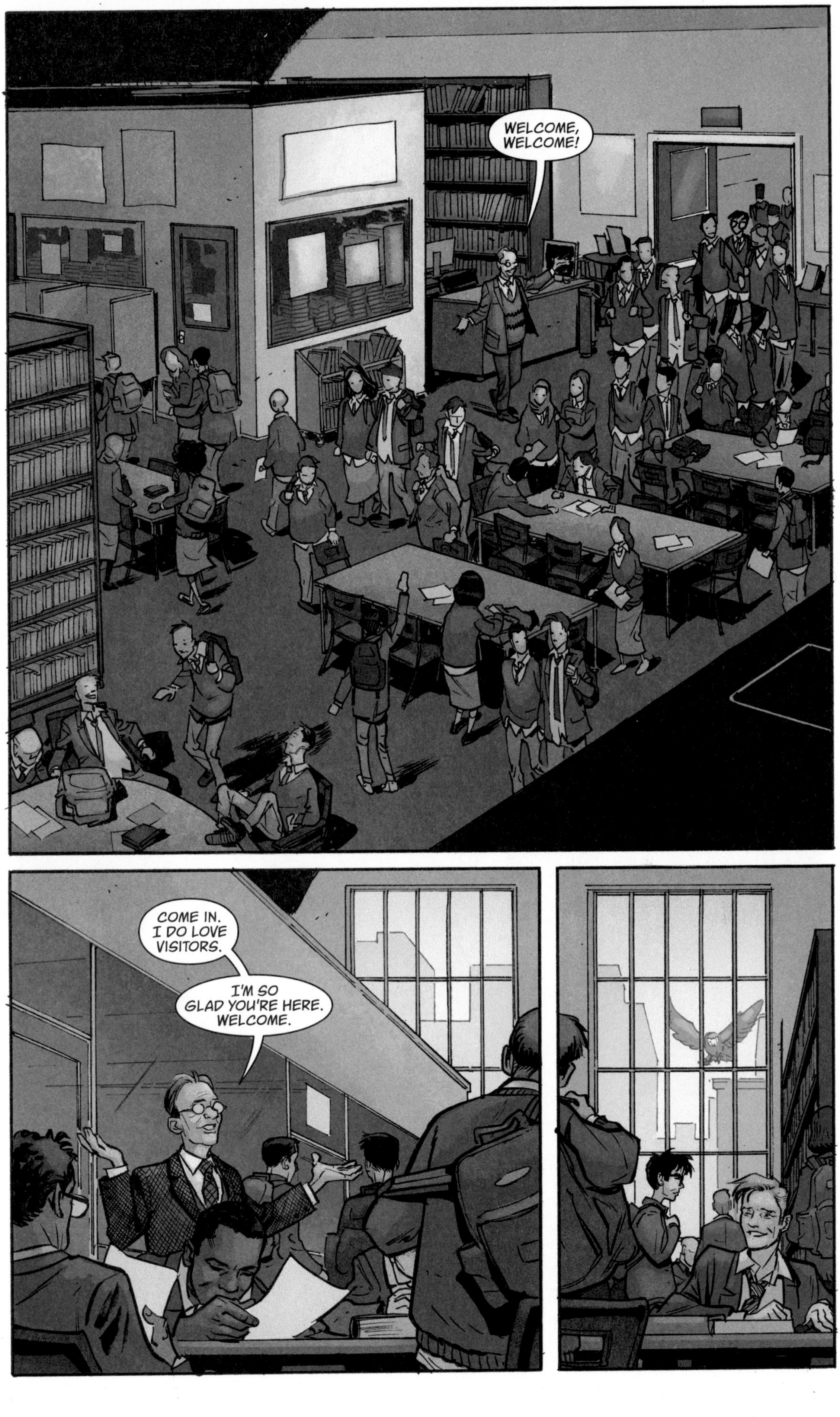
WELCOME, WELCOME!
COME IN. I DO LOVE VISITORS.
I'M SO GLAD YOU'RE HERE. WELCOME.

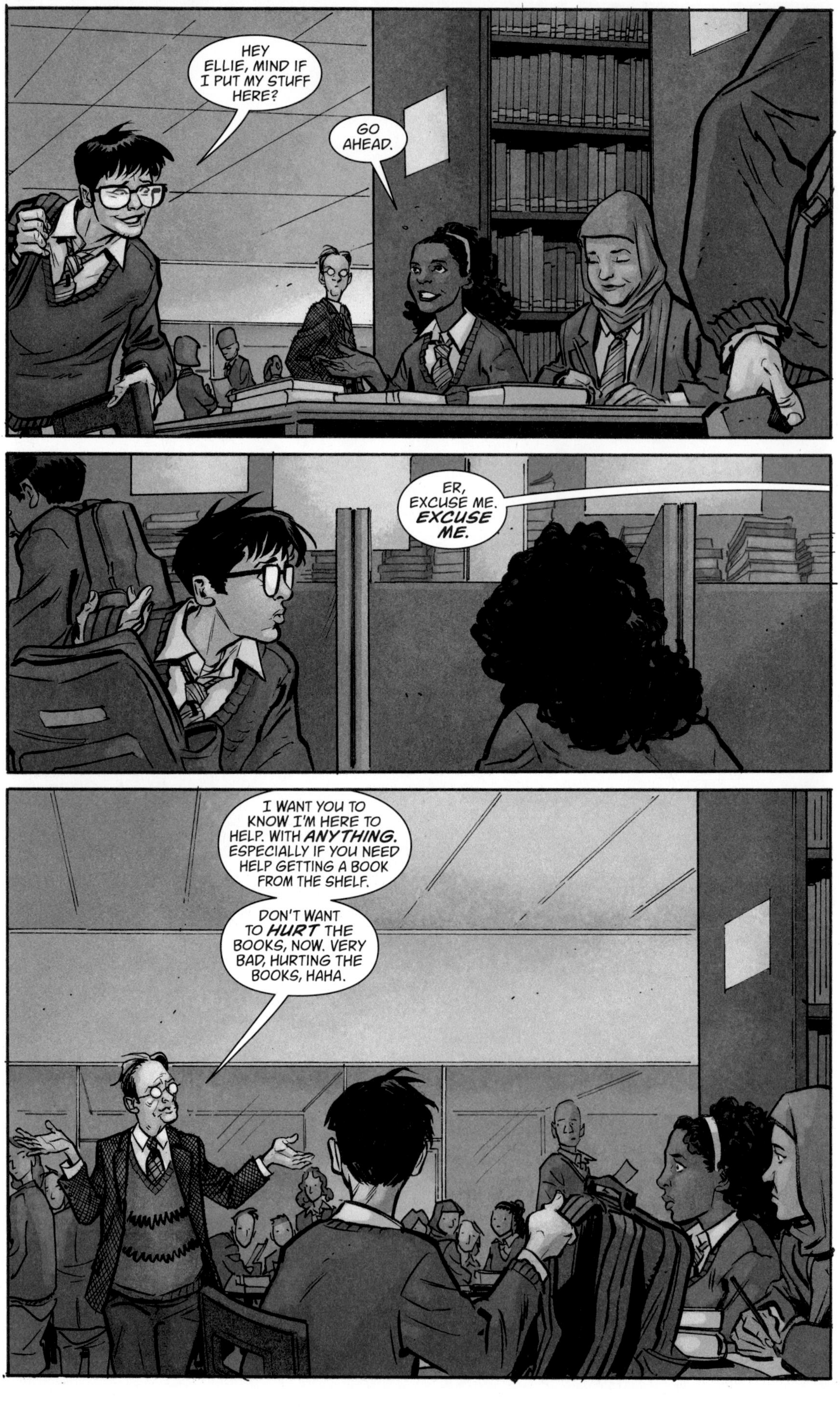
HEY ELLIE, MIND IF I PUT MY STUFF HERE?
GO AHEAD.
ER, EXCUSE ME. **EXCUSE ME.**
I WANT YOU TO KNOW I'M HERE TO HELP. WITH **ANYTHING.** ESPECIALLY IF YOU NEED HELP GETTING A BOOK FROM THE SHELF.
DON'T WANT TO **HURT** THE BOOKS, NOW. VERY BAD, HURTING THE BOOKS, HAHA.

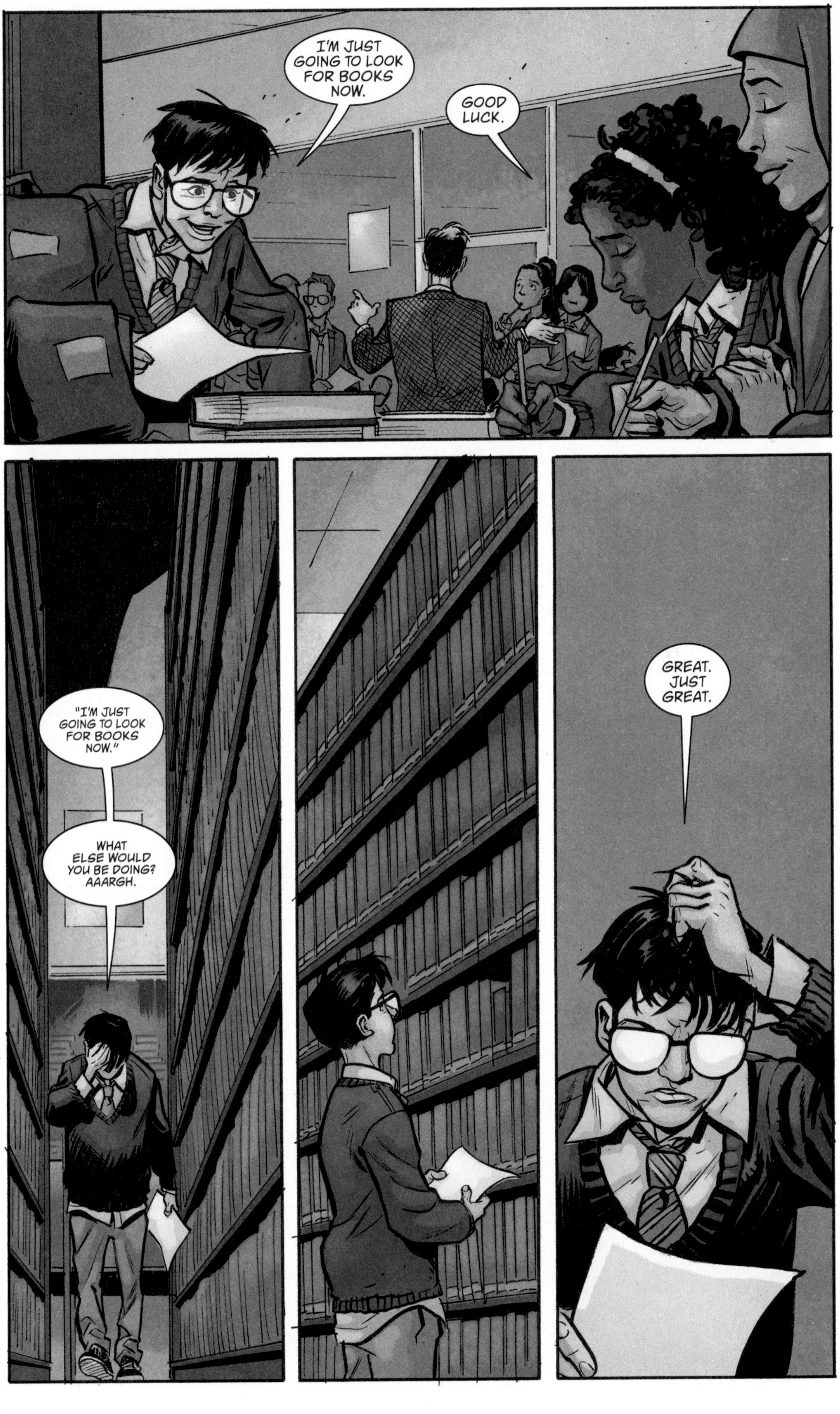
I'M JUST GOING TO LOOK FOR BOOKS NOW.
GOOD LUCK.
"I'M JUST GOING TO LOOK FOR BOOKS NOW."
WHAT ELSE WOULD YOU BE DOING? AAARGH.
GREAT. JUST GREAT.

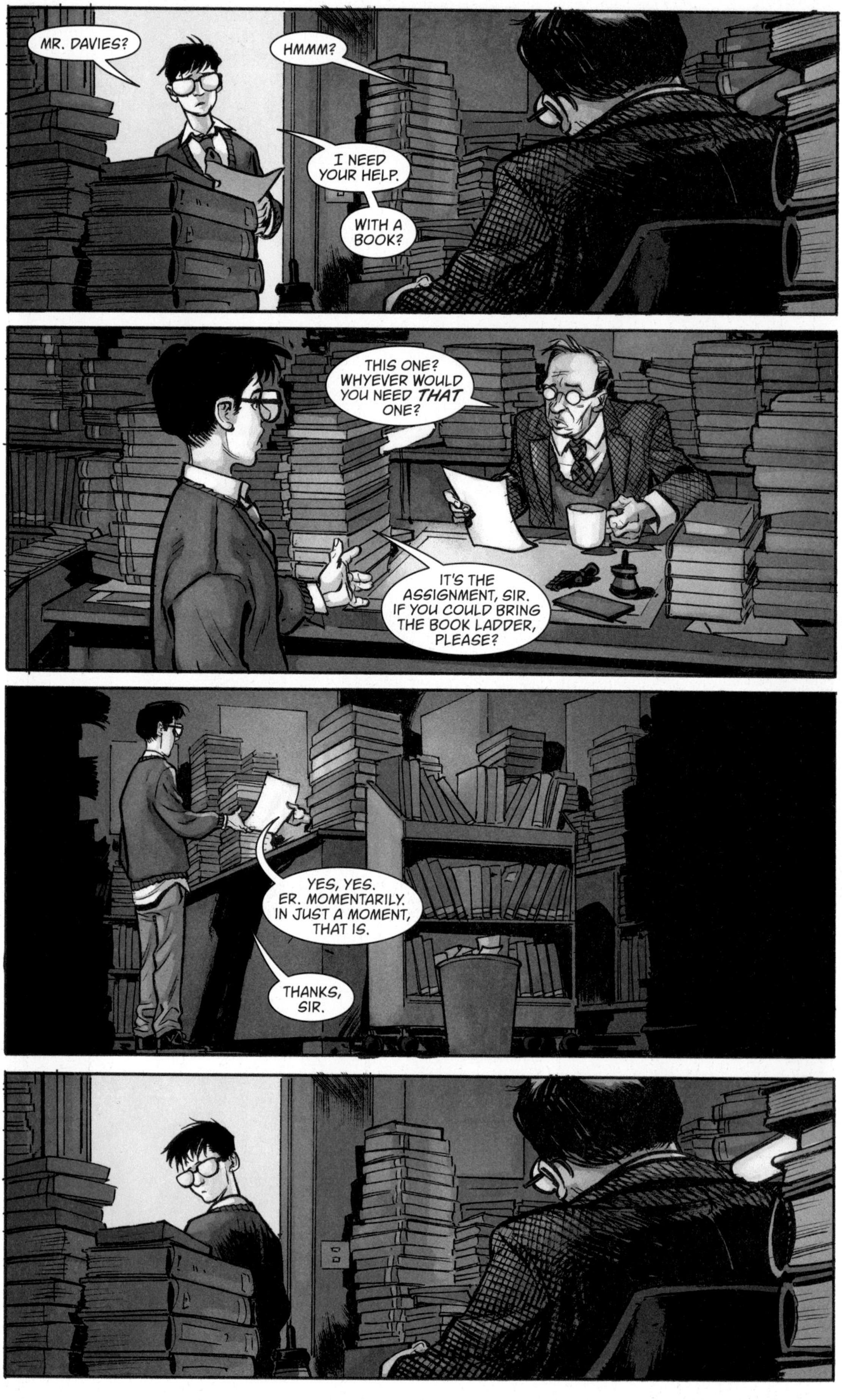
MR. DAVIES?
HMMM?
I NEED YOUR HELP.
WITH A BOOK?
THIS ONE? WHYEVER WOULD YOU NEED *THAT* ONE?
IT'S THE ASSIGNMENT, SIR. IF YOU COULD BRING THE BOOK LADDER, PLEASE?
YES, YES. ER. MOMENTARILY. IN JUST A MOMENT, THAT IS.
THANKS, SIR.

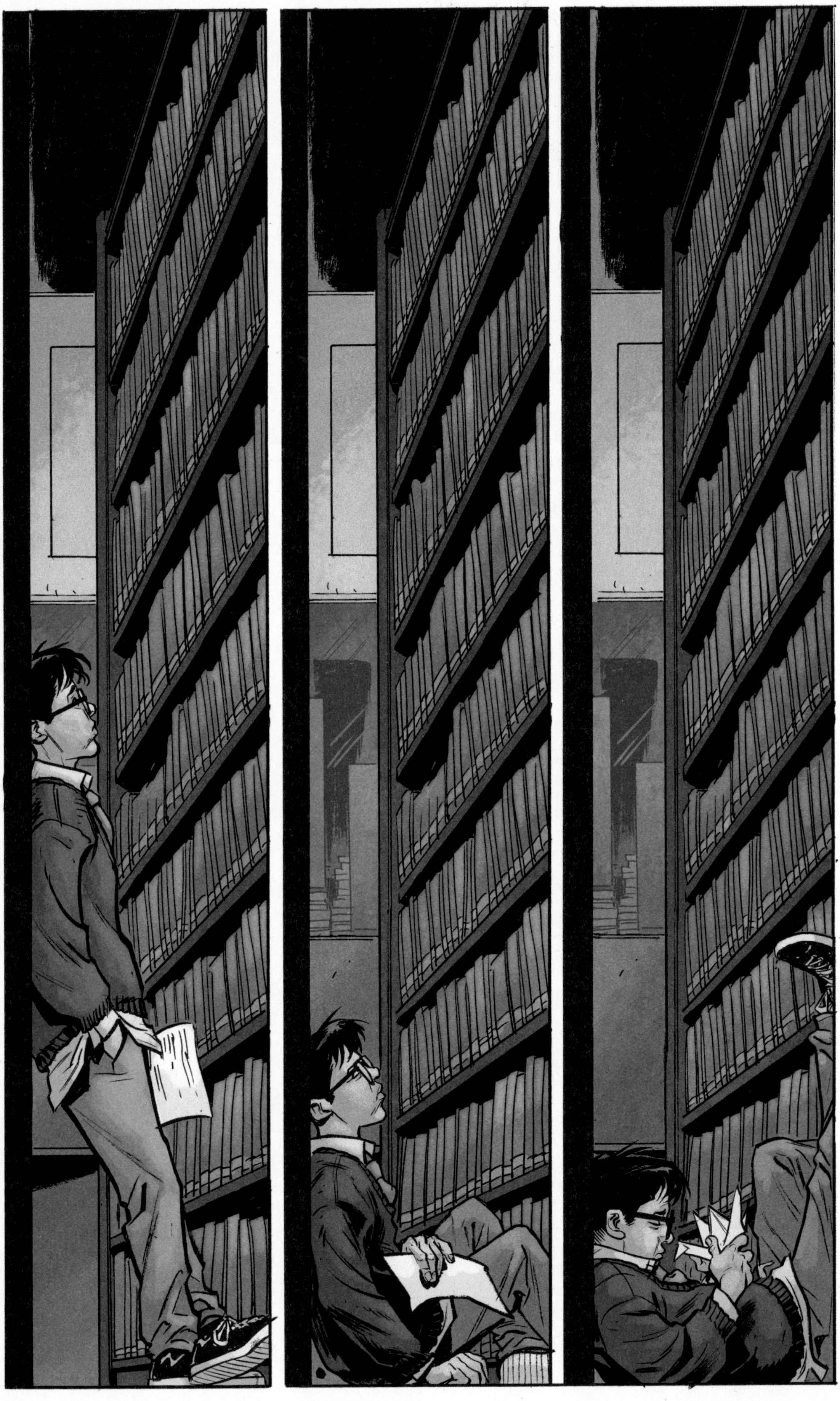

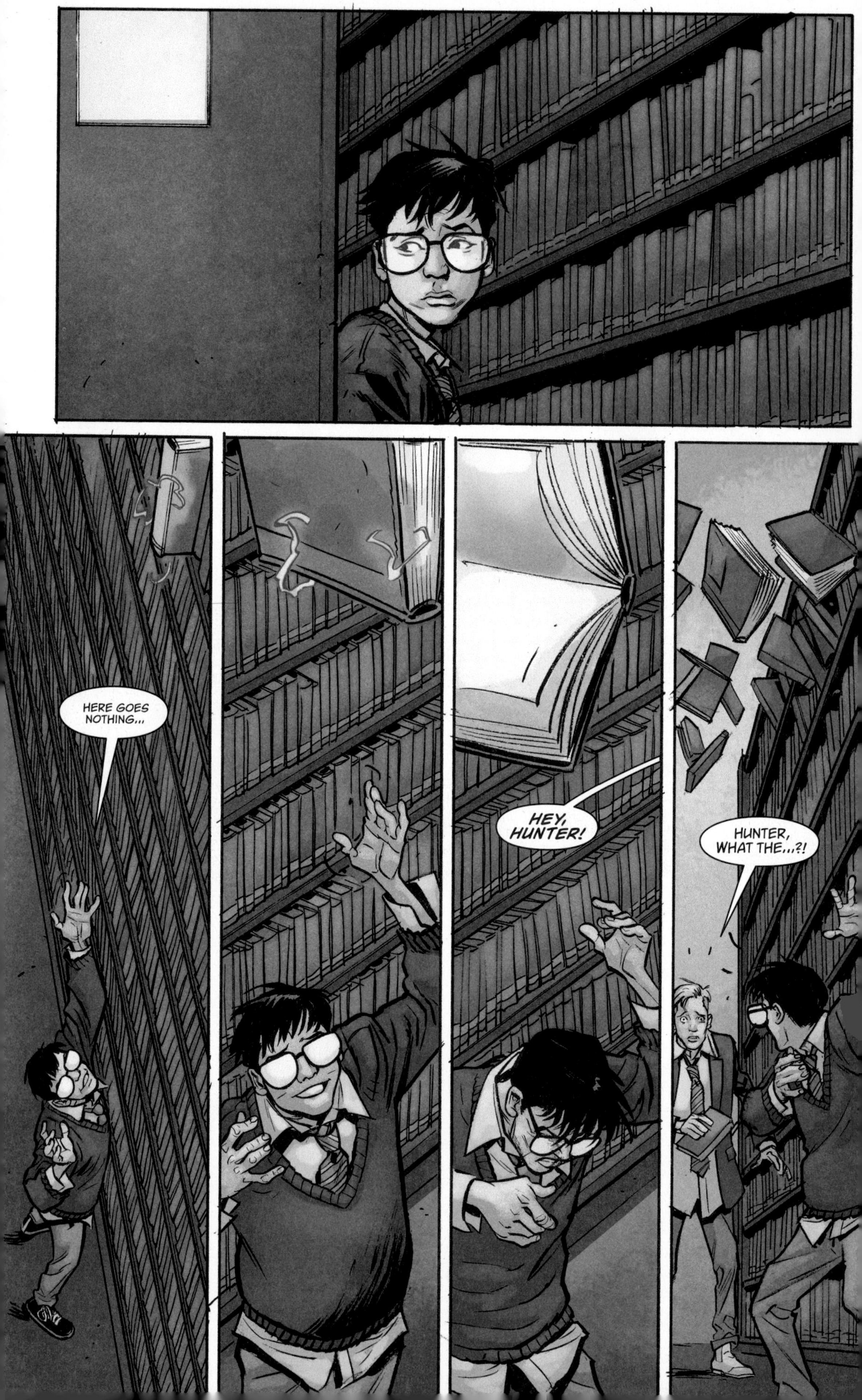
HERE GOES NOTHING...
HEY, HUNTER!
HUNTER, WHAT THE...?!

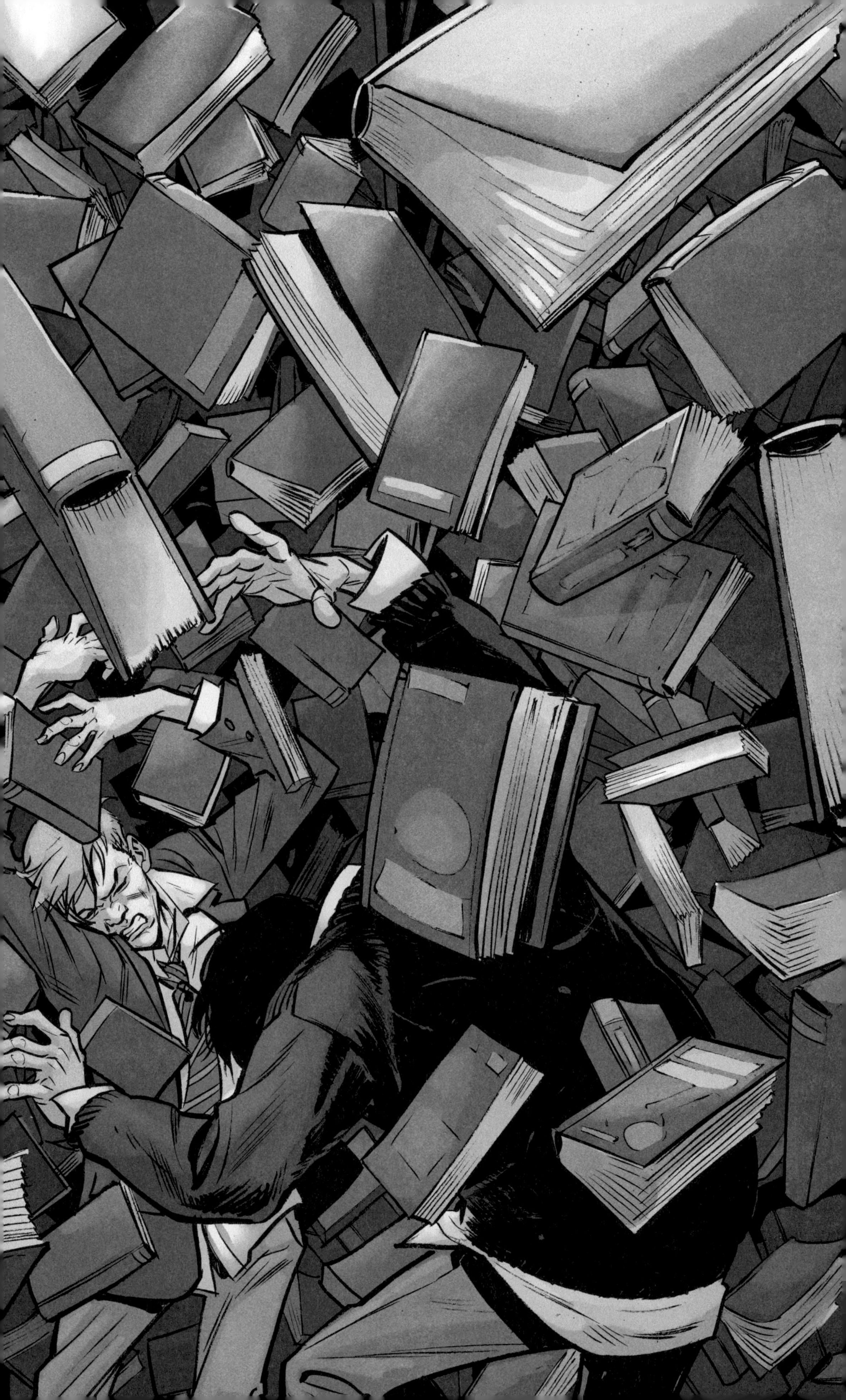

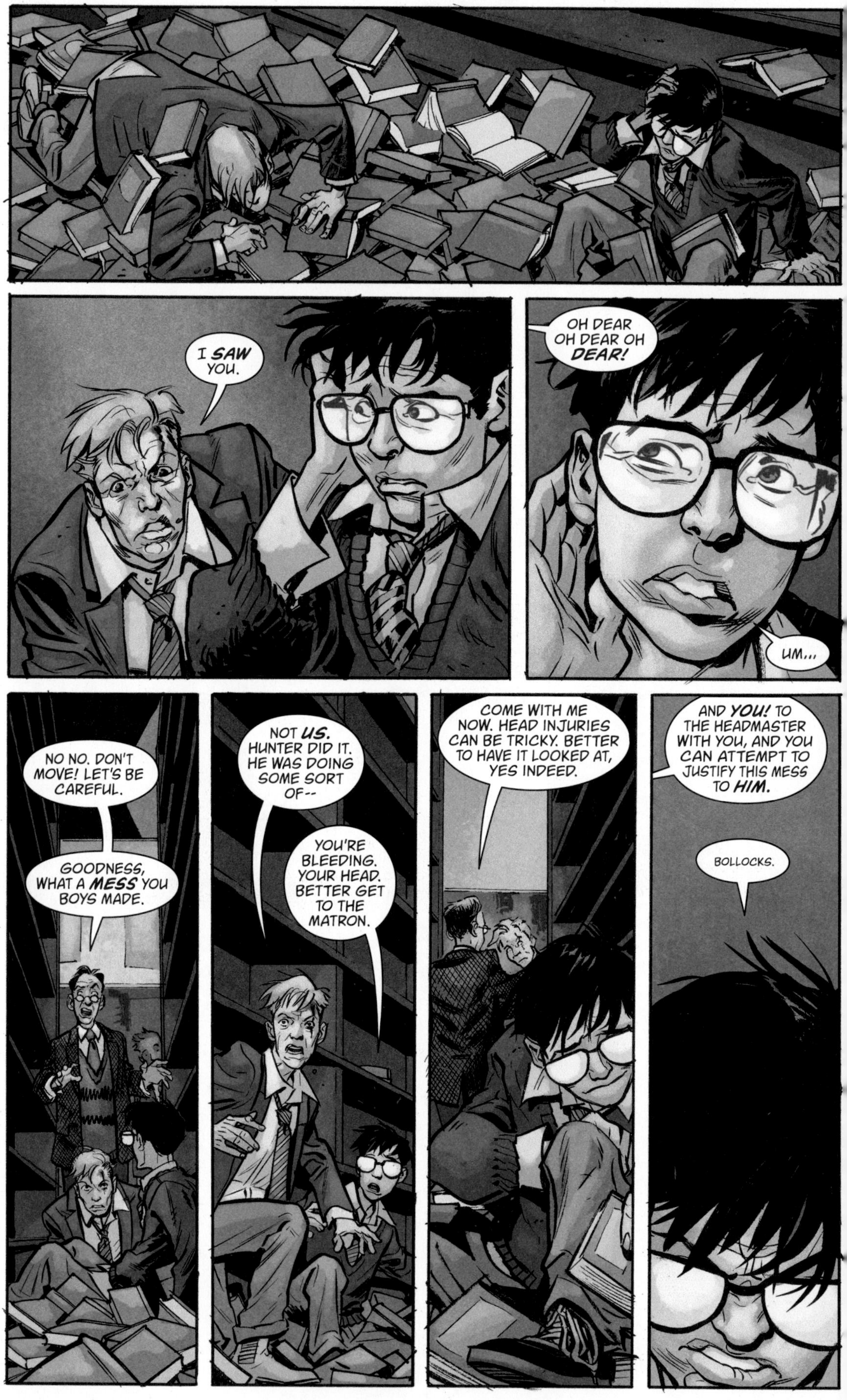

I SAW YOU.
OH DEAR OH DEAR OH DEAR!
UM...
NO NO. DON'T MOVE! LET'S BE CAREFUL.
GOODNESS, WHAT A MESS YOU BOYS MADE.
NOT US. HUNTER DID IT. HE WAS DOING SOME SORT OF--
YOU'RE BLEEDING. YOUR HEAD. BETTER GET TO THE MATRON.
COME WITH ME NOW. HEAD INJURIES CAN BE TRICKY. BETTER TO HAVE IT LOOKED AT, YES INDEED.
AND YOU! TO THE HEADMASTER WITH YOU, AND YOU CAN ATTEMPT TO JUSTIFY THIS MESS TO HIM.
BOLLOCKS.

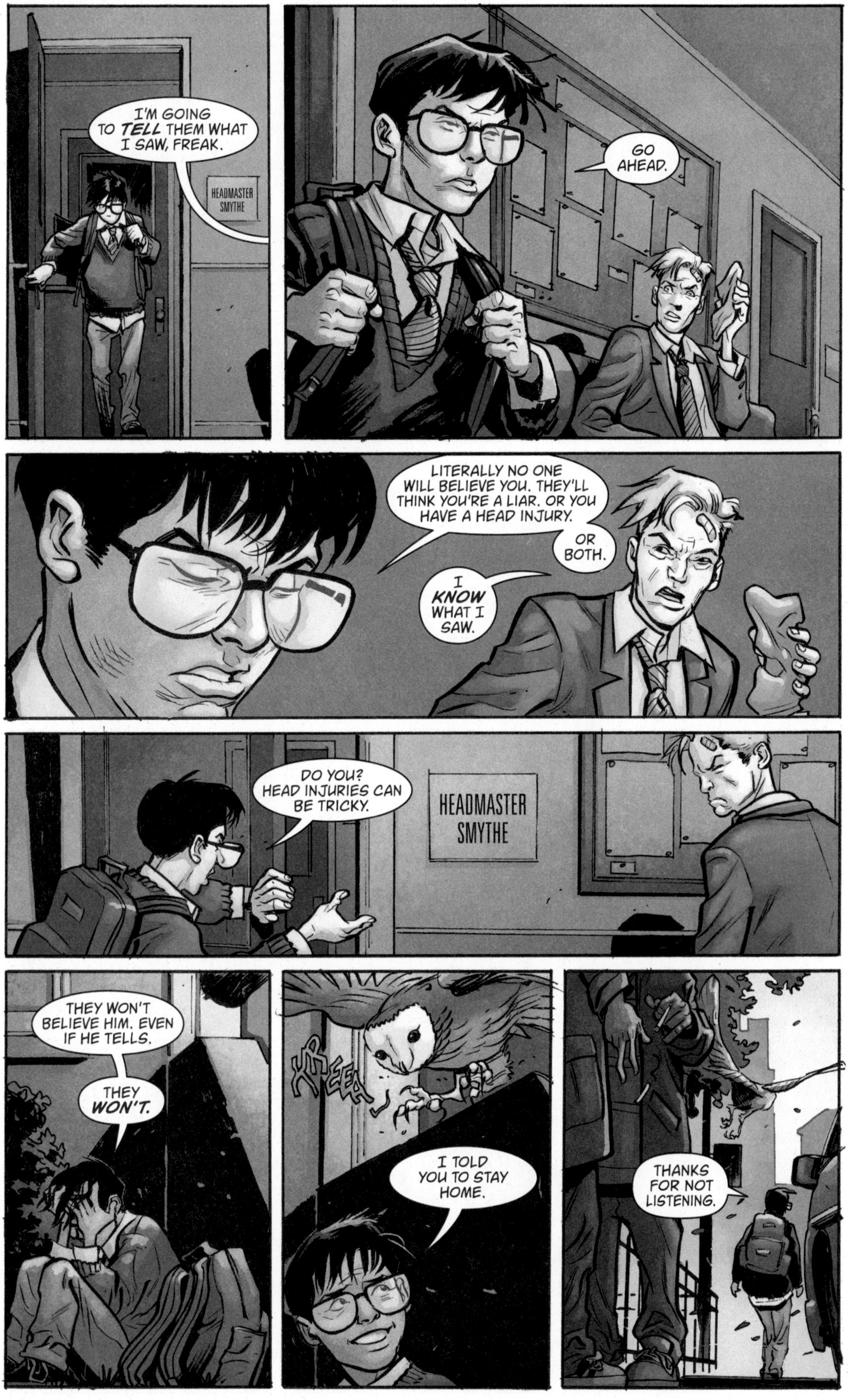
I'M GOING TO TELL THEM WHAT I SAW, FREAK.
HEADMASTER SMYTHE
GO AHEAD.
LITERALLY NO ONE WILL BELIEVE YOU. THEY'LL THINK YOU'RE A LIAR. OR YOU HAVE A HEAD INJURY.
OR BOTH.
I KNOW WHAT I SAW.
DO YOU? HEAD INJURIES CAN BE TRICKY.
HEADMASTER SMYTHE
THEY WON'T BELIEVE HIM. EVEN IF HE TELLS.
THEY WON'T.
KREEEA
I TOLD YOU TO STAY HOME.
THANKS FOR NOT LISTENING.

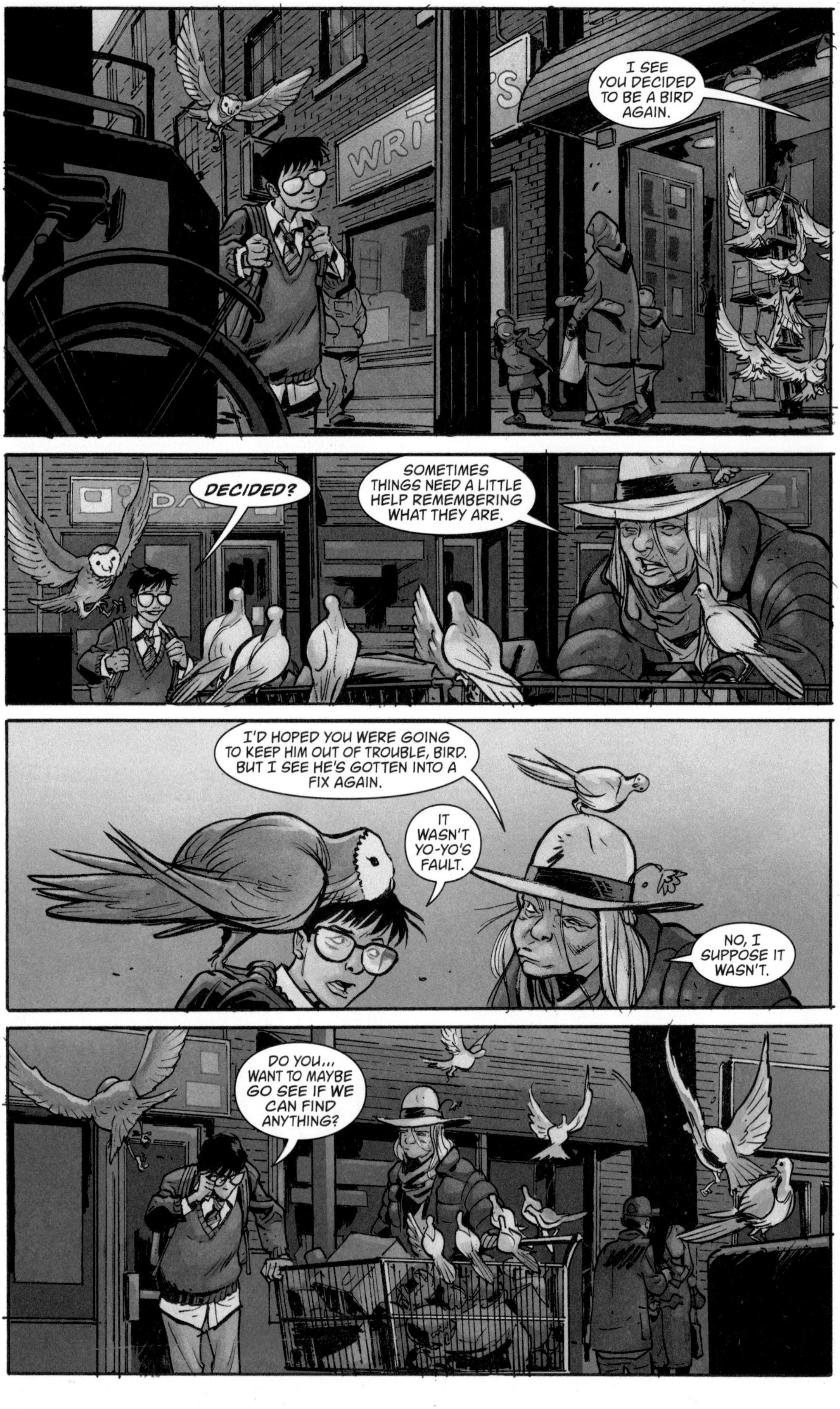

I SEE YOU DECIDED TO BE A BIRD AGAIN.
DECIDED?
SOMETIMES THINGS NEED A LITTLE HELP REMEMBERING WHAT THEY ARE.
I'D HOPED YOU WERE GOING TO KEEP HIM OUT OF TROUBLE, BIRD. BUT I SEE HE'S GOTTEN INTO A FIX AGAIN.
IT WASN'T YO-YO'S FAULT.
NO, I SUPPOSE IT WASN'T.
DO YOU... WANT TO MAYBE GO SEE IF WE CAN FIND ANYTHING?

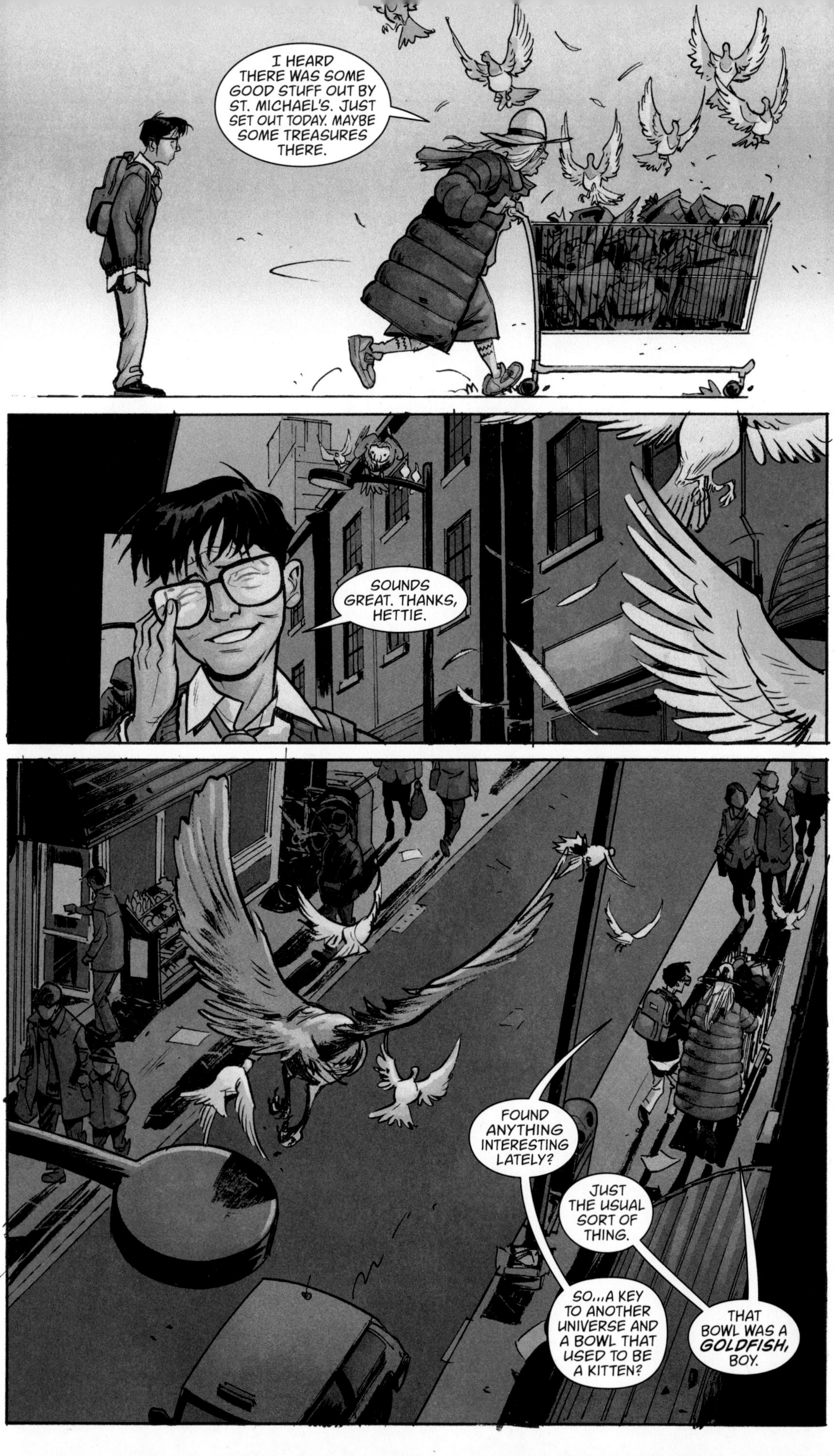
I HEARD THERE WAS SOME GOOD STUFF OUT BY ST. MICHAEL'S. JUST SET OUT TODAY. MAYBE SOME TREASURES THERE.
SOUNDS GREAT. THANKS, HETTIE.
FOUND ANYTHING INTERESTING LATELY?
JUST THE USUAL SORT OF THING.
SO...A KEY TO ANOTHER UNIVERSE AND A BOWL THAT USED TO BE A KITTEN?
THAT BOWL WAS A **GOLDFISH,** BOY.

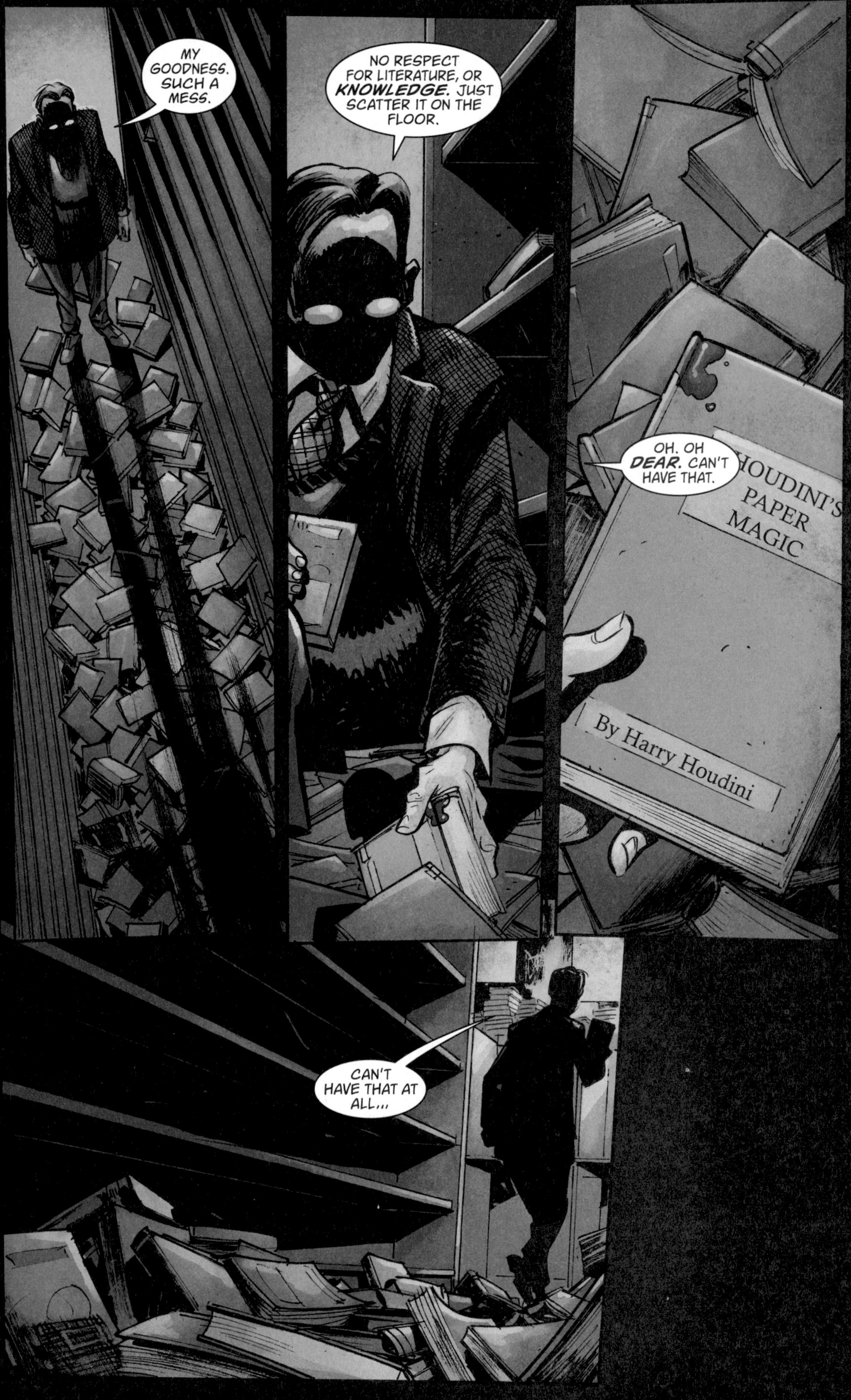
MY GOODNESS. SUCH A MESS.
NO RESPECT FOR LITERATURE, OR KNOWLEDGE. JUST SCATTER IT ON THE FLOOR.
OH. OH DEAR. CAN'T HAVE THAT.
HOUDINI'S PAPER MAGIC
By Harry Houdini
CAN'T HAVE THAT AT ALL...

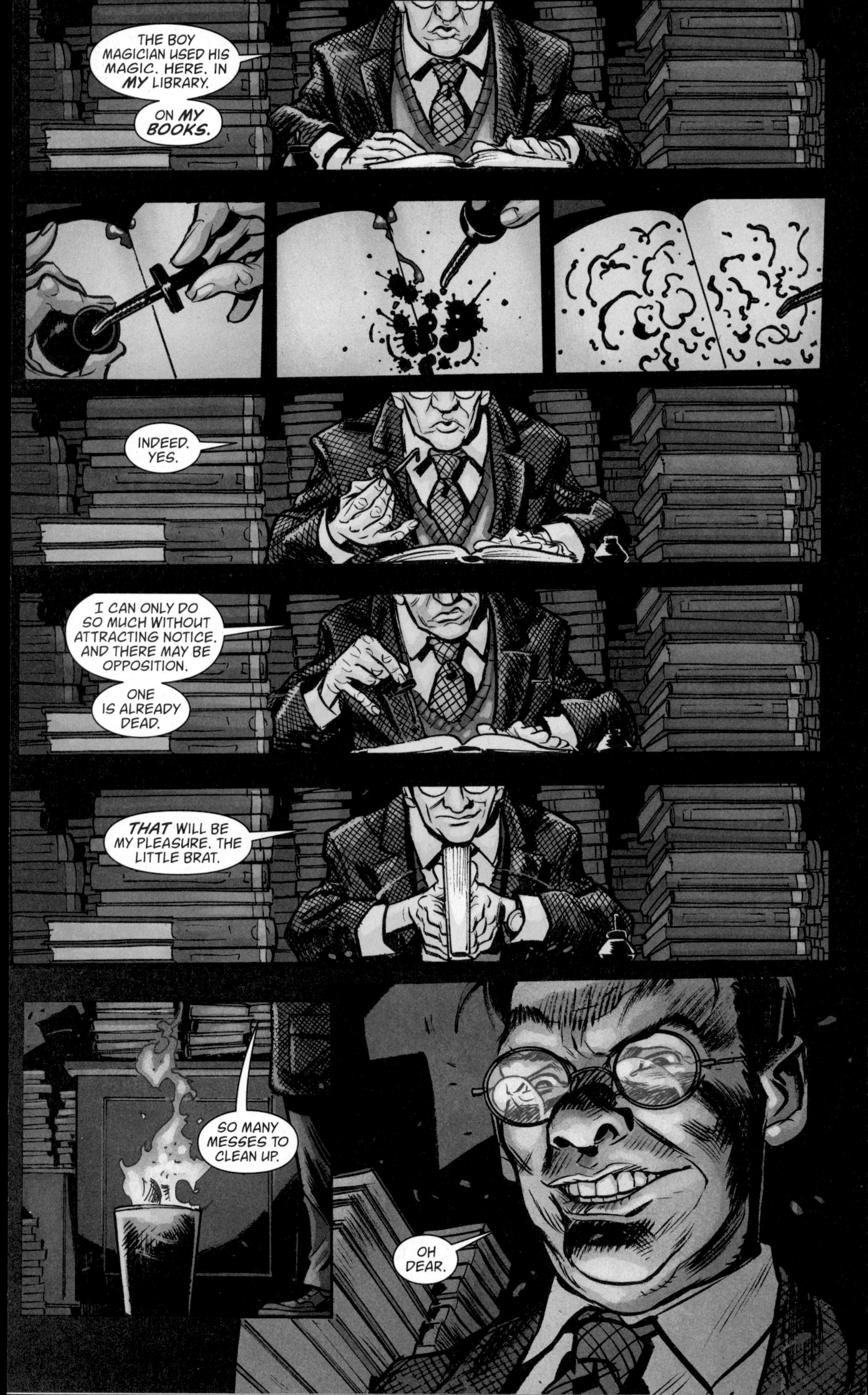
THE BOY MAGICIAN USED HIS MAGIC. HERE. IN *MY* LIBRARY.
ON *MY* *BOOKS*.
INDEED. YES.
I CAN ONLY DO SO MUCH WITHOUT ATTRACTING NOTICE. AND THERE MAY BE OPPOSITION.
ONE IS ALREADY DEAD.
THAT WILL BE MY PLEASURE. THE LITTLE BRAT.
SO MANY MESSES TO CLEAN UP.
OH DEAR.

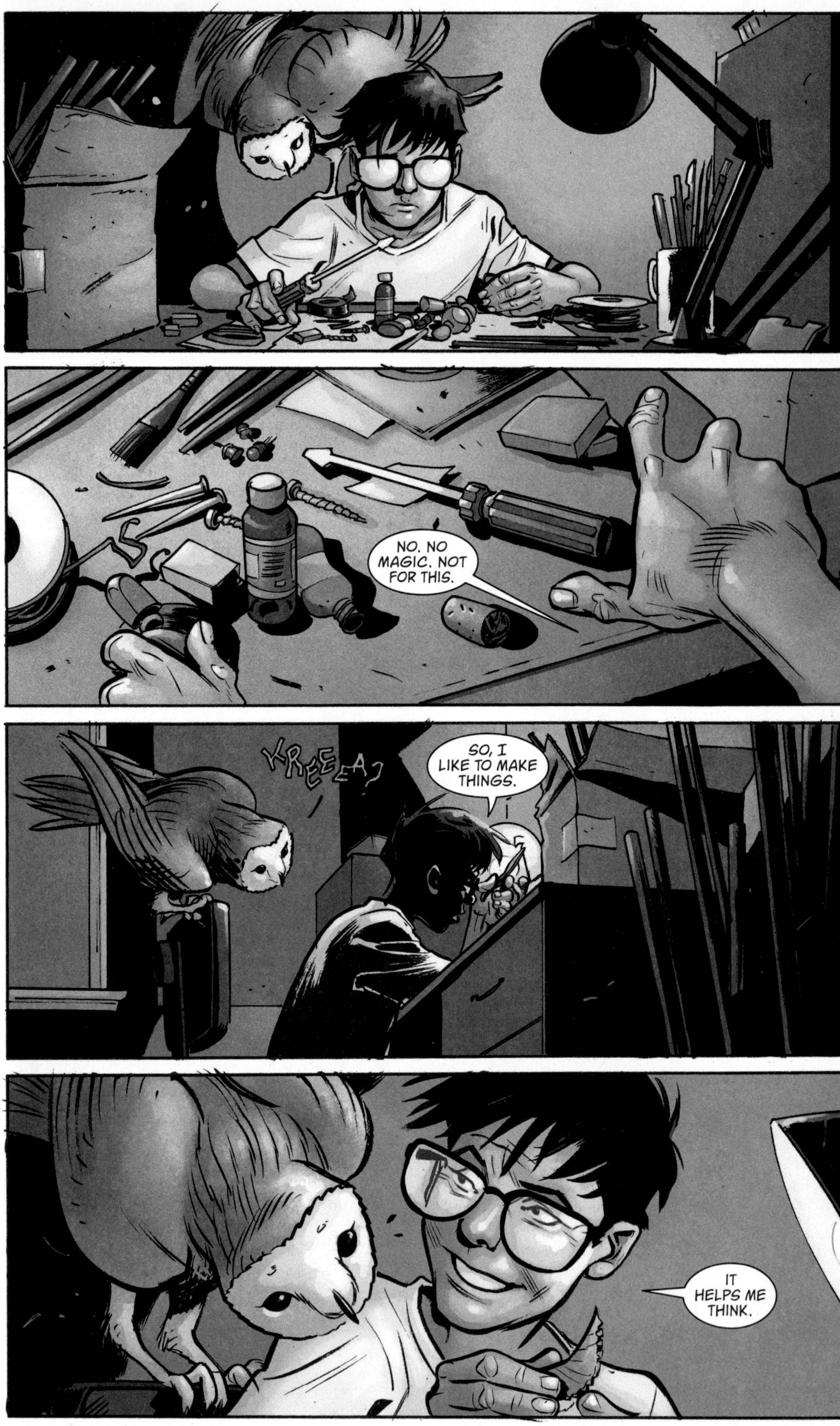
NO. NO MAGIC. NOT FOR THIS.
KREEEAA
SO, I LIKE TO MAKE THINGS.
IT HELPS ME THINK.

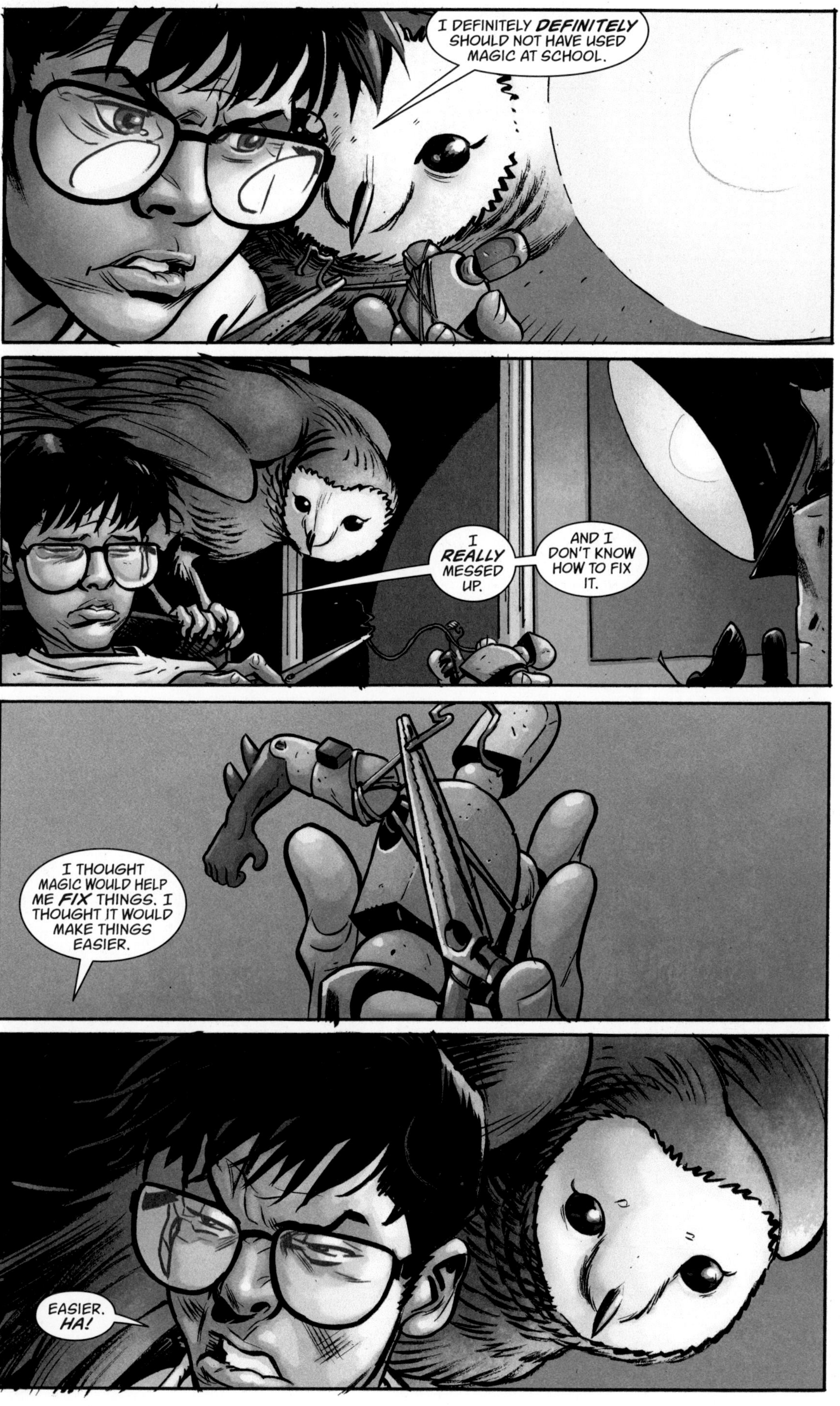
I DEFINITELY DEFINITELY SHOULD NOT HAVE USED MAGIC AT SCHOOL.
I REALLY MESSED UP.
AND I DON'T KNOW HOW TO FIX IT.
I THOUGHT MAGIC WOULD HELP ME FIX THINGS. I THOUGHT IT WOULD MAKE THINGS EASIER.
EASIER. HA!

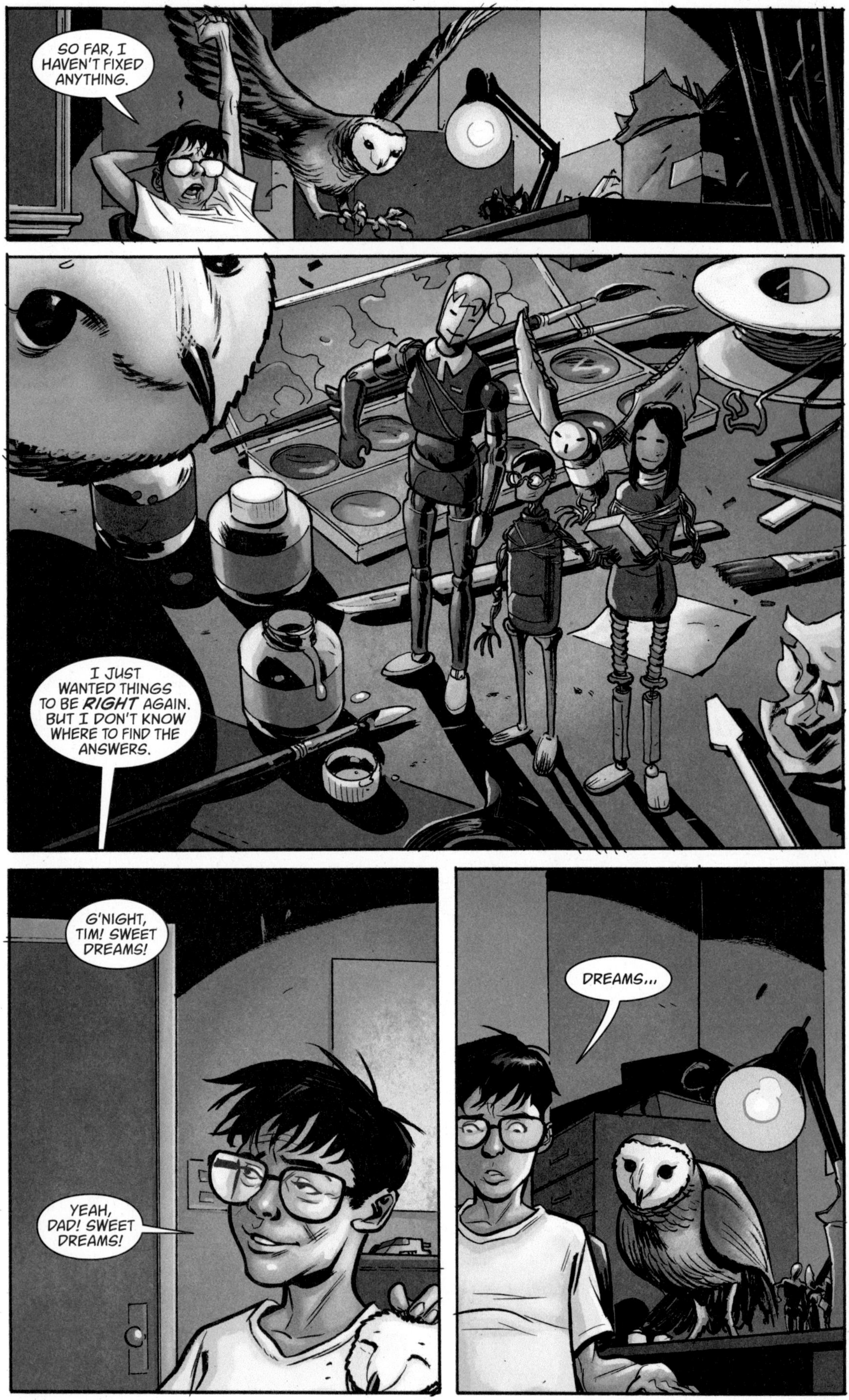
SO FAR, I HAVEN'T FIXED ANYTHING.
I JUST WANTED THINGS TO BE RIGHT AGAIN. BUT I DON'T KNOW WHERE TO FIND THE ANSWERS.
G'NIGHT, TIM! SWEET DREAMS!
YEAH, DAD! SWEET DREAMS!
DREAMS...

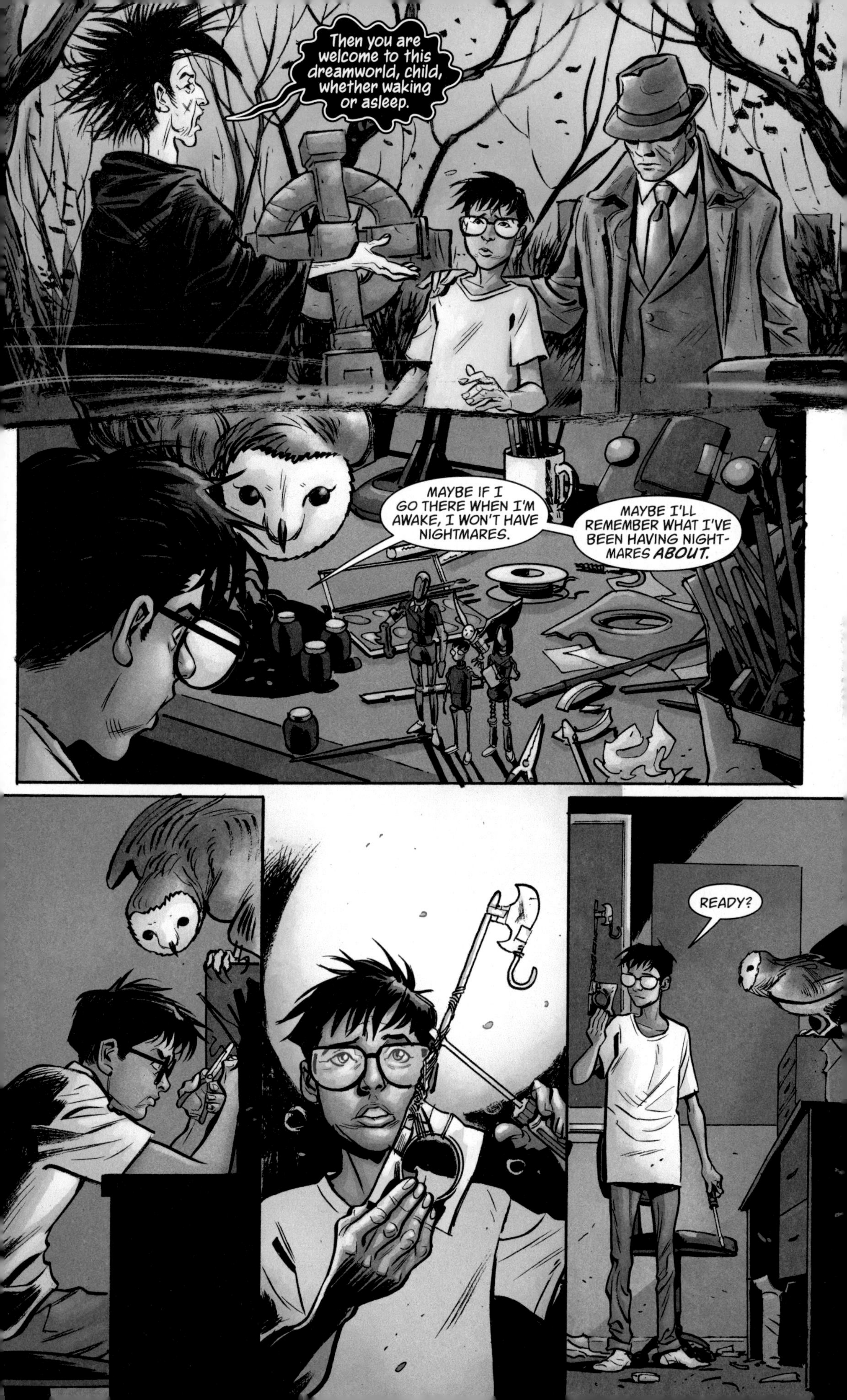
Then you are welcome to this dreamworld, child, whether waking or asleep.
MAYBE IF I GO THERE WHEN I'M AWAKE, I WON'T HAVE NIGHTMARES.
MAYBE I'LL REMEMBER WHAT I'VE BEEN HAVING NIGHT-MARES ***ABOUT.***
READY?

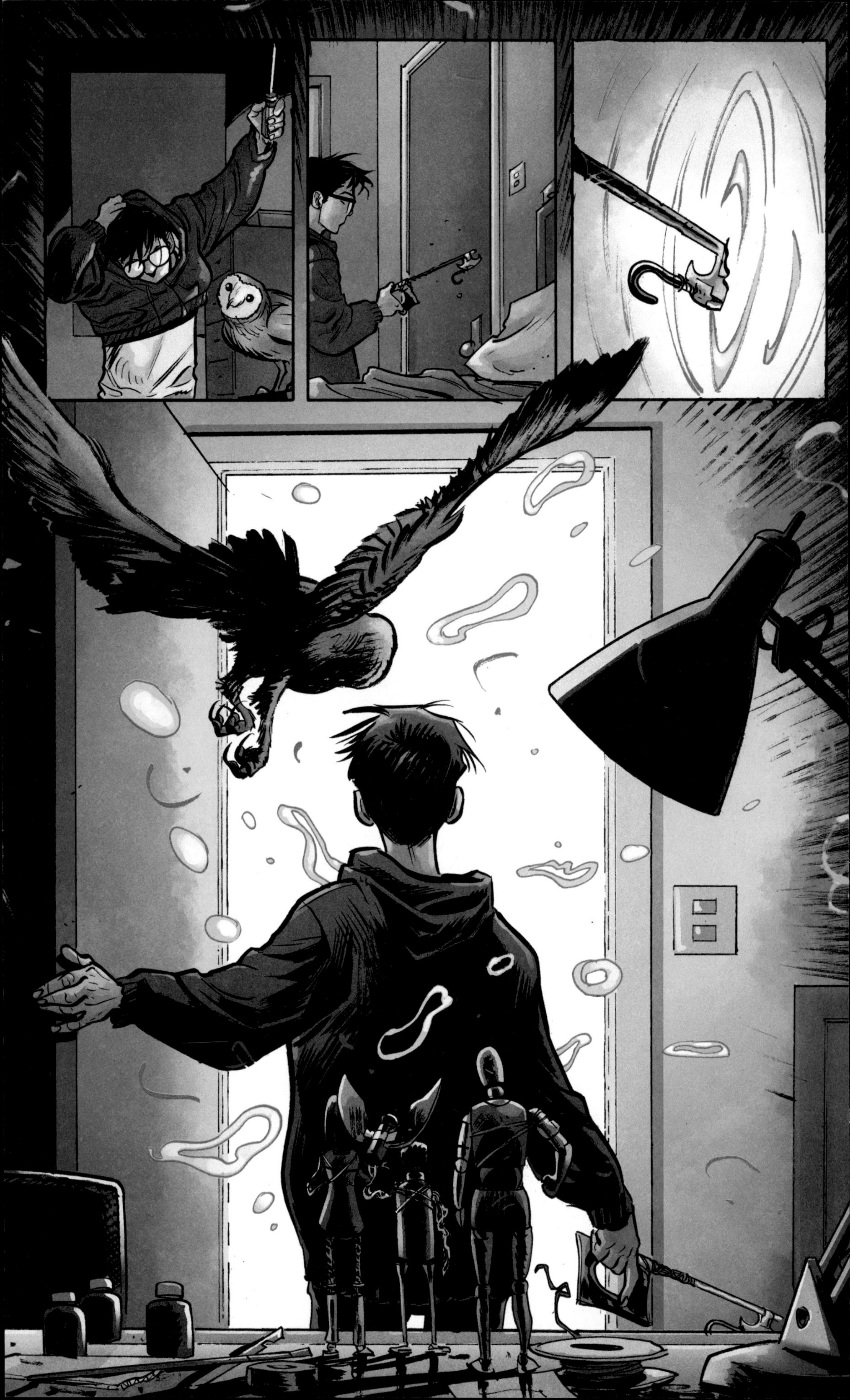

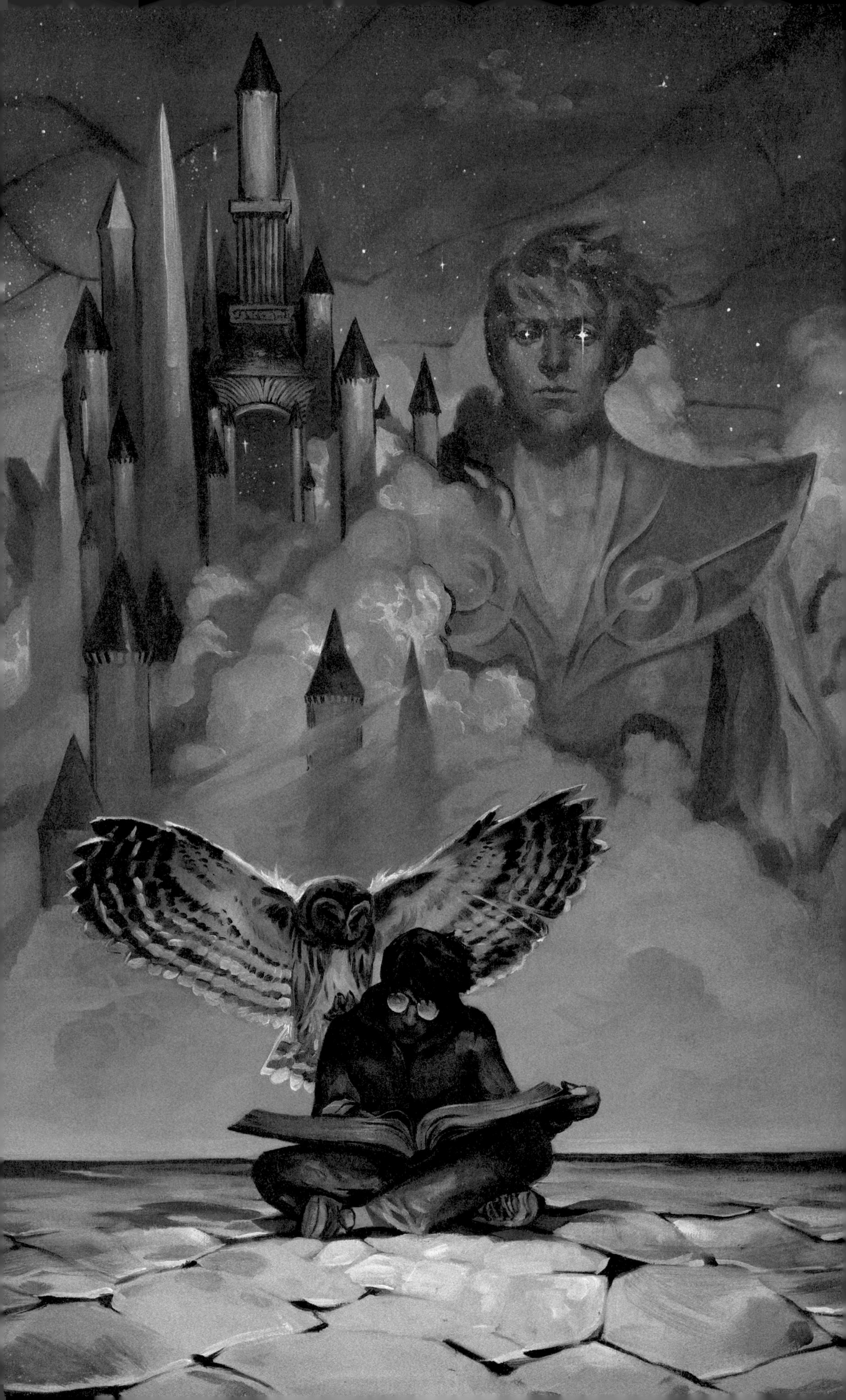

BOOKS OF MAGIC

A Twist in the Narrative

WRITTEN BY
Kat Howard

ILLUSTRATED BY
Tom Fowler

COLORS BY
Jordan Boyd

LETTERS BY
Todd Klein

COVER ART BY
Kai Carpenter

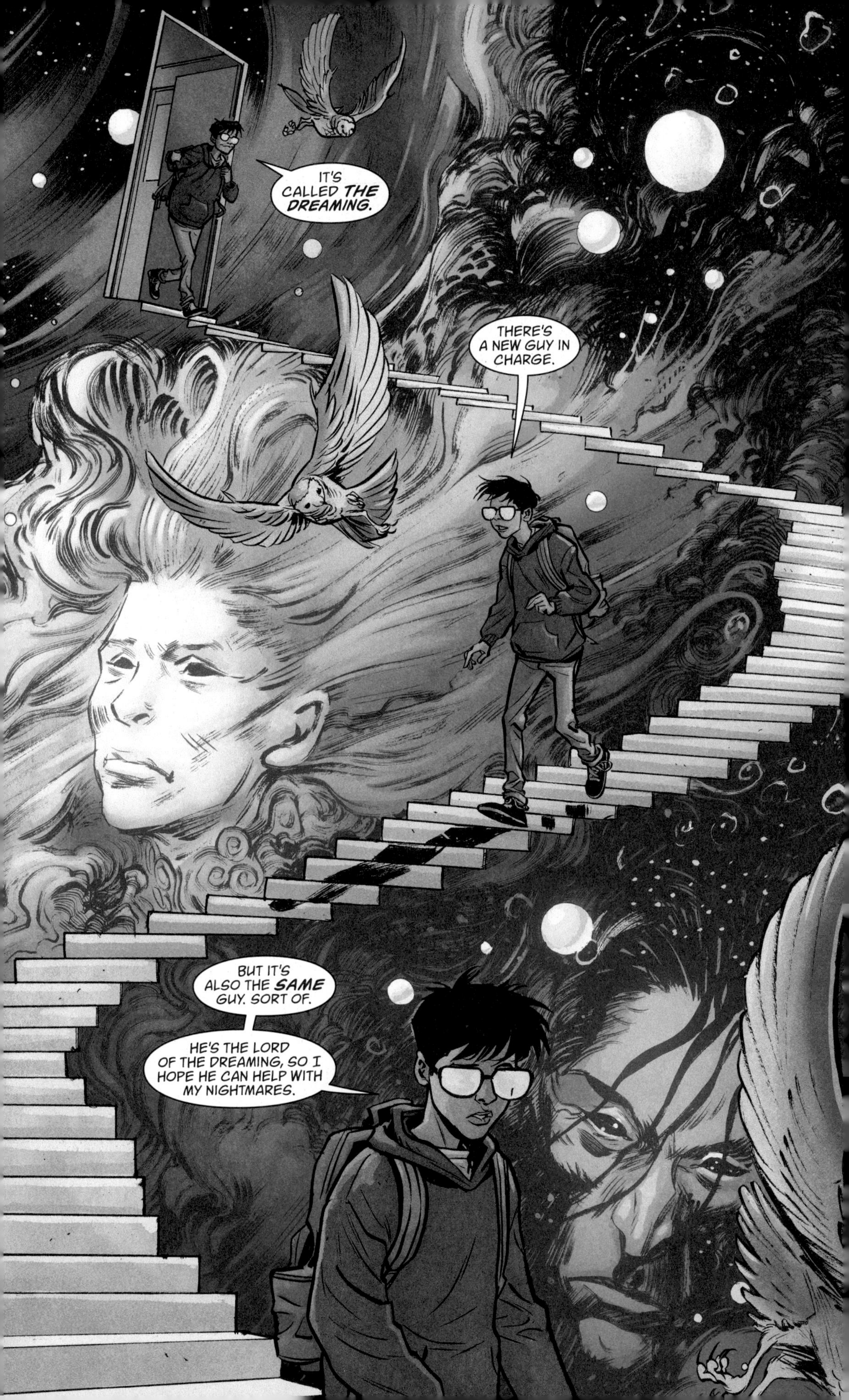
IT'S CALLED *THE DREAMING.*
THERE'S A NEW GUY IN CHARGE.
BUT IT'S ALSO THE *SAME* GUY. SORT OF.
HE'S THE LORD OF THE DREAMING, SO I HOPE HE CAN HELP WITH MY NIGHTMARES.

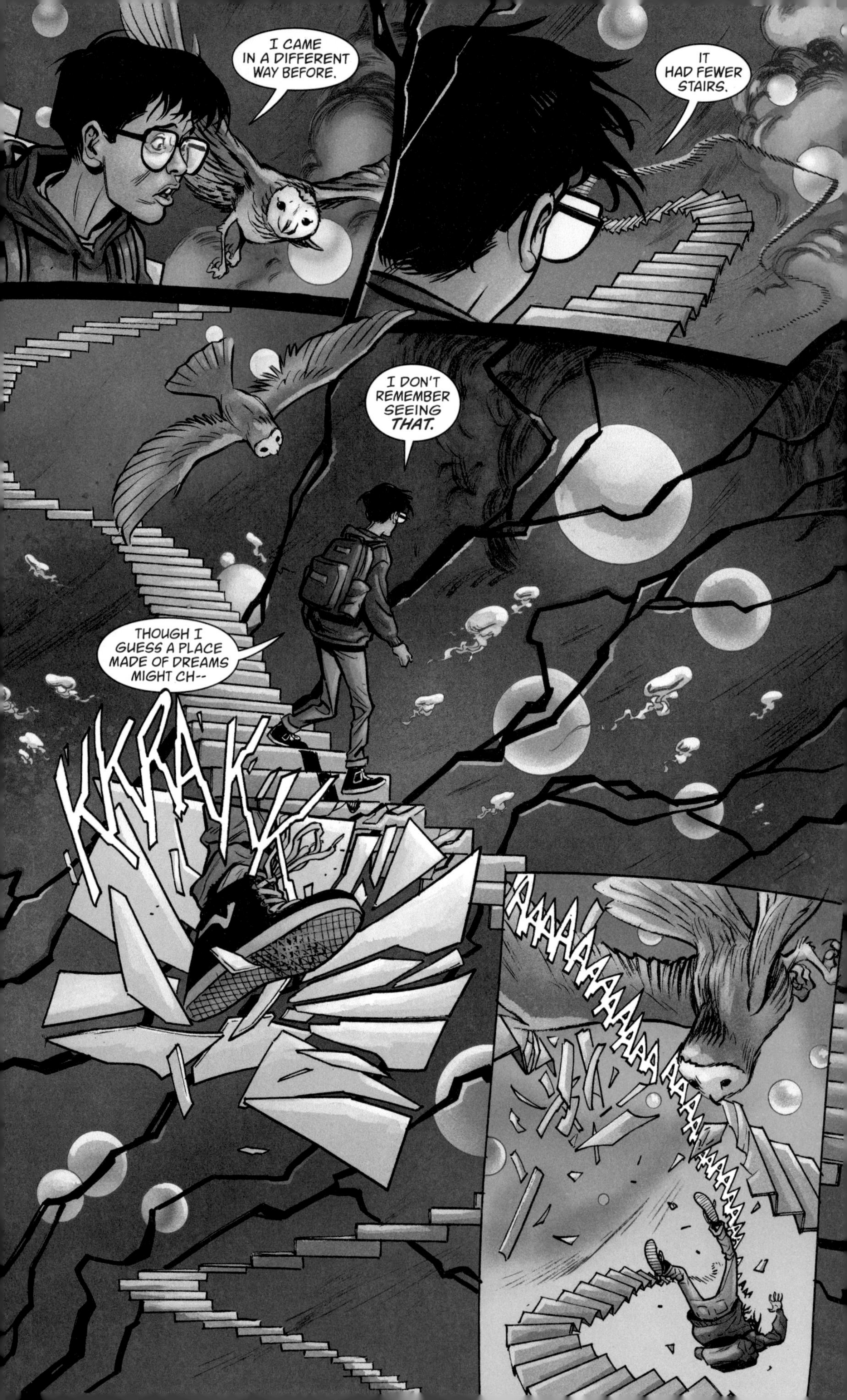

I CAME IN A DIFFERENT WAY BEFORE.
IT HAD FEWER STAIRS.
I DON'T REMEMBER SEEING *THAT.*
THOUGH I GUESS A PLACE MADE OF DREAMS MIGHT CH--
KKRAKK
AAAAAAAAAAAAAAAAAAAAAAAAAAAAAAAAAAAAAAAAAAAAAAAAAAAAAAA

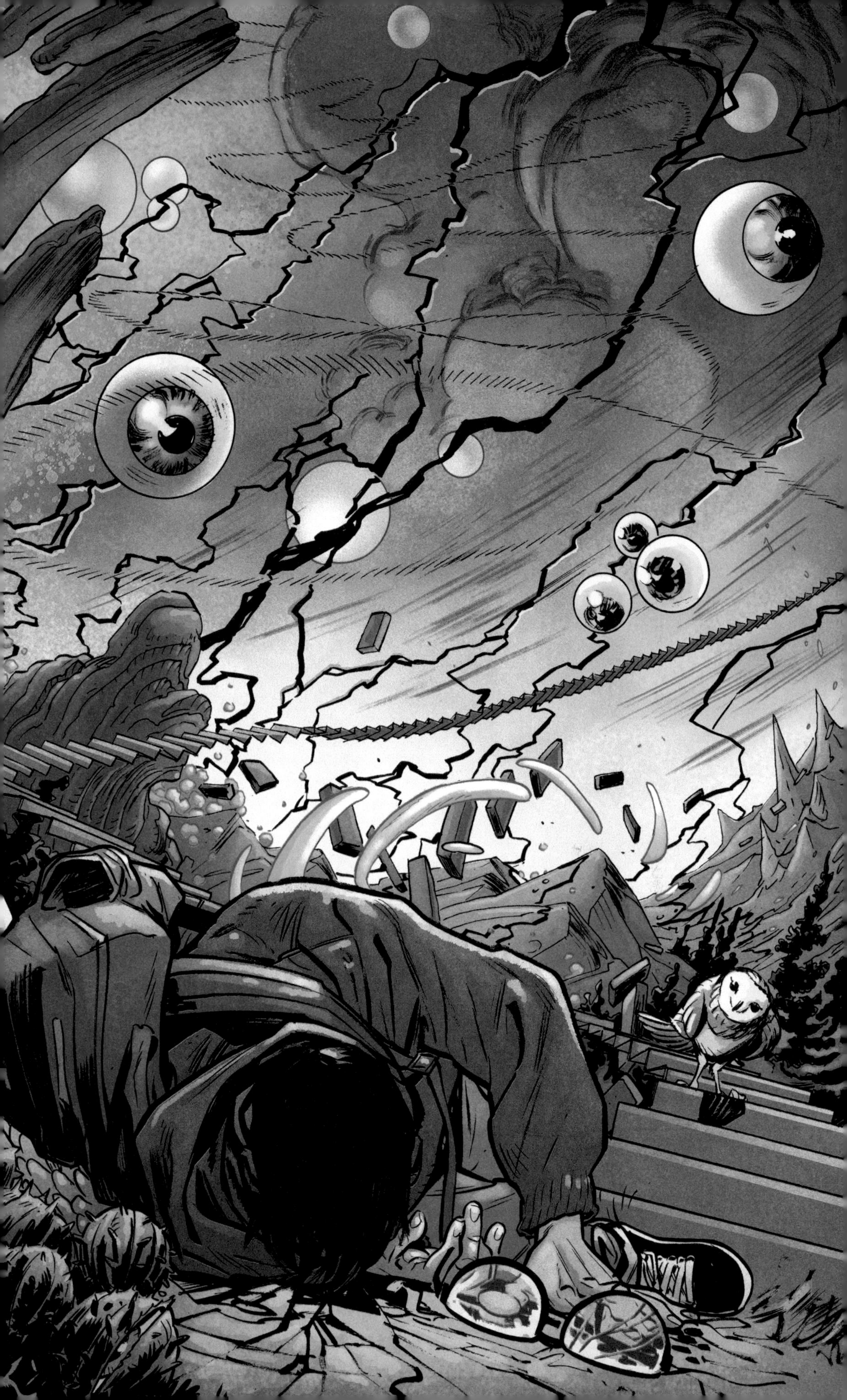

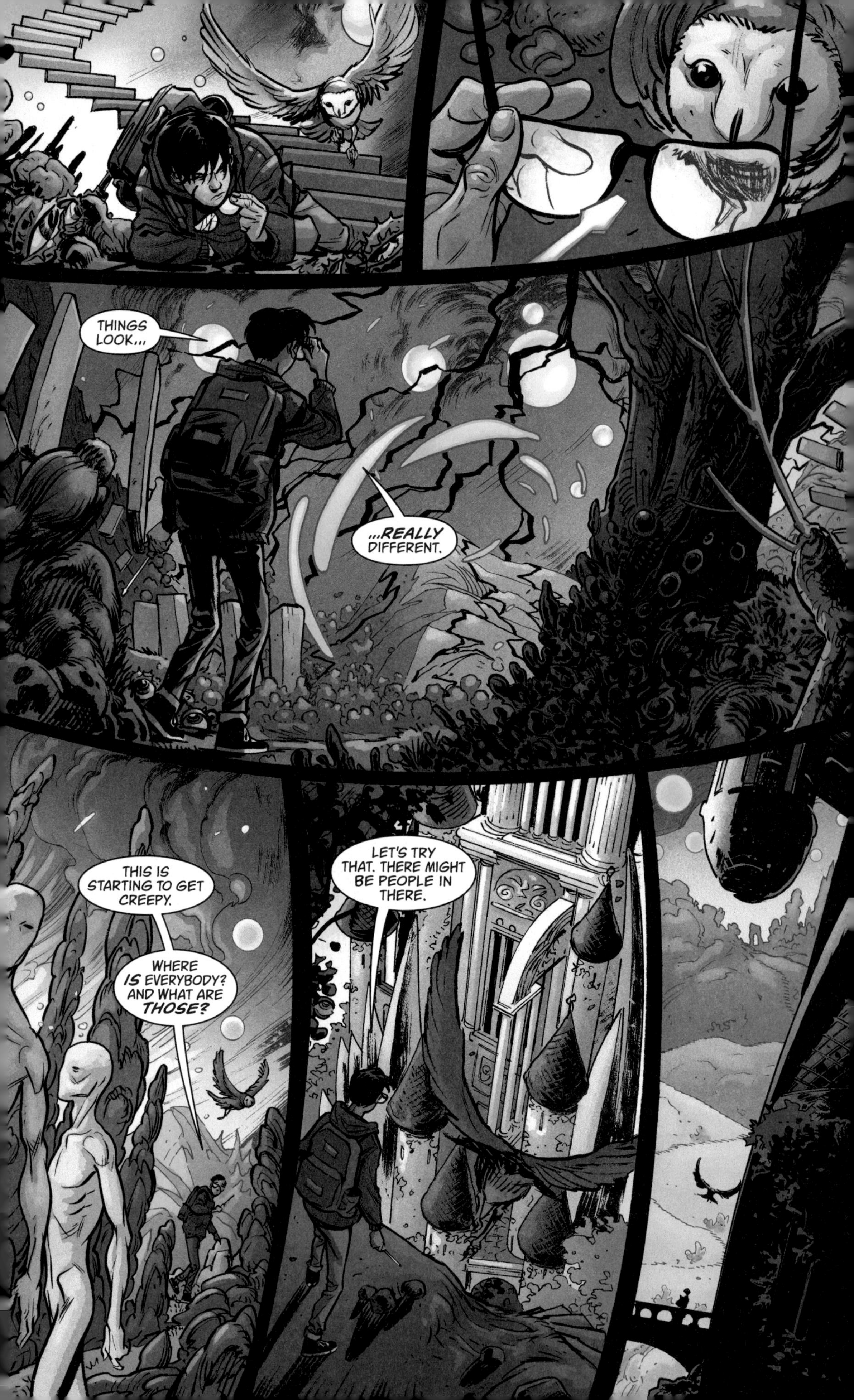
THINGS LOOK...
...REALLY DIFFERENT.
THIS IS STARTING TO GET CREEPY.
WHERE IS EVERYBODY? AND WHAT ARE THOSE?
LET'S TRY THAT. THERE MIGHT BE PEOPLE IN THERE.

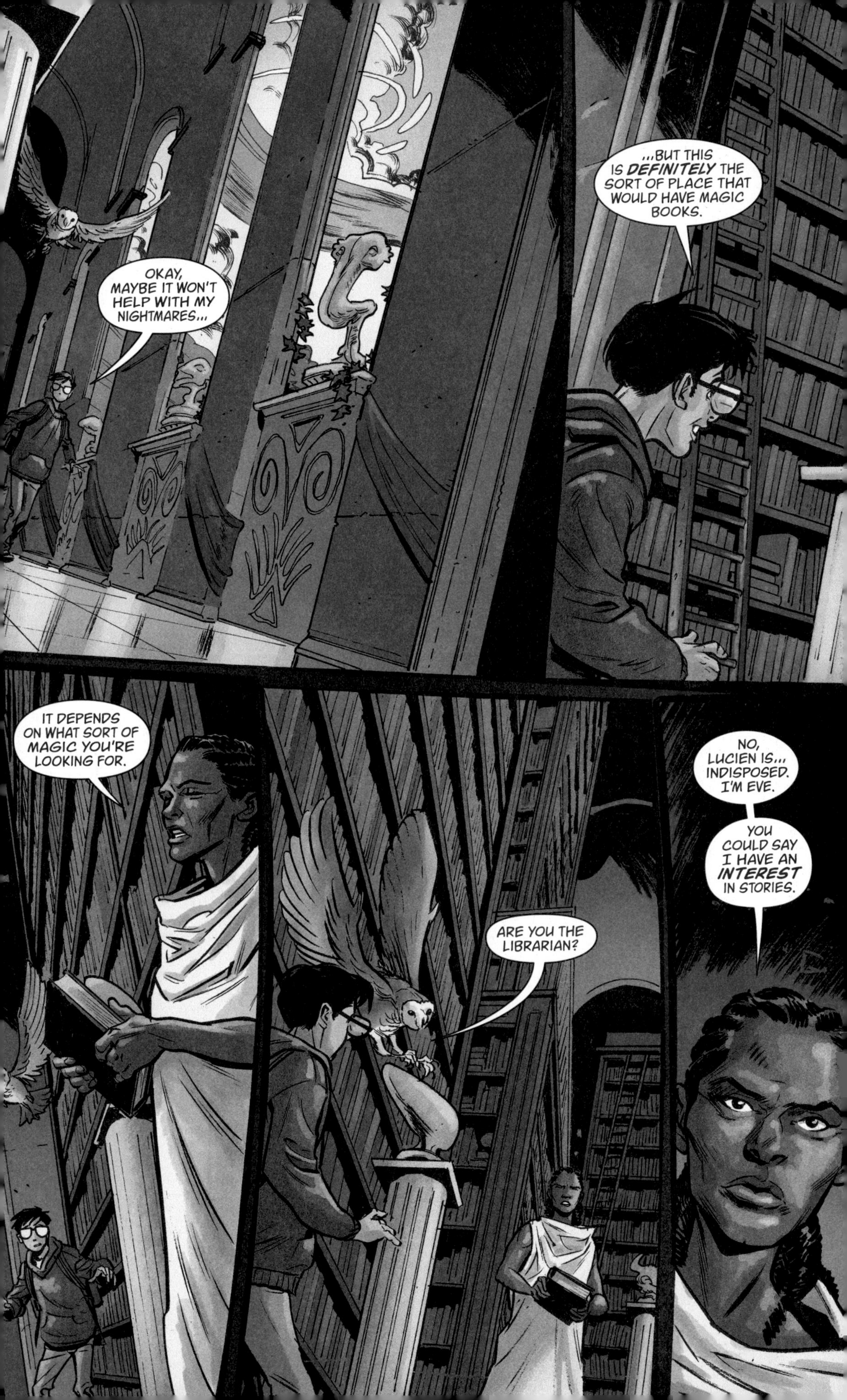
OKAY, MAYBE IT WON'T HELP WITH MY NIGHTMARES...
...BUT THIS IS DEFINITELY THE SORT OF PLACE THAT WOULD HAVE MAGIC BOOKS.
IT DEPENDS ON WHAT SORT OF MAGIC YOU'RE LOOKING FOR.
ARE YOU THE LIBRARIAN?
NO, LUCIEN IS... INDISPOSED. I'M EVE.
YOU COULD SAY I HAVE AN INTEREST IN STORIES.

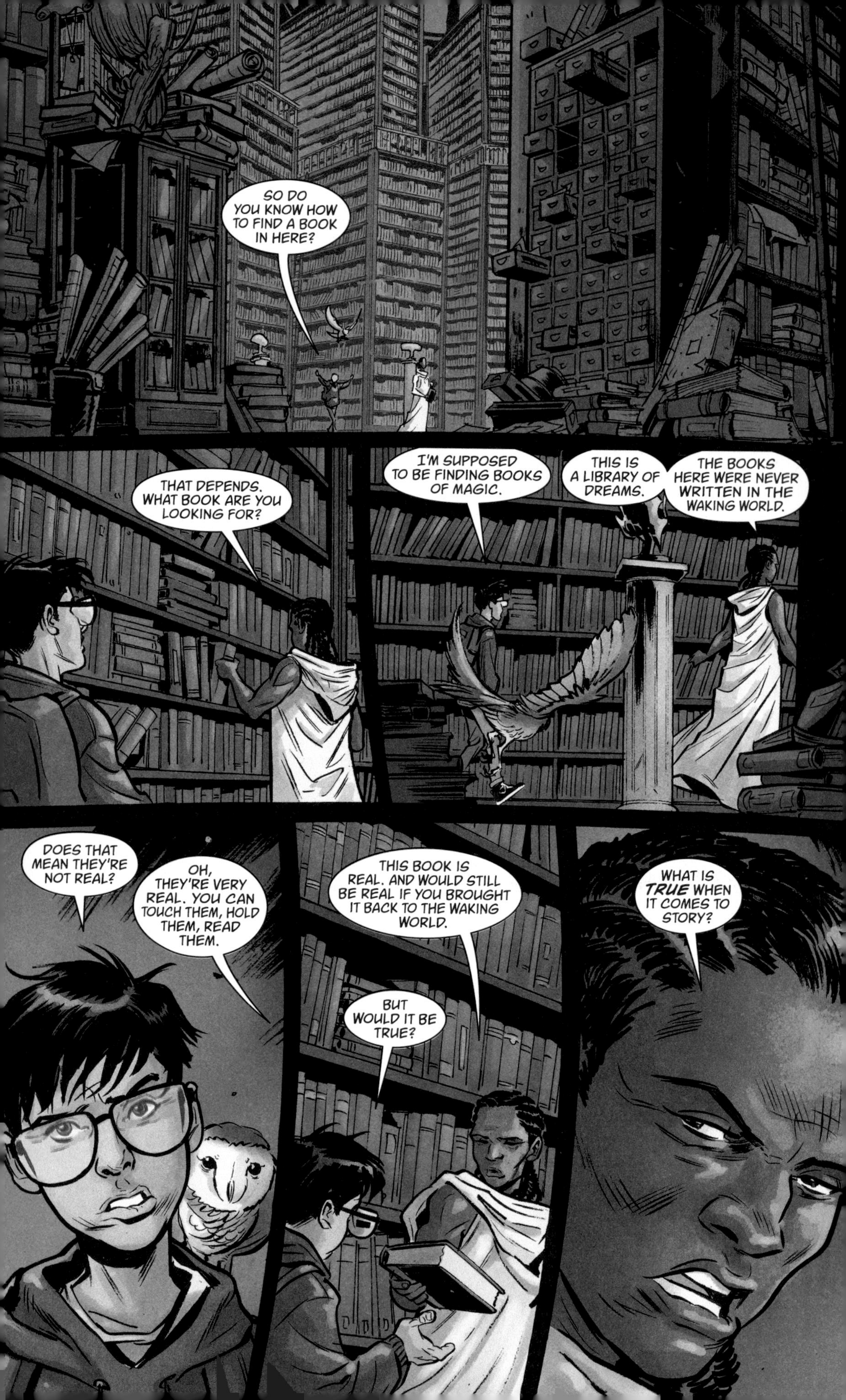
SO DO YOU KNOW HOW TO FIND A BOOK IN HERE?
THAT DEPENDS. WHAT BOOK ARE YOU LOOKING FOR?
I'M SUPPOSED TO BE FINDING BOOKS OF MAGIC.
THIS IS A LIBRARY OF DREAMS.
THE BOOKS HERE WERE NEVER WRITTEN IN THE WAKING WORLD.
DOES THAT MEAN THEY'RE NOT REAL?
OH, THEY'RE VERY REAL. YOU CAN TOUCH THEM, HOLD THEM, READ THEM.
THIS BOOK IS REAL. AND WOULD STILL BE REAL IF YOU BROUGHT IT BACK TO THE WAKING WORLD.
BUT WOULD IT BE TRUE?
WHAT IS ***TRUE*** WHEN IT COMES TO STORY?

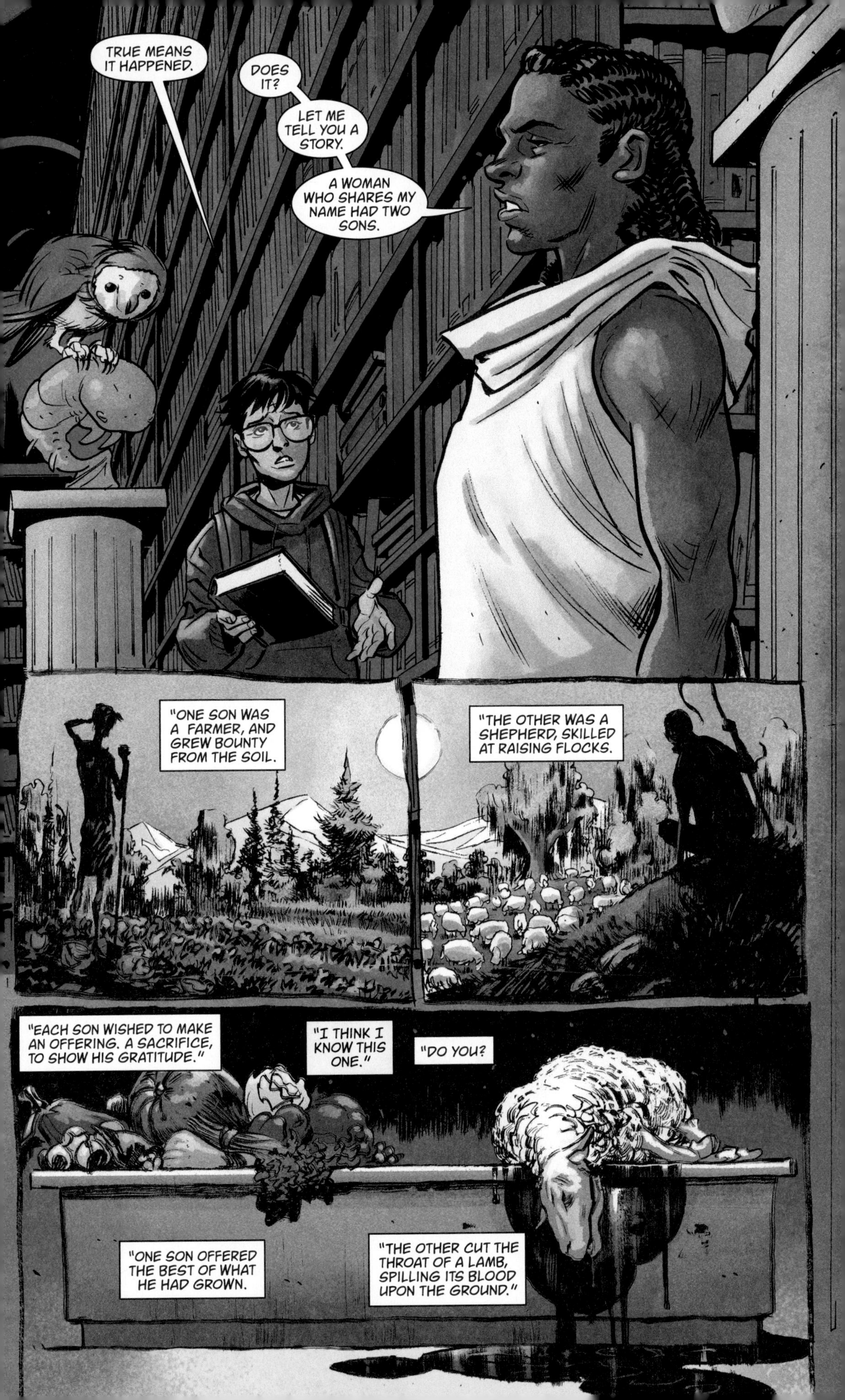
TRUE MEANS IT HAPPENED.
DOES IT?
LET ME TELL YOU A STORY.
A WOMAN WHO SHARES MY NAME HAD TWO SONS.
"ONE SON WAS A FARMER, AND GREW BOUNTY FROM THE SOIL.
"THE OTHER WAS A SHEPHERD, SKILLED AT RAISING FLOCKS.
"EACH SON WISHED TO MAKE AN OFFERING. A SACRIFICE, TO SHOW HIS GRATITUDE."
"I THINK I KNOW THIS ONE."
"DO YOU?
"ONE SON OFFERED THE BEST OF WHAT HE HAD GROWN.
"THE OTHER CUT THE THROAT OF A LAMB, SPILLING ITS BLOOD UPON THE GROUND."

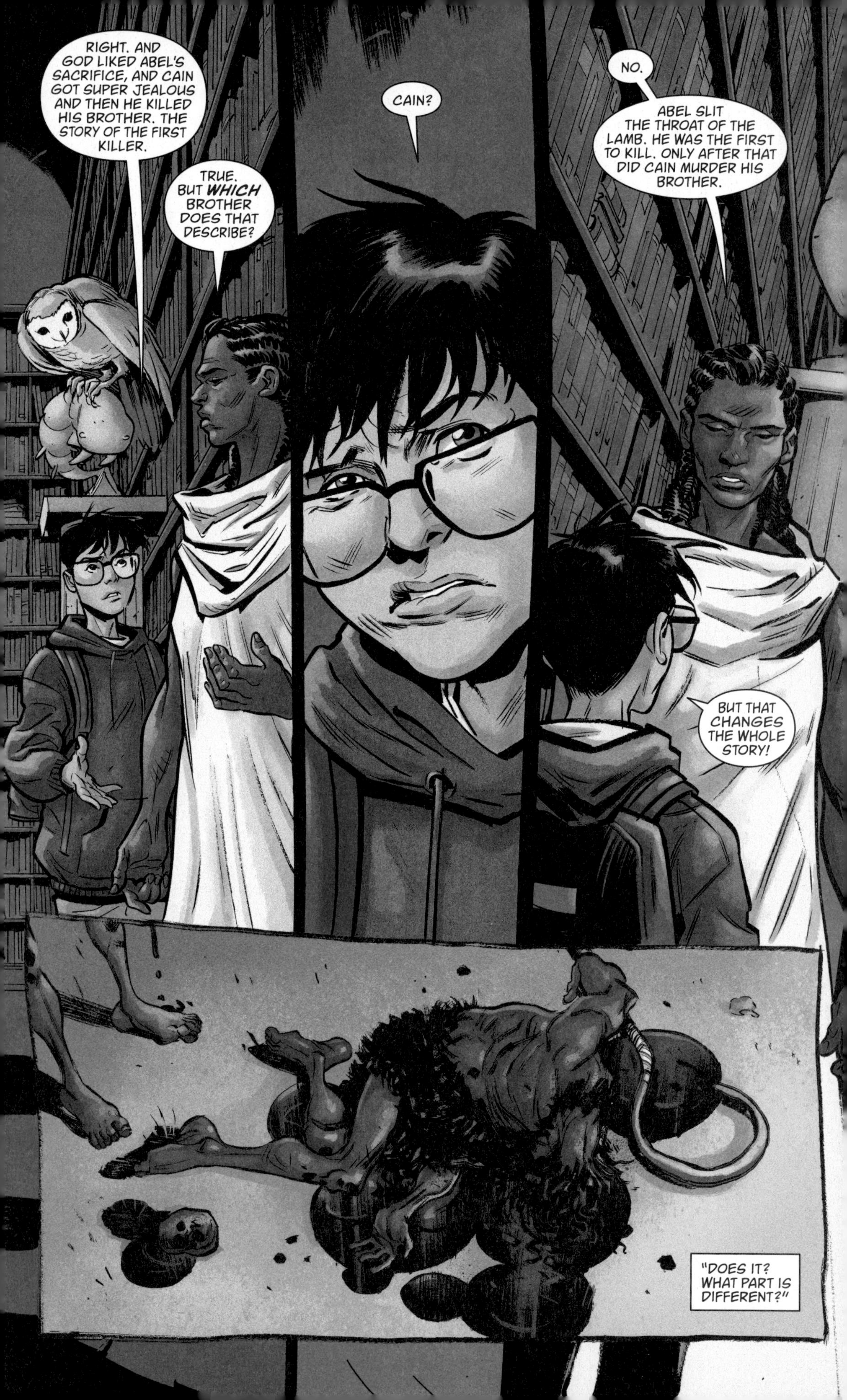
RIGHT. AND GOD LIKED ABEL'S SACRIFICE, AND CAIN GOT SUPER JEALOUS AND THEN HE KILLED HIS BROTHER. THE STORY OF THE FIRST KILLER.
TRUE. BUT WHICH BROTHER DOES THAT DESCRIBE?
CAIN?
NO.
ABEL SLIT THE THROAT OF THE LAMB. HE WAS THE FIRST TO KILL. ONLY AFTER THAT DID CAIN MURDER HIS BROTHER.
BUT THAT CHANGES THE WHOLE STORY!
"DOES IT? WHAT PART IS DIFFERENT?"

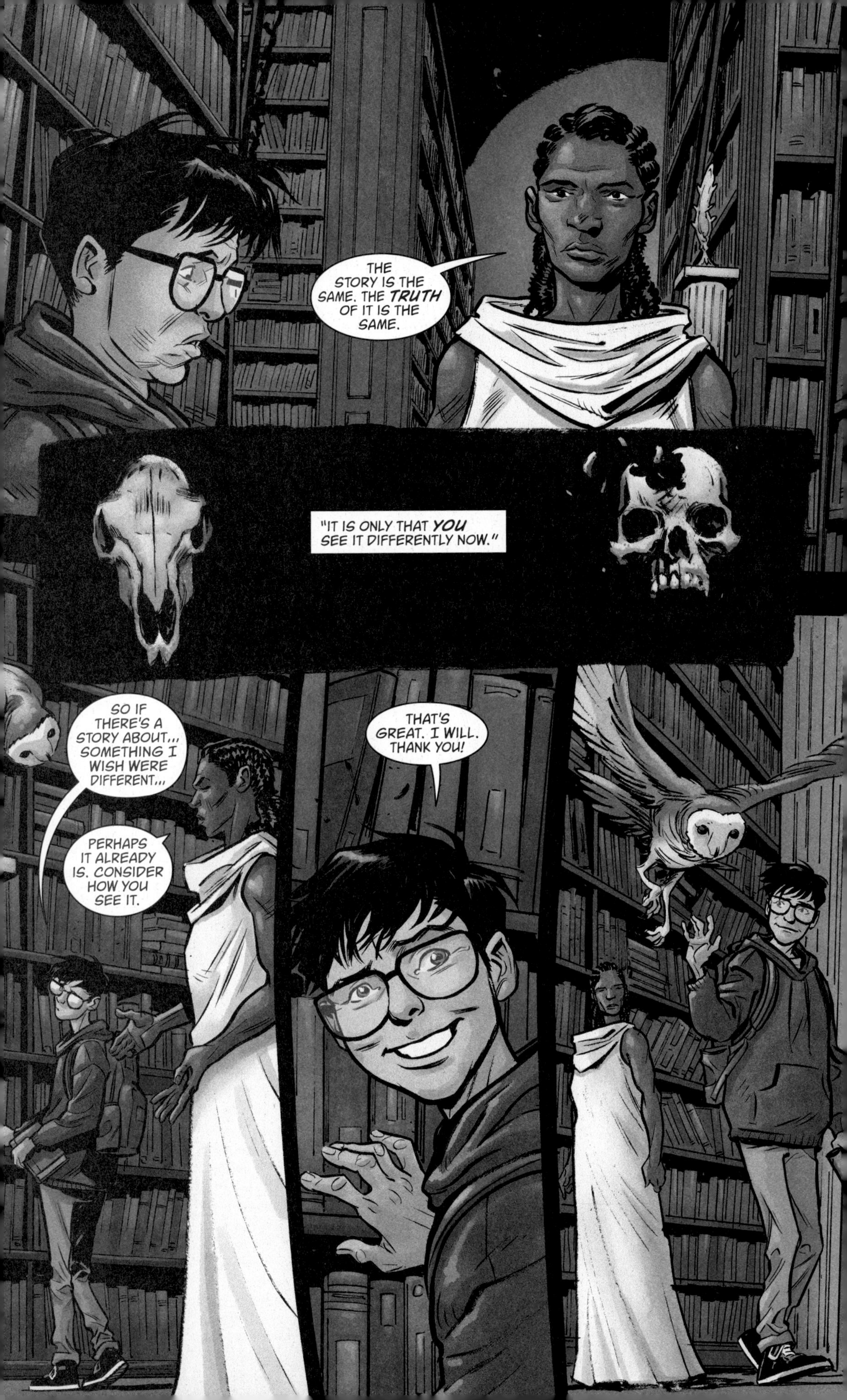
THE STORY IS THE SAME. THE TRUTH OF IT IS THE SAME.
"IT IS ONLY THAT YOU SEE IT DIFFERENTLY NOW."
SO IF THERE'S A STORY ABOUT... SOMETHING I WISH WERE DIFFERENT...
PERHAPS IT ALREADY IS. CONSIDER HOW YOU SEE IT.
THAT'S GREAT. I WILL. THANK YOU!

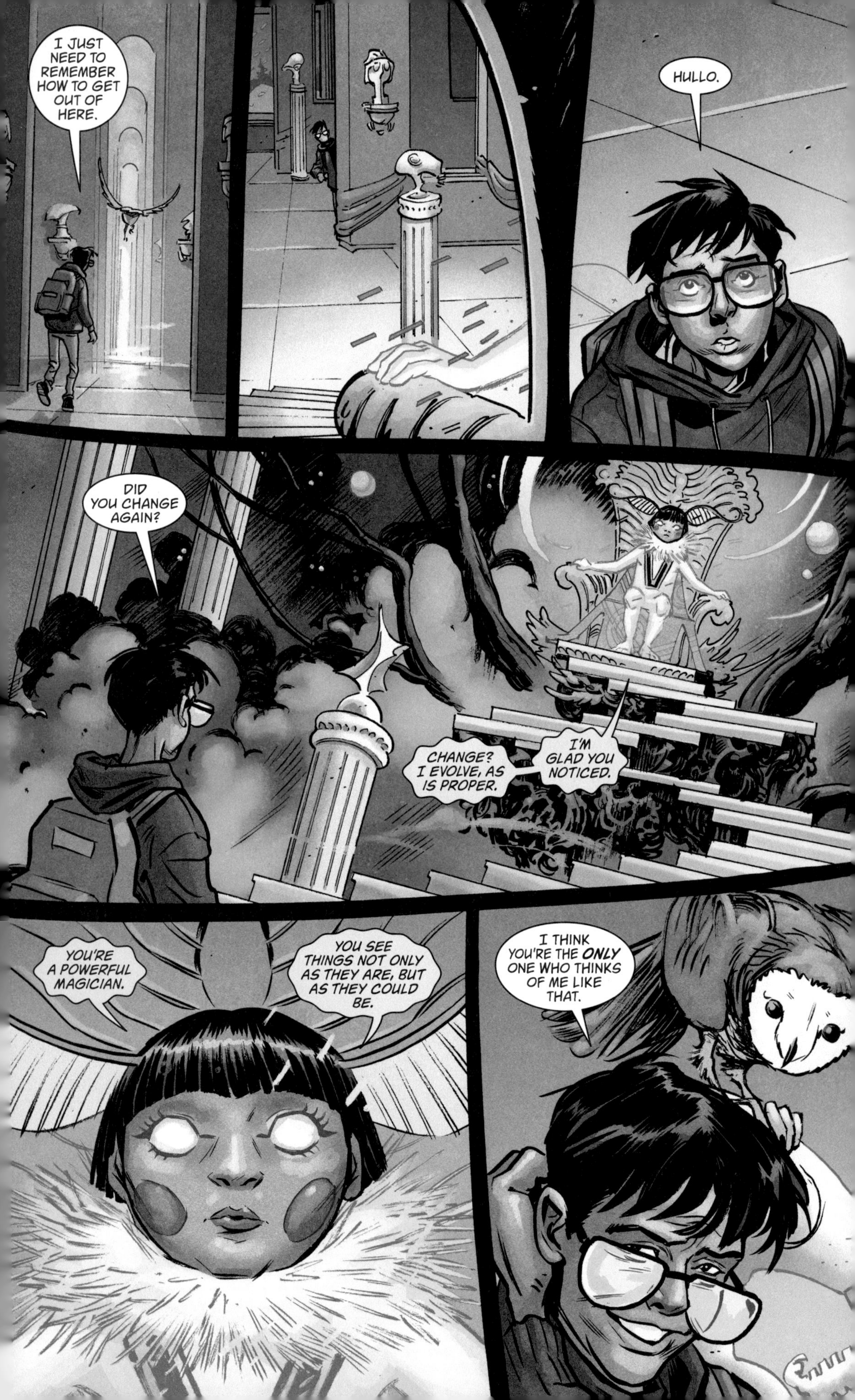
I JUST NEED TO REMEMBER HOW TO GET OUT OF HERE.
HULLO.
DID YOU CHANGE AGAIN?
CHANGE? I EVOLVE, AS IS PROPER.
I'M GLAD YOU NOTICED.
YOU'RE A POWERFUL MAGICIAN.
YOU SEE THINGS NOT ONLY AS THEY ARE, BUT AS THEY COULD BE.
I THINK YOU'RE THE ONLY ONE WHO THINKS OF ME LIKE THAT.

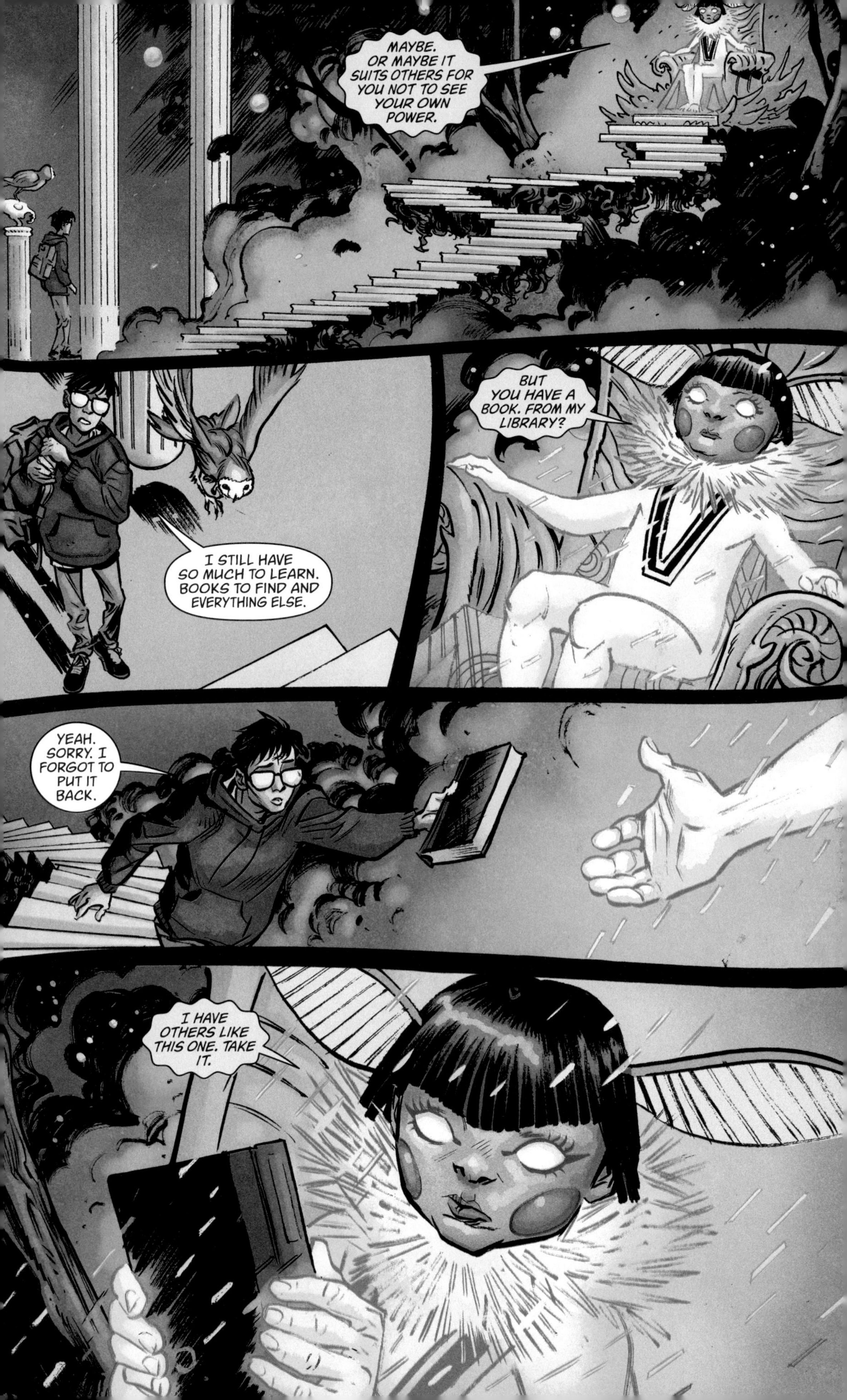
MAYBE. OR MAYBE IT SUITS OTHERS FOR YOU NOT TO SEE YOUR OWN POWER.
I STILL HAVE SO MUCH TO LEARN. BOOKS TO FIND AND EVERYTHING ELSE.
BUT YOU HAVE A BOOK. FROM MY LIBRARY?
YEAH. SORRY. I FORGOT TO PUT IT BACK.
I HAVE OTHERS LIKE THIS ONE. TAKE IT.

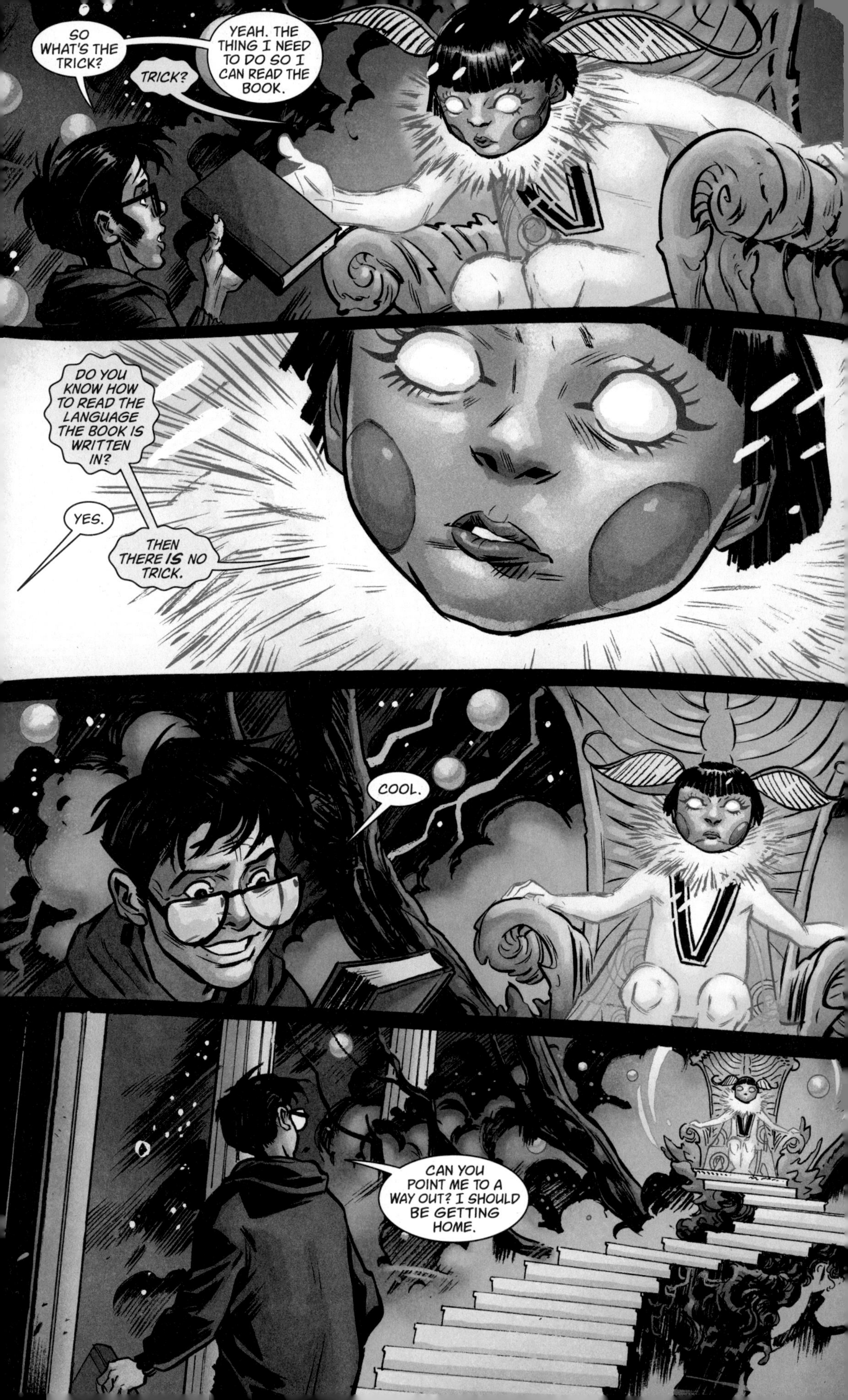
SO WHAT'S THE TRICK?
YEAH. THE THING I NEED TO DO SO I CAN READ THE BOOK.
TRICK?
DO YOU KNOW HOW TO READ THE LANGUAGE THE BOOK IS WRITTEN IN?
YES.
THEN THERE IS NO TRICK.
COOL.
CAN YOU POINT ME TO A WAY OUT? I SHOULD BE GETTING HOME.

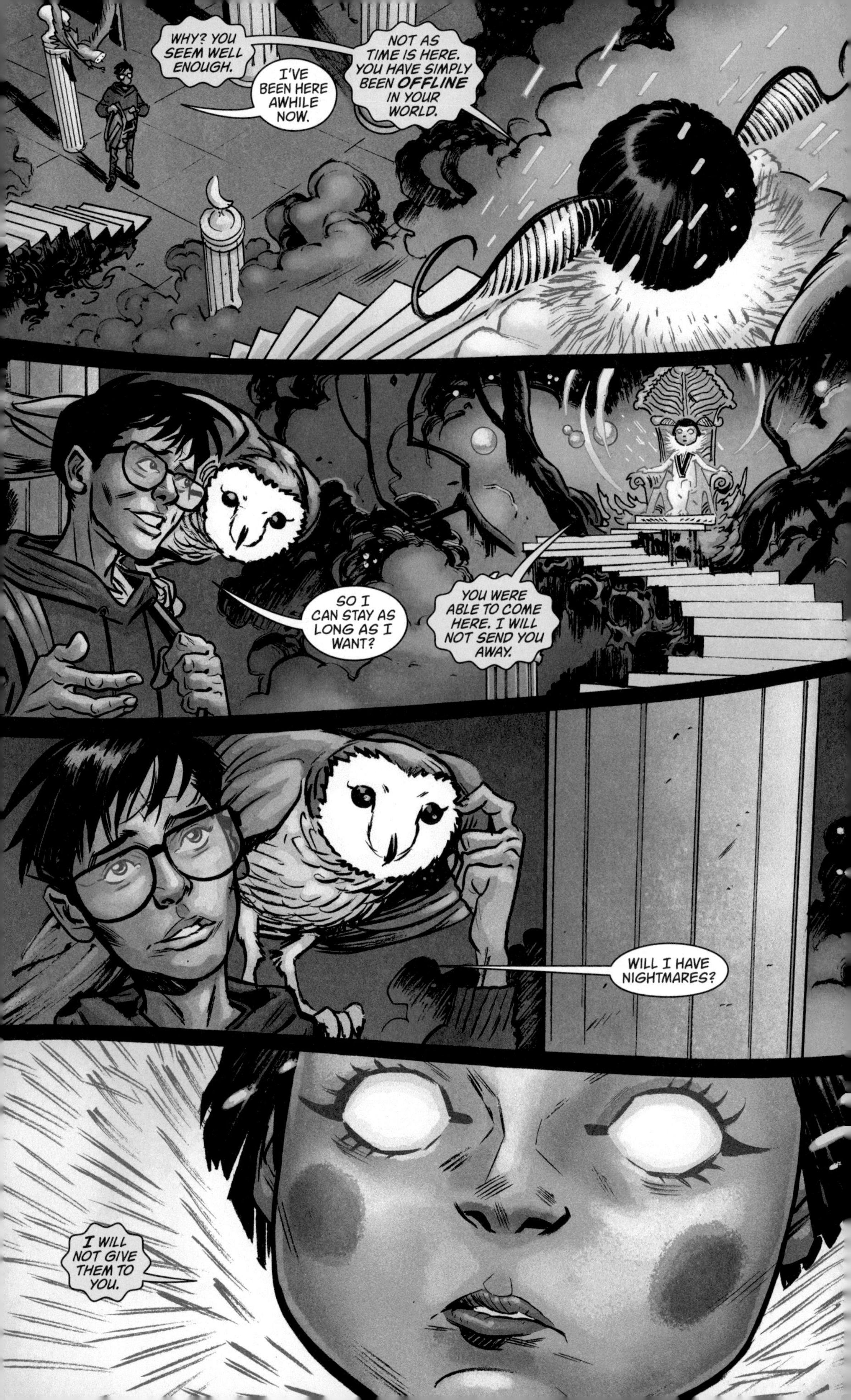
WHY? YOU SEEM WELL ENOUGH.
I'VE BEEN HERE AWHILE NOW.
NOT AS TIME IS HERE. YOU HAVE SIMPLY BEEN OFFLINE IN YOUR WORLD.
SO I CAN STAY AS LONG AS I WANT?
YOU WERE ABLE TO COME HERE. I WILL NOT SEND YOU AWAY.
WILL I HAVE NIGHTMARES?
I WILL NOT GIVE THEM TO YOU.

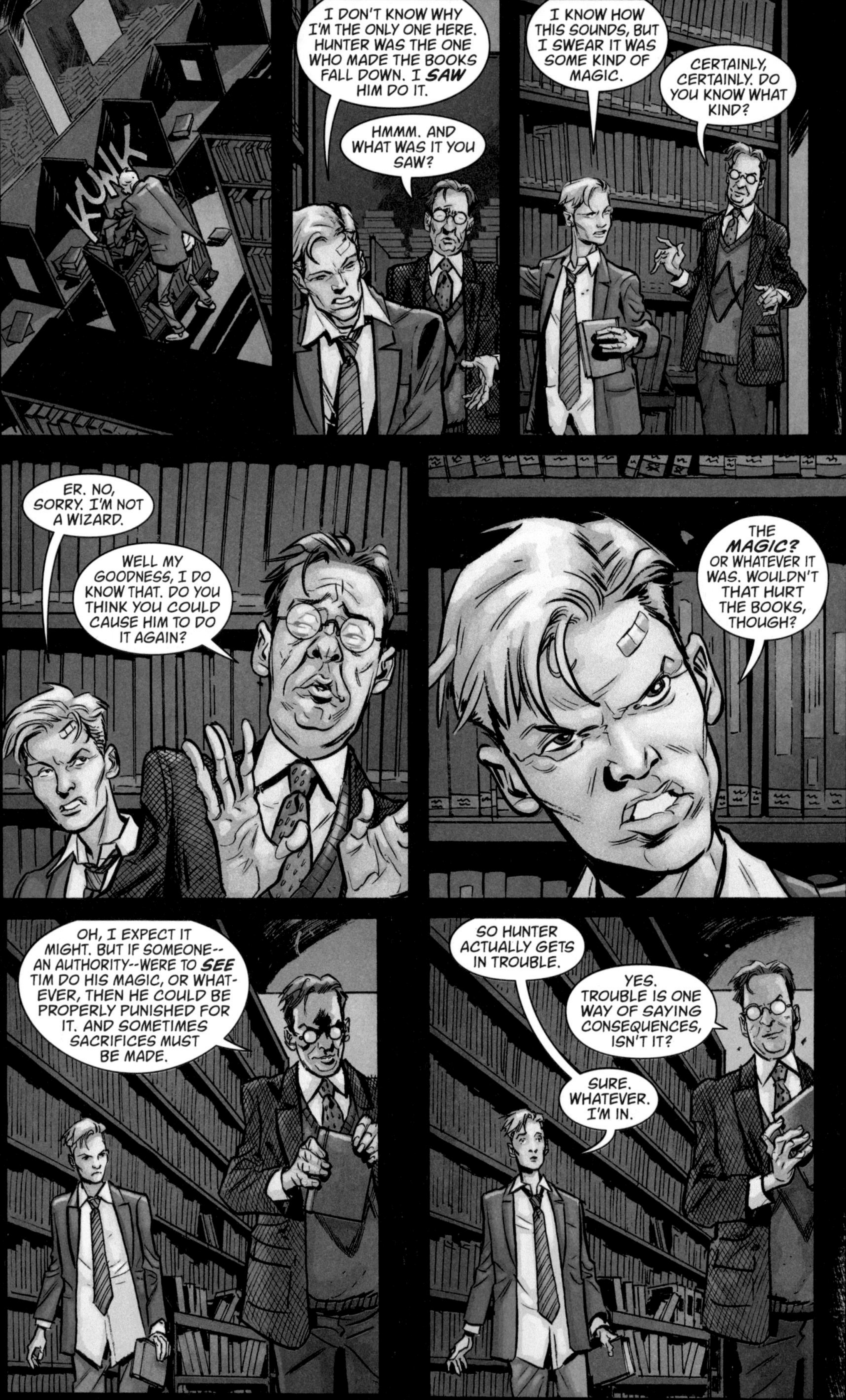
KUNK
I DON'T KNOW WHY I'M THE ONLY ONE HERE. HUNTER WAS THE ONE WHO MADE THE BOOKS FALL DOWN. I *SAW* HIM DO IT.
HMMM. AND WHAT WAS IT YOU SAW?
I KNOW HOW THIS SOUNDS, BUT I SWEAR IT WAS SOME KIND OF MAGIC.
CERTAINLY, CERTAINLY. DO YOU KNOW WHAT KIND?
ER. NO, SORRY. I'M NOT A WIZARD.
WELL MY GOODNESS, I DO KNOW THAT. DO YOU THINK YOU COULD CAUSE HIM TO DO IT AGAIN?
THE *MAGIC?* OR WHATEVER IT WAS. WOULDN'T THAT HURT THE BOOKS, THOUGH?
OH, I EXPECT IT MIGHT. BUT IF SOMEONE--AN AUTHORITY--WERE TO *SEE* TIM DO HIS MAGIC, OR WHAT-EVER, THEN HE COULD BE PROPERLY PUNISHED FOR IT. AND SOMETIMES SACRIFICES MUST BE MADE.
SO HUNTER ACTUALLY GETS IN TROUBLE.
YES. TROUBLE IS ONE WAY OF SAYING CONSEQUENCES, ISN'T IT?
SURE. WHATEVER. I'M IN.

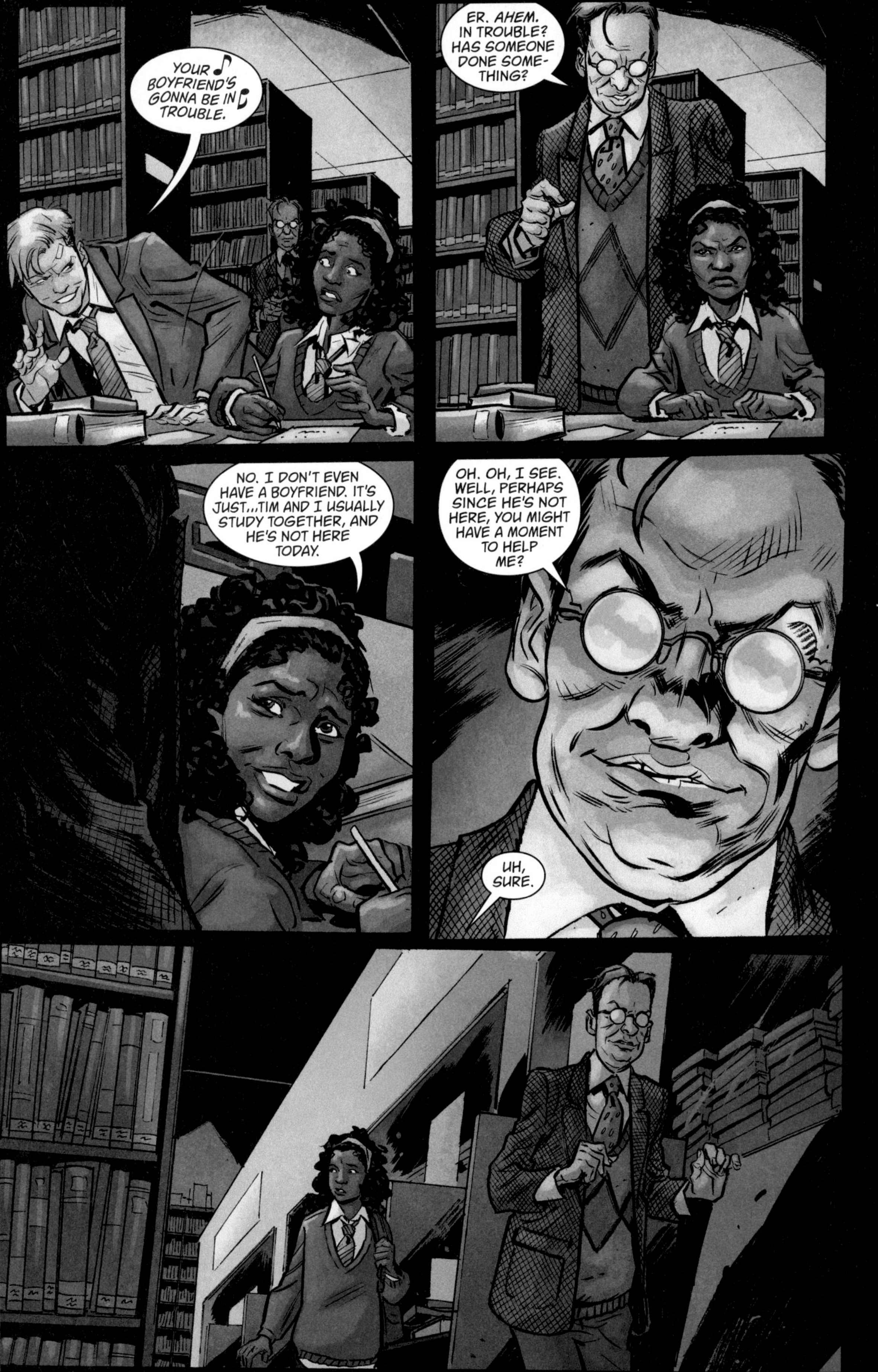
YOUR ♪ BOYFRIEND'S GONNA BE IN ♫ TROUBLE.
ER. AHEM. IN TROUBLE? HAS SOMEONE DONE SOMETHING?
NO. I DON'T EVEN HAVE A BOYFRIEND. IT'S JUST...TIM AND I USUALLY STUDY TOGETHER, AND HE'S NOT HERE TODAY.
OH. OH, I SEE. WELL, PERHAPS SINCE HE'S NOT HERE, YOU MIGHT HAVE A MOMENT TO HELP ME?
UH, SURE.

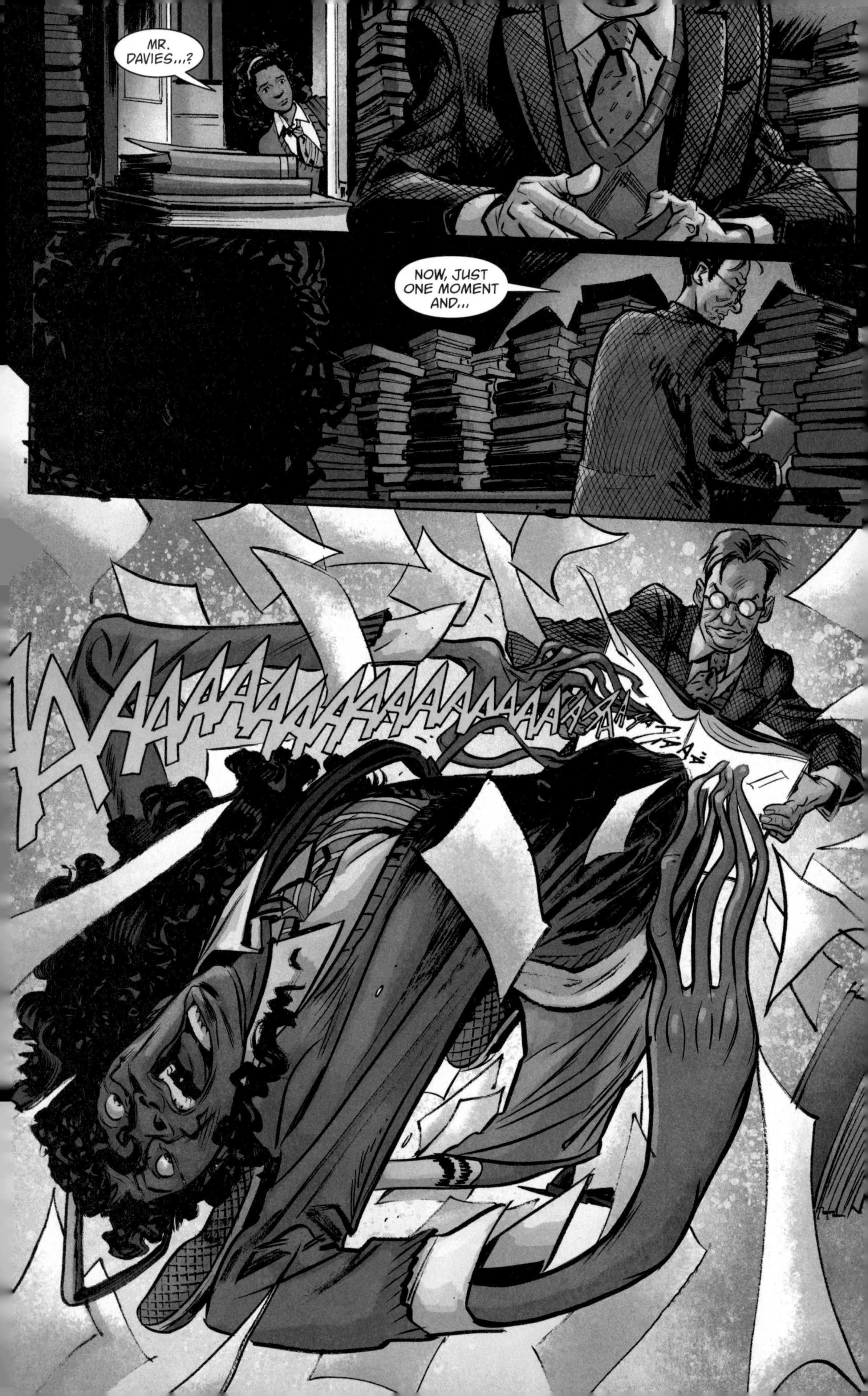
MR. DAVIES...?
NOW, JUST ONE MOMENT AND...
AAAAAAAAAAAAAAAAAA

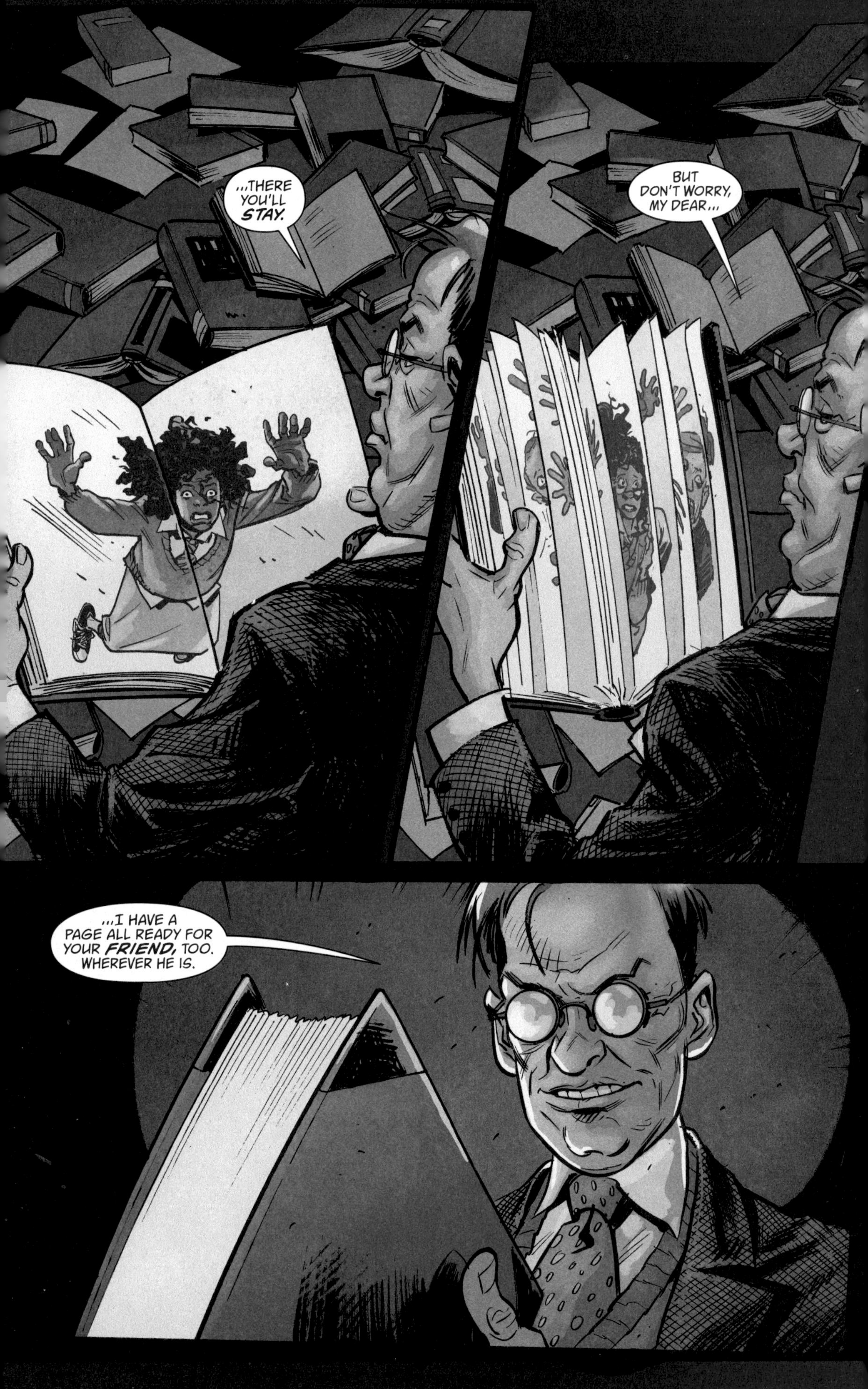
...THERE YOU'LL STAY.
BUT DON'T WORRY, MY DEAR...
...I HAVE A PAGE ALL READY FOR YOUR FRIEND, TOO. WHEREVER HE IS.

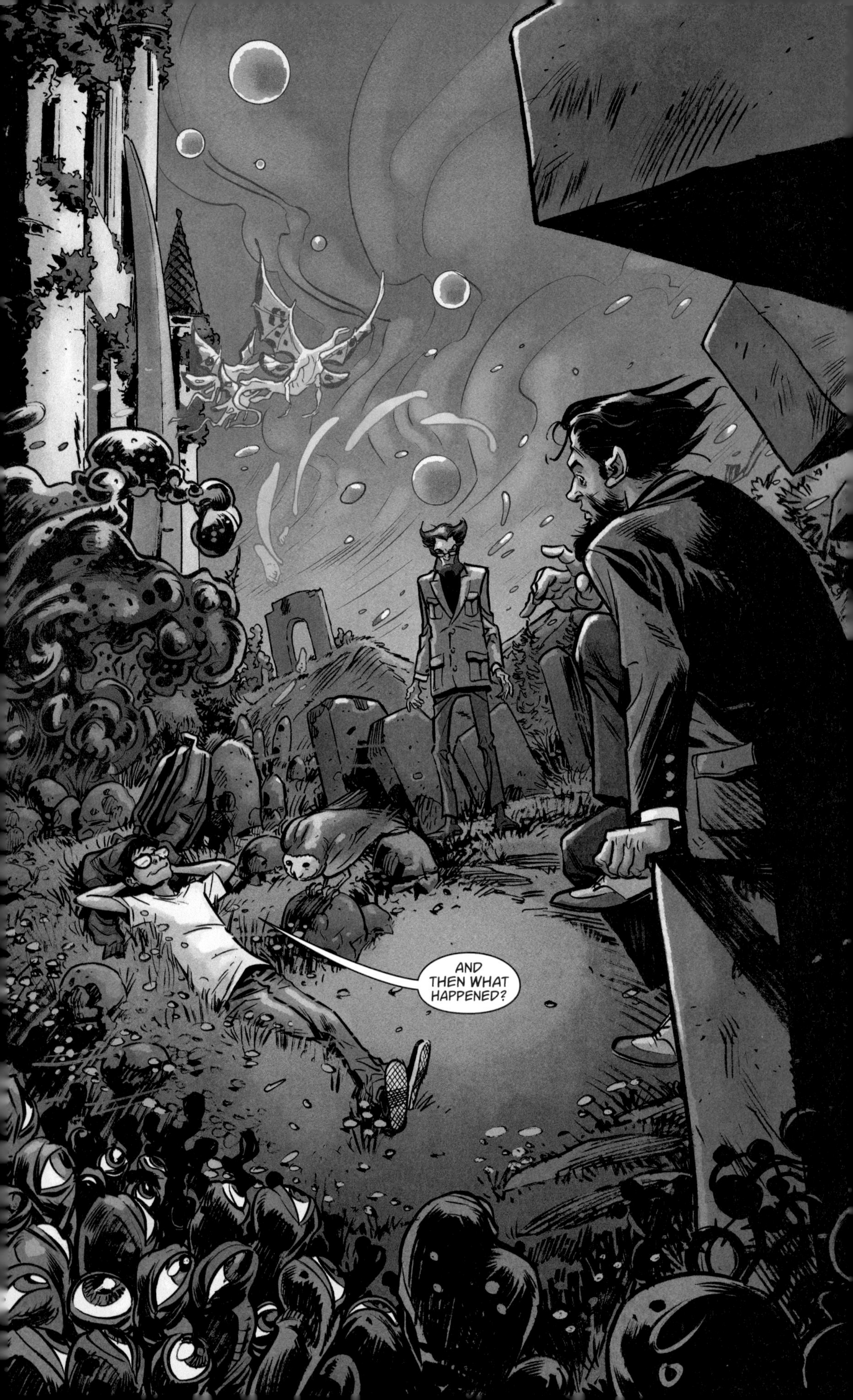
AND THEN WHAT HAPPENED?

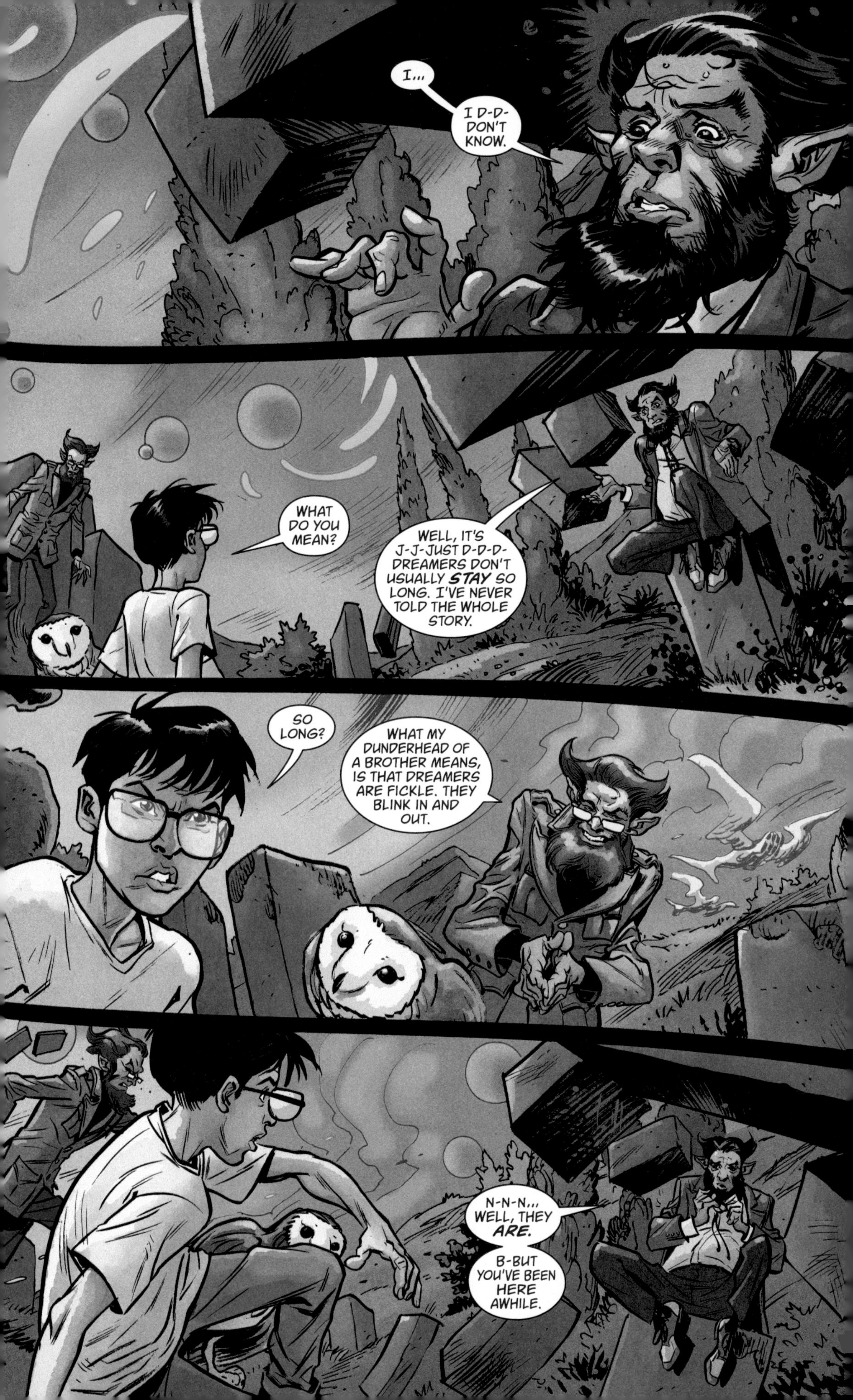
I...
I D-D-DON'T KNOW.
WHAT DO YOU MEAN?
WELL, IT'S J-J-JUST D-D-D-DREAMERS DON'T USUALLY STAY SO LONG. I'VE NEVER TOLD THE WHOLE STORY.
SO LONG?
WHAT MY DUNDERHEAD OF A BROTHER MEANS, IS THAT DREAMERS ARE FICKLE. THEY BLINK IN AND OUT.
N-N-N... WELL, THEY ARE.
B-BUT YOU'VE BEEN HERE AWHILE.

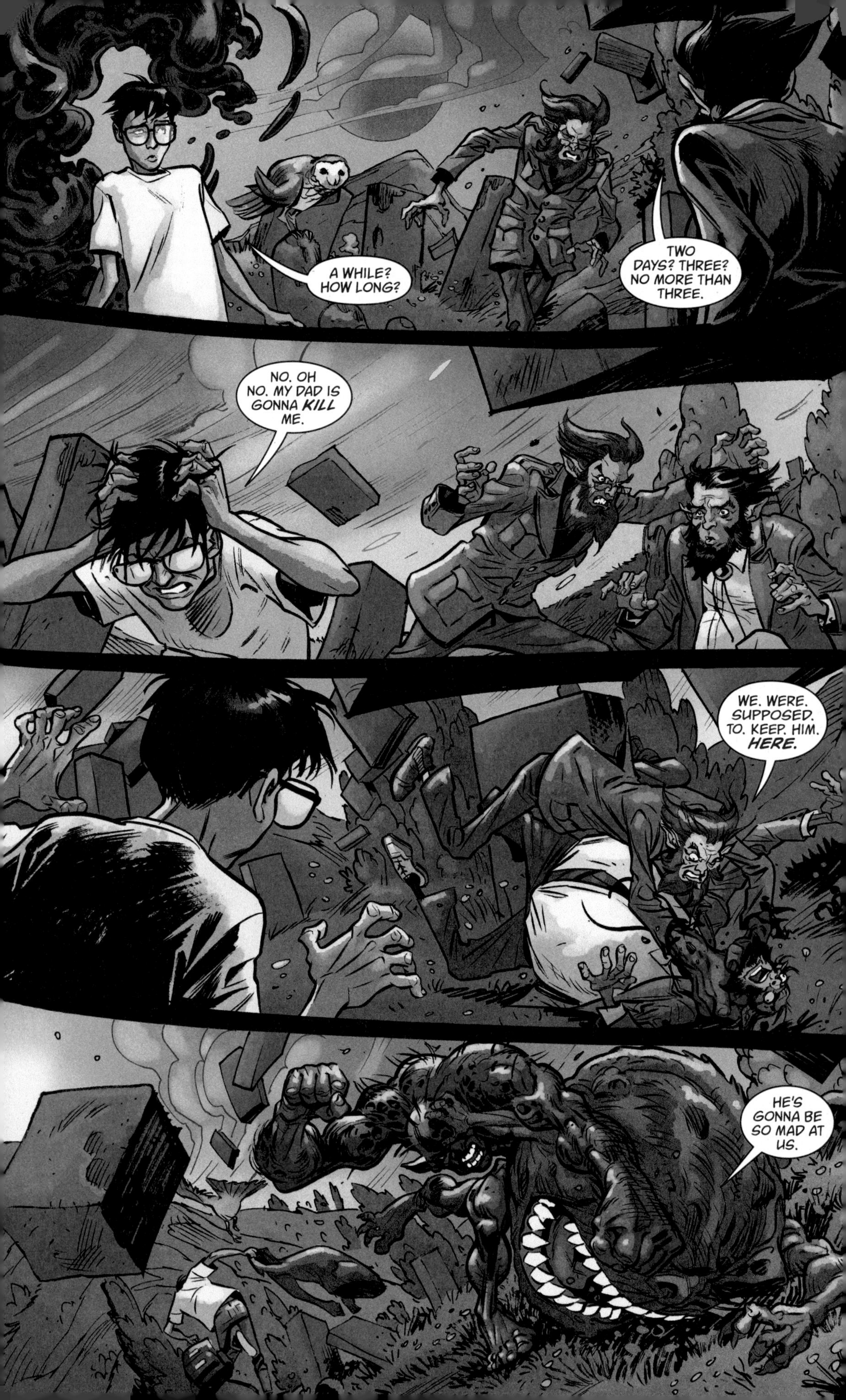
A WHILE? HOW LONG?
TWO DAYS? THREE? NO MORE THAN THREE.
NO. OH NO. MY DAD IS GONNA **KILL** ME.
WE. WERE. SUPPOSED. TO. KEEP. HIM. **HERE.**
HE'S GONNA BE SO MAD AT US.

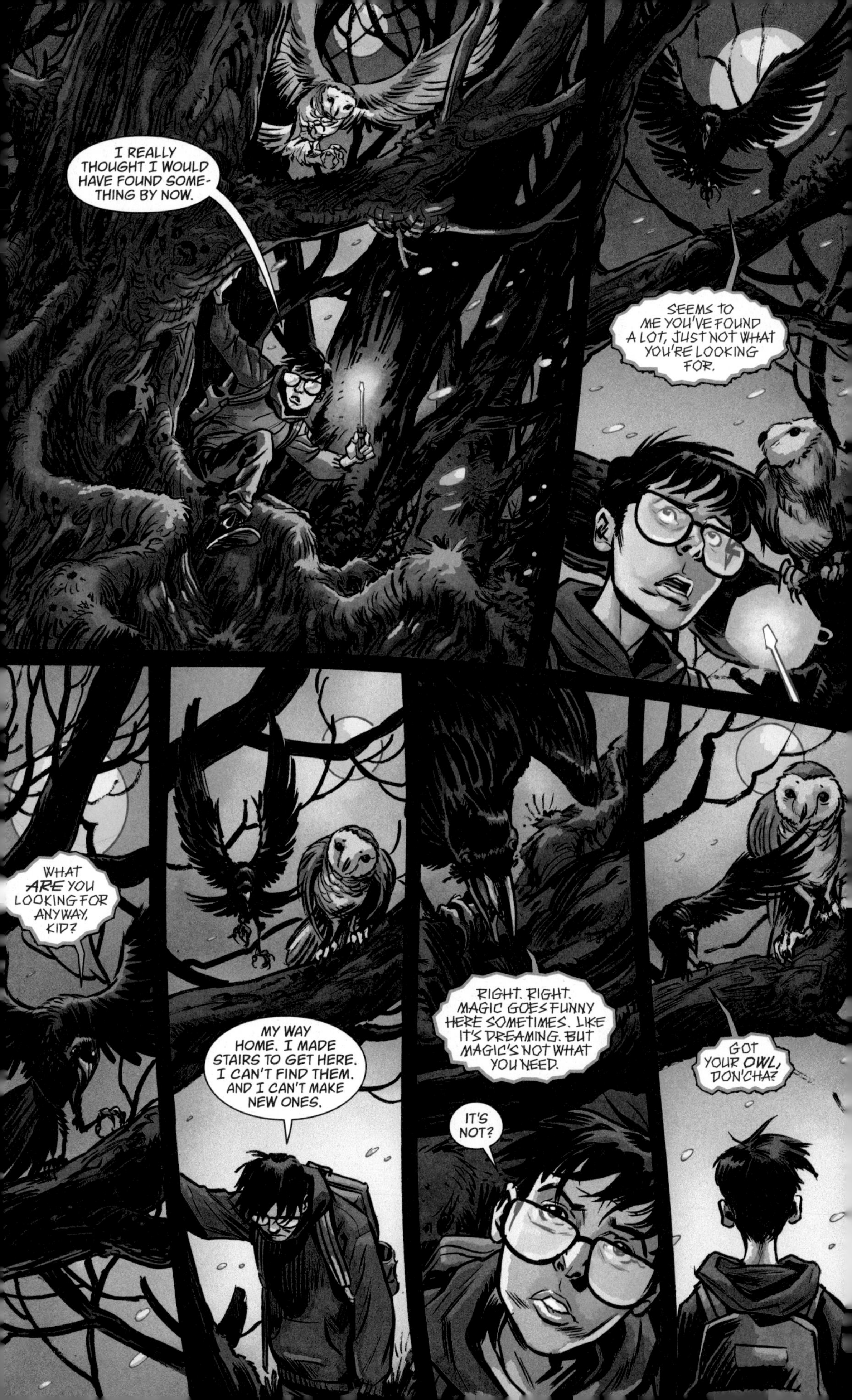
I REALLY THOUGHT I WOULD HAVE FOUND SOME-THING BY NOW.
SEEMS TO ME YOU'VE FOUND A LOT, JUST NOT WHAT YOU'RE LOOKING FOR.
WHAT ARE YOU LOOKING FOR ANYWAY, KID?
MY WAY HOME. I MADE STAIRS TO GET HERE. I CAN'T FIND THEM. AND I CAN'T MAKE NEW ONES.
RIGHT. RIGHT. MAGIC GOES FUNNY HERE SOMETIMES. LIKE IT'S DREAMING. BUT MAGIC'S NOT WHAT YOU NEED.
IT'S NOT?
GOT YOUR OWL, DON'CHA?

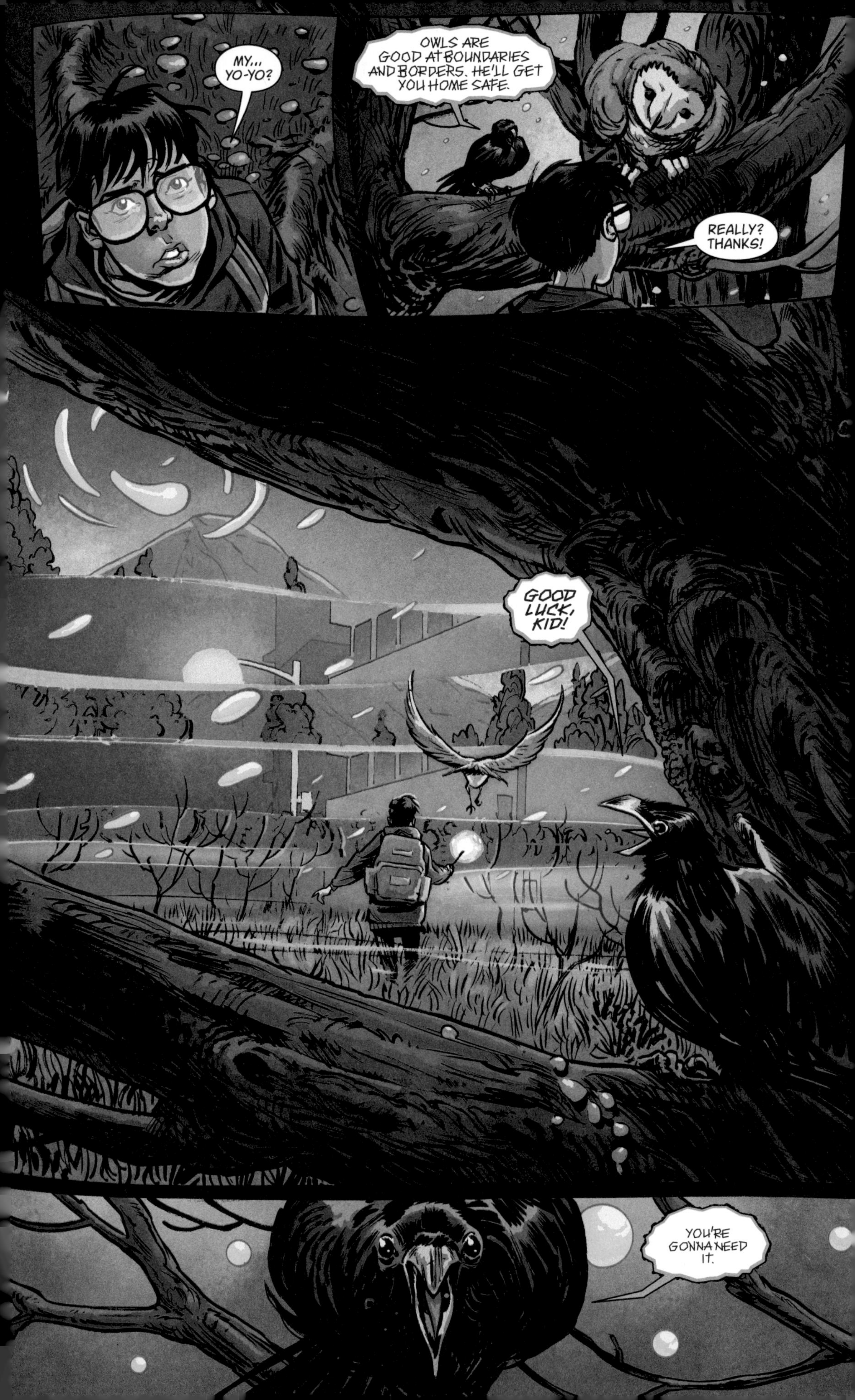
MY... YO-YO?
OWLS ARE GOOD AT BOUNDARIES AND BORDERS. HE'LL GET YOU HOME SAFE.
REALLY? THANKS!
GOOD LUCK, KID!
YOU'RE GONNA NEED IT.

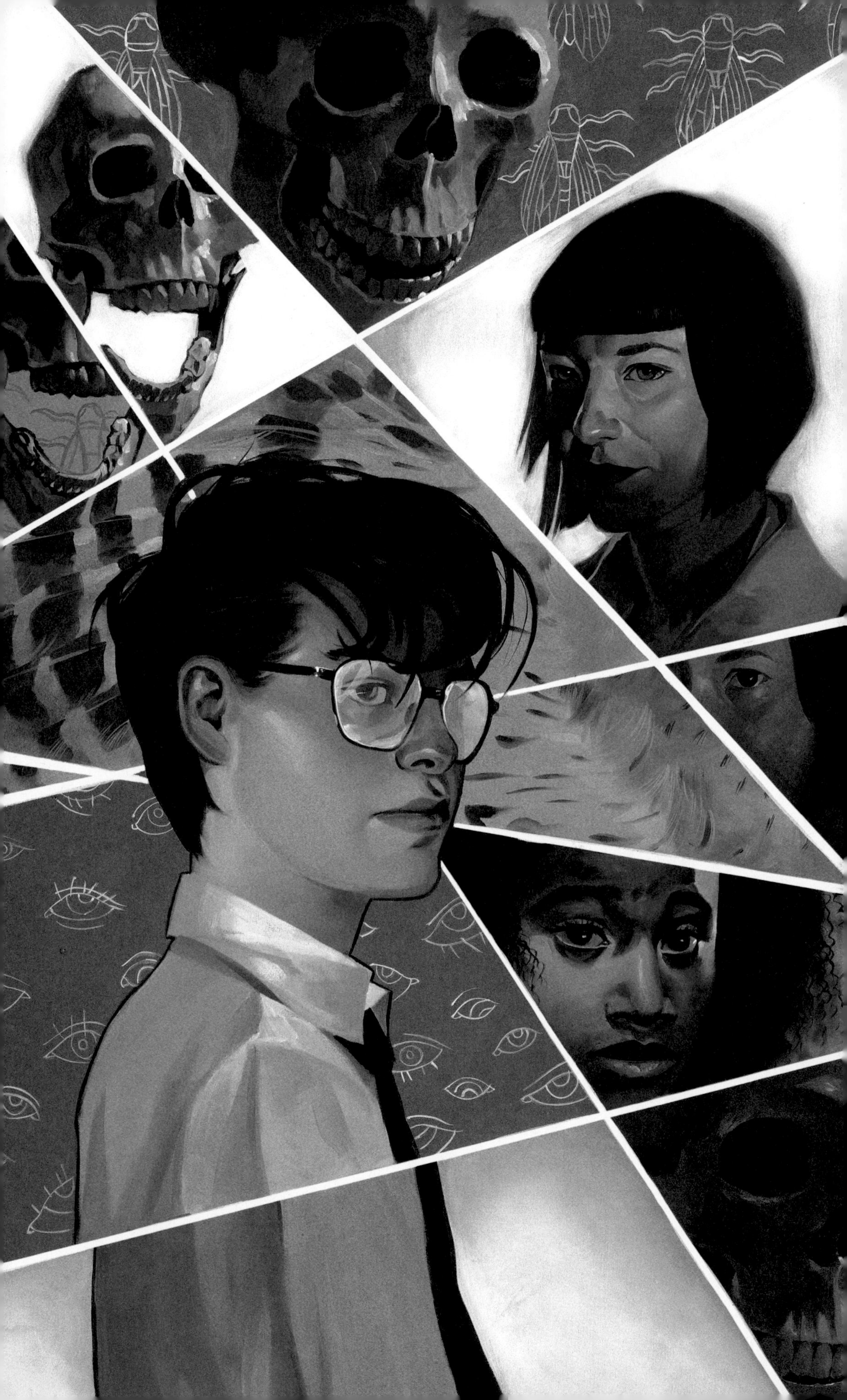

BOOKS OF MAGIC

The End of Chapter One

WRITTEN BY
Kat Howard

ILLUSTRATED BY
Tom Fowler

COLORS BY
Jordan Boyd

LETTERS BY
Todd Klein

COVER ART BY
Kai Carpenter

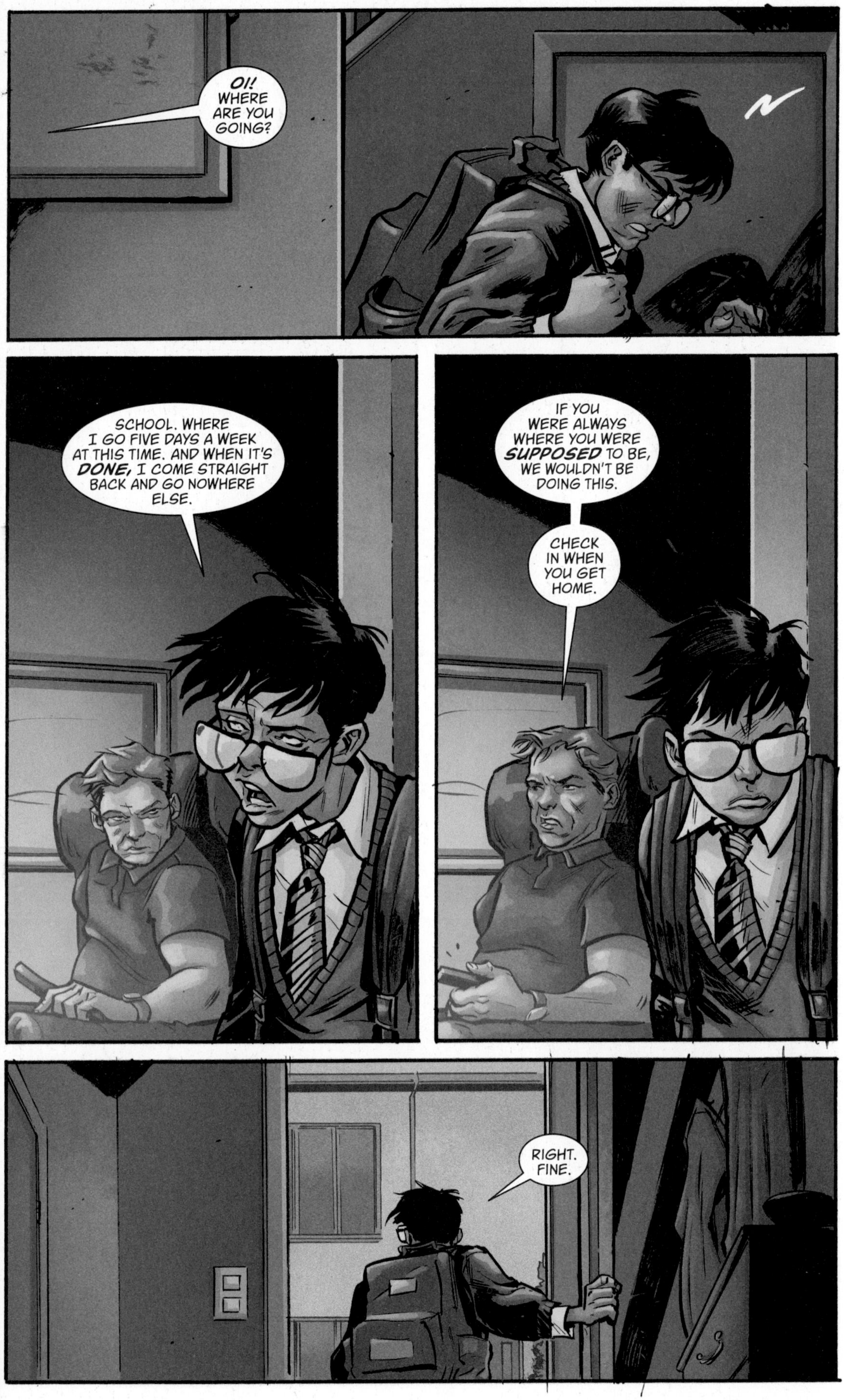
OI! WHERE ARE YOU GOING?
SCHOOL. WHERE I GO FIVE DAYS A WEEK AT THIS TIME. AND WHEN IT'S DONE, I COME STRAIGHT BACK AND GO NOWHERE ELSE.
IF YOU WERE ALWAYS WHERE YOU WERE SUPPOSED TO BE, WE WOULDN'T BE DOING THIS.
CHECK IN WHEN YOU GET HOME.
RIGHT. FINE.

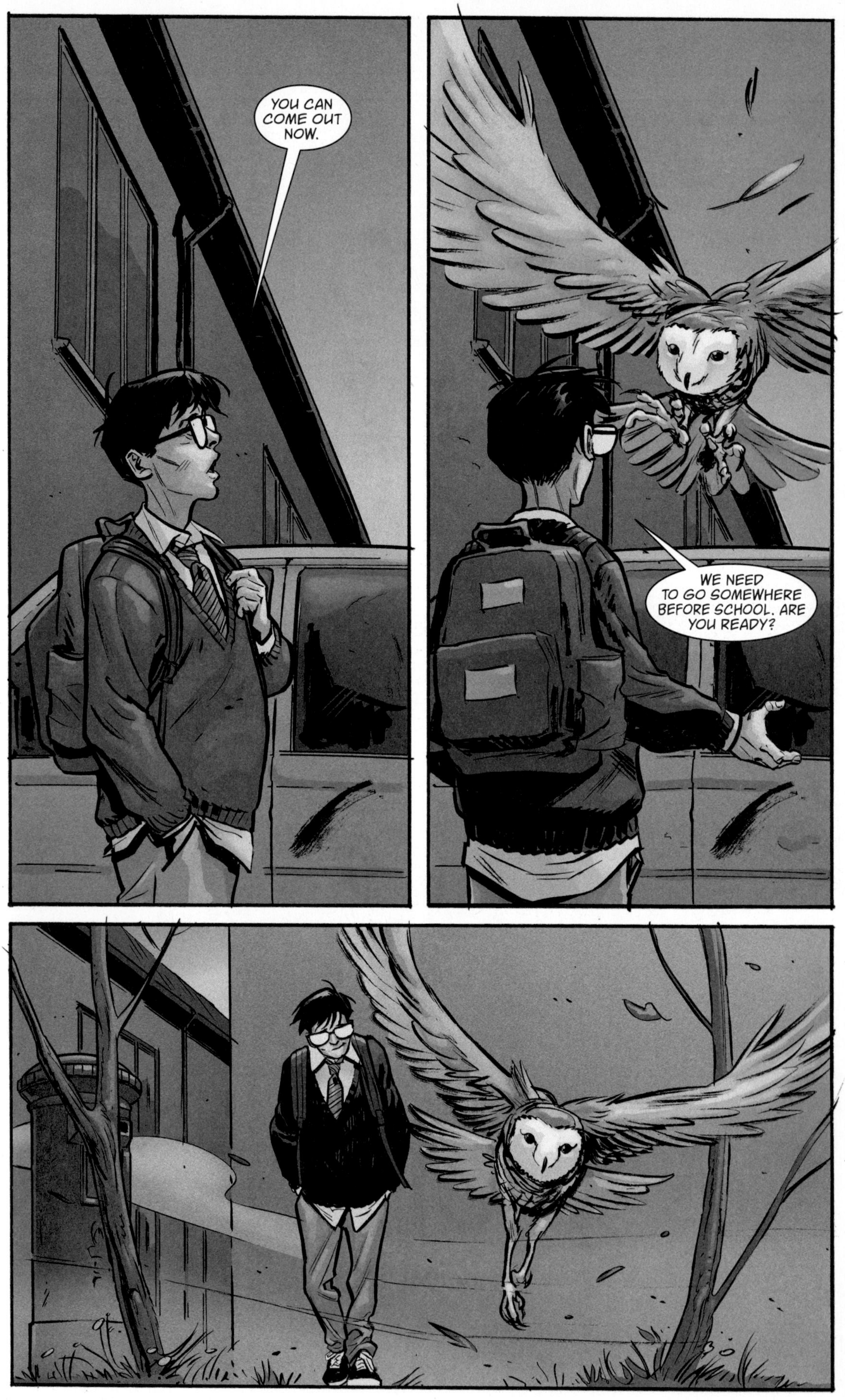
YOU CAN COME OUT NOW.
WE NEED TO GO SOMEWHERE BEFORE SCHOOL. ARE YOU READY?

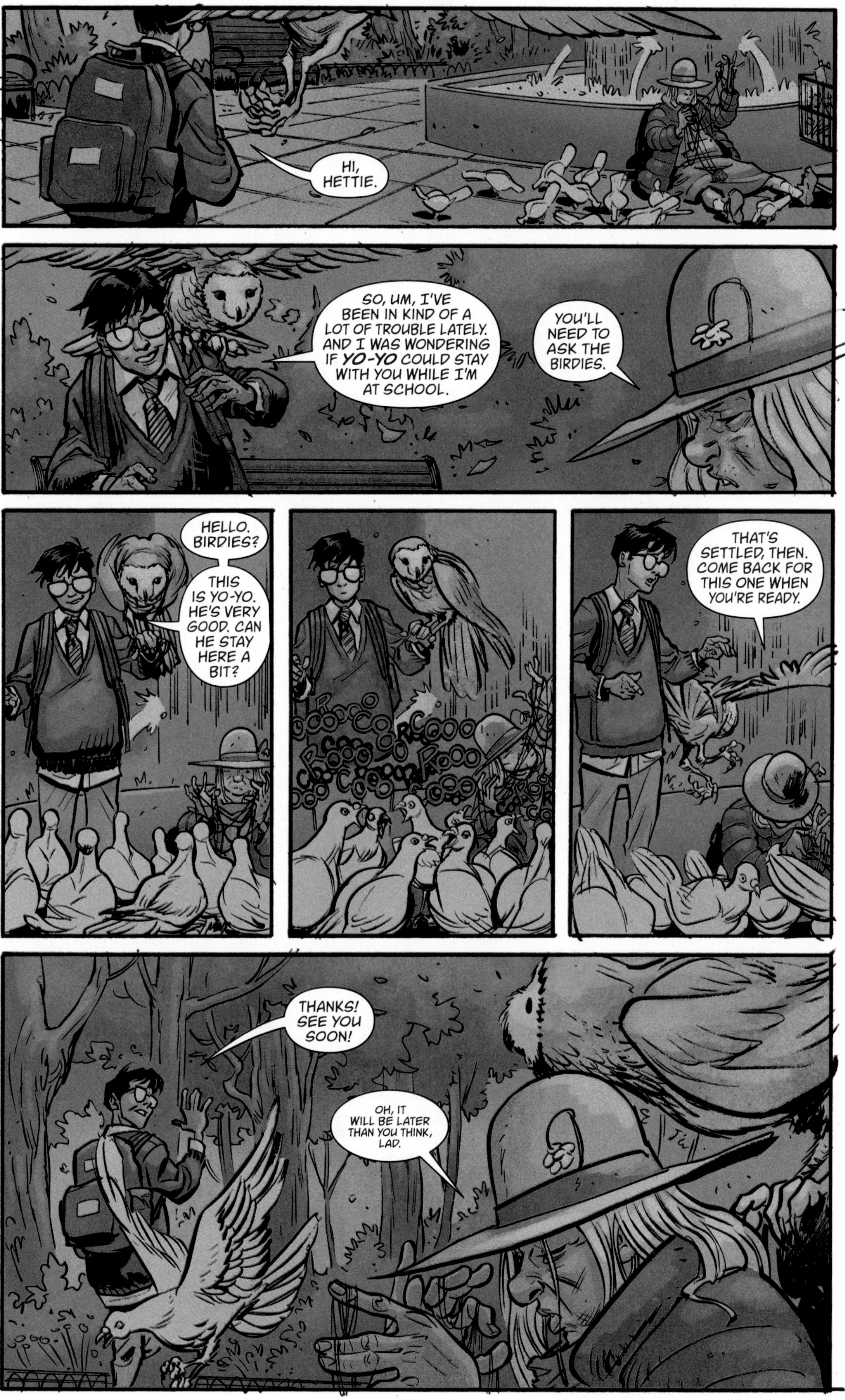
HI, HETTIE.
SO, UM, I'VE BEEN IN KIND OF A LOT OF TROUBLE LATELY. AND I WAS WONDERING IF *YO-YO* COULD STAY WITH YOU WHILE I'M AT SCHOOL.
YOU'LL NEED TO ASK THE BIRDIES.
HELLO. BIRDIES?
THIS IS YO-YO. HE'S VERY GOOD. CAN HE STAY HERE A BIT?
THAT'S SETTLED, THEN. COME BACK FOR THIS ONE WHEN YOU'RE READY.
THANKS! SEE YOU SOON!
OH, IT WILL BE LATER THAN YOU THINK, LAD.

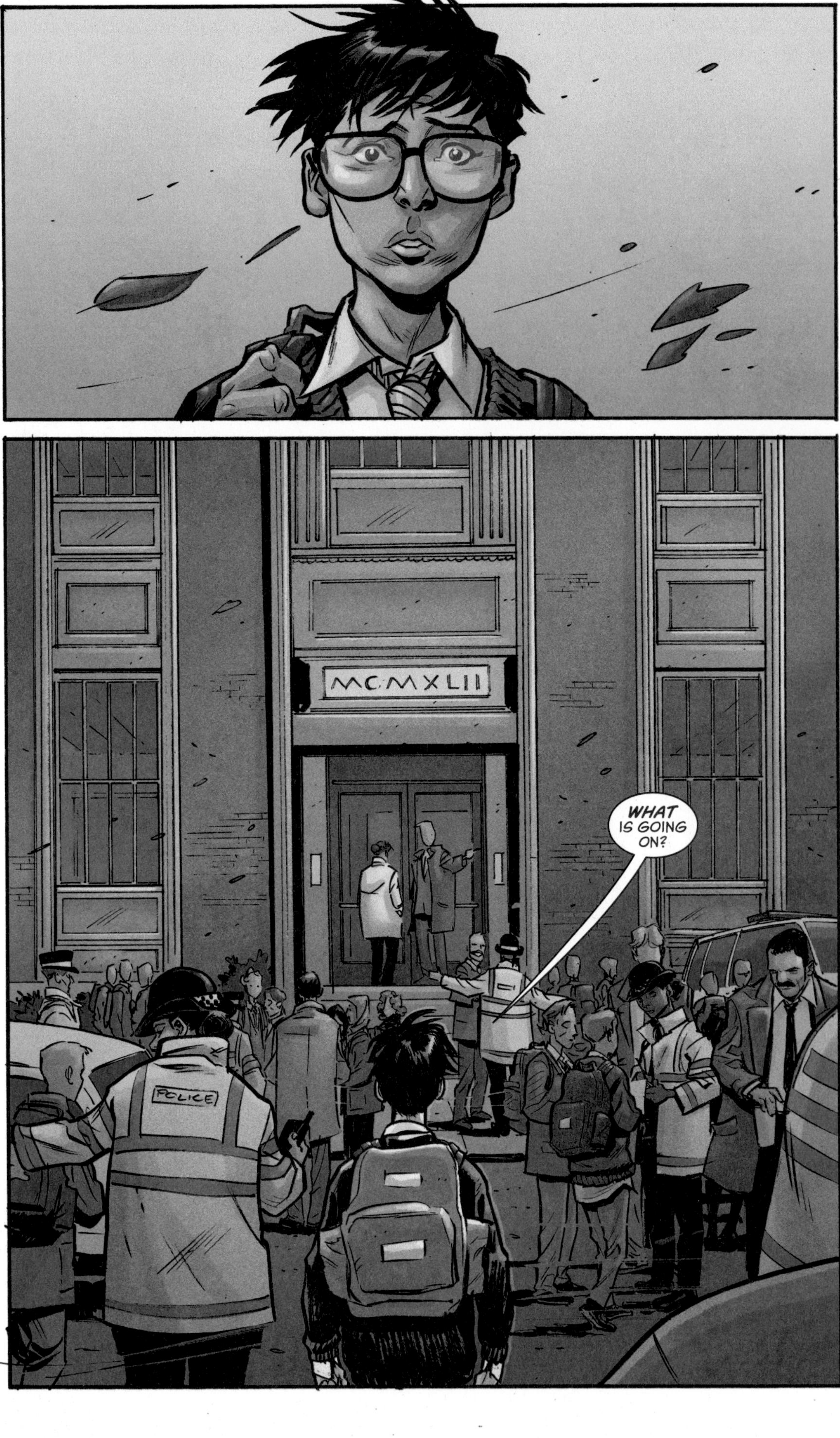
MCMXLII
WHAT IS GOING ON?
POLICE

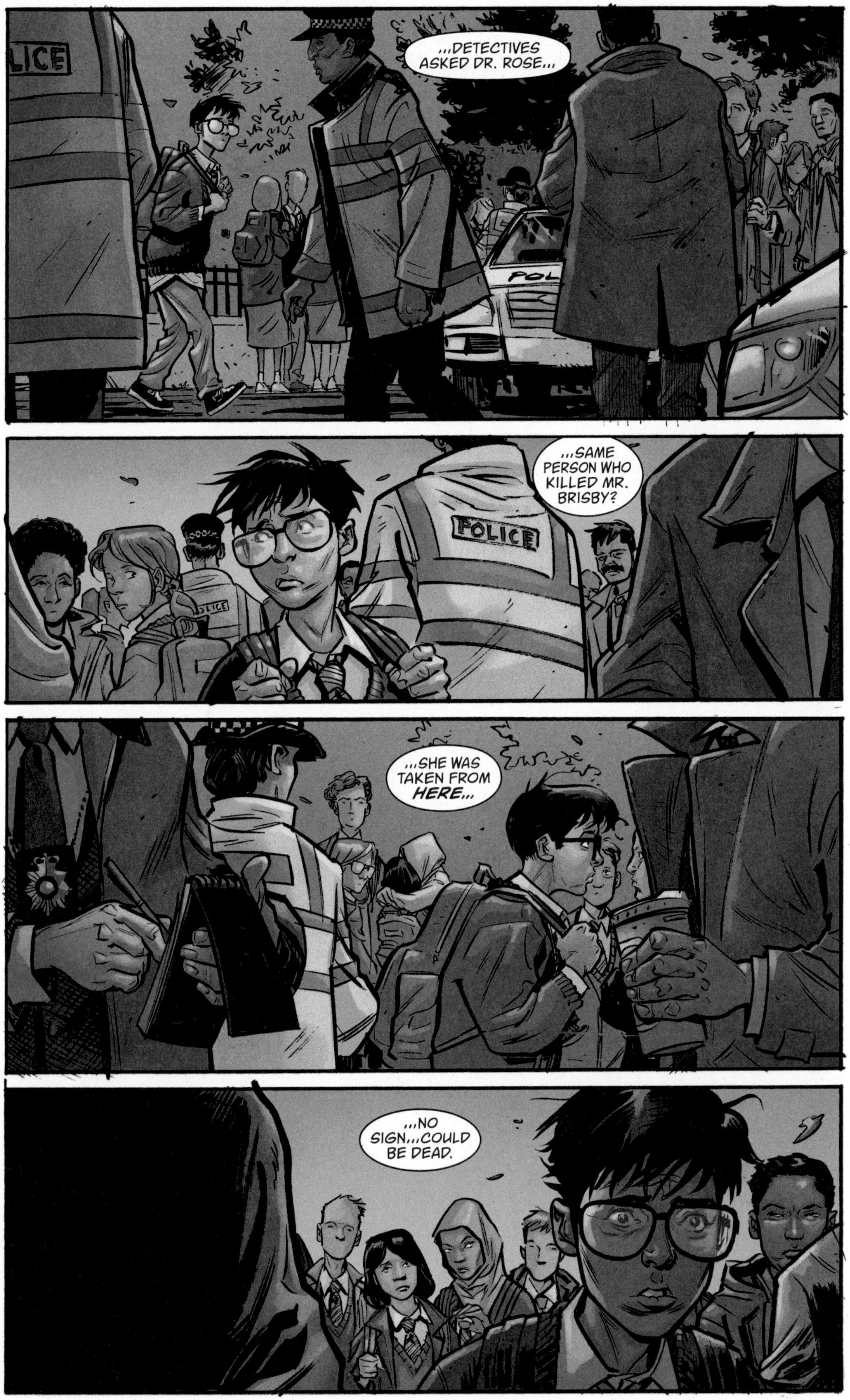
LICE
...DETECTIVES ASKED DR. ROSE...
POL
...SAME PERSON WHO KILLED MR. BRISBY?
POLICE
...SHE WAS TAKEN FROM HERE...
...NO SIGN...COULD BE DEAD.

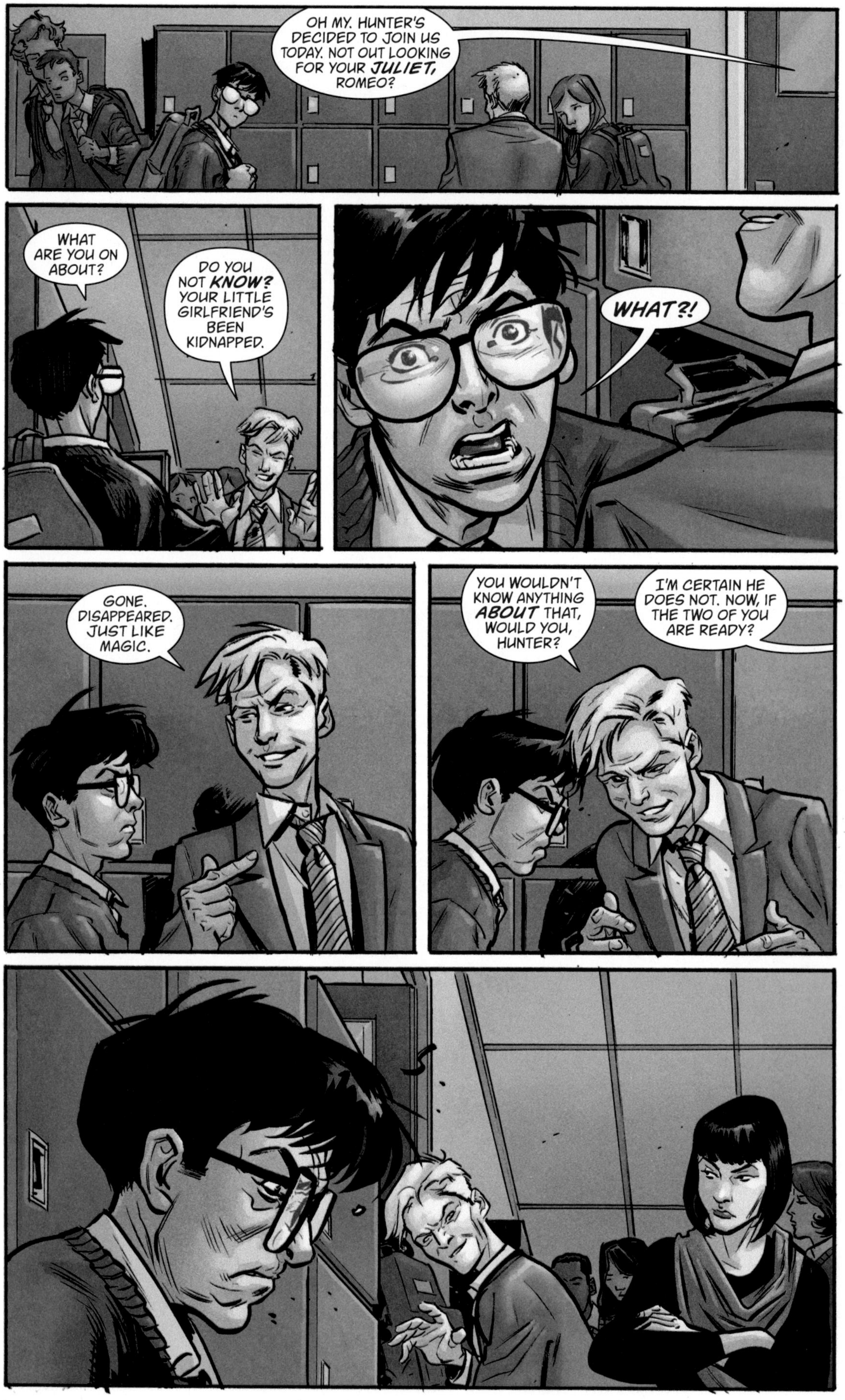
OH MY. HUNTER'S DECIDED TO JOIN US TODAY. NOT OUT LOOKING FOR YOUR JULIET, ROMEO?
WHAT ARE YOU ON ABOUT?
DO YOU NOT KNOW? YOUR LITTLE GIRLFRIEND'S BEEN KIDNAPPED.
WHAT?!
GONE. DISAPPEARED. JUST LIKE MAGIC.
YOU WOULDN'T KNOW ANYTHING ABOUT THAT, WOULD YOU, HUNTER?
I'M CERTAIN HE DOES NOT. NOW, IF THE TWO OF YOU ARE READY?

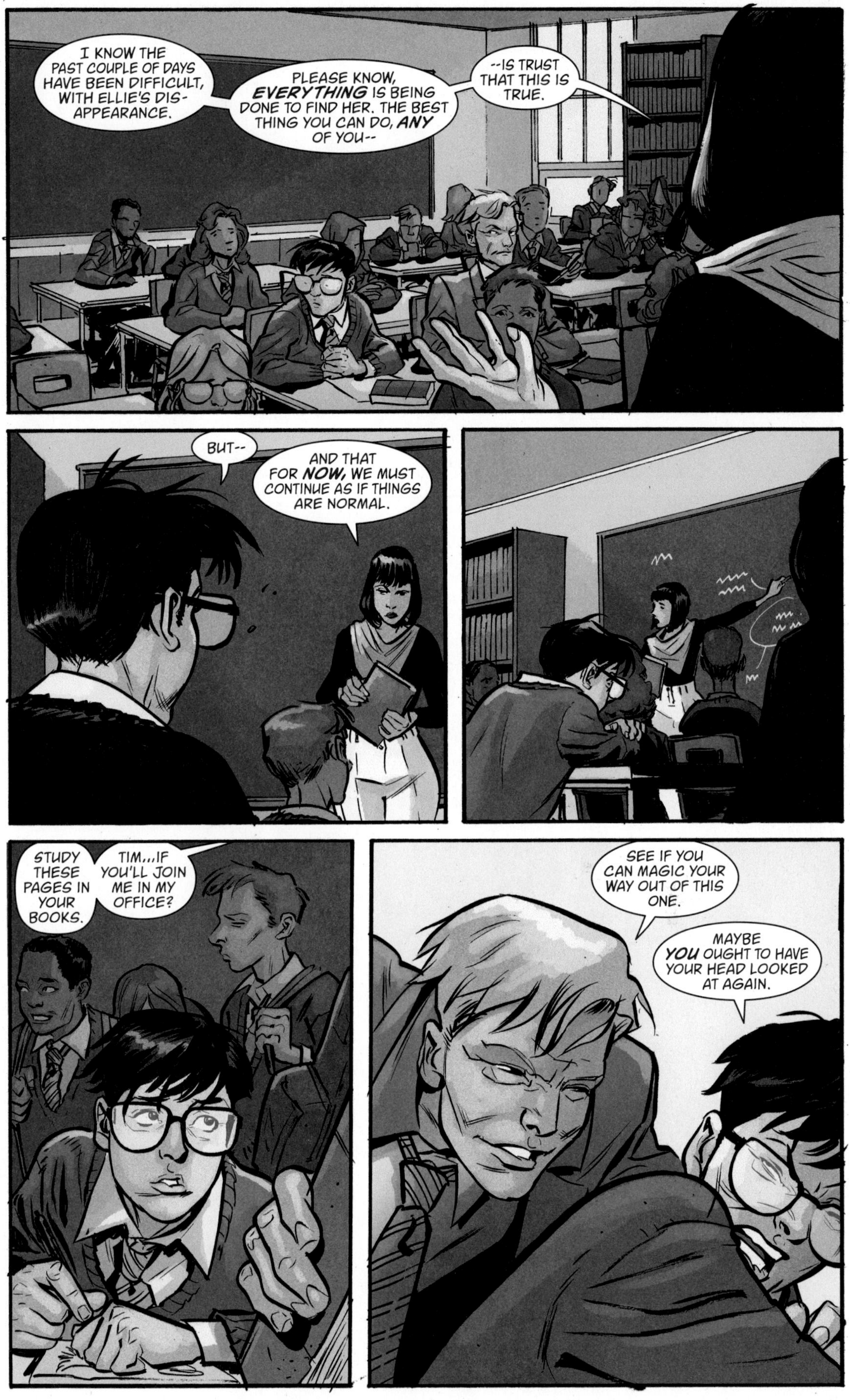
I KNOW THE PAST COUPLE OF DAYS HAVE BEEN DIFFICULT, WITH ELLIE'S DIS-APPEARANCE.
PLEASE KNOW, EVERYTHING IS BEING DONE TO FIND HER. THE BEST THING YOU CAN DO, ANY OF YOU--
--IS TRUST THAT THIS IS TRUE.
BUT--
AND THAT FOR NOW, WE MUST CONTINUE AS IF THINGS ARE NORMAL.
STUDY THESE PAGES IN YOUR BOOKS.
TIM...IF YOU'LL JOIN ME IN MY OFFICE?
SEE IF YOU CAN MAGIC YOUR WAY OUT OF THIS ONE.
MAYBE YOU OUGHT TO HAVE YOUR HEAD LOOKED AT AGAIN.

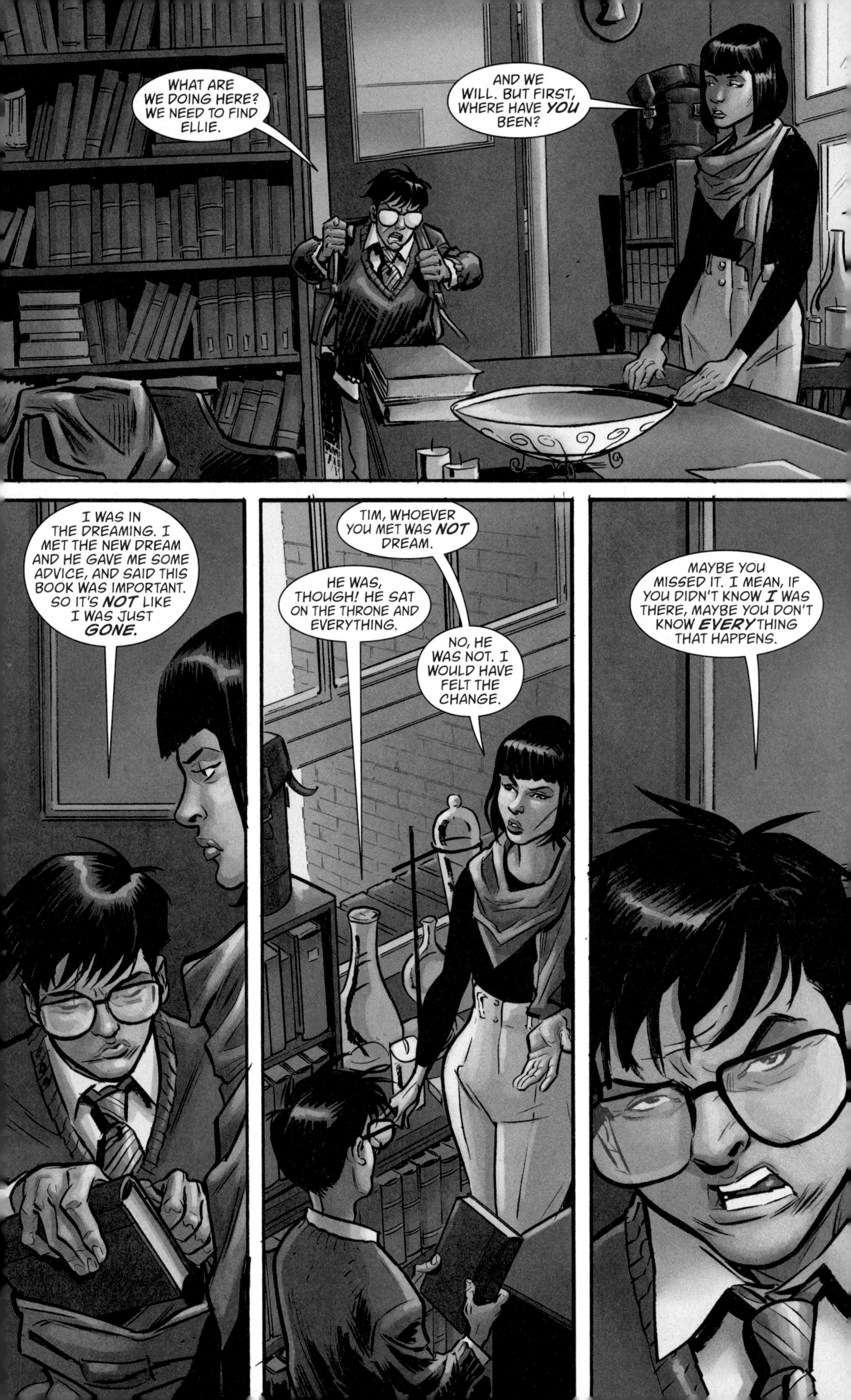
WHAT ARE WE DOING HERE? WE NEED TO FIND ELLIE.
AND WE WILL. BUT FIRST, WHERE HAVE **YOU** BEEN?
I WAS IN THE DREAMING. I MET THE NEW DREAM AND HE GAVE ME SOME ADVICE, AND SAID THIS BOOK WAS IMPORTANT. SO IT'S **NOT** LIKE I WAS JUST **GONE.**
TIM, WHOEVER YOU MET WAS **NOT** DREAM.
HE WAS, THOUGH! HE SAT ON THE THRONE AND EVERYTHING.
NO, HE WAS NOT. I WOULD HAVE FELT THE CHANGE.
MAYBE YOU MISSED IT. I MEAN, IF YOU DIDN'T KNOW **I** WAS THERE, MAYBE YOU DON'T KNOW **EVERY**THING THAT HAPPENS.

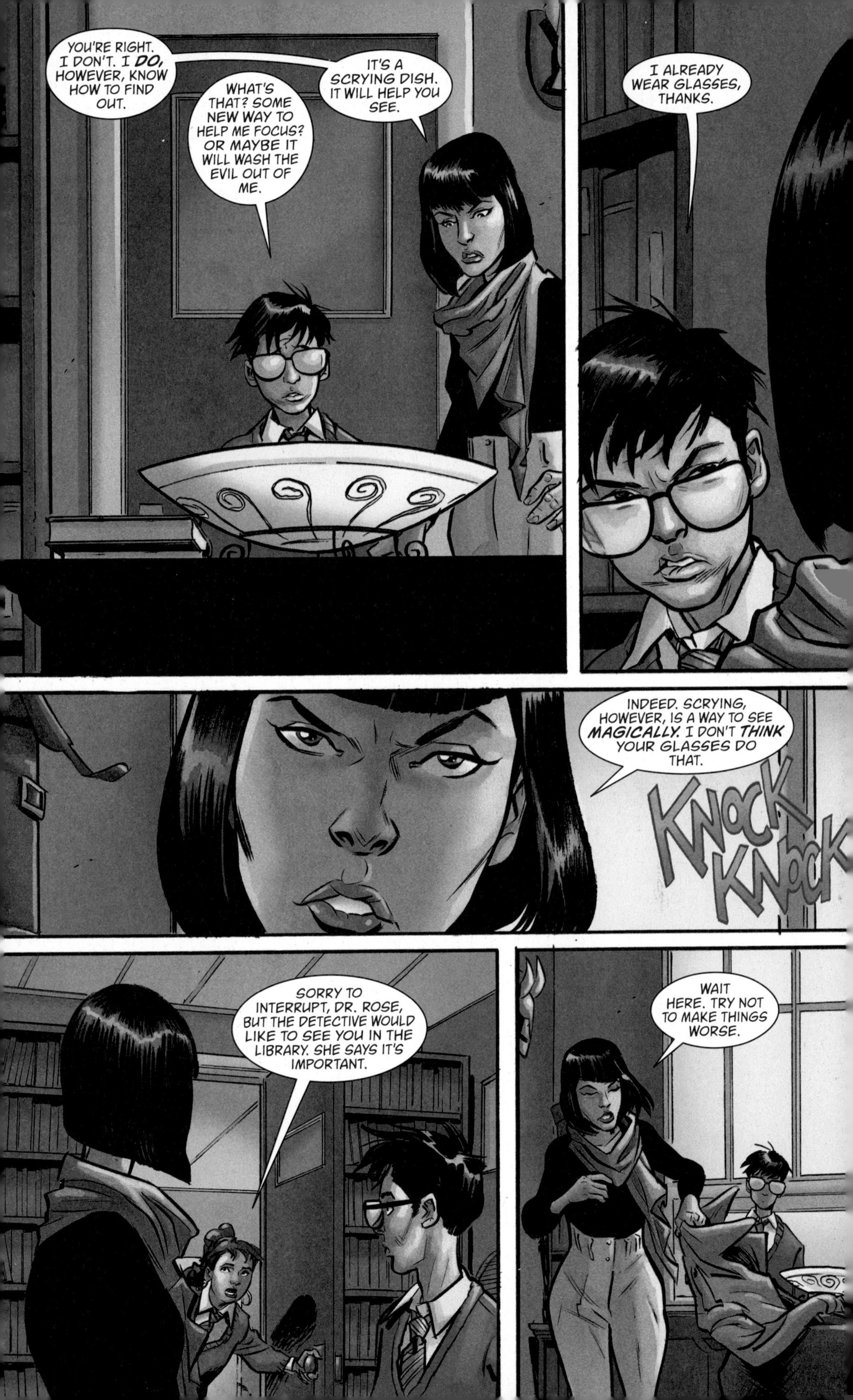
YOU'RE RIGHT. I DON'T. I DO, HOWEVER, KNOW HOW TO FIND OUT.
WHAT'S THAT? SOME NEW WAY TO HELP ME FOCUS? OR MAYBE IT WILL WASH THE EVIL OUT OF ME.
IT'S A SCRYING DISH. IT WILL HELP YOU SEE.
I ALREADY WEAR GLASSES, THANKS.
INDEED. SCRYING, HOWEVER, IS A WAY TO SEE MAGICALLY. I DON'T THINK YOUR GLASSES DO THAT.
KNOCK KNOCK
SORRY TO INTERRUPT, DR. ROSE, BUT THE DETECTIVE WOULD LIKE TO SEE YOU IN THE LIBRARY. SHE SAYS IT'S IMPORTANT.
WAIT HERE. TRY NOT TO MAKE THINGS WORSE.

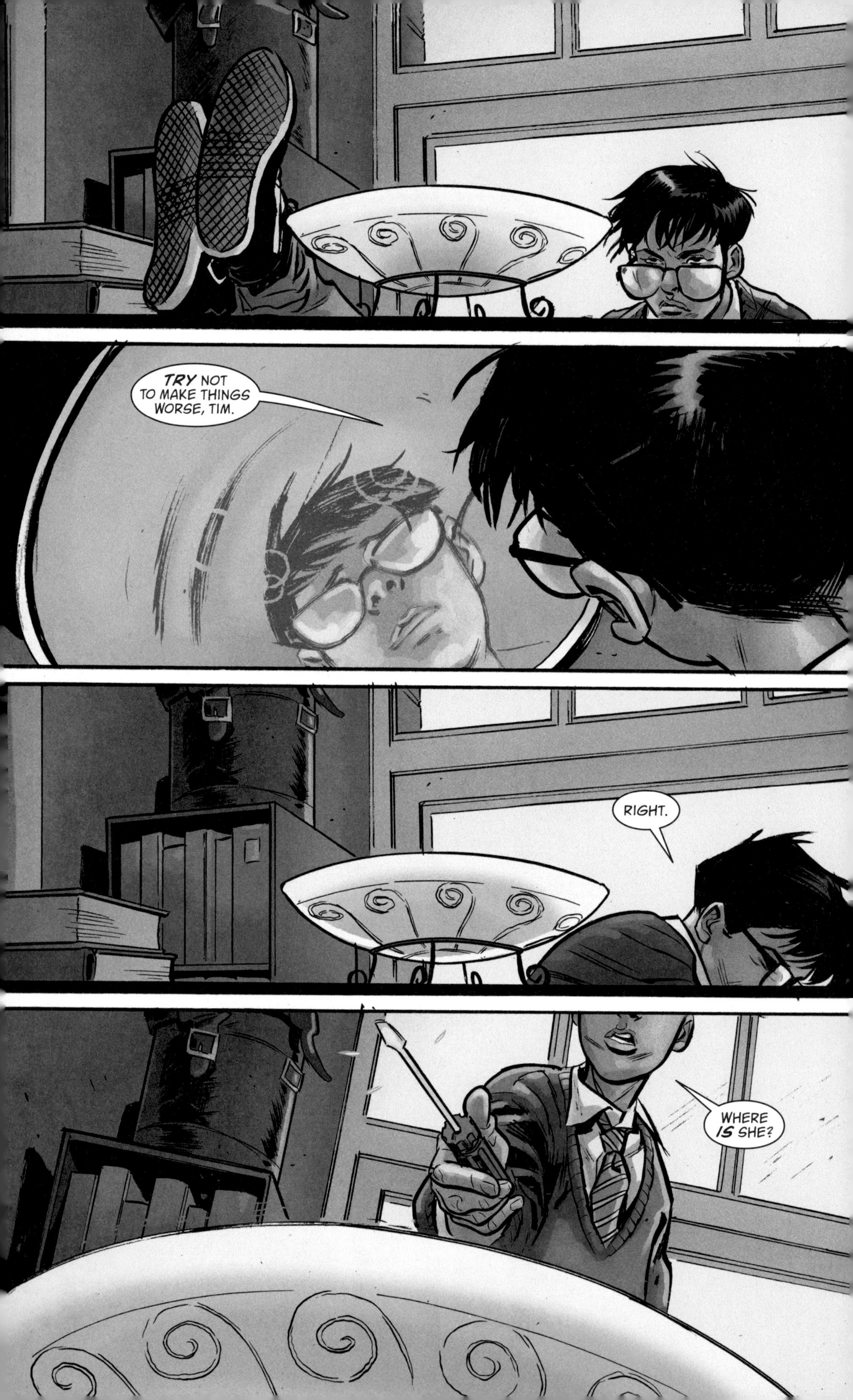

TRY NOT TO MAKE THINGS WORSE, TIM.
RIGHT.
WHERE IS SHE?

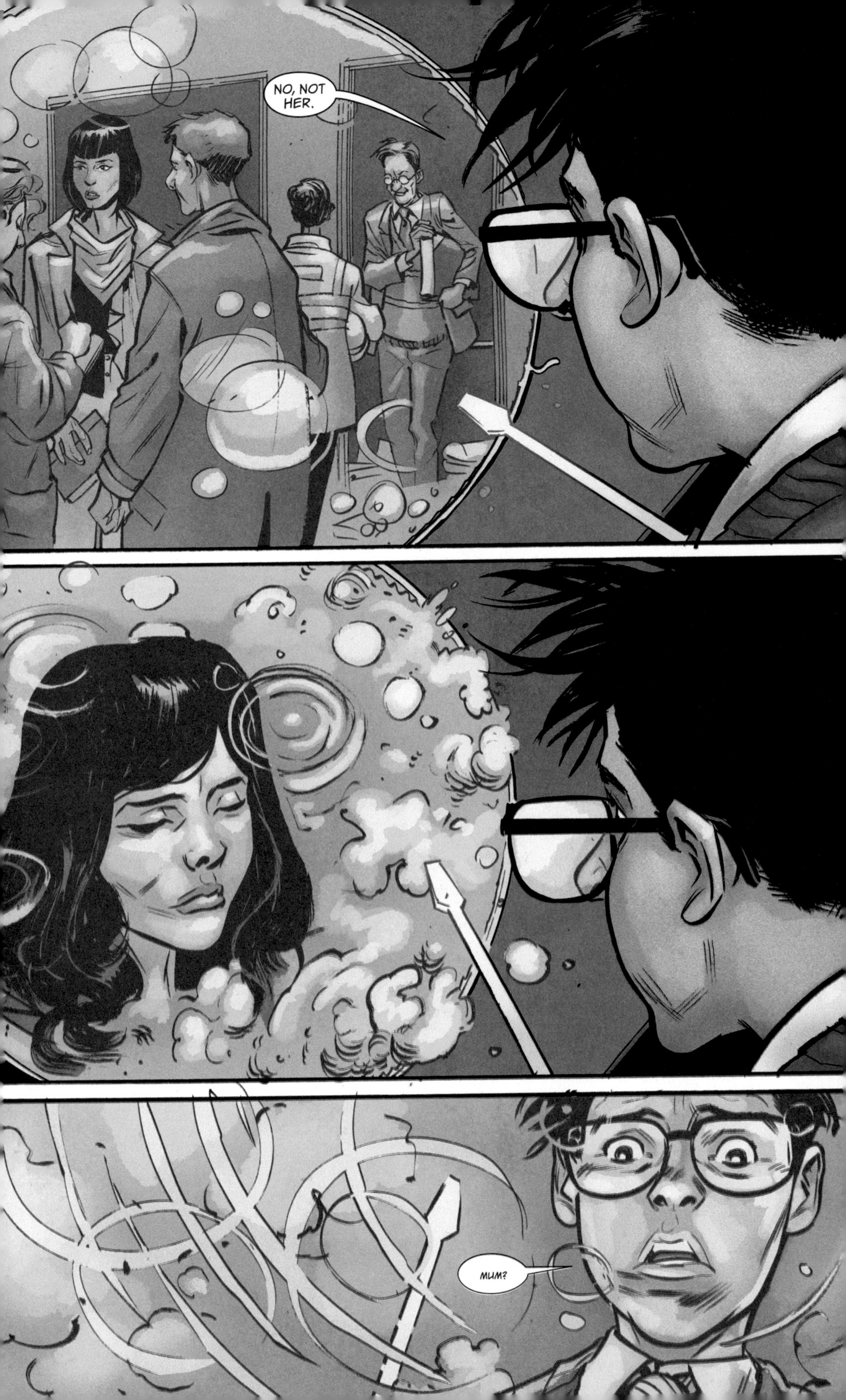
NO, NOT HER.
MUM?

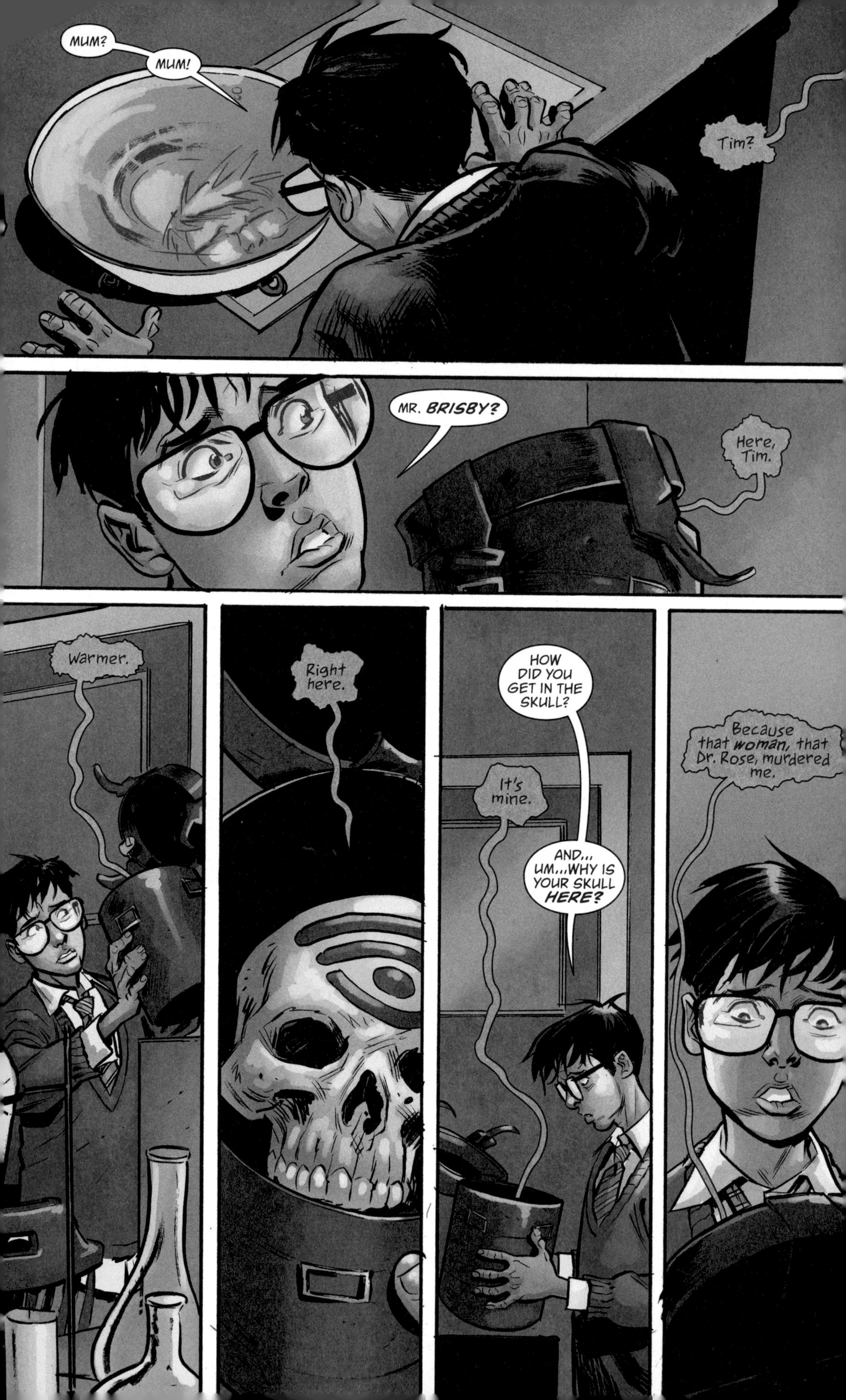
MUM?
MUM!
Tim?
MR. BRISBY?
Here, Tim.
Warmer.
Right here.
HOW DID YOU GET IN THE SKULL?
It's mine.
AND... UM...WHY IS YOUR SKULL HERE?
Because that woman, that Dr. Rose, murdered me.

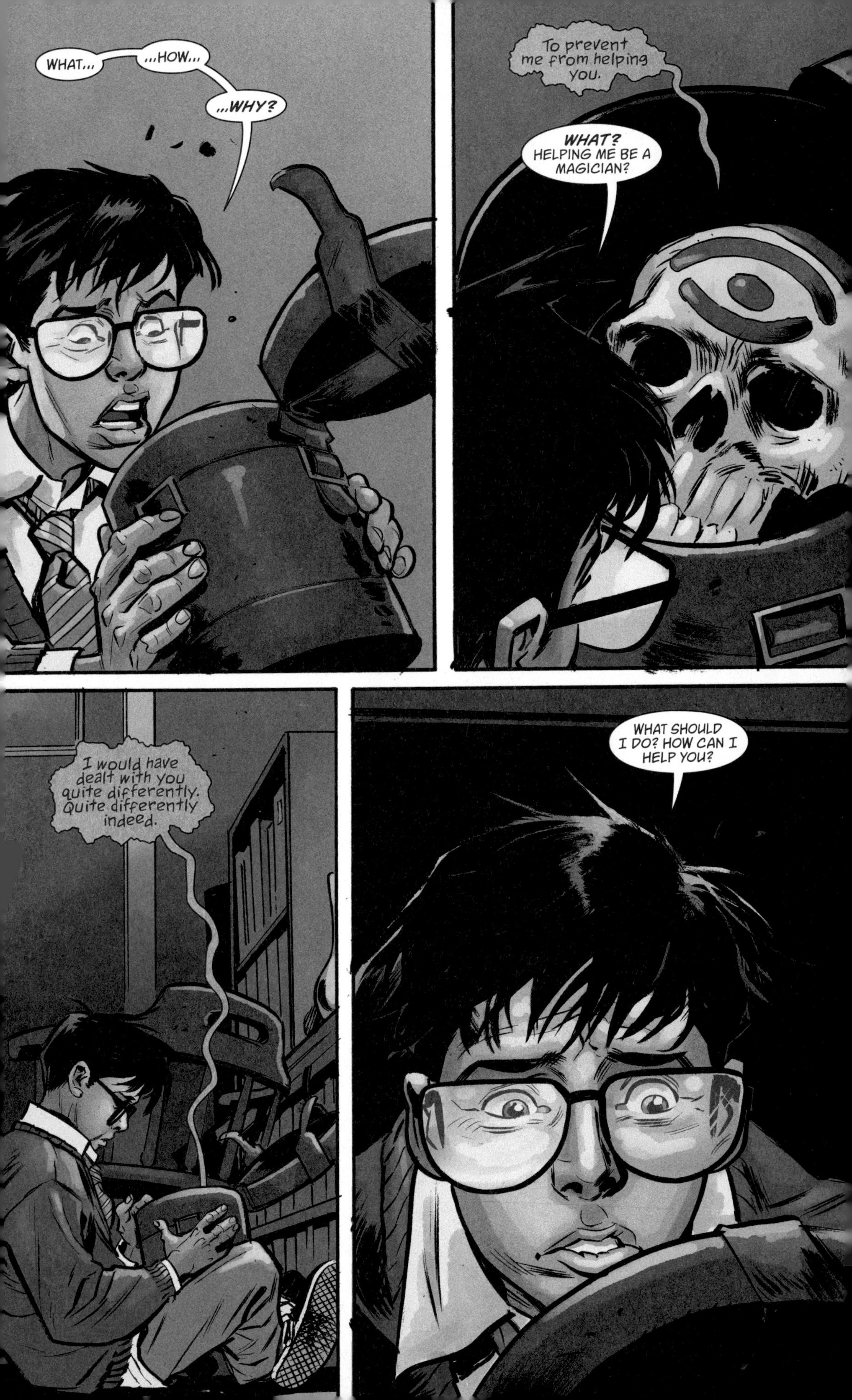
WHAT...
...HOW...
...WHY?
To prevent me from helping you.
WHAT? HELPING ME BE A MAGICIAN?
I would have dealt with you quite differently. Quite differently indeed.
WHAT SHOULD I DO? HOW CAN I HELP YOU?

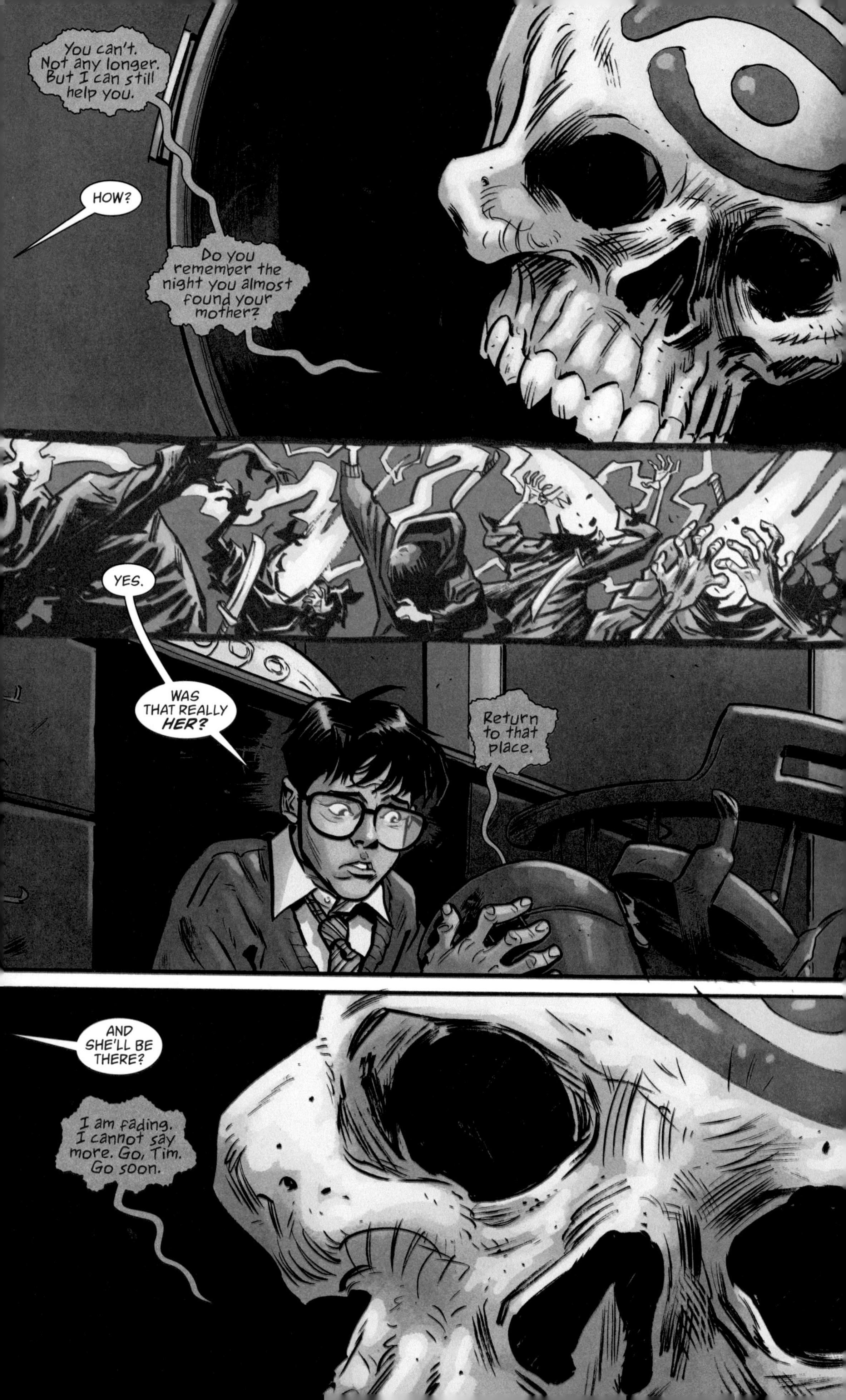
You can't. Not any longer. But I can still help you.
HOW?
Do you remember the night you almost found your mother?
YES.
WAS THAT REALLY *HER?*
Return to that place.
AND SHE'LL BE THERE?
I am fading. I cannot say more. Go, Tim. Go soon.

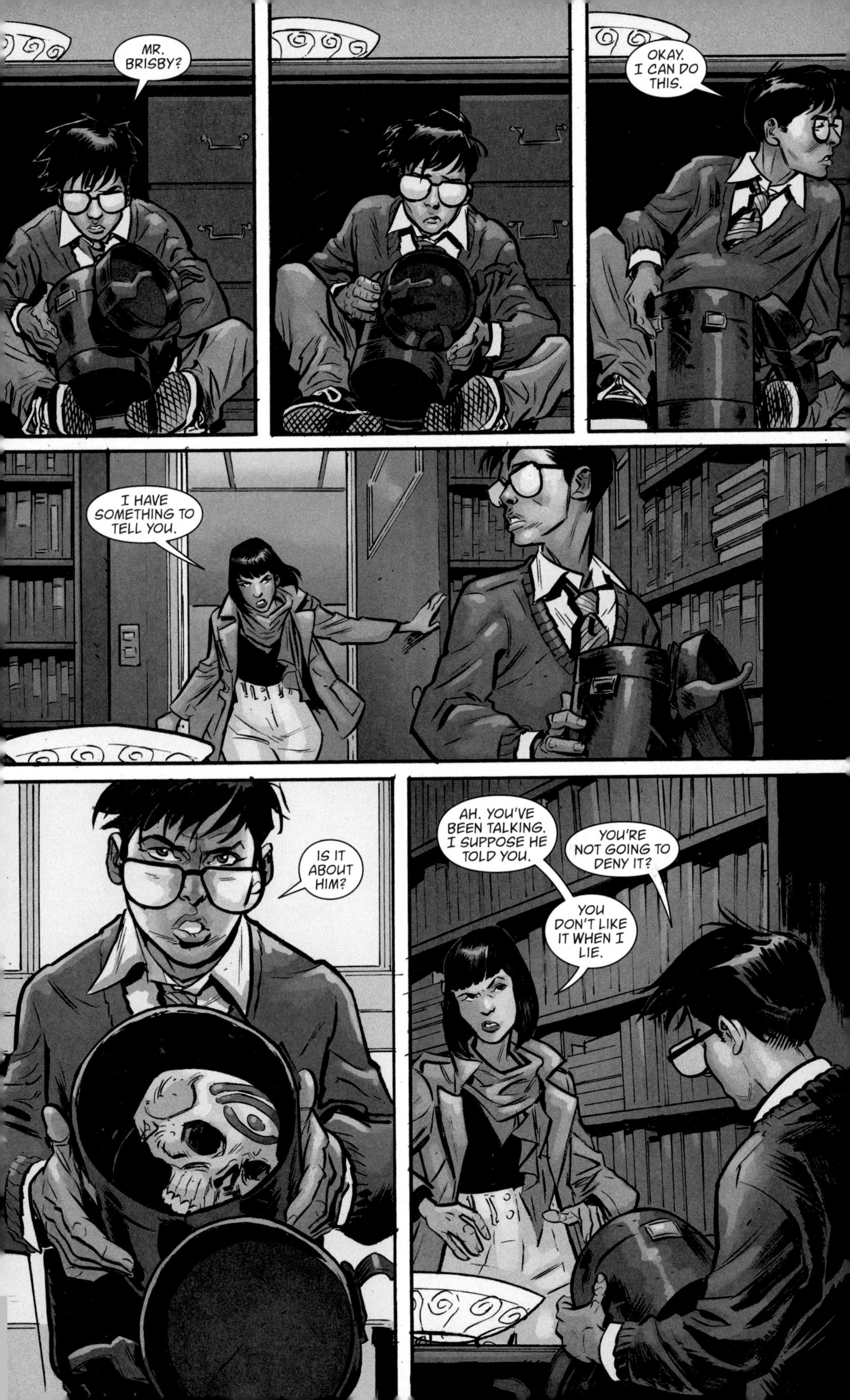
MR. BRISBY?
OKAY. I CAN DO THIS.
I HAVE SOMETHING TO TELL YOU.
IS IT ABOUT HIM?
AH. YOU'VE BEEN TALKING. I SUPPOSE HE TOLD YOU.
YOU'RE NOT GOING TO DENY IT?
YOU DON'T LIKE IT WHEN I LIE.

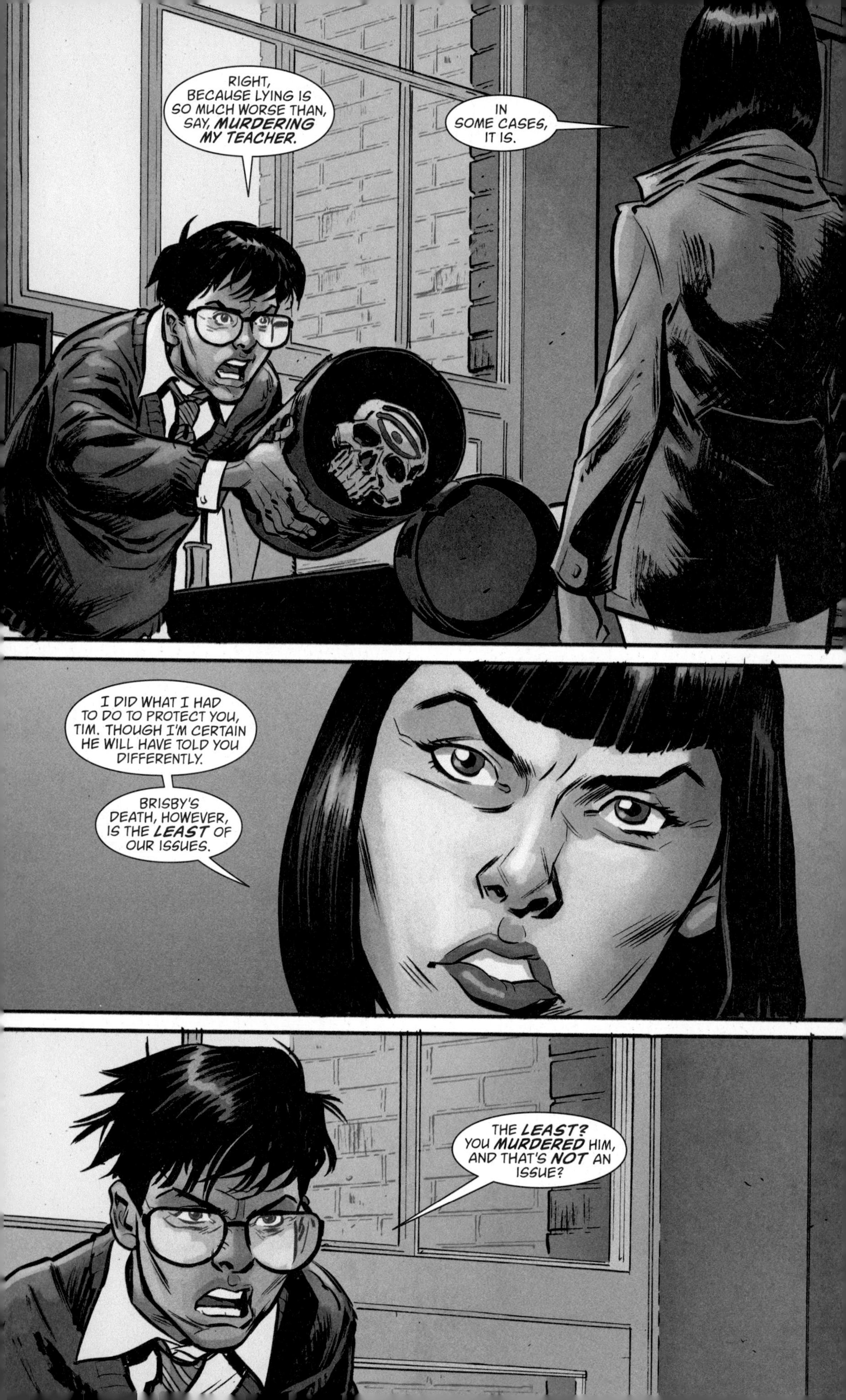
RIGHT, BECAUSE LYING IS SO MUCH WORSE THAN, SAY, **MURDERING MY TEACHER.**
IN SOME CASES, IT IS.
I DID WHAT I HAD TO DO TO PROTECT YOU, TIM. THOUGH I'M CERTAIN HE WILL HAVE TOLD YOU DIFFERENTLY.
BRISBY'S DEATH, HOWEVER, IS THE **LEAST** OF OUR ISSUES.
THE **LEAST?** YOU **MURDERED** HIM, AND THAT'S **NOT** AN ISSUE?

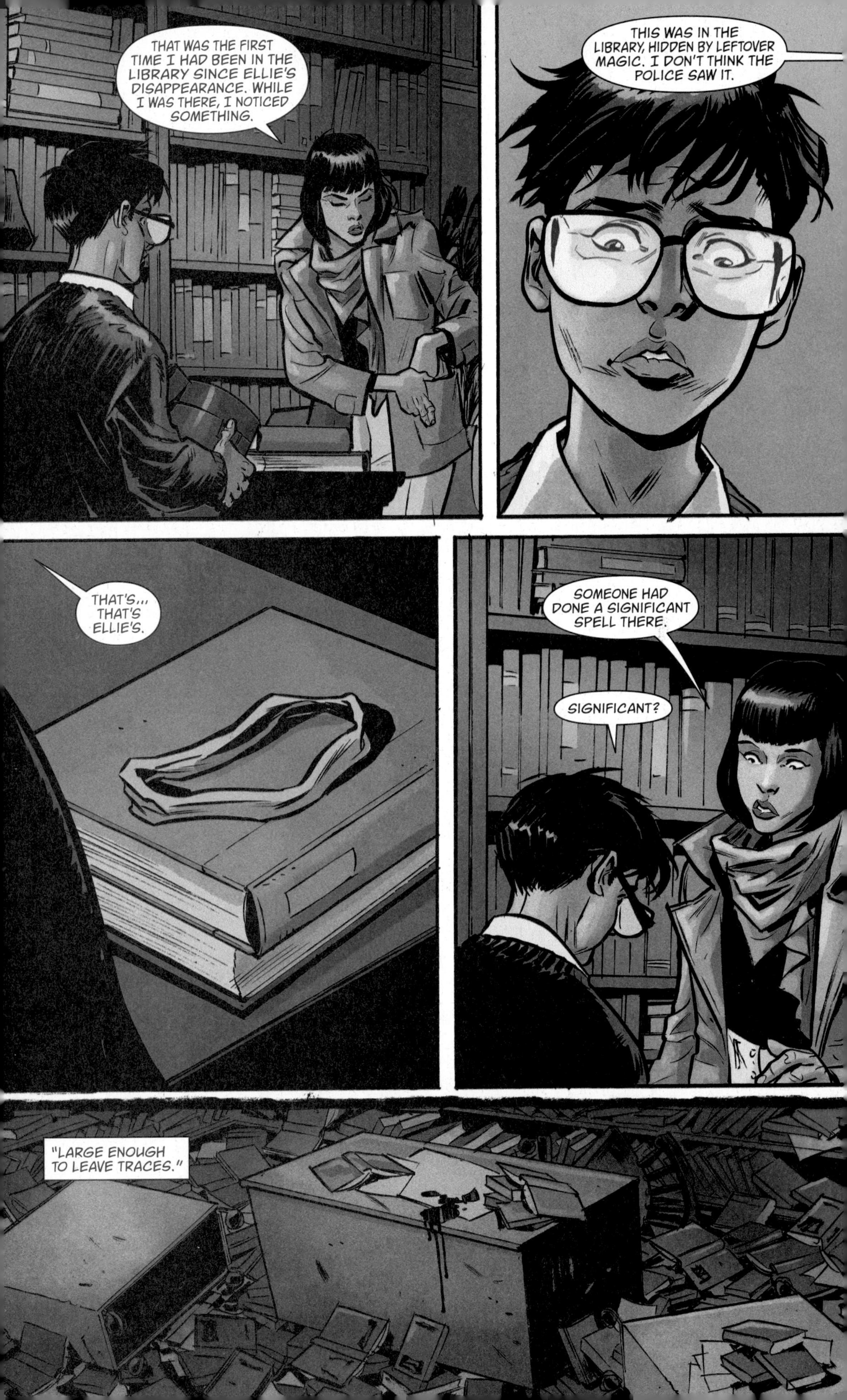
THAT WAS THE FIRST TIME I HAD BEEN IN THE LIBRARY SINCE ELLIE'S DISAPPEARANCE. WHILE I WAS THERE, I NOTICED SOMETHING.
THIS WAS IN THE LIBRARY, HIDDEN BY LEFTOVER MAGIC. I DON'T THINK THE POLICE SAW IT.
THAT'S... THAT'S ELLIE'S.
SOMEONE HAD DONE A SIGNIFICANT SPELL THERE.
SIGNIFICANT?
"LARGE ENOUGH TO LEAVE TRACES."

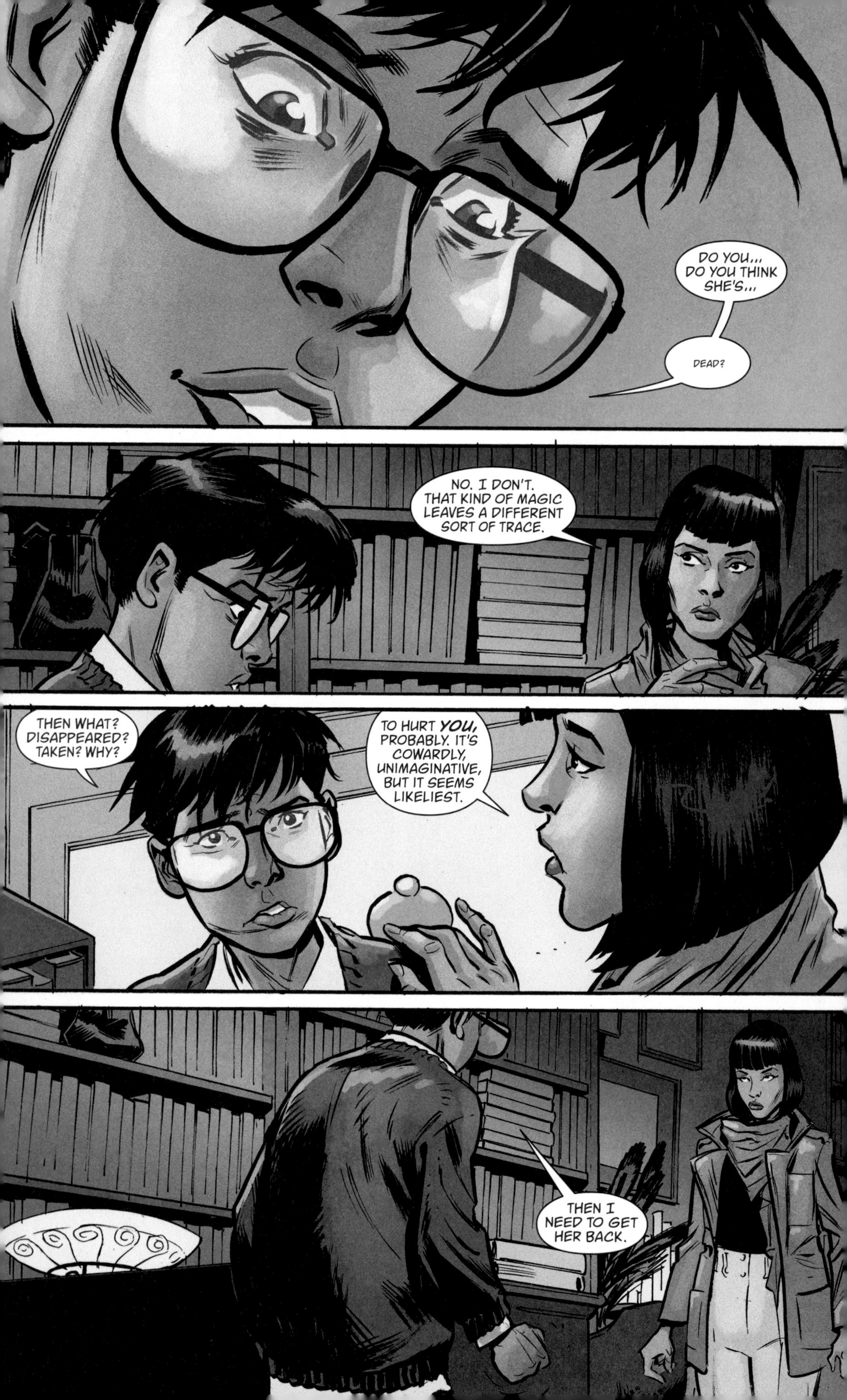
DO YOU... DO YOU THINK SHE'S...
DEAD?
NO. I DON'T. THAT KIND OF MAGIC LEAVES A DIFFERENT SORT OF TRACE.
THEN WHAT? DISAPPEARED? TAKEN? WHY?
TO HURT *YOU,* PROBABLY. IT'S COWARDLY, UNIMAGINATIVE, BUT IT SEEMS LIKELIEST.
THEN I NEED TO GET HER BACK.

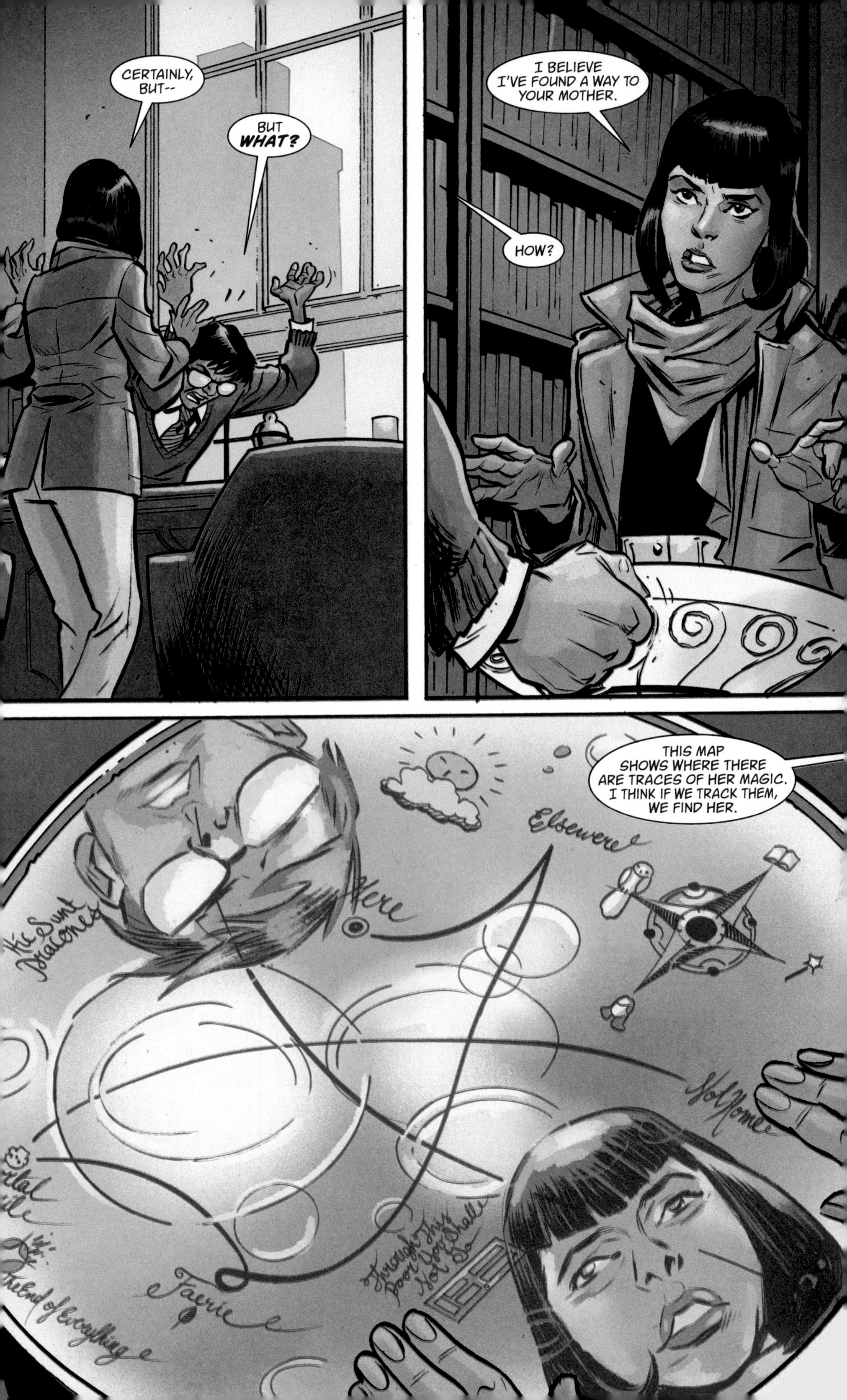
CERTAINLY, BUT--
BUT WHAT?
I BELIEVE I'VE FOUND A WAY TO YOUR MOTHER.
HOW?
THIS MAP SHOWS WHERE THERE ARE TRACES OF HER MAGIC. I THINK IF WE TRACK THEM, WE FIND HER.
Elsewere
Here
Not Home
Faerie
The End of Everything

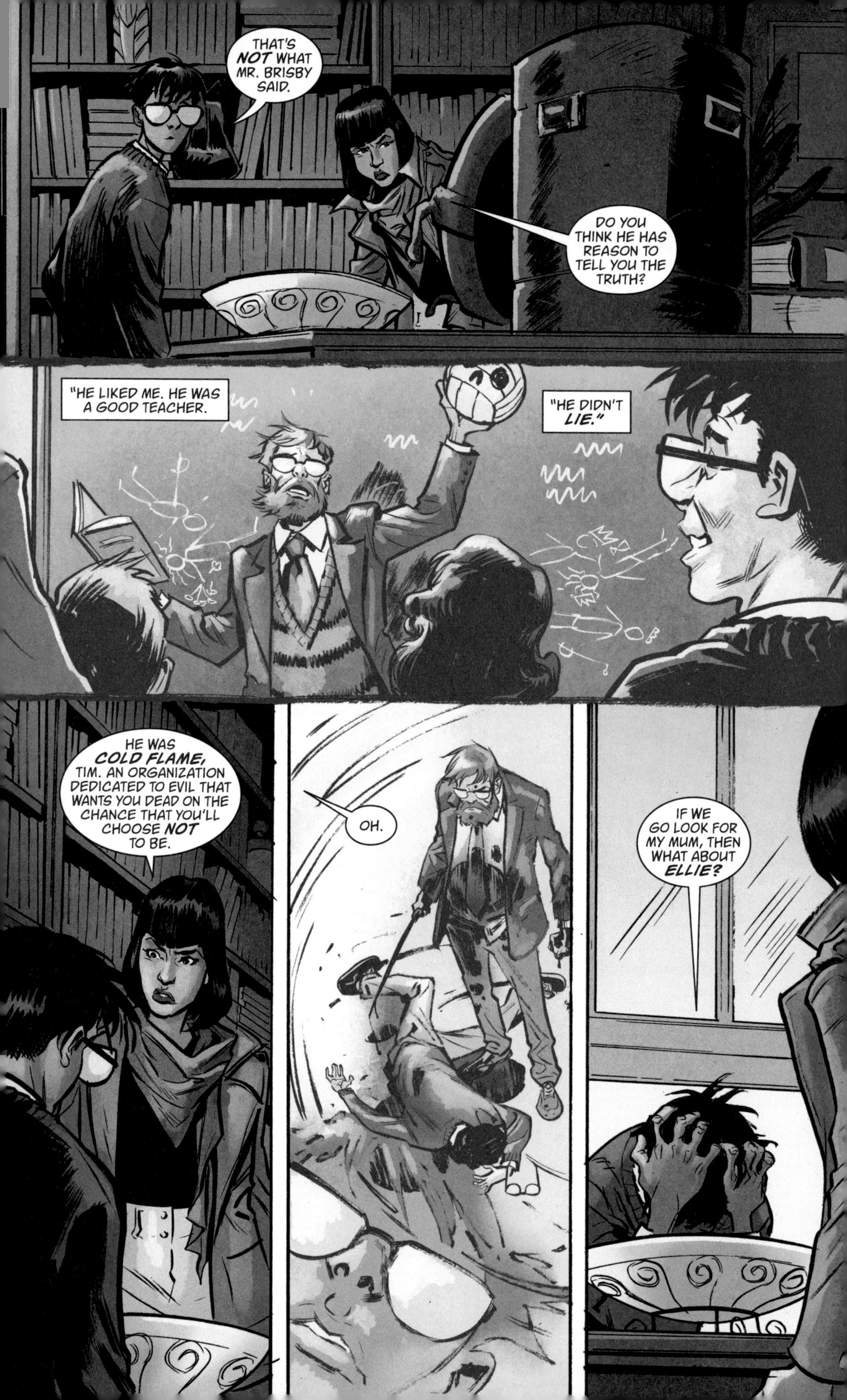
THAT'S NOT WHAT MR. BRISBY SAID.
DO YOU THINK HE HAS REASON TO TELL YOU THE TRUTH?
"HE LIKED ME. HE WAS A GOOD TEACHER.
"HE DIDN'T LIE."
HE WAS COLD FLAME, TIM. AN ORGANIZATION DEDICATED TO EVIL THAT WANTS YOU DEAD ON THE CHANCE THAT YOU'LL CHOOSE NOT TO BE.
OH.
IF WE GO LOOK FOR MY MUM, THEN WHAT ABOUT ELLIE?

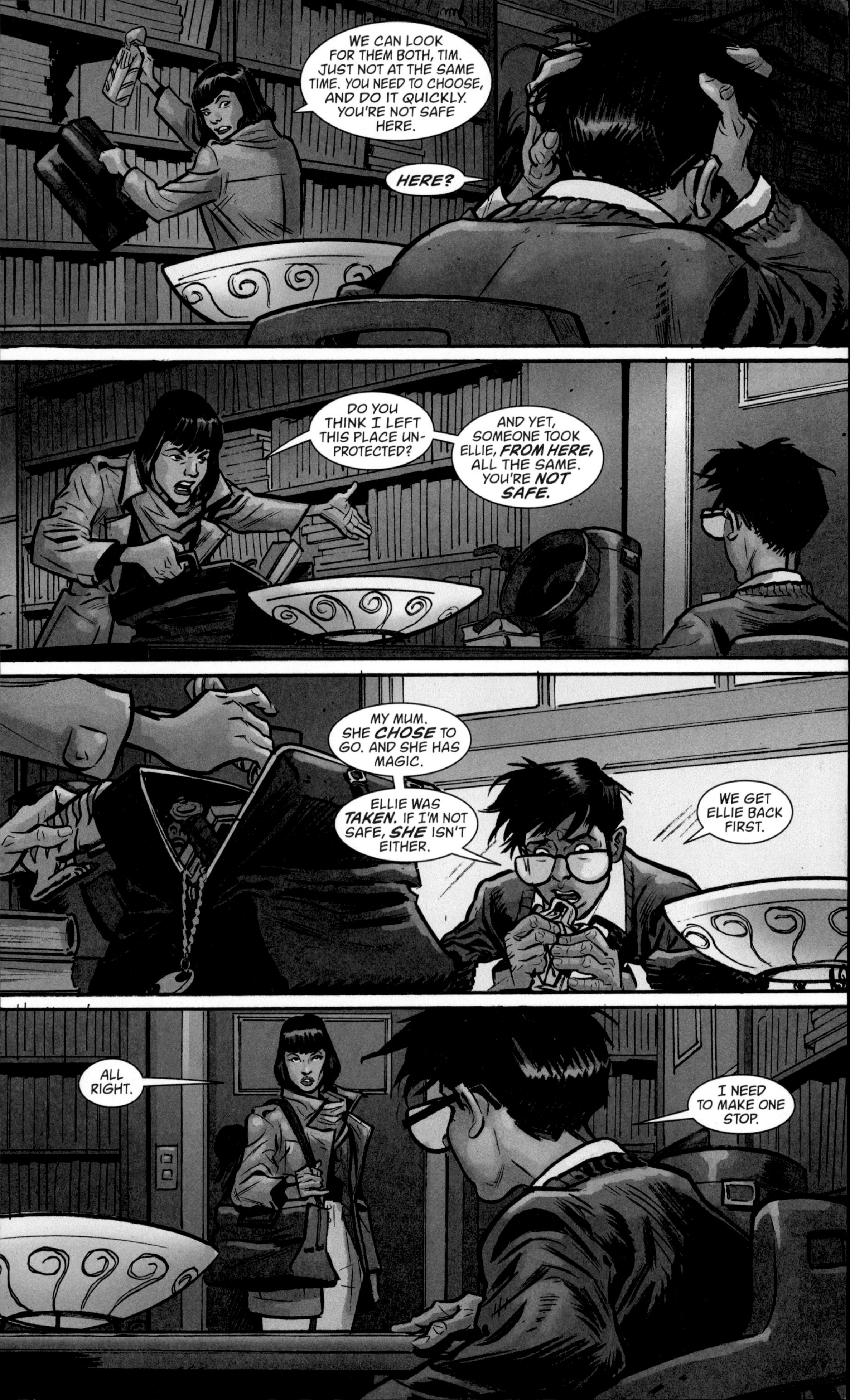
WE CAN LOOK FOR THEM BOTH, TIM. JUST NOT AT THE SAME TIME. YOU NEED TO CHOOSE, AND DO IT QUICKLY. YOU'RE NOT SAFE HERE.
HERE?
DO YOU THINK I LEFT THIS PLACE UN-PROTECTED?
AND YET, SOMEONE TOOK ELLIE, FROM HERE, ALL THE SAME. YOU'RE NOT SAFE.
MY MUM. SHE CHOSE TO GO. AND SHE HAS MAGIC.
ELLIE WAS TAKEN. IF I'M NOT SAFE, SHE ISN'T EITHER.
WE GET ELLIE BACK FIRST.
ALL RIGHT.
I NEED TO MAKE ONE STOP.

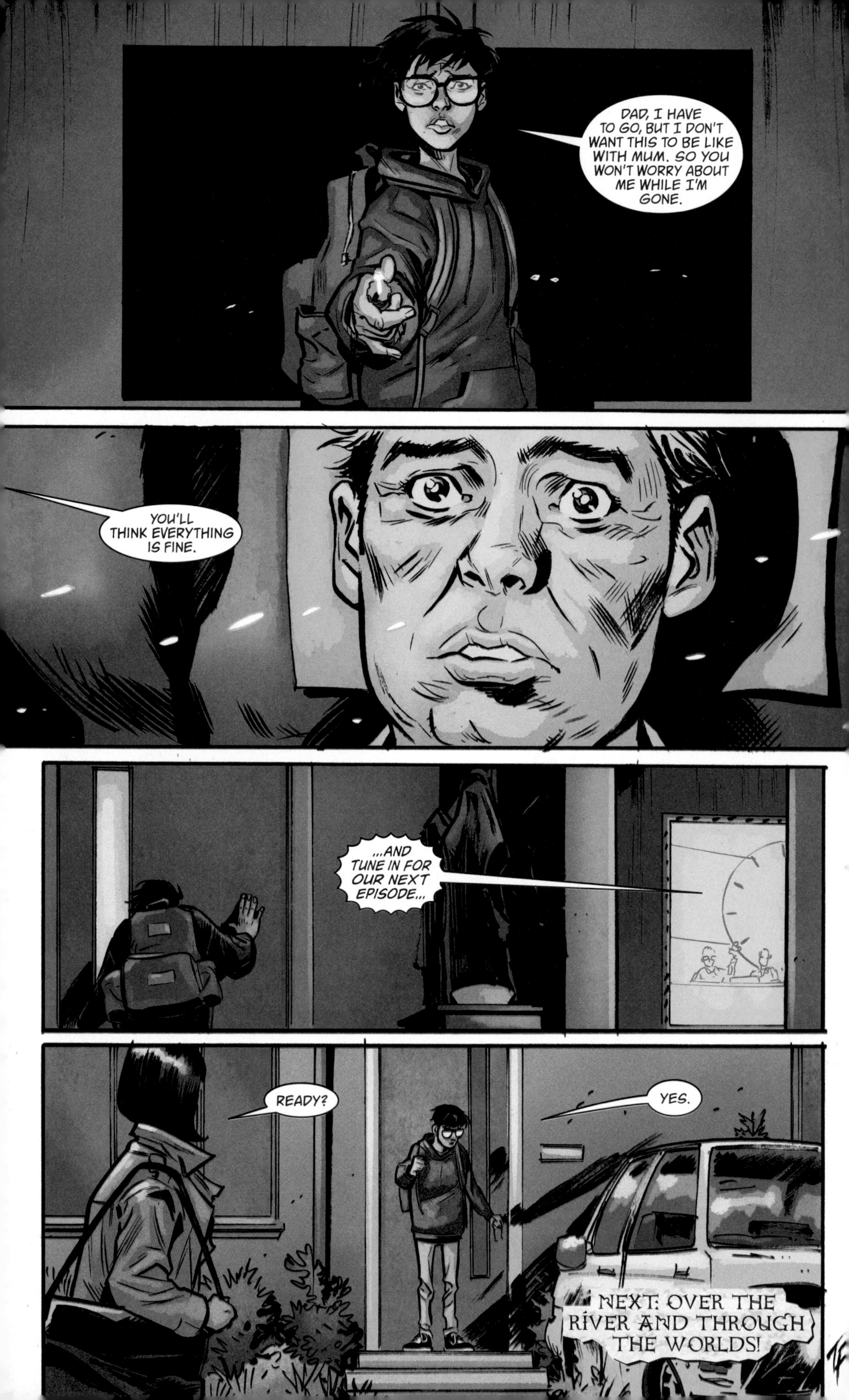
DAD, I HAVE TO GO, BUT I DON'T WANT THIS TO BE LIKE WITH MUM. SO YOU WON'T WORRY ABOUT ME WHILE I'M GONE.
YOU'LL THINK EVERYTHING IS FINE.
...AND TUNE IN FOR OUR NEXT EPISODE...
READY?
YES.
NEXT: OVER THE RIVER AND THROUGH THE WORLDS!

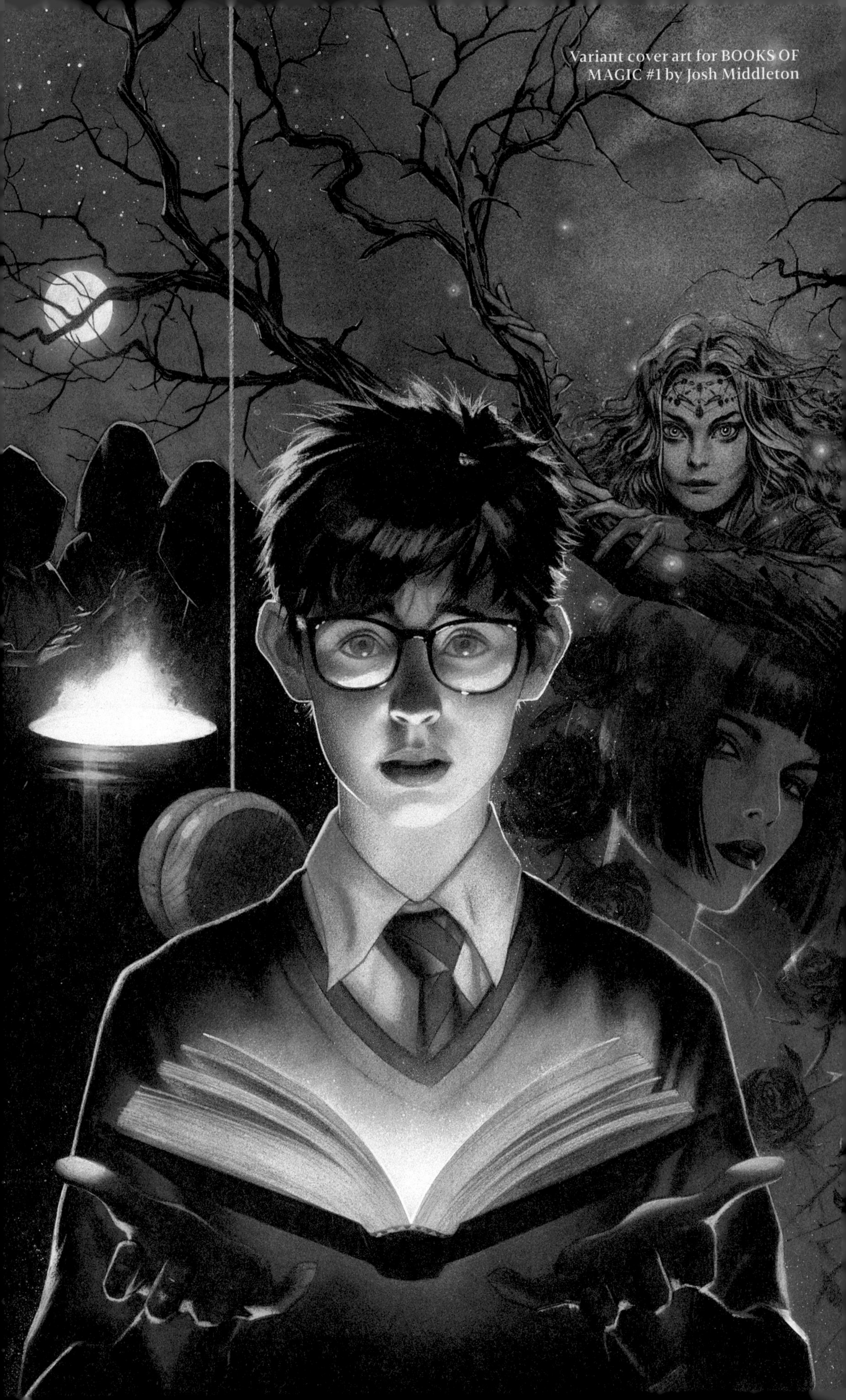

Variant cover art for BOOKS OF MAGIC #1 by Josh Middleton

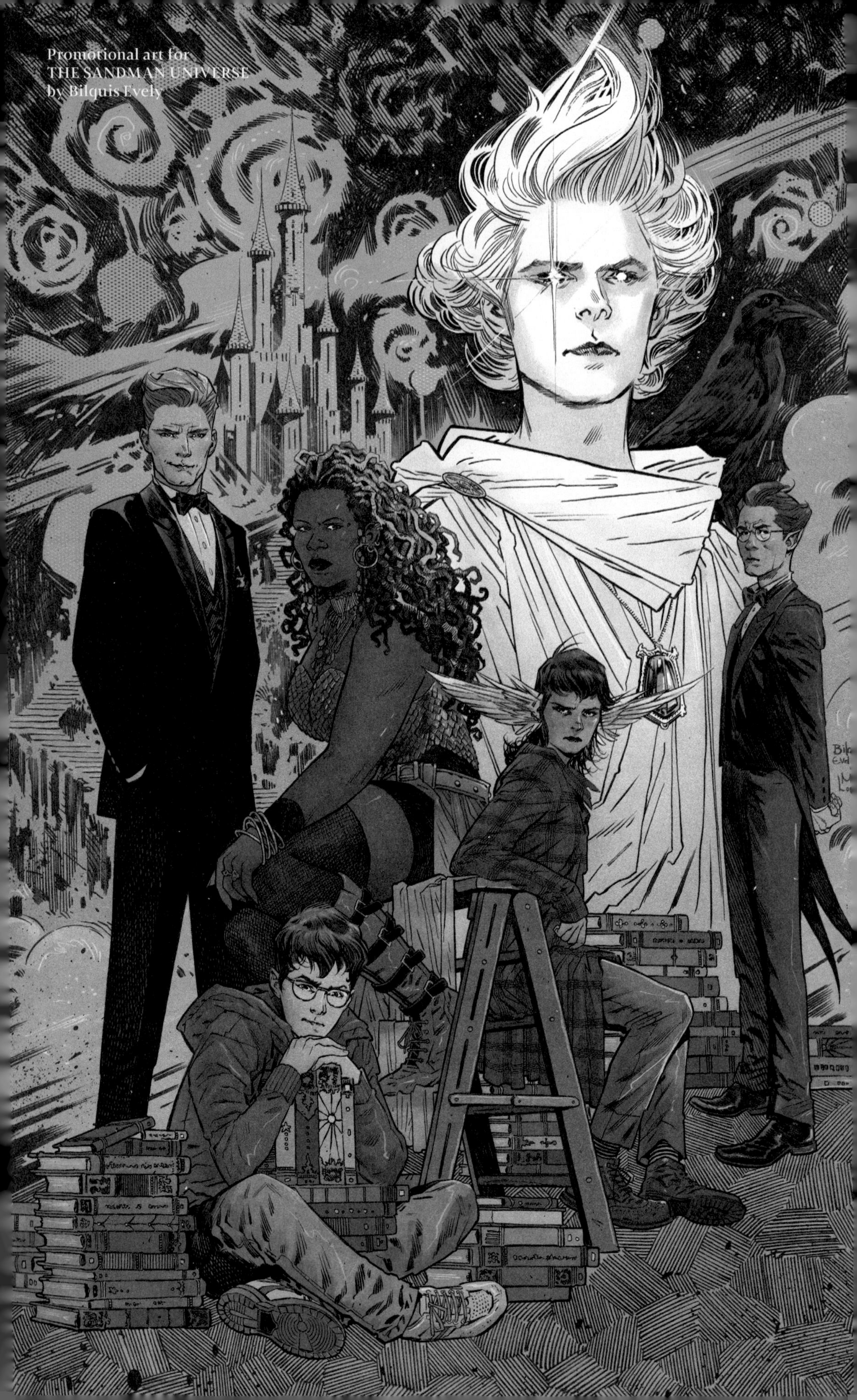

Promotional art for
THE SANDMAN UNIVERSE
by Bilquis Evely

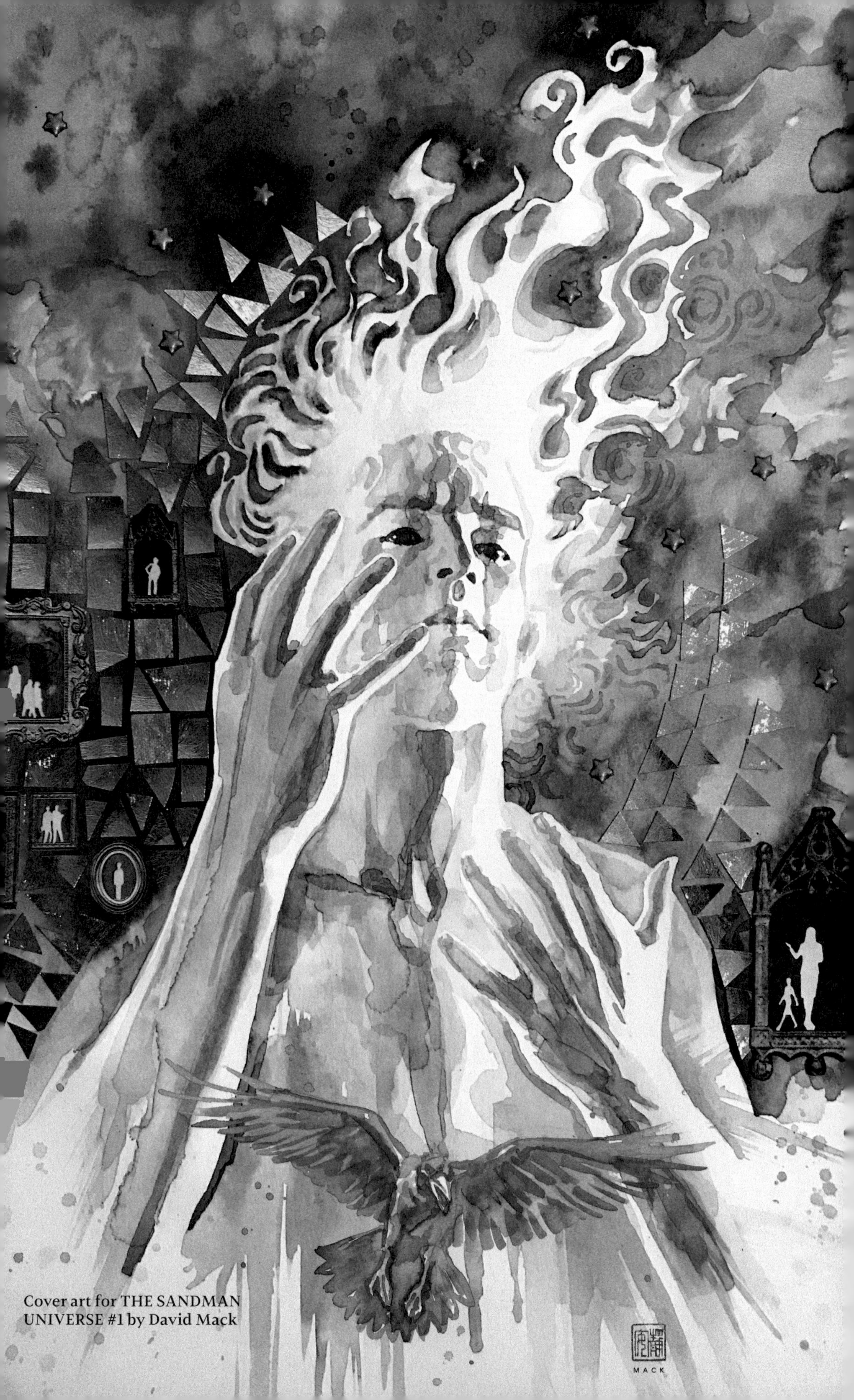
MACK

Cover art for THE SANDMAN UNIVERSE #1 by David Mack

Cover art for THE SANDMAN
UNIVERSE #1 by Sam Kieth

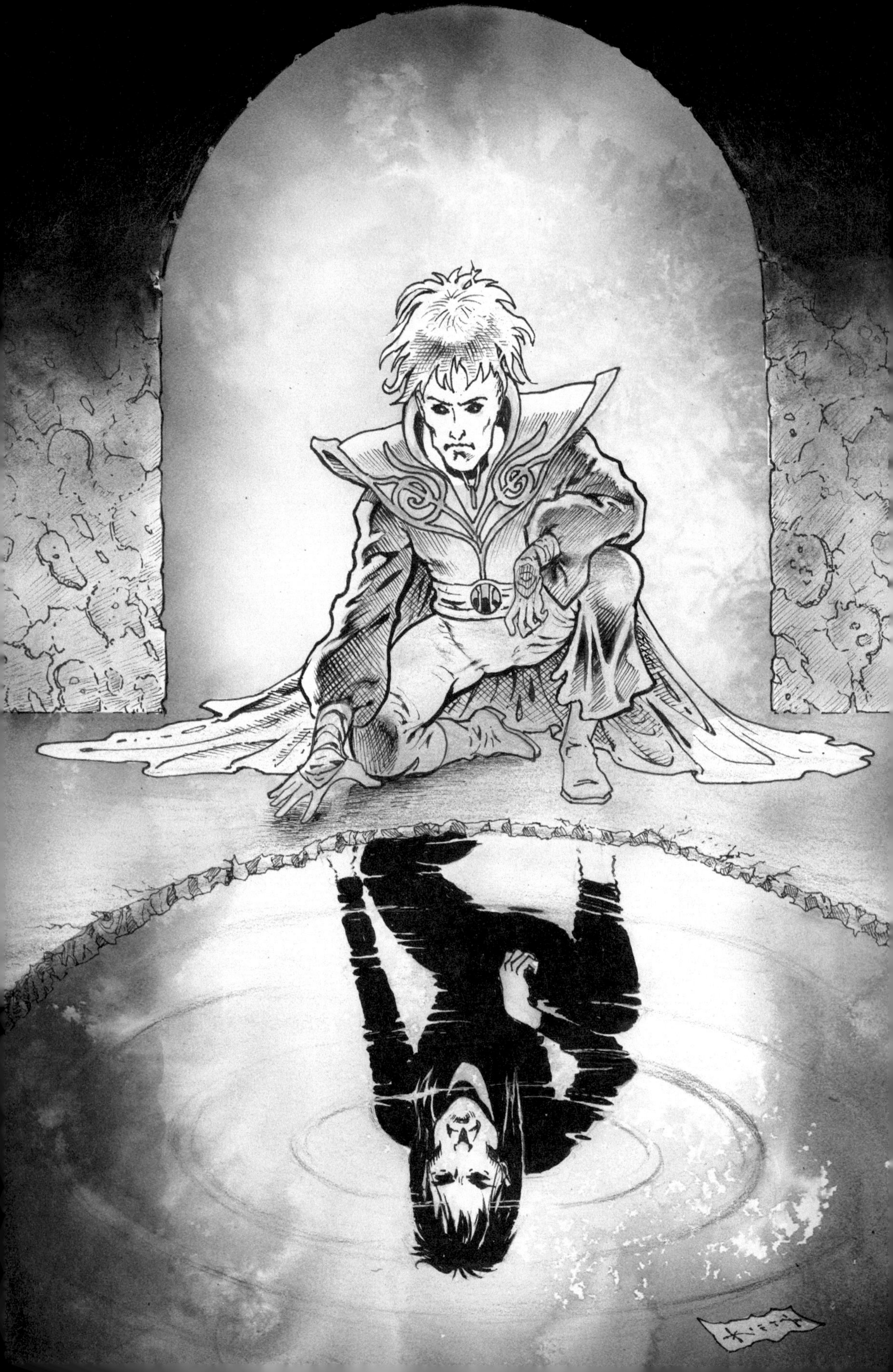

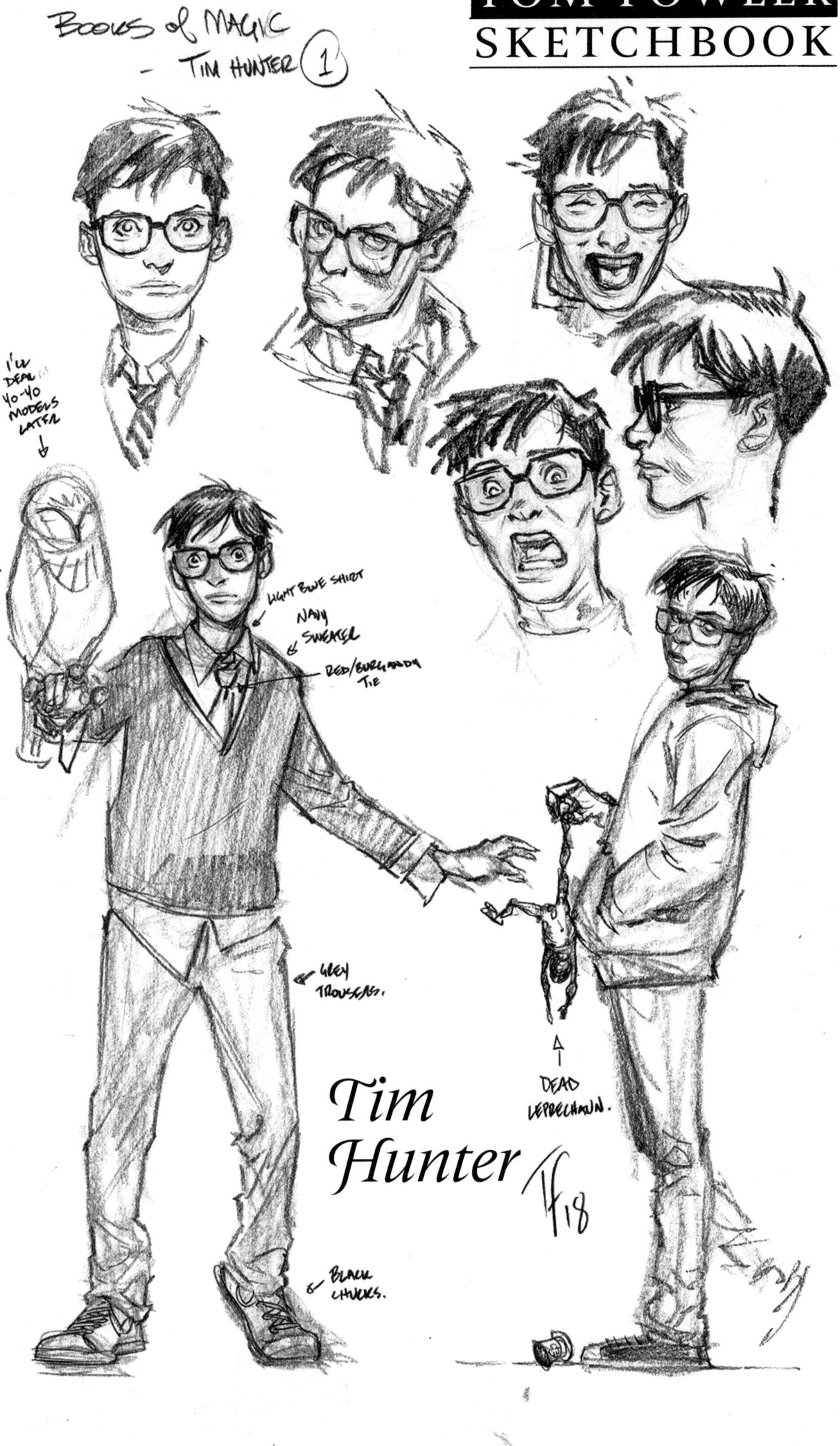
BOOKS OF MAGIC
- TIM HUNTER 1
I'LL DEAL YO-YO MODELS LATER
LIGHT BLUE SHIRT
NAVY SWEATER
RED/BURGANDY TIE
GREY TROUSERS.
BLACK CHUCKS.
DEAD LEPRECHAUN.
TF '18

Tim Hunter

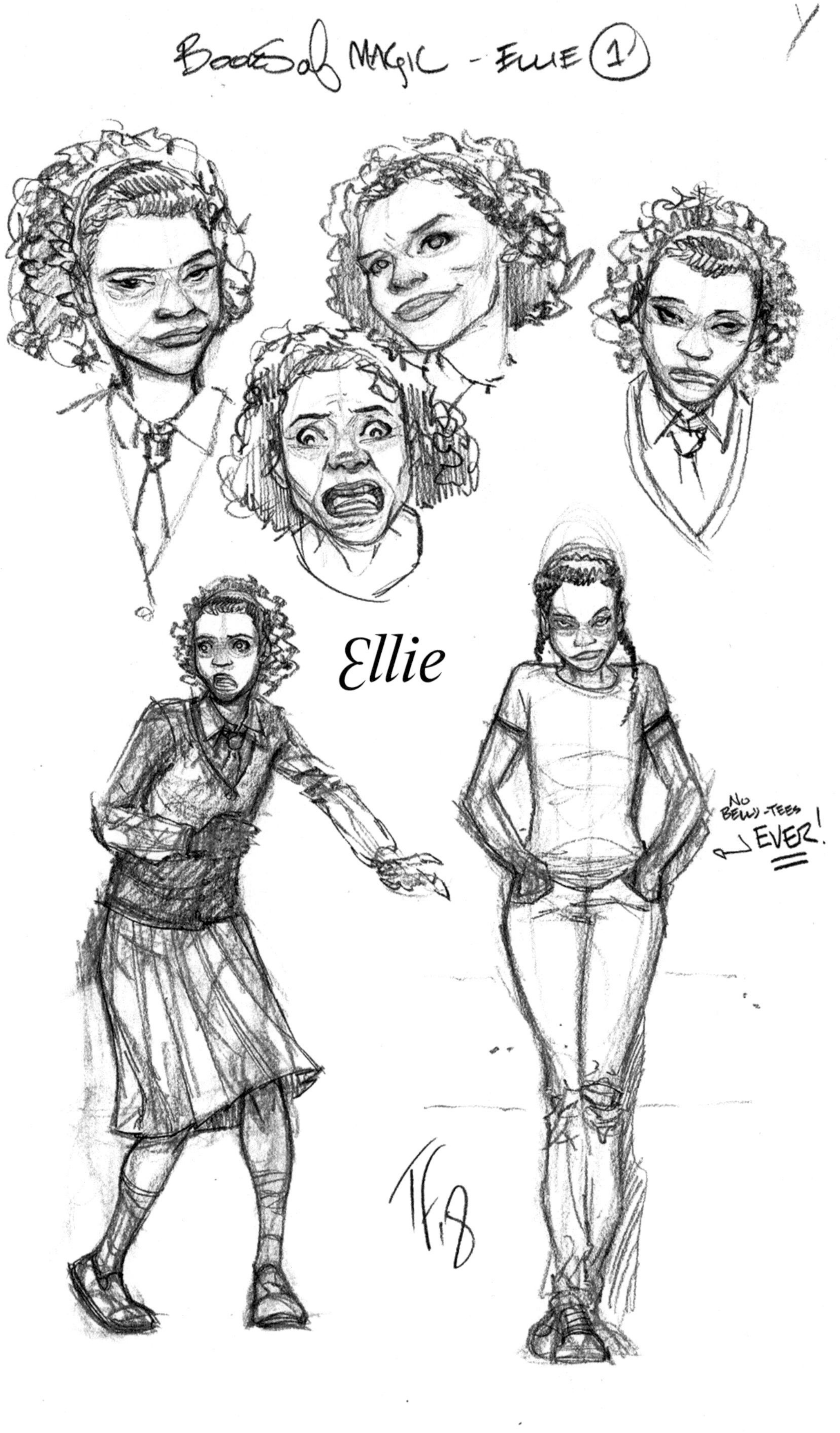
BOOKS of MAGIC - ELLIE 1
NO BELLY-TEES
EVER!

Ellie

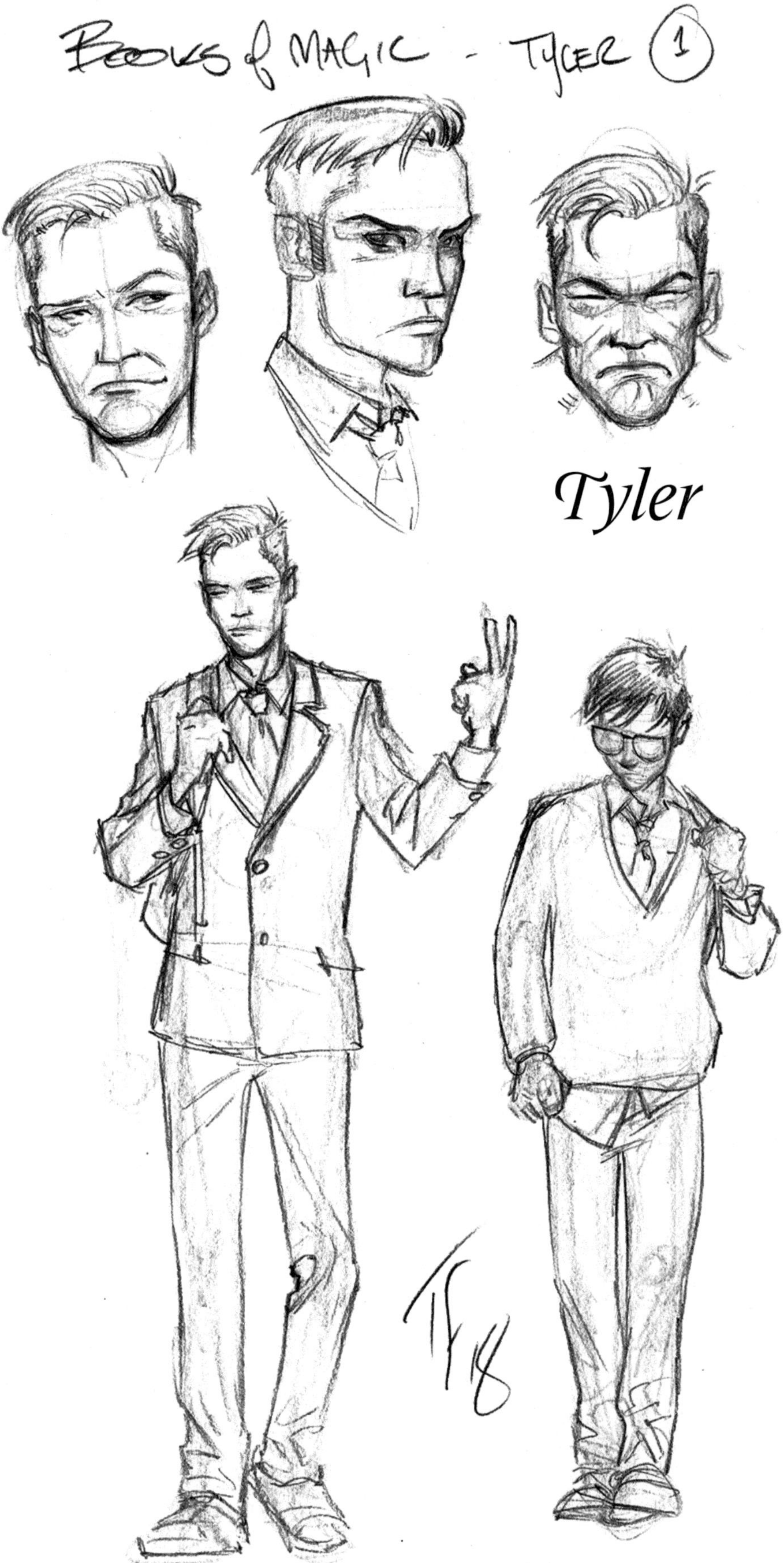
BOOKS of MAGIC - TYLER 1
Tyler
TF 18

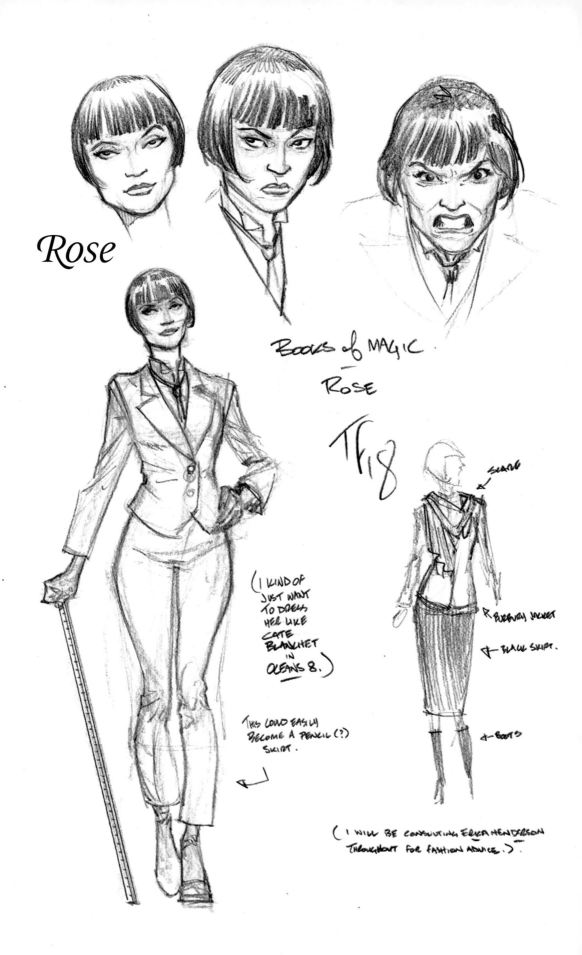

Rose

BOOKS of MAGIC
- ROSE

TF18

(I KIND OF
JUST WANT
TO DRESS
HER LIKE
CATE
BLANCHET
IN
OCEANS 8.)

THIS COULD EASILY
BECOME A PENCIL (?)
SKIRT.

← SCARF

R BURBURY JACKET

← BLACK SKIRT.

← BOOTS

(I WILL BE CONSULTING ERIKA HENDERSON
THROUGHOUT FOR FASHION ADVICE.)

UNIFORM
COLOR GUIDE

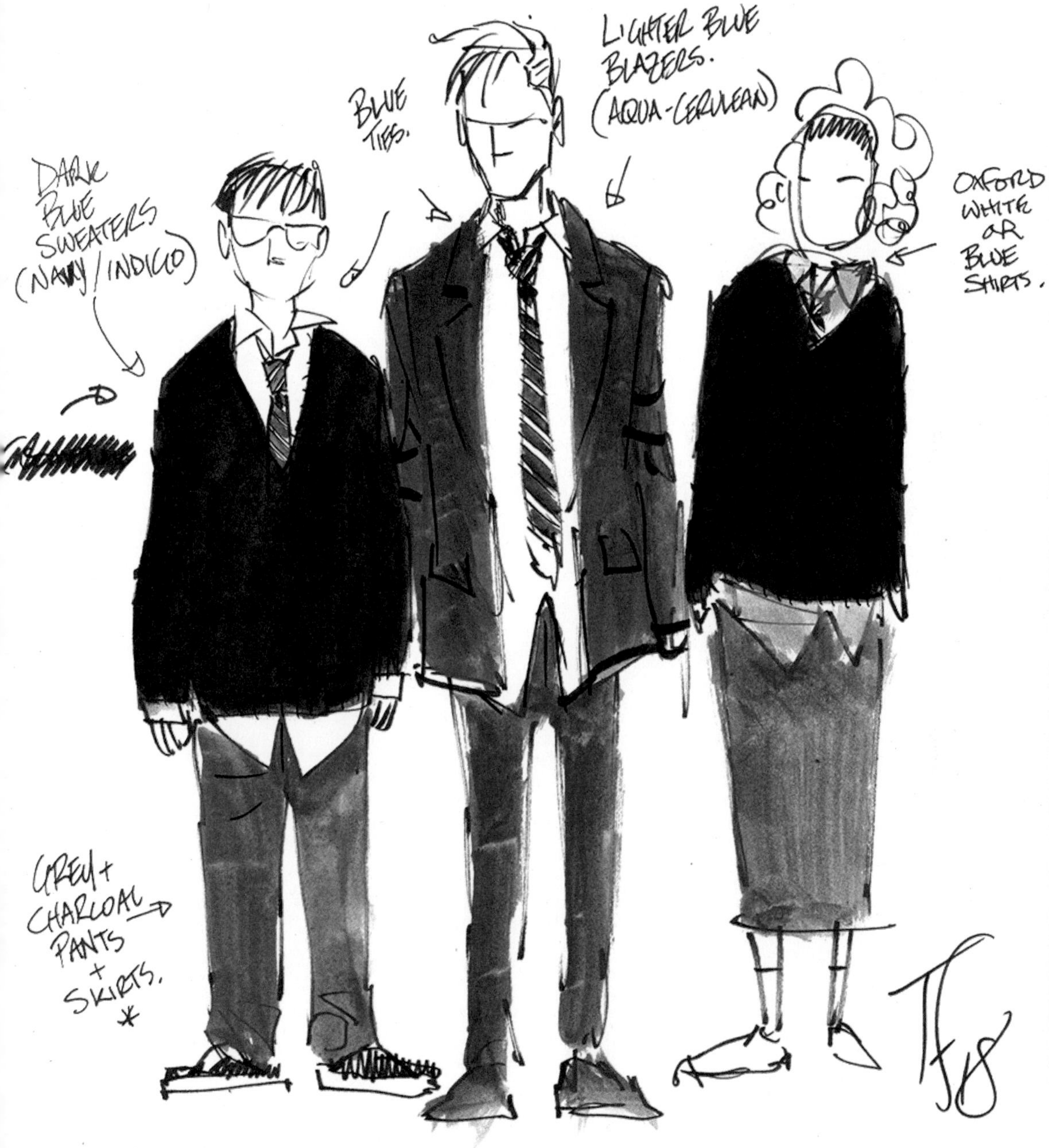
DARK BLUE SWEATERS (NAVY/INDIGO)
BLUE TIES.
LIGHTER BLUE BLAZERS. (AQUA-CERULEAN)
OXFORD WHITE OR BLUE SHIRTS.
GREY + CHARCOAL PANTS + SKIRTS. *

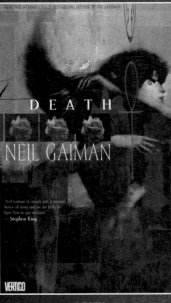